THE NOBLE
QUR'AN

A New Rendering of
its Meaning in English

by
Abdalhaqq and Aisha Bewley

© 1426/ 2005 Bookwork
Revised edition.

Production: Bookwork, Norwich
Cover design: Aarlsen Design, Norwich

Published by:
Bookwork
Norwich
abewley@tesco.net

ISBN 0-9538639-3-X

Printed at: Biddles, Kings Lynn, Norfolk, UK

Translators' Preface

We first embarked on this project at the suggestion of our guide and teacher, Shaykh 'Abdalqadir as-Sufi, in 1975 and we would like to state clearly that had it not been for his constant guidance, instruction, encouragement and occasional timely reminder, we would certainly never have brought it to fruition. May Allah prolong his life and reward him in the best possible way.

It has never been a work of mere academic endeavour but has rather grown out of more than two decades of continuous contact with the Qur'an as a living guidance, almost twenty-five years of regular daily recitation and reference, during which we have continually grappled with arriving at the best way of expressing the meaning of its ayats in English.

We discovered very early on that none of the available English versions conveyed the meaning of Allah's words in a way that fulfilled our needs. There is no doubt that the Qur'an spoke clearly and directly to the community to which it was first revealed and has continued to do so in its original form to every subsequent generation of Muslims ever since. When we read the existing translations, however, although the meaning came across, the language always seemed to get in its way. So instead of coming straight through as it does in the original, the meaning always came 'through a glass darkly'. This is in no way intended to denigrate the work of our predecessors, most of whom did a meticulous and admirable job, it is rather a comment on the constantly evolving nature of the English language. This, then, was perhaps our main objective in presenting this new rendering: to allow the meaning of the original, as far as possible, to come straight through with as little linguistic interface as possible so that the English used does not get in the way of the direct transmission of the meaning.

While, as it itself makes clear, the Qur'an is not poetry in any formal sense and cannot be defined or qualified linguistically in any way whatsoever, Allah, may He be exalted, nevertheless makes full and free use of the natural rhythms and rhymes of the Arabic language to the extent that these form an integral part of the Qur'anic Message and are definitely an important factor in the way its meaning is conveyed to the heart of both reciters and listeners. Therefore, to convey the meaning in plain dry prose would not be faithful to the original. For this reason we have attempted, by using the natural rhythms of the English language combined with a particular kind of layout on the page, to pass on to the reader at least a taste of this essential attribute of the original text.

On a more specific note, readers will immediately notice that several key terms have not been translated and remain in the text in a transliterated Arabic form. Wherever Islam has spread in areas whose mother tongue is not Arabic – and that, in fact, comprises the vast majority of Muslim lands – you find that a certain number of key Qur'anic terms are always retained in their original Arabic form, whether the language concerned is Turkish or Urdu or Malay or Hausa or any of the other myriad languages spoken by Muslims throughout the world. In more recent times exactly the same phenomenon has occurred with English so that English speaking Muslims have assimilated into the language various Arabic words which are either untranslatable or words whose English equivalents have become so imbued with a meaning other than that intended by the original Arabic that to use them would be to mislead rather than give the correct significance.

Since this rendering is intended primarily as a tool for English speaking Muslims we have incorporated many of these words into it, so that rather than, for instance, using the words 'faith' and 'believers' we have used the terms 'iman' and 'muminun'; instead of 'disbelief' and 'unbelievers', we have used the terms 'kufr' and 'kafirun' or 'kuffar'; and the same applies to all the other arabic terminology employed in the text, definitions of which will be found in the small glossary at the end.

Another point which should be mentioned is that the Arabic text used for this rendering is the *riwaya* from Imam Warsh from Nafi‘, the great reciter of the second generation of Muslims in Madina. We have used this reading because, originating in Madina, it undoubtedly connects directly to the most ancient tradition of recitation and is known to be the reading closest to the Qurayshi dialect in which the Qur'an was revealed. This does, however, mean that there are slight variations of meaning between it and the reading of Imam Hafs which is what has been used, as far as we know, as the basis of most, if not all, of the previous English versions. This means that in a few instances there will be differences between this and previous English renderings. For instance, we find that in Surat Yunus, ayat 45 reads in our rendering, 'On the Day *We* gather them together,' whereas in other versions you will find, 'On the Day *He* gathers them together,' or something similar, with the pronoun changed from We to He. This is because the orthography of the original Arabic allows for such slight variations in meaning and the Qur'anic revelation is vast enough to be able to contain all of them within its compass, all of them being considered correct. The reason we are mentioning this here is so that if a reader notices such a difference between this rendering and a previous one, they should not immediately assume it is a mistake but should rather check it against the Warsh reading. The ayat numbering also tends to vary between the different readings.

One further point which needs to be mentioned is the use in the text of certain anthropomorphic expressions in connection with Allah, may He be glorified and exalted. You will find references to Allah's Hands, and His Eyes and His Face and other similar things. Arabic is like English in that such expressions can be validly used in a metaphorical sense as you find, for instance, in the English expression 'he had a hand in everything that happened'. This obviously does not mean that the person concerned physically touched everything referred to or had several pairs of hands! The same applies in Arabic so that when these matters are mentioned they are not to be taken as literally referring to any sort of physical characteristic but rather to an attribute or quality indicated by the expression used.

Before closing this brief preface we would first like to follow all our predecessors in acknowledging the complete impossibility of adequately conveying the meanings of the Qur'an in English or indeed in any other language. Allah, may He be exalted, chose pure classical Arabic as the linguistic vehicle for His final Revelation to mankind because of its unique capacity of retaining and conveying great depth of meaning in a multi-faceted way which is beyond the scope of any other language, particularly in the debased form to which they have arrived in the time in which we live.

We are indebted to the European Arabic lexicographers, Hans Wehr and E.W. Lane, and to their great Arab predecessors who compiled *al-Lisan al-'Arab*. We also owe a great debt of gratitude to the great mufassirun of the past who spent so much time and energy in unearthing, preserving and passing on the meaning of Allah's Book and in protecting it from unacceptable interpretation and deviation. In particular we have made much use of the *Jalalayn* with Sawi's gloss, the *Kitab at-Tas'hil* of Ibn Juzayy al-Kalbi, the *Jami' li-Ahkam al-Qur'an* of al-Qurtubi and the *Ahkam al-Qur'an* of Abu Bakr Ibn al-'Arabi, but we have also consulted many others during the course of our work.

Although this has hopefully safeguarded us from error and kept us well within the parameters of acceptable meaning, we can only admit along with all our predecessors that the result falls far short of being anything like a complete exposition of the meanings of the Qur'an. Nevertheless, we hope that this rendering will give people of this time, and in particular English speaking Muslims, a more direct access to the meaning of the Book of Allah and encourage them to go further and discover from the original Arabic the inexhaustible fund of light and wisdom it contains.

We would also like to thank Dr Yasin Dutton for his painstaking reading of much of the draft manuscript and for the many comments and suggestions he made, most of which have been incorporated into the final text. And finally our heartfelt thanks go to Shaykh Hamdan Al Maktoum bin Rashid, under whose auspices this first edition is being printed. We ask Allah to bless and protect him and all his family.

We praise and thank Allah for enabling us to complete this work, seek His forgiveness for the shortcomings it possesses, and ask Him to accept it from us. May the peace and blessings of Allah be upon His Messenger Muhammad and his family and Companions and all who follow in their footsteps until the Last Day.

Abdalhaqq and Aisha Bewley
Norwich, England. 1420/1999

Table of Contents

Contents

THE NOBLE
QUR'AN

Sura 1

Al-Fatiha

In the name of Allah, All-Merciful, Most Merciful

1	Praise be to Allah, the Lord of all the worlds,
2	the All-Merciful, the Most Merciful,
3	the King of the Day of Repayment.
4	You alone we worship.
	You alone we ask for help.
5	Guide us on the Straight Path,
6	the Path of those You have blessed,
7	not of those with anger on them,
	nor of the misguided.

Sura 2

Al-Baqara
The Cow

In the name of Allah, All-Merciful, Most Merciful

1   Alif Lam Mim
2   That is the Book, without any doubt.
     In it is guidance for the godfearing:
3   those who believe in the Unseen and establish the prayer
         and spend from what We have provided for them;
4   those who believe in what has been sent down to you
         and what was sent down before you,
             and are certain about the Next World.
5   They are the people guided by their Lord.
         They are the successful.

6   As for those who disbelieve, it makes no difference to them
         whether you warn them or do not warn them,
             they will not believe.

7   Allah has sealed up their hearts and hearing
         and over their eyes is a blindfold.
     They will have a terrible punishment.

8   Among the people there are some who say,
         'We believe in Allah and the Last Day,'
             when they are not believers.

9   They think they deceive Allah and those who believe.
         They deceive no one but themselves
             but they are not aware of it.

10   There is a sickness in their hearts
        and Allah has increased their sickness.
     They will have a painful punishment
        on account of their denial.

11   When they are told, 'Do not cause corruption on the earth,'
        they say, 'We are only putting things right.'

12   No indeed! They are the corrupters,
        but they are not aware of it.

13   When they are told, 'Believe
        in the way that the people believe,'
     they say, 'What! Are we to believe
        in the way that fools believe?'
     No indeed! They are the fools, but they do not know it.

14   When they meet those who believe, they say,
        'We believe.'
     But then when they go apart with their shaytans,
        they say, 'We are really with you.
            We were only mocking.'

15   But Allah is mocking them, and drawing them on,
        as they wander blindly in their excessive insolence.

16   Those are the people who have sold guidance for misguidance.
        Their trade has brought no profit; they are not guided.

17   Their likeness is that of people who light a fire,
        and then when it has lit up all around them,
            Allah removes their light
        and leaves them in darkness, unable to see.

18   Deaf, dumb, blind.
        They will not return.

19   Or that of a storm-cloud in the sky,
        full of darkness, thunder and lightning.
     They put their fingers in their ears against the thunderclaps,
        fearful of death.
     Allah encompasses the unbelievers.

20   The lightning all but takes away their sight.
        Whenever they have light, they walk in it
   but whenever darkness covers them, they halt.
       If Allah wished, He could take away
           their hearing and their sight.
       Allah has power over all things.

21   Mankind! worship your Lord,
        who created you and those before you,
   so that hopefully you will be godfearing.

22   It is He who made the earth a couch for you,
        and the sky a dome.
   He sends down water from the sky
        and by it brings forth fruits for your provision.
   Do not, then, knowingly make others equal to Allah.

23   If you have doubts about what We have sent down to Our slave,
        produce another sura equal to it,
   and call your witnesses, besides Allah,
        if you are telling the truth.

24   If you do not do that – and you will not do it –
        then fear the Fire whose fuel is people and stones,
           made ready for the unbelievers.

25   Give good news
        to those who believe and do right actions
   that they will have Gardens
        with rivers flowing under them.
   When they are given fruit there as provision,
        they will say, 'This is what we were given before.'
           But they were only given a simulation of it.
   They will have there spouses of perfect purity
        and will remain there timelessly, for ever.

26   Allah is not ashamed to make an example of a gnat
        or of an even smaller thing.
   As for those who believe,
        they know it is the truth from their Lord.
   But as for those who disbelieve,
        they say, 'What does Allah mean by this example?'
   He misguides many by it and guides many by it.
        But He only misguides the deviators.

27   Those who break Allah's contract after it has been agreed,
          and sever what Allah has commanded to be joined,
              and cause corruption on the earth,
          it is they who are the lost.

28   How can you reject Allah,
          when you were dead and then He gave you life,
      then He will make you die and then give you life again,
          then you will be returned to Him?

29   It is He who created everything on the earth for you
          and then directed His attention up to heaven
      and arranged it into seven regular heavens.
          He has knowledge of all things.

30   When your Lord said to the angels,
          'I am putting a khalif on the earth,'
      they said, 'Why put on it one who will cause corruption on it
              and shed blood
          when we glorify You with praise
              and proclaim Your purity?'
      He said, 'I know what you do not know.'

31   He taught Adam the names of all things.
          Then He arrayed them before the angels and said,
      'Tell me the names of these if you are telling the truth.'

32   They said, 'Glory be to You! We have no knowledge
          except what You have taught us.
      You are the All-Knowing, the All-Wise.'

33   He said, 'Adam, tell them their names.'
          When he had told them their names,
      He said, 'Did I not tell you that I know
              the Unseen of the heavens and the earth,
          and I know what you make known
              and what you hide?'

34   We said to the angels, 'Prostrate to Adam!'
          and they prostrated, with the exception of Iblis.
      He refused and was arrogant and was one of the unbelievers.

35   We said, 'Adam, live in the Garden, you and your wife,
          and eat freely from it wherever you will.

But do not approach this tree and so become wrongdoers.'

36 But Shaytan made them slip up by means of it,
   expelling them from where they were.
We said, 'Go down from here as enemies to each other!
   You will have residence on the earth
      and enjoyment for a time.'

37 Then Adam received some words from his Lord
   and He turned towards him.
He is the Ever-Relenting, the Most Merciful.

38 We said, 'Go down from it, every one of you!
   Then when guidance comes to you from Me,
      those who follow My guidance
   will feel no fear and know no sorrow.'

39 But those who disbelieve and deny Our Signs
   are the Companions of the Fire,
      remaining in it timelessly, for ever.

40 Tribe of Israel! remember the blessing I conferred on you.
   Honour My contract and I will honour your contract.
      Have dread of Me alone.

41 Believe in what I have sent down,
   confirming what is with you.
      Do not be the first to reject it
   and do not sell My Signs for a paltry price.
      Have taqwa of Me alone.

42 Do not mix up truth with falsehood
   and knowingly hide the truth.

43 Establish the prayer and pay zakat
   and bow with those who bow.

44 Do you order people to devoutness and forget yourselves,
   when you recite the Book?
Will you not use your intellect?

45 Seek help in steadfastness and the prayer.
   But that is a very hard thing,
      except for the humble:

46   those who are aware that they will meet their Lord
          and that they will return to Him.

47   Tribe of Israel! remember the blessing I conferred on you
          and that I preferred you over all other beings.

48   Have fear of a Day when no self
          will be able to compensate for another in any way.
      No intercession will be taken from it,
          no ransom accepted from it,
              and none will be helped.

49   Remember when We rescued you from the people of Pharaoh.
          They were inflicting an evil punishment on you –
              slaughtering your sons and letting your women live.
      In that there was a terrible trial for you from your Lord.

50   And when We parted the sea for you and rescued you,
          and drowned the people of Pharaoh while you watched.

51   And when We allotted to Musa forty nights.
          Then you adopted the Calf when he had gone
              and you were wrongdoers.

52   Then We pardoned you after that
          so that perhaps you would show thanks.

53   Remember when We gave Musa the Book and discrimination
          so that perhaps you would be guided.

54   And when Musa said to his people, 'My people,
          You wronged yourselves by adopting the Calf
              so turn towards your Maker and kill yourselves.
          That is the best thing for you in your Maker's sight.'
              And He turned towards you.
          He is the Ever-Returning, the Most Merciful.

55   And when you said, 'Musa, we will not believe in you
          until we see Allah with our own eyes.'
      So the thunder-bolt struck you dead
          while you were looking.

56   Then We brought you back to life after your death,
          so that perhaps you would show thanks.

57   And We shaded you with clouds
            and sent down manna and quails to you:
        'Eat of the good things We have provided for you.'
            They did not wrong Us;
        rather it was themselves they were wronging.

58   Remember when We said, 'Enter this town.
            and eat from it wherever you like, freely.
        Enter the gate prostrating and say, "Relieve us of our burdens!"
            Your mistakes will be forgiven.
        We will grant increase to all good-doers.'
59   But those who did wrong substituted words
                    other than those they had been given.
                So We sent down a plague from heaven
                    on those who did wrong
                because they were deviators.

60   And when Musa was seeking water for his people,
            We said, 'Strike the rock with your staff.'
        Then twelve fountains gushed out from it
            and all the people knew their drinking place.
        'Eat and drink of Allah's provision
            and do not go about the earth corrupting it.'

61   And when you said, 'Musa, we will not put up with
                just one kind of food
        so ask your Lord to supply to us some of
            what the earth produces –
        its green vegetables, cucumbers,
            grains, lentils and onions,'
        he said, 'Do you want to replace what is better
            with something inferior?
        Go back to Egypt, then you will have what you are asking for.'
            Abasement and destitution were stamped upon them.
                They brought down anger from Allah upon themselves.
        That was because they rejected Allah's Signs
            and killed the Prophets without any right to do so.
        That was because they rebelled and went beyond the limits.

62   Those who believe, those who are Jews,
            and the Christians and Sabaeans,
        all who believe in Allah and the Last Day and act rightly,
            will have their reward with their Lord.
        They will feel no fear and they will know no sorrow.

63   Remember when We made the covenant with you
            and lifted up the Mount above your heads:
      'Take hold vigorously of what We have given you
            and pay heed to what is in it,
        so that hopefully you may be godfearing.'

64   Then after that you turned away,
            and were it not for Allah's favour to you
                and His mercy,
        you would have been among the lost.

65   You are well aware of those of you who broke the Sabbath.
        We said to them, 'Be apes, despised, cast out.'

66   We made it an exemplary punishment for those there then,
            and those coming afterwards,
        and a warning to the godfearing.

67   And when Musa said to his people,
            'Allah commands you to sacrifice a cow,'
      they said, 'What! Are you making a mockery of us?'
            He said, 'I seek refuge with Allah
                from being one of the ignorant!'

68   They said, 'Ask your Lord to make it clear to us
            what it should be like.'
      He said, 'He says it should be a cow,
            not old or virgin, but somewhere between the two.
        So do as you have been told.'

69   They said, 'Ask your Lord to make it clear to us
            what colour it should be.'
      He said, 'He says it should be a yellow cow,
            the colour of sorrel,
        a pleasure to all who look.'

70   They said, 'Ask your Lord to make it clear to us
            what it should be like.
      Cows are all much the same to us.
            Then, if Allah wills, we will be guided.'

71   He said, 'He says it should be a cow
            not trained to plough or irrigate the fields –
                completely sound, without a blemish on it.'

They said, 'Now you have brought the truth.'
So they sacrificed it – but they almost did not do it.

72 Remember when you killed someone
 and violently accused each other of it,
and Allah brought out what you were hiding.

73 We said, 'Hit him with part of it!'
 In that way Allah gives life to the dead
  and He shows you His Signs
 so that hopefully you will understand.

74 Then your hearts became hardened after that,
 so they were like rocks or even harder still.
There are some rocks from which rivers gush out,
 and others which split open and water pours out,
  and others which crash down from fear of Allah.
 Allah is not unaware of what you do.

75 Do you really hope they will follow you in faith
 when a group of them heard Allah's Word
and then, after grasping it, knowingly distorted it?

76 When they meet those who believe, they say,
 'We believe.'
But when they go apart with one another, they say,
 'Why do you speak to them about
  what Allah has disclosed to you,
 so they can use it as an argument against you
  before your Lord?
 Will you not use your intellect?'

77 Do they not know that Allah knows what they keep secret
 and what they make public?

78 Some of them are illiterate,
 knowing nothing of the Book but wishful thinking.
  They only speculate.

79 Woe to those who write the Book with their own hands
 and then say 'This is from Allah'
  to sell it for a paltry price.
Woe to them for what their hands have written!
 Woe to them for what they earn!

80 They say, 'The Fire will only touch us for a number of days.'
Say, 'Have you made a contract with Allah –
then Allah will not break His contract –
or are you rather saying about Allah what you do not know?'

81 No indeed! Those who accumulate bad actions
and are surrounded by their mistakes,
such people are the Companions of the Fire,
remaining in it timelessly, for ever;
82 whereas those who believe and do right actions,
such people are the Companions of the Garden,
remaining in it timelessly, for ever.

83 Remember when We made a covenant with the tribe of Israel:
'Worship none but Allah and be good to your parents
and to relatives and orphans and the very poor.
And speak good words to people.
And establish the prayer and pay zakat.'
But then you turned away – except a few of you –
you turned aside.

84 And when We made a covenant with you not to shed your blood
and not to expel one another from your homes,
you agreed and were all witnesses.

85 Then you are the people who are killing one another
and expelling a group among you from their homes,
ganging up against them in wrongdoing and enmity.
Yet if they are brought to you as captives, you ransom them,
when it was forbidden for you to expel them in the first place!
Do you, then, believe in one part of the Book
and reject the other?
What repayment will there be for any of you who do that
except disgrace in this world?
And on the Day of Rising, they will be returned
to the harshest of punishments.
Allah is not unaware of what they do.

86 Those are the people who trade the Next World for this world.
The punishment will not be lightened for them.
They will not be helped.

87 We gave Musa the Book
and sent a succession of Messengers after him.

We gave 'Isa, son of Maryam, the Clear Signs
    and reinforced him with the Purest Ruh.
Why then, whenever a Messenger came to you
    with something your lower selves did not desire,
        did you grow arrogant,
    and deny some of them and murder others?

88   They say, 'Our hearts are uncircumcised.'
        Rather, Allah has cursed them for their unbelief.
            What little faith they have!

89   When a Book does come to them from Allah,
        confirming what is with them –
    even though before that they were praying
        for victory over the unbelievers –
    yet when what they recognise does come to them,
        they reject it.
    Allah's curse is on the unbelievers.

90   What an evil thing they have sold themselves for
        in rejecting what Allah has sent down,
    outraged that Allah should send down His favour
        on whichever of His slaves He wills.
    They have brought down anger upon anger on themselves.
        The unbelievers will have a humiliating punishment.

91   When they are told, 'Believe in what Allah has sent down,'
        they say, 'We believe is in what was sent down to us,'
            and they reject anything beyond that,
    even though it is the truth, confirming what they have.
        Say, 'Why then, if you are believers,
    did you previously kill the Prophets of Allah?'

92   Musa brought you the Clear Signs;
        then, after he left, you adopted the Calf
            and were wrongdoers.

93   Remember when We made a covenant with you
        and lifted up the Mount above your heads:
    'Take hold vigorously of what We have given you and listen.'
        They said, 'We hear and disobey.'
    They were made to drink the Calf into their hearts
        because of their unbelief.

Say, 'If you are believers, what an evil thing
 your belief has made you do.'

94 Say, 'If the abode of the Next World with Allah is for you alone,
 to the exclusion of all others,
then long for death if you are telling the truth.'

95 But they will never ever long for it
 because of what they have done.
Allah knows the wrongdoers.

96 Rather you will find them the people greediest for life,
 along with the idolators.
Any of them would love to be allowed to live a thousand years.
 But being allowed to live would not save him
  from the punishment.
 Allah sees what they do.

97 Say, 'Anyone who is the enemy of Jibril should know
 that it was he who brought it down upon your heart,
  by Allah's authority,
 confirming what came before,
and as guidance and good news for the believers.
98 Anyone who is the enemy of Allah and of His angels,
  and of His Messengers and of Jibril and Mika'il,
 should know that Allah is the enemy of the unbelievers.'

99 We have sent down Clear Signs to you
 and no one rejects them except the deviators.

100 Why is it that, whenever they make a contract,
 a group of them disdainfully tosses it aside?
  No indeed! Most of them do not believe.

101 When a Messenger comes to them from Allah
 confirming what is with them,
a group of those who have been given the Book
 disdainfully toss the Book of Allah behind their backs,
  just as if they did not know.

102 They follow what the shaytans recited in the reign of Sulayman.
 Sulayman did not disbelieve, but the shaytans did,
  teaching people sorcery
 and what had been sent down to Harut and Marut,

the two angels in Babylon,
who taught no one without first saying to him,
'We are merely a trial and temptation,
so do not disbelieve.'
People learned from them how to separate a man and his wife
but they cannot harm anyone by it,
except with Allah's permission.
They have learned what will harm them
and will not benefit them.
They know that any who deal in it
will have no share in the Next World.
What an evil thing they have sold themselves for
if they only knew!

103   If only they had believed and been godfearing!
A reward from Allah is better, if they only knew.

104   You who believe! do not say, *'Ra'ina,'*
say, *'Undhurna,'* and listen well.
The unbelievers will have a painful punishment.

105   Those of the People of the Book who disbelieve
and the idolators
do not like anything good to be sent down to you
from your Lord.
But Allah selects for His mercy whomever He wills.
Allah's favour is truly vast.

106   Whenever We abrogate an ayat or cause it to be forgotten,
We bring one better than it or equal to it.
Do you not know that Allah has power over all things?

107   Do you not know that Allah is He to Whom
the kingdom of the heavens and the earth belongs
and that, besides Allah,
you have no protector and no helper?

108   Or do you want to question your Messenger
as Musa was questioned before?
Anyone who exchanges faith for unbelief
has definitely gone astray from the level way.

---

* Two Arabic words meaning "Look at us." But the former can be ambiguously construed in a derogatory way whereas the latter cannot.

109   Many of the People of the Book would love it
            if they could make you revert to being unbelievers
                after you have become believers,
        showing their innate envy now that the truth is clear to them.
            But you should pardon and overlook
                until Allah gives His command.
            Truly Allah has power over all things.

110   Establish the prayer and pay zakat.
            Any good you send ahead for yourselves,
                you will find with Allah.
            Certainly Allah sees what you do.

111   They say, 'No one will enter the Garden
            except for Jews and Christians.'
                Such is their vain hope.
        Say, 'Produce your evidence if you are telling the truth.'

112   Not so! All who submit themselves completely to Allah
                and are good-doers
            will find their reward with their Lord.
        They will feel no fear and they will know no sorrow.

113   The Jews say, 'The Christians have nothing to stand on,'
            and the Christians say, 'The Jews have nothing to stand on,'
                yet they both recite the Book.
            Those who do not know say the same as they say.
        Allah will judge between them on the Day of Rising
            regarding the things about which they differ.

114   Who could do greater wrong than someone
            who bars access to the mosques of Allah,
        preventing His name from being remembered in them,
            and goes about destroying them?
        Such people will never be able to enter them – except in fear.
            They will have disgrace in this world
        and in the Next World they will have a terrible punishment.

115   Both East and West belong to Allah,
            so wherever you turn,
                the Face of Allah is there.
        Allah is All-Encompassing, All-Knowing.

116   They say, 'Allah has a son.'
       Glory be to Him!
  No, everything in the heavens and earth belongs to Him.
       Everything is obedient to Him,
117   the Originator of the heavens and earth.
       When He decides on something,
  He just says to it, 'Be!' and it is.

118   Those who do not know say, 'If only Allah would speak to us,
       or some sign come to us!'
  just like those before them who said the same as they say.
       Their hearts are much the same.
  We have made the Signs clear for people who have certainty.

119   We have sent you with the Truth,
       bringing good news and giving warning.
  Do not ask about the inhabitants of the Blazing Fire.

120   The Jews and the Christians will never be pleased with you
       until you follow their religion.
  Say, 'Allah's guidance is the true guidance.'
       If you were to follow their whims and desires,
          after the knowledge that has come to you,
       you would find no protector or helper against Allah.

121   Those to whom We have given the Book,
       who recite it in the way it should be recited,
          such people believe in it.
  As for those who reject it, they are the losers.

122   Tribe of Israel! remember the blessing I conferred on you,
       and that I preferred you over all other beings.

123   Have fear of a Day when no self
       will be able to compensate for another
          in any way,
       and no ransom will be accepted from it,
          and no intercession benefit it,
             and they will not be helped.

124   Remember when Ibrahim was tested by his Lord
       with certain instructions which he carried out completely.
  He said, 'I will make you a model for mankind.'

He asked, 'And what of my descendants?'
He said, 'My contract does not include wrongdoers.'

125   And when We made the House* a place of return,
          a sanctuary for mankind:
They took the Maqam of Ibrahim as a place of prayer.
    We contracted with Ibrahim and Isma'il:
'Purify My House for those who circle it,
          and those who stay there,
          and those who bow and who prostrate.'

126   And when Ibrahim said, 'My Lord, make this a place of safety
          and provide its inhabitants with fruits –
                all of them who believe
                      in Allah and the Last Day,'
He said, 'I will let anyone who disbelieves
          enjoy himself a little
but then I will drive him to the punishment of the Fire.
    What an evil destination!'

127   And when Ibrahim built
          the foundations of the House with Isma'il:
'Our Lord, accept this from us!
    You are the All-Hearing, the All-Knowing.
128   Our Lord, make us both Muslims submitted to You,
          and our descendants a Muslim community submitted to You.
Show us our rites of worship and turn towards us.
    You are the Ever-Relenting, the Most Merciful.
129   Our Lord, raise up among them a Messenger from them
          to recite Your Signs to them
                and teach them the Book and Wisdom
                      and purify them.
          You are the Almighty, the All-Wise.'

130   Who would deliberately renounce the religion of Ibrahim
          except someone who reveals himself to be a fool?
          We chose him in this world
          and in the Next World he will be one of the righteous.

131   When his Lord said to him, 'Become a Muslim!'
          he said, 'I am a Muslim who has submitted
                to the Lord of all the worlds.'

---

* The Ka'ba in Makka.

132   Ibrahim directed his sons to this, as did Ya'qub:
             'My sons! Allah has chosen this deen for you,
                  so do not die except as Muslims.'
133   Or were you present when death came to Ya'qub
             and he said to his sons,
                  'What will you worship when I have gone?'
         They said, 'We will worship your God,
             the God of your forefathers,
                  Ibrahim, Isma'il and Ishaq –
                       one God.
             We are Muslims submitted to Him.'

134   That was a community which has long since passed away.
             It has what it earned.
                  You have what you have earned.
             You will not be questioned about what they did.

135   They say, 'Be Jews or Christians and you will be guided.'
             Say, 'Rather adopt the religion of Ibrahim,
                  a man of natural pure belief.
             He was not one of the idolators.'

136   Say, 'We believe in Allah
             and what has been sent down to us
         and what was sent down to Ibrahim
             and Isma'il and Ishaq
                  and Ya'qub and the Tribes,
             and what Musa and 'Isa were given,
         and what all the Prophets were given by their Lord.
             We do not differentiate between any of them.
                  We are Muslims submitted to Him.'

137   If their faith is the same as yours
             then they are guided.
         But if they turn away,
             they are entrenched in hostility.
         Allah will be enough for you against them.
             He is the All-Hearing, the All-Knowing.

138   The colouring of Allah –
             and what colouring could be better than Allah's?
                  It is Him we worship.

139   Say, 'Do you argue with us about Allah
         when He is our Lord and your Lord?
      We have our actions and you have your actions.
         We act for Him alone.'

140   Or do they say that Ibrahim and Isma'il and Ishaq
         and Ya'qub and the Tribes were Jews or Christians?
      Say, 'Do you know better or does Allah?'
         Who could do greater wrong than someone who hides
            the evidence he has been given by Allah?
         Allah is not unaware of what you do.

141   That was a community which has long since passed away.
         It has what it earned.
            You have what you have earned.
         You will not be questioned about what they did.

142   The fools among the people will ask,
         'What has made them turn round
            from the direction they used to face?'*
      Say, 'Both East and West belong to Allah.
         He guides whoever He wills to a straight path.'

143   In this way We have made you a middlemost community,
         so that you may act as witnesses against mankind
         and the Messenger as a witness against you.
      We only appointed the direction you used to face
         in order to distinguish those who follow the Messenger
         from those who turn round on their heels.
      Though in truth it is a very hard thing –
         except for those Allah has guided.
      Allah would never let your faith go to waste.
         Allah is All-Gentle, Most Merciful to mankind.

144   We have seen you looking up into heaven,
         turning this way and that,
      so We will turn you towards a direction which will please you.
         Turn your face, therefore, towards the Masjid al-Haram.
      Wherever you all are, turn your faces towards it.
         Those given the Book know it is the truth from their Lord.
         Allah is not unaware of what they do.

145   If you were to bring every Sign to those given the Book,
         they still would not follow your direction.

---

* Referring to when the direction faced in the prayer was changed from Jerusalem to Makka.

You do not follow their direction.
    They do not follow each other's direction.
If you followed their whims and desires,
    after the knowledge that has come to you,
you would then be one of the wrongdoers.

146   Those We have given the Book recognise it
         as they recognise their own sons.
     Yet a group of them knowingly conceal the truth.

147   The truth is from your Lord,
         so on no account be among the doubters.

148   Each person faces a particular direction
         so race each other to the good.
     Wherever you are, Allah will bring you all together.
         Truly Allah has power over all things.

149   Wherever you come from, turn your face to the Masjid al-Haram.
         This is certainly the truth from your Lord.
             Allah is not unaware of what you do.

150   Wherever you come from, turn your face to the Masjid al-Haram.
         Wherever you are, turn your faces towards it
             so that people will have no argument against yourselves
         except for those among them who do wrong
     and then you should not fear them but rather fear Me –
         and so that I may complete My blessing upon you
             so that hopefully you will be guided.

151   For this We sent a Messenger to you from among you
         to recite Our Signs to you and purify you
             and teach you the Book and Wisdom
         and teach you things you did not know before.

152   Remember Me – I will remember you.
         Give thanks to Me and do not be ungrateful.

153   You who believe! seek help in steadfastness and the prayer.
         Allah is with the steadfast.

154   Do not say of those killed in the Way of Allah
         that they are dead.

On the contrary, they are alive
   but you are not aware of it.

155   We will test you with a certain amount of fear and hunger
         and loss of wealth and life and fruits.
      But give good news to the steadfast:

156   Those who, when disaster strikes them, say,
         'We belong to Allah and to Him we will return.'

157   Those are the people who will have blessings and mercy
         from their Lord;
      they are the ones who are guided.

158   Safa and Marwa are among the Landmarks of Allah,
         so anyone who goes on hajj to the House or does 'umra
      incurs no wrong in going back and forth between them.
         If anyone spontaneously does good,
      Allah is All-Thankful, All-Knowing.

159   Those who hide the Clear Signs and Guidance
               We have sent down,
         after We have made it clear to people in the Book,
            Allah curses them, and the cursers curse them –
160   except for those who repent
         and put things right and make things clear.
            I turn towards them.
         I am the Ever-Relenting, the Most Merciful.

161   But as for those who disbelieve and die as unbelievers,
         the curse of Allah is upon them
      and that of the angels and all mankind.
162   They will be under it for ever.
      The punishment will not be lightened for them.
         They will be granted no reprieve.

163   Your God is One God.
         There is no god but Him,
      the All-Merciful, the Most Merciful.

164   In the creation of the heavens and earth,
         and the alternation of the night and day,
         and the ships which sail the seas to people's benefit,
         and the water which Allah sends down from the sky –

by which He brings the earth to life when it was dead
    and scatters about in it creatures of every kind –
and the varying direction of the winds,
and the clouds subservient between heaven and earth,
there are Signs for people who use their intellect.

165   Some people set up equals to Allah,
            loving them as they should love Allah.
        But those who believe have greater love for Allah.
            If only you could see those who do wrong
        at the time when they see the punishment,
            and that truly all strength belongs to Allah,
        and that Allah is severe in punishment.

166   When those who were followed
            disown those who followed them,
                and they see the punishment,
        and the connection between them is cut,
167   those who followed will say,
        'If only we could have another chance,
                we would disown them
            just as they have disowned us.'
        In that way Allah will show them their actions
            as a cause of anguish and remorse for them.
        They will never emerge from the Fire.

168   Mankind! eat what is good and lawful on the earth.
            And do not follow in the footsteps of Shaytan.
                He truly is an outright enemy to you.

169   He only commands you to do evil and indecent acts
            and to say about Allah what you do not know.

170   When they are told, 'Follow what Allah has sent down to you,'
            They say, 'We are following what we found our fathers doing.'
        What, even though their fathers did not understand a thing
            and were not guided!

171   The likeness of those who disbelieve is that of someone
            who yells out to something which cannot hear –
                it is nothing but a cry and a call.
            Deaf – dumb – blind.
                They do not use their intellect.

172   You who believe! eat of the good things
              We have provided for you
       and give thanks to Allah if you worship Him alone.
173   He has only forbidden you carrion, blood and pork
       and what has been consecrated to other than Allah.
       But anyone who is forced to eat it –
          without desiring it or going to excess in it –
             commits no crime.
       Allah is Ever-Forgiving, Most Merciful.

174   Those who conceal what Allah has sent down of the Book
              and sell it cheap,
          take nothing into their bellies but the Fire.
       On the Day of Rising Allah will not speak to them
          or purify them.
       They will have a painful punishment.

175   Those are the ones who have sold guidance for misguidance
              and forgiveness for punishment.
       How steadfastly they will endure the Fire!

176   That is because Allah has sent down the Book with truth
              and those who differ from the Book
                 are entrenched in hostility.

177   Goodness does not lie in turning your faces
              to the East or to the West.
          Rather, those with true devoutness are those who believe
       in Allah and the Last Day, the Angels, the Book and the Prophets,
          and who, despite their love for it, give away their wealth
       to their relatives and to orphans and the very poor,
              and to travellers and beggars and to set slaves free,
                 and who establish the prayer and pay zakat;
       those who honour their contracts when they make them,
          and are steadfast in poverty and illness and in battle.
       Those are the people who are true.
          They are the people who are godfearing.

178   You who believe! retaliation is prescribed for you
              in the case of people killed:
                 free man for free man,
                    slave for slave,
                 female for female.
       But if someone is absolved by his brother,

blood-money should be claimed with correctness
    and paid with good will.
That is an easement and a mercy from your Lord.
    Anyone who goes beyond the limits after this
        will receive a painful punishment.

179   There is life for you in retaliation, people of intelligence,
    so that hopefully you will be godfearing.

180   It is prescribed for you,
    when death approaches one of you
        and if he has some goods to leave,
to make a will in favour of his parents and relatives,
    correctly and fairly:
a duty for the godfearing.

181   Then if anyone alters it after hearing it,
    the crime is on the part of those who alter it.
Allah is All-Hearing, All-Knowing.

182   But if anyone fears bias or wrongdoing
    on the part of the person making the will,
and puts things right between the people involved,
    in that case he has not committed any crime.
Allah is Ever-Forgiving, Most Merciful.

183   You who believe! fasting is prescribed for you,
    as it was prescribed for those before you –
        so that hopefully you will be godfearing –
184   for a specified number of days.
But any of you who are ill or on a journey
    should fast a number of other days.
For those who are able to fast,
    their fidya is to feed the poor.
And if someone does good of his own accord,
    it is better for him.
But that you should fast is better for you,
    if you only knew.

185   The month of Ramadan is the one in which the Qur'an
    was sent down as guidance for mankind,
with Clear Signs containing guidance and discrimination.
    Any of you who are resident for the month should fast it.
But any of you who are ill or on a journey
    should fast a number of other days.

Allah desires ease for you;
　　He does not desire difficulty for you.
You should complete the number of days
　　and proclaim Allah's greatness
　　　　for the guidance He has given you
　　so that hopefully you will be thankful.

186　If My slaves ask you about Me, I am near.
　　I answer the call of the caller when he calls on Me.
They should therefore respond to Me and believe in Me
　　so that hopefully they will be rightly guided.

187　On the night of the fast it is lawful for you
　　to have sexual relations with your wives.
　　　　They are clothing for you and you for them.
Allah knows that you have been betraying yourselves
　　and He has turned towards you and excused you.
Now you may have sexual intercourse with them
　　and seek what Allah has written for you.
Eat and drink until you can clearly discern
　　the white thread from the black thread of the dawn,
　　　　then fulfil the fast until the night appears.
But do not have sexual intercourse with them
　　while you are in retreat in the mosques.
These are Allah's limits, so do not go near them.
　　In this way does Allah make His Signs clear to people
　　so that hopefully they will be godfearing.

188　Do not devour one another's property by false means
　　nor offer it to the judges as a bribe,
trying through crime to knowingly usurp
　　a portion of other people's property.

189　They will ask you about the crescent moons.
　　Say, 'They are set times for mankind and for the hajj.'
It is not devoutness for you to enter houses by the back.
　　Rather devoutness is possessed by those who are godfearing.
So come to houses by their doors and have taqwa of Allah,
　　so that hopefully you will be successful.

190　Fight in the Way of Allah against those who fight you,
　　but do not go beyond the limits.
Allah does not love those who go beyond the limits.

191   Kill them wherever you come across them
            and expel them from where they expelled you.
                Fitna is worse than killing.
        Do not fight them in the Masjid al-Haram
            until they fight you there.
        But if they do fight you, then kill them.
            That is how the unbelievers should be repaid.

192   But if they cease, Allah is Ever-Forgiving, Most Merciful.

193   Fight them until there is no more fitna
            and the deen belongs to Allah alone.
        If they cease, there should be no enmity
            towards any but wrongdoers.

194   Sacred month in return for sacred month –
            sacred things are subject to retaliation.
        So if anyone oversteps the limits against you,
            overstep against him the same as he did to you.
                But have taqwa of Allah.
        Know that Allah is with those who are godfearing.

195   Spend in the Way of Allah.
            Do not cast yourselves into destruction.
        And do good: Allah loves good-doers.

196   Perform the hajj and 'umra for Allah.
            If you are forcibly prevented,
                make whatever sacrifice is feasible.
        But do not shave your heads until the sacrificial animal
            has reached the place of sacrifice.
        If any of you are ill or have a head injury, the expiation
            is fasting or sadaqa or sacrifice
                when you are safe and well again.
        Anyone who comes out of ihram between 'umra and hajj
            should make whatever sacrifice is feasible.
        For any one who cannot, there are three days' fast on hajj
            and seven on your return – that is ten in all.
        That is for anyone whose family does not live near
            the Masjid al-Haram.
        Have taqwa of Allah and know
            that Allah is severe in retribution.

197   The hajj takes place during certain well-known months.
        If anyone undertakes the obligation of hajj in them,
there must be no sexual intercourse, no wrongdoing,
        nor any quarrelling during hajj.
Whatever good you do, Allah knows it.
        Take provision;
            but the best provision
                is taqwa of Allah.
So have taqwa of Me, people of intelligence!

198   There is nothing wrong in seeking bounty from your Lord.
        When you pour down from Arafat,
            remember Allah at the Sacred Landmark.*
Remember Him because He has guided you,
        even though before this you were astray.

199   Then press on from where the people press on
        and ask Allah's forgiveness.
Allah is Ever-Forgiving, Most Merciful.

200   When you have completed your rites, remember Allah
        as you used to remember your forefathers – or even more.
There are some people who say,
        'Our Lord, give us good in this world.'
        They will have no share in the Next World.

201   And there are others who say,
        'Our Lord, give us good in this world,
            and good in the Next World,
        and safeguard us from the punishment of the Fire.'

202   They will have a good share from what they have earned.
        Allah is swift at reckoning.

203   Remember Allah on the designated days.
        Those who hurry on in two days have done no wrong,
and those who stay another day have done no wrong –
        those of them who are godfearing.
        So have taqwa of Allah.
And know that you will be gathered back to Him.

204   Among the people there is someone whose words
        about the life of this world excite your admiration,

---

* Referring to Muzdalifa, a place between Arafat and Mina on hajj.

and he calls Allah to witness what is in his heart,
     while he is in fact the most hostile of adversaries.

205   When he leaves you, he goes about the earth corrupting it,
     destroying crops and animals.
       Allah does not love corruption.

206   When he is told to have taqwa of Allah,
     he is seized by pride
which drives him to wrongdoing.
     Hell will be enough for him!
What an evil resting-place!

207   And among the people there are some who give up everything,
     desiring the good pleasure of Allah.
Allah is Ever-Gentle with His slaves.

208   You who believe! enter Islam totally.
     Do not follow in the footsteps of Shaytan.
       He is an outright enemy to you.

209   If you backslide after the Clear Signs have come to you,
     know that Allah is Almighty, All-Wise.

210   What are they waiting for but for Allah to come to them
     in the shadows of the clouds, together with the angels,
       in which case the matter will have been settled?
     All matters return to Allah.

211   Ask the tribe of Israel how many Clear Signs We gave to them.
     If anyone alters Allah's blessing after it has come to him,
       Allah is fierce in retribution.

212   To those who disbelieve, the life of this world
     is painted in glowing colours
       and they laugh at those who believe.
But on the Day of Rising those who fear Allah will be over them.
     Allah provides for whomever He wills without any reckoning.

213   Mankind was a single community.
     Then Allah sent out Prophets
       bringing good news and giving warning,
     and with them He sent down the Book with truth
       to decide between people regarding their differences.

Only those who were given it differed about it,
  after the Clear Signs had come to them, envying one another.
Then, by His permission, Allah guided those who believe
  to the truth of that about which they had differed.
Allah guides whomever He wills to a straight path.

214 Or did you suppose that you would enter the Garden
       without facing the same as those who came before you?
     Poverty and illness afflicted them
       and they were shaken to the point
     that the Messenger and those who believed with him said,
       'When is Allah's help coming?'
     Be assured that Allah's help is very near.

215 They will ask you what they should give away.
       Say, 'Any wealth you give away should go
         to your parents and relatives
         and to orphans and the very poor and travellers.'
     Whatever good you do, Allah knows it.

216 Fighting is prescribed for you even if it is hateful to you.
       It may be that you hate something when it is good for you
     and it may be that you love something when it is bad for you.
       Allah knows and you do not know.

217 They will ask you about the Sacred Month
       and fighting in it.
     Say, 'Fighting in it is a serious matter;
       but barring access to the Way of Allah
         and rejecting Him
       and barring access to the Masjid al-Haram
         and expelling its people from it
     are far more serious in the sight of Allah.
       Fitna is worse than killing.'
     They will not stop fighting you until
       they make you revert from your deen,
         if they are able.
     As for any of you who reverts from his deen
       and dies an unbeliever,
     his actions will come to nothing
       in this world and the Next World.
     Such people are the Companions of the Fire,
       remaining in it timelessly, for ever.

218   Those who believe and make hijra
            and do jihad in the Way of Allah
                can expect Allah's mercy.
       Allah is Ever-Forgiving, Most Merciful.

219   They will ask you about alcoholic drinks and gambling.
            Say, 'There is great wrong in both of them
                and also certain benefits for mankind.
            But the wrong in them is greater than the benefit.'
       They will ask you what they should give away.
            Say, 'Whatever is surplus to your needs.'
       In this way Allah makes the Signs clear to you,
            so that hopefully you will reflect
220   on this world and the Next World.
       They will ask you about the property of orphans.
            Say, 'Managing it in their best interests is best.'
       If you mix your property with theirs, they are your brothers.
            Allah knows a squanderer from a good manager.
       If Allah had wanted, He could have been hard on you.
            Allah is Almighty, All-Wise.

221   Do not marry women of the idolators until they believe.
            A slavegirl who is a believer is better for you
                than a woman of the idolators,
            even though she may attract you.
       And do not give (your women) in marriage
                to men of the idolators until they believe.
            A slave who is a believer is better for you
                than a man of the idolators,
            even though he may attract you.
       Such people call you to the Fire
            whereas Allah calls you, with His permission,
                to the Garden and forgiveness.
       He makes His Signs clear to people
            so that hopefully they will pay heed.

222   They will ask you about menstruation.
            Say, 'It is an impurity,
       so keep apart from women during menstruation
            and do not approach them
       until they have purified themselves.
            But once they have purified themselves,
       then go to them in the way that Allah has enjoined on you.'

Allah loves those who turn back from wrongdoing
and He loves those who purify themselves.

223   Your women are fertile fields for you,
so come to your fertile fields however you like.
Send good ahead for yourselves and have taqwa of Allah.
Know that you are going to meet Him.
And give good news to the believers.

224   Do not, by your oaths, make Allah a pretext
to avoid good action and having taqwa
and putting things right between people.
Allah is All-Hearing, All-Knowing.

225   Allah will not take you to task for
inadvertent statements in your oaths,
but He will take you to task for
the intention your hearts have made.
Allah is Ever-Forgiving, All-Forbearing.

226   Those who swear to abstain from
sexual relations with their wives
can wait for a period of up to four months.
If they then retract their oath,
Allah is Ever-Forgiving, Most Merciful.

227   If they are determined to divorce,
Allah is All-Hearing, All-Knowing.

228   Divorced women should wait by themselves
for three menstrual cycles;
and it is not lawful for them to conceal
what Allah has created in their wombs
if they believe in Allah and the Last Day.
Their husbands have the right
to take them back within that time,
if they desire to be reconciled.
Women possess rights similar to those held over them
to be honoured with fairness;
but men have a degree above them.
Allah is Almighty, All-Wise.

229   Divorce can be pronounced two times;
in which case wives may be retained

with correctness and courtesy
or released with good will.
It is not lawful for you to keep anything you have given them
    unless a couple fear that they will not remain
        within Allah's limits.
If you fear that they will not remain within Allah's limits,
    there is nothing wrong in the wife ransoming herself
        with some of what she received.
These are Allah's limits, so do not overstep them.
    Those who overstep Allah's limits are wrongdoers.

230   But if a man divorces his wife a third time,
    she is not halal for him after that
        until she has married another husband.
Then if he divorces her, there is nothing wrong
    in the original couple getting back together
provided they think they will remain within Allah's limits.
    These are Allah's limits
which He has made clear to people who know.

231   When you divorce women and they are near the end of their 'idda,
    then either retain them with correctness and courtesy
        or release them with correctness and courtesy.
Do not retain them by force, thus overstepping the limits.
    Anyone who does that has wronged himself.
        Do not make a mockery of Allah's Signs.
Remember Allah's blessing upon you and the Book and Wisdom
    He has sent down to you to admonish you.
        Have taqwa of Allah
    and know that Allah has knowledge of all things.

232   When you divorce women and they are near the end of their 'idda,
    do not prevent them from marrying their first husbands
        if they have mutually agreed to it
            with correctness and courtesy.
    This is an admonition for those of you
        who believe in Allah and the Last Day.
    That is better and purer for you.
        Allah knows and you do not know.

233   Mothers should nurse their children for two full years –
    for those who wish to complete the full term of nursing.
It is the duty of the fathers to feed and clothe them
    with correctness and courtesy –
        no self is charged with more than it can bear.

No mother should be put under pressure in respect of her child
  nor any father in respect of his child.
    The same duty is incumbent on the heir.
If the couple both wish weaning to take place
  after mutual agreement and consultation,
    there is nothing wrong in their doing so.
If you wish to find wet-nurses for your children,
  there is nothing wrong in your doing so
provided you hand over to them what you have agreed to give
  with correctness and courtesy.
Have taqwa of Allah and know that Allah sees what you do.

234 Those of you who die leaving wives behind:
       they should wait by themselves
         for four months and ten nights.
     When their 'idda comes to an end,
       you are not to blame for anything they do with themselves
         with correctness and courtesy.
       Allah is aware of what you do.

235 Nor is there anything wrong in any allusion to marriage
           you make to a woman,
             nor for any you keep to yourself.
     Allah knows that you will say things to them.
     But do not make secret arrangements with them,
       rather only speak with correctness and courtesy.
     Do not finally decide on the marriage contract
       until the prescribed period has come to its end.
     Know that Allah knows what is in your selves,
       so beware of Him!
     And know that Allah is Ever-Forgiving, All-Forbearing.

236 There is nothing wrong in your divorcing women
       before you have touched them
         or allotted a dowry to them.
     But give them a gift –
       he who is wealthy according to his means
         and he who is less well off according to his means –
     a gift to be given with correctness and courtesy:
       a duty for all good-doers.

237 If you divorce them before you have touched them
       but have already allotted them a dowry,
     they should have half the amount which you allotted,

unless they forgo it
or the one in charge of the marriage contract forgoes it.
   To forgo it is closer to taqwa.
Do not forget to show generosity to one another.
   Allah sees what you do.

238   Safeguard the prayer – especially the middle one.
        Stand in obedience to Allah.

239   If you are afraid, then pray on foot or mounted.
            But when you are safe,
        remember Allah in the way He taught you
            when previously you did not know.

240   Those of you who die leaving wives behind
            should make a bequest to their wives
                of maintenance for a year
            without them having to leave their homes.
        But if they do leave you are not to blame
            for anything they do with themselves
                with correctness and courtesy.
            Allah is Almighty, All-Wise.

241   Divorced women should receive maintenance
            given with correctness and courtesy:
                a duty for all who are godfearing.

242   In this way Allah makes His Signs clear to you,
            so that hopefully you will use your intellect.

243   What do you think about those who left their homes in thousands
            in fear of death?
        Allah said to them, 'Die!' and then brought them back to life.
            Allah shows great favour to mankind,
                but most people are not grateful.

244   Fight in the Way of Allah.
            Know that Allah is All-Hearing, All-Knowing.

245   Is there anyone who will make Allah a generous loan
            so that He can multiply it for him many times over?
        Allah both restricts and expands.
            And you will be returned to Him.

246   What do you think about the council of the tribe of Israel
            after Musa's time
        when they said to one of their Prophets, 'Give us a king
            and we will fight in the Way of Allah!'?
        He said, 'Is it not possible that if fighting were prescribed for you,
            you would not fight?'
        They said, 'How could we not fight in the way of Allah
            when we have been driven from our homes and children?'
        But then when fighting was prescribed for them,
            they turned their backs – except for a few of them.
                Allah knows the wrongdoers.

247   Their Prophet said to them,
            'Allah has appointed Saul to be your king.'
        They said, 'How can he be our king
            when we have much more right to kingship than he does?
                He has not even much wealth!'
        He said, 'Allah has chosen him over you
            and increased him greatly in knowledge and physical strength.
                Allah gives kingship to anyone He wills.
            Allah is All-Encompassing, All-Knowing.'

248   Their Prophet said to them,
            'The sign of his kingship is that the Ark will come to you,
                containing serenity from your Lord
            and certain relics left by the families of Musa and Harun.
                It will be borne by angels.
            There is a sign for you in that if you are believers.'

249   When Saul marched out with the army, he said,
            'Allah will test you with a river.
        Anyone who drinks from it is not with me.
            But anyone who does not taste it is with me –
        except for him who merely scoops up a little in his hand.'
            But they drank from it – except for a few of them.
        Then when he and those who believed with him had crossed it,
            they said, 'We do not have the strength
                to face Goliath and his troops today.'
        But those who were sure that they were going to meet Allah
            said, 'How many a small force has triumphed over
                a much greater one by Allah's permission!
            Allah is with the steadfast.

250   When they came out against Goliath and his troops,
         they said, 'Our Lord, pour down steadfastness upon us,
             and make our feet firm,
         and help us against this unbelieving people.'

251   And with Allah's permission they routed them.
         Dawud killed Goliath
and Allah gave him kingship and wisdom
         and taught him whatever He willed.
If it were not for Allah's driving some people back
         by means of others,
         the earth would have been corrupted.
But Allah shows favour to all the worlds.

252   Those are Allah's Signs which We recite to you with truth.
         You are indeed one of the Messengers.

253   These Messengers: We favoured some of them over others.
         Allah spoke directly to some of them
             and raised up some of them in rank.
We gave Clear Signs to 'Isa, son of Maryam,
         and reinforced him with the Purest Ruh.
If Allah had willed, those who came after them
         would not have fought each other
             after the Clear Signs came to them,
             but they differed.
Among them there are those who believe
         and among them there are those who disbelieve.
If Allah had willed, they would not have fought each other.
         But Allah does whatever He desires.

254   You who believe! give away
         some of what We have provided for you
before a Day arrives on which
         there is no trading,
            no close friendship
              and no intercession.
It is the unbelievers who are the wrongdoers.

255   Allah,
there is no god but Him,
         the Living, the Self-Sustaining.
He is not subject to drowsiness or sleep.
         Everything in the heavens and the earth belongs to Him.

Who can intercede with Him except by His permission?
He knows what is before them and what is behind them
but they cannot grasp any of His knowledge save what He wills.
His Footstool encompasses the heavens and the earth
and their preservation does not tire Him.
He is the Most High, the Magnificent.

256   There is no compulsion where the deen is concerned.
Right guidance has become clearly distinct from error.
Anyone who rejects false gods and believes in Allah
has grasped the Firmest Handhold,
which will never give way.
Allah is All-Hearing, All-Knowing.

257   Allah is the Protector of those who believe.
He brings them out of the darkness into the light.
But those who disbelieve have false gods as protectors.
They take them from the light into the darkness.
Those are the Companions of the Fire
remaining in it timelessly, for ever.

258   What about the one who argued with Ibrahim about his Lord,
on the basis that Allah had given him sovereignty?
Ibrahim said, 'My Lord is He who gives life and causes to die.'
He said, 'I too give life and cause to die.'
Ibrahim said, 'Allah makes the sun come from the East.
Make it come from the West.'
And the one who disbelieved was dumbfounded.
Allah does not guide wrongdoing people.

259   Or the one who passed by a town which had fallen into ruin?
He asked, 'How can Allah restore this to life
when it has died?'
Allah caused him to die a hundred years
then brought him back to life.
Then He asked, 'How long have you been here?'
He replied, 'I have been here a day or part of a day.'
He said, 'Not so! You have been here a hundred years.
Look at your food and drink – it has not gone bad –
and look at your donkey
so We can make you a Sign for all mankind.
Look at the bones –
how We raise them up and clothe them in flesh.'

When it had become clear to him, he said,
'Now I know that Allah has power over all things.'

260   When Ibrahim said, 'My Lord, show me
how You bring the dead to life.'
He asked, 'Do you not then believe?'
He replied, 'Indeed I do!
But so that my heart may be at peace.'
He said, 'Take four birds and train them to yourself.
Then put a part of them on each mountain and call to them;
they will come rushing to you.
Know that Allah is Almighty, All-Wise.'

261   The metaphor of those who spend their wealth
in the Way of Allah
is that of a grain which produces seven ears;
in every ear there are a hundred grains.
Allah gives such multiplied increase to whomever He wills.
Allah is All-Encompassing, All-Knowing.

262   Those who spend their wealth in the Way of Allah,
and then do not follow what they have spent
by demands for gratitude or insulting words
will have their reward with their Lord.
They will feel no fear and they will know no sorrow.

263   Correct and courteous words accompanied by forgiveness
are better than sadaqa followed by insulting words.
Allah is Rich Beyond Need, All-Forbearing.

264   You who believe! do not nullify your sadaqa
by demands for gratitude or insulting words,
like him who spends his wealth, showing off to people
and not believing in Allah and the Last Day.
His likeness is that of a smooth rock coated with soil,
which, when heavy rain falls on it, is left stripped bare.
They have no power over anything they have earned.
Allah does not guide unbelieving people.

265   The metaphor of those who spend their wealth,
desiring the pleasure of Allah and firmness for themselves,
is that of a garden on a hillside.
When heavy rain falls on it, it doubles its produce;

and if heavy rain does not fall, there is dew.
Allah sees what you do.

266   Would any of you like to have a garden of dates and grapes,
with rivers flowing underneath
containing all kinds of fruits,
then to be stricken with old age
and have children who are weak,
and then for a fierce whirlwind containing fire
to come and strike it
so that it goes up in flames?
In this way Allah makes His Signs clear to you,
so that hopefully you will reflect.

267   You who believe! give away
some of the good things you have earned
and some of what We have produced
for you from the earth.
Do not have recourse to bad things when you give,
things you would only take with your eyes tight shut!
Know that Allah is Rich Beyond Need, Praiseworthy.

268   Shaytan promises you poverty and commands you to avarice.
Allah promises you forgiveness from Him and abundance.
Allah is All-Encompassing, All-Knowing.

269   He gives wisdom to whoever He wills
and he who has been given wisdom
has been given great good.
But no one pays heed but people of intelligence.

270   Whatever amount you spend or vow you make,
Allah knows it.
The wrongdoers have no helpers.

271   If you make your sadaqa public, that is good.
But if you conceal it and give it to the poor,
that is better for you,
and We will erase some of your bad actions from you.
Allah is aware of what you do.

272   You are not responsible for their guidance,
but Allah guides whomever He wills.
Whatever good you give away is to your own benefit,

when you give desiring only the Face of Allah.
Whatever good you give away will be repaid to you in full.
You will not be wronged.

273   It is for the poor who are held back in the Way of Allah,
            unable to travel in the land.
        The ignorant consider them rich because of their reticence.
            You will know them by their mark.
                They do not ask from people insistently.
            Whatever good you give away, Allah knows it.
274   Those who give away their wealth by night and day,
                secretly and openly,
            will have their reward with their Lord.
        They will feel no fear and they will know no sorrow.

275   Those who practise riba will not rise from the grave
            except as someone driven mad by Shaytan's touch.
        That is because they say, 'Trade is the same as riba.'
            But Allah has permitted trade and He has forbidden riba.
        Whoever is given a warning by his Lord and then desists,
            may keep what he received in the past
                and his affair is Allah's concern.
        But all who return to it will be the Companions of the Fire,
            remaining in it timelessly, for ever.

276   Allah obliterates riba but makes sadaqa grow in value!
            Allah does not love any persistently ungrateful wrongdoer.

277   Those who believe and do right actions
            and establish the prayer and pay zakat,
                will have their reward with their Lord.
        They will feel no fear and they will know no sorrow.

278   You who believe! have taqwa of Allah
            and forgo any remaining riba
                if you are believers.

279   If you do not, know that it means war from Allah
            and from His Messenger.
        But if you repent you may have your capital,
            without wronging and without being wronged.

280   If someone is in difficult circumstances,
            there should be a deferral until things are easier.

But making a free gift of it would be better for you
if you only knew.

281 Have fear of a Day when you will be returned to Allah.
Then every self will be paid in full for what it earned.
They will not be wronged.

282 You who believe! when you take on a debt
for a specified period, write it down.
A writer should write it down between you justly.
No writer should refuse to write;
as Allah has taught him, so he should write.
The one incurring the debt should dictate
and should have taqwa of Allah his Lord
and not reduce it in any way.
If the person incurring the debt is incompetent or weak
or unable to dictate,
then his guardian should dictate for him justly.
Two men among you should act as witnesses.
But if there are not two men, then a man and two women
with whom you are satisfied as witnesses;
then if one of them forgets, the other can remind her.
Witnesses should not refuse when they are called upon.
Do not think it too trivial to write down,
whether small or large,
with the date that it falls due.
Doing that is more just in Allah's sight
and more helpful when bearing witness
and more likely to eliminate any doubt –
unless it is an immediate transaction hand to hand,
taken and given without delay.
There is nothing wrong in your not writing that down.
Call witnesses when you trade.
Neither writer nor witness should be put under pressure.
If you do that, it is deviancy on your part.
Have taqwa of Allah and Allah will give you knowledge.
Allah has knowledge of all things.

283 If you are on a journey and cannot find a writer,
something can be left as a security.
If you leave things on trust with one another
the one who is trusted must deliver up his trust
and have taqwa of Allah his Lord.
Do not conceal testimony.

If someone does conceal it, his heart commits a crime.
Allah knows what you do.

284   Everything in the heavens
            and everything in the earth belongs to Allah.
        Whether you divulge what is in yourselves or keep it hidden,
                Allah will still call you to account for it.
        He forgives whoever He wills and He punishes whoever He wills.
            Allah has power over all things.

285   The Messenger believes in what has been
            sent down to him from his Lord,
                and so do the believers.
        Each one believes in Allah and His angels
            and His Books and His Messengers.
        We do not differentiate between any of His Messengers.
            They say, 'We hear and we obey.
                Forgive us, our Lord!
        You are our journey's end.'

286   Allah does not impose on any self
            any more than it can stand.
        For it, is what it has earned;
            against it, what it has merited.
        Our Lord, do not take us to task
            if we forget or make a mistake!
        Our Lord, do not place on us a load
            like the one You placed on those before us!
        Our Lord, do not place on us a load
            we have not the strength to bear!
        And pardon us;
            and forgive us;
                and have mercy on us.
        You are our Master,
            so help us against the people of the unbelievers.

Sura 3

Al 'Imran
The Family of 'Imran

In the name of Allah, All-Merciful, Most Merciful

1   Alif Lam Mim
     Allah,
there is no god but Him,
     the Living, the Self-Sustaining.

2   He has sent down the Book to you with truth,
     confirming what was there before it.
And He sent down the Torah and the Injil,
3   previously, as guidance for mankind,
and He has sent down the Discrimination.*

4   Those who reject Allah's Signs
     will have a terrible punishment.
Allah is Almighty, Exactor of Revenge.

5   Allah – Him from Whom nothing is hidden,
     either on earth or in heaven.

6   It is He who forms you in the womb however He wills.
     There is no god but Him, the Almighty, the All-Wise.

7   It is He who sent down the Book to you from Him:
     ayats containing clear judgements –
         they are the core of the Book –
     and others which are open to interpretation.
Those with deviation in their hearts
     follow what is open to interpretation in it,

---

* Furqan, Another name for the Qur'an.

desiring conflict,
    seeking its inner meaning.
No one knows its inner meaning but Allah.
    Those firmly rooted in knowledge say,
'We believe in it. All of it is from our Lord.'
    But only people of intelligence pay heed.

8   'Our Lord, do not make our hearts swerve aside
    after You have guided us.
And give us mercy from You.
    You are the Ever-Giving.
9   Our Lord, You are the Gatherer of mankind
    to a Day of which there is no doubt.
Allah will not break His promise.'

10   As for those who disbelieve, their wealth and children
    will not help them against Allah in any way.
       They are fuel for the Fire,
11   as was the case with the people of Pharaoh
    and those before them.
They denied Our Signs
    so Allah seized them for their wrong actions.
       Allah is fierce in retribution.

12   Say to those who disbelieve:
    'You will be overwhelmed and crowded into Hell.
       What an evil resting-place!'

13   There was a sign for you in the two parties which met face to face,
    one party fighting in the Way of Allah
    and the other unbelievers.
You saw them as twice their number with your own eyes.
    Allah reinforces with His help whoever He wills.
There is instruction in that for people of insight.

14   To mankind the love of worldly appetites
    is painted in glowing colours:
       women and children,
and heaped-up mounds of gold and silver,
    and horses with fine markings,
       and livestock and fertile farmland.
All that is merely the enjoyment of the life of this world.
    The best homecoming is in the presence of Allah.

15   Say, 'Shall I tell you of something better than that?'
            The godfearing will have Gardens with their Lord,
                with rivers flowing under them,
            remaining in them timelessly, for ever,
                and purified wives,
                    and the Pleasure of Allah.
            Allah sees His slaves:
16   those who say, 'Our Lord, we believe,
            so forgive us our wrong actions
        and safeguard us from the punishment of the Fire.

17   The steadfast, the truthful, the obedient, the givers,
            and those who seek forgiveness before dawn.'

18   Allah bears witness that there is no god but Him,
            as do the angels and the people of knowledge,
                upholding justice.
        There is no god but Him,
            the Almighty, the All-Wise.

19   The deen in the sight of Allah is Islam.
            Those given the Book only differed
                after knowledge had come to them,
                    envying one another.
            As for those who reject Allah's Signs,
                Allah is swift at reckoning.

20   If they argue with you, say,
            'I have submitted myself completely to Allah,
                and so have all who follow me.'
        Say to those given the Book and those who have no Book,
            'Have you become Muslim?'
        If they become Muslim, they have been guided.
        If they turn away, you are only responsible for transmission.
            Allah sees His slaves.

21   As for those who reject Allah's Signs,
            and kill the Prophets without any right to do so,
                and kill those who command justice,
            give them news of a painful punishment.

22   They are the ones whose actions come to nothing
            in this world or the Next World.
        They will have no helpers.

23   Do you not see those who have been given a portion of the Book
          being invited to let Allah's Book be the judge between them?
            But then a group of them turn away.

24   That is because they say,
          'The Fire will only touch us for a number of days.'
       Their inventions have deluded them in their deen.

25   But how will it be when We gather them all together
          for a Day about which there is no doubt?
       Every self will be paid in full for what it earned.
          They will not be wronged.

26   Say, 'O Allah! Master of the Kingdom!
          You give sovereignty to whoever You will
          You take sovereignty from whoever You will.
          You exalt whoever You will
          You abase whoever You will.
            All good is in Your hands.
          You have power over all things.
27   You merge the night into the day.
          You merge the day into the night.
          You bring out the living from the dead.
          You bring out the dead from the living.
          You provide for whoever You will
            without any reckoning.'

28   The believers should not take unbelievers as friends
          rather than believers.
       Anyone who does that
          has nothing to do with Allah at all –
            unless it is because you are afraid of them.
       Allah advises you to beware of Him.
          Allah is the final destination.

29   Say, 'Whether you conceal what is in your breasts
          or make it known,
            Allah knows it.
       He knows what is in the heavens
          and what is on earth.
       Allah has power over all things.'

30   On the Day that each self finds the good it did,
          and the evil it did,

present there in front of it,
it will wish there were an age between it and then.
    Allah advises you to beware of Him.
Allah is Ever-Gentle with His slaves.

31   Say, 'If you love Allah, then follow me
        and Allah will love you and forgive you
            for your wrong actions.
    Allah is Ever-Forgiving, Most Merciful.'

32   Say, 'Obey Allah and the Messenger.'
        Then if they turn away,
    Allah does not love the unbelievers.

33   Allah chose Adam and Nuh
        and the family of Ibrahim
            and the family of 'Imran
        over all other beings –
34   descendants one of the other.
        Allah is All-Hearing, All-Knowing.

35   Remember when the wife of 'Imran said,
        'My Lord, I have pledged to You
            what is in my womb,
        devoting it to Your service.
            Please accept my prayer.
        You are the All-Hearing, the All-Knowing.'

36   When she gave birth, she said,
        'My Lord! I have given birth to a girl' –
    and Allah knew very well what she had given birth to,
        male and female are not the same –
    'and I have named her Maryam and placed her and her children
        in Your safekeeping from the accursed Shaytan.'

37   Her Lord accepted her with approval
        and made her grow in health and beauty.
        And Zakariyya became her guardian.
    Every time Zakariyya visited her in the Upper Room,
        he found food with her.
    He said, 'Maryam, how did you come by this?'
        She said, 'It is from Allah.
            Allah provides for whoever He wills
                without any reckoning.'

38   Then and there Zakariyya called on his Lord and said,
            'O Lord, grant me by Your favour an upright child.
                You are the Hearer of Prayer.'

39   The angels called out to him
            while he was standing in prayer in the Upper Room:
        'Allah gives you the good news of Yahya,
            who will come to confirm a Word from Allah,
                and will be a leader and a celibate,
            a Prophet and one of the righteous.'

40   He said, 'My Lord, how can I possibly have a son
            when I have reached old age and my wife is barren?'
        He said, 'It will be so.
            Allah does whatever He wills.'

41   He said, 'My Lord, appoint a Sign for me.'
            He said, 'Your Sign is that not to speak
                to people for three days,
                    except by gesture.
            Remember your Lord much and glorify Him
                in the evening and after dawn.'

42   And when the angels said, 'Maryam, Allah has chosen you
                and purified you.
            He has chosen you over all other women.
43   Maryam, obey your Lord and prostrate
            and bow with those who bow.'

44   This is news from the Unseen which We reveal to you.
            You were not with them when they cast their reeds
        to see which of them would be the guardian of Maryam.
            You were not with them when they quarrelled.

45   When the angels said, 'Maryam, Allah
            gives you good news of a Word from Him.
        His name is the Messiah, 'Isa, son of Maryam,
            of high esteem in this world and the Next World,
                and one of those brought near.
46   He will speak to people in the cradle,
            and also when fully grown,
                and will be one of the righteous,'
47   she said, 'My Lord! How can I have a son
            when no man has ever touched me?'

He said, 'It will be so.'
  Allah creates whatever He wills.
When He decides on something,
  He just says to it, 'Be!' and it is.

48 He will teach him the Book and Wisdom,
  and the Torah and the Injil,

49 as a Messenger to the tribe of Israel, saying:
  'I have brought you a Sign from your Lord.
I will create the shape of a bird out of clay for you
  and then breathe into it and it will be a bird
    by Allah's permission.
I will heal the blind and lepers,
  and bring the dead to life,
    by Allah's permission.
I will tell you what you eat
  and what you store up in your homes.
There is a Sign for you in that if you are believers.

50 I come confirming the Torah I find already there,
    and to make lawful for you
  some of what was previously forbidden to you.
I have brought you a Sign from your Lord.
  So have taqwa of Allah and obey me.

51 Allah is my Lord and your Lord so worship Him.
  That is a straight path.'

52 When 'Isa sensed unbelief on their part,
    he said, 'Who will be my helpers to Allah?'
The disciples said, 'We are Allah's helpers.
    We believe in Allah.
  Bear witness that we are Muslims.

53 Our Lord, we believe in what You have sent down
    and have followed the Messenger,
  so write us down among the witnesses.'

54 They plotted and Allah plotted.
  But Allah is the best of plotters.*

55 When Allah said, ''Isa, I will take you back
    and raise you up to Me
  and purify you of those who disbelieve.
And I will place the people who follow you
    above those who disbelieve until the Day of Rising.

---

* This ayat refers to the Jews who rejected 'Isa.

Then you will all return to Me,
    and I will judge between you
regarding the things about which you differed.
56   As for those who disbelieve,
I will punish them with a harsh punishment
    in this world and the Next World.
        They will have no helpers.'

57   As for those who believe and do right actions,
    We will pay them their wages in full.
        Allah does not love wrongdoers.

58   That is what We recite to you
    of the Signs and the wise Reminder.

59   The likeness of 'Isa in Allah's sight is the same as Adam.
    He created him from earth
and then He said to him, 'Be!' and he was.

60   It is the truth from your Lord
    so do not be among the doubters.

61   If anyone argues with you about him
    after the knowledge that has come to you,
say, 'Come then! Let us summon our sons and your sons,
    our women and your women,
        ourselves and yourselves.
    Then let us make earnest supplication
and call down the curse of Allah upon the liars.'

62   This is the true account:
    there is no other god besides Allah.
Allah – He is the Almighty, the All-Wise.

63   And if they turn away,
    Allah knows the corrupters.

64   Say, 'People of the Book! come to a proposition
    which is the same for us and you –
that we should worship none but Allah
    and not associate any partners with Him
        and not take one another as lords besides Allah.'
If they turn away, say, 'Bear witness that we are Muslims.'

65   'People of the Book! why do you argue concerning Ibrahim
         when the Torah and Injil were only sent down after him?
         Why do you not use your intellect?

66   You are people arguing about something
         of which you have no knowledge.
      Why do you argue about something
         of which you have no knowledge?
            Allah knows; you do not know.'

67   Ibrahim was neither a Jew nor a Christian.
         but a man of pure natural belief – a Muslim.
      He was not one of the idolators.

68   The people with the strongest claim to Ibrahim
         are those who followed him
            and this Prophet
         and those who believe.
      Allah is the Protector of the believers.

69   A group of the People of the Book
         would love to misguide you.
      They only misguide themselves
         but they are not aware of it.

70   People of the Book! why do you reject Allah's Signs
         when you yourselves are there as witnesses?

71   People of the Book! why do you mix truth with falsehood
         and knowingly conceal the truth?

72   A group of the People of the Book say,
         'At the beginning of the day, you should claim to believe
            in what was sent down to those who believe,
         and then at the end of the day, you should reject it,
            so that hopefully they will revert.

73   Do not trust anyone except for those
         who follow your deen.'
      Say, 'Allah's guidance is true guidance.
         But you think it is impossible for anyone
      to be given the same as you were given,
         or to argue with you before your Lord.'
      Say, 'All favour is in Allah's Hand
         and He gives it to whoever He wills.
      Allah is All-Encompassing, All-Knowing.

74   He picks out for His mercy whoever He wills.
            Allah's favour is indeed immense.'

75   Among the People of the Book there are some who,
                if you entrust them with a pile of gold,
                    will return it to you.
            But there are others among them who,
                if you entrust them with just a single dinar,
                    will not return it to you,
                unless you stay standing over them.
            That is because they say,
                'We are under no obligation
                    where the gentiles are concerned.'
            They tell a lie against Allah and they know it.

76   No, the truth is, if people honour their contracts
                and have taqwa of Him,
            Allah loves those who are godfearing.

77   Those who sell Allah's contract and their own oaths
                    for a paltry price,
                such people will have no portion in the Next World
            and on the Day of Rising Allah will not speak to them
                or look at them
                    or purify them.
            They will have a painful punishment.

78   Among them is a group who distort the Book with their tongues
                so that you think it is from the Book
                    when it is not from the Book.
            They say, 'It is from Allah,' but it is not from Allah.
                They tell a lie against Allah and they know it.

79   It is not right for any human being
                that Allah should give him the Book
                    and Judgement and Prophethood,
            and then that he should say to people,
                'Be worshippers of me rather than Allah.'
            Rather he will say, 'Be people of the Lord
                because of your knowledge of the Book
                    and because you study.'

80   He would never command you to take
                the angels and Prophets as Lords.

Would He command you to disbelieve
after being Muslim?

81   Remember when Allah made a covenant with the Prophets:
'Now that We have given you a share
of the Book and Wisdom,
and then a Messenger comes to you
confirming what is with you,
you must believe in him and help him.'
He asked, 'Do you agree and undertake My commission
on that condition?'
They replied, 'We agree.'
He said, 'Bear witness, then.
I am with you as one of the witnesses.'

82   Any who turn away after that
are deviators.

83   Is it other than the deen of Allah that you desire,
when everything in the heavens and earth,
willingly or unwillingly,
submits to Him
and to Him you will be returned?

84   Say, 'We believe in Allah
and what has been sent down to us
and what was sent down to Ibrahim, Isma'il and Ishaq
and Ya'qub and the Tribes,
and what Musa and 'Isa and all the Prophets
were given by their Lord.
We do not differentiate between any of them.
We are Muslims submitted to Him.'

85   If anyone desires anything other than Islam as a deen,
it will not be accepted from him,
and in the Next World he will be among the losers.

86   How can Allah guide a people
who have disbelieve after having believed?
They bore witness that the Messenger was true
and that the Clear Signs had come to them.
Allah does not guide people who are wrongdoers.

87   The repayment of such people is that Allah's curse is on them
            and that of the angels and of all mankind.

88   They will be under it for ever.
            Their punishment will not be lightened.
                They will be granted no reprieve.

89   Except for those who, after that, repent
            and put things right.
        Truly Allah is Ever-Forgiving, Most Merciful.

90   Those who disbelieve after having believed
            and then increase in their unbelief,
        their repentance will not be accepted.
            They are the misguided.

91   As for those who disbelieve and die as unbelievers,
            the whole earth filled with gold would not be accepted
        from any of them if they were to offer it as a ransom.
            They will have a painful punishment.
                They will have no helpers.

92   You will not attain true goodness
            until you give of what you love.
        Whatever you give away, Allah knows it.

93   All food was lawful for the tribe of Israel
            except what Israel made unlawful for himself
                before the Torah was sent down.
        Say, 'Bring the Torah and read it out
            if you are telling the truth.'

94   So any who, after this, invent a lie against Allah
            are indeed wrongdoers.

95   Say, 'Allah speaks the truth,
            so follow the religion of Ibrahim,
                a man of pure natural belief.
            He was not one of the idolators.'

96   The first House established for mankind was that at Bakka,
            a place of blessing and a guidance for all beings.

97   In it are Clear Signs – the Maqam of Ibrahim.
            All who enter it are safe.

Hajj to the House is a duty owed to Allah by all mankind –
    those who can find a way to do it.
But if anyone disbelieves,
    Allah is Rich Beyond Need of any being.

98   Say, 'People of the Book, why do you reject Allah's Signs
    when Allah is witness of everything you do?'

99   Say, 'People of the Book, why do you bar
    those who believe from the Way of Allah,
      desiring to make it crooked,
    when you yourselves are witnesses to it?
Allah is not unaware of what you do.'

100   You who believe! if you obey a group of those given the Book,
    they will make you revert to being unbelievers
      after you have believed.

101   How can you disbelieve, when Allah's Signs are recited to you
    and the Messenger is there among you?
Whoever holds fast to Allah
    has been guided to a straight path.

102   You who believe! have taqwa of Allah
    with the taqwa due to Him
      and do not die except as Muslims.

103   Hold fast to the rope of Allah all together,
    and do not separate.
Remember Allah's blessing to you when you were enemies
    and He joined your hearts together
so that you became brothers by His blessing.
You were on the very brink of a pit of the Fire
    and He rescued you from it.
In this way Allah makes His Signs clear to you,
    so that hopefully you will be guided.

104   Let there be a community among you
    who call to the good,
      and enjoin the right,
        and forbid the wrong.
They are the ones who are successful.

105   Do not be like those who split up and differed
    after the Clear Signs came to them.
They will have a terrible punishment

106   on the Day when faces are whitened
           and faces are blackened.
      As for those whose faces are blackened:
      'What! Did you disbelieve after having believed?
      Taste the punishment for your unbelief!'

107   As for those whose faces are whitened,
           they are in Allah's mercy,
      remaining in it timelessly, for ever.

108   These are Allah's Signs which We recite to you with truth.
           Allah desires no wrong for any being.

109   Everything in the heavens
           and everything in the earth
              belongs to Allah.
      All matters return to Allah.

110   You are the best nation ever to be produced before mankind.
           You enjoin the right,
              forbid the wrong
                 and believe in Allah.
      If the People of the Book were to believe,
           it would be better for them.
      Some of them are believers
           but most of them are deviators.

111   They will not harm you
           except with abusive words.
      If they fight you,
           they will turn their backs on you.
      Then they will not be helped.

112   They will be plunged into abasement wherever they are found,
           unless they have a treaty with Allah and with the people.
      They have brought down anger from Allah upon themselves,
           and they have been plunged into destitution.
      That was because they rejected Allah's Signs
           and killed the Prophets without any right to do so.
      That was because they disobeyed
           and went beyond the limits.
113   They are not all the same.
      There is a community among the People of the Book
           who are upright.

They recite Allah's Signs throughout the night,
    and they prostrate.

114   They believe in Allah and the Last Day,
    and enjoin the right
        and forbid the wrong,
            and compete in doing good.
    They are among the righteous.

115   You will not be denied the reward
        for any good thing you do.
    Allah knows the godfearing.

116   As for those who disbelieve, their wealth and children
        will not help them against Allah in any way.
    They are the Companions of the Fire.
        remaining in it timelessly, for ever.

117   The metaphor of what they spend
        in their life in this world
    is that of a wind with an icy bite to it
        which strikes the crops of a people
            who have wronged themselves
                and destroys them.
        Allah did not wrong them;
    rather it was themselves they were wronging.

118   You who believe! do not take
        any outside yourselves as intimates.
    They will do anything to harm you.
        They love what causes you distress.
    Hatred has appeared out of their mouths,
        but what their breasts hide is far worse.
    We have made the Signs clear to you
        if you use your intellect.

119   There you are, loving them when they do not love you,
        even though you believe in all the Books.
    When they meet you, they say, 'We believe.'
        But when they leave they bite their fingers
            out of rage against you.
        Say, 'Die in your rage.'
    Allah knows what your hearts contain.

120   If something good happens to you, it galls them.
            If something bad strikes you, they rejoice at it.
        But if you are steadfast and are godfearing,
            their scheming will not harm you in any way.
        Allah encompasses what they do.

121   Remember when you left your family early in the day
            to instal the believers in their battle stations.*
        Allah is All-Hearing, All-Knowing.

122   And remember when two of your clans
            were on the point of losing heart
                and Allah was their Protector.
        Let the believers put their trust in Allah.

123   Allah helped you at Badr when you were weak
            so have taqwa of Allah,
        so that hopefully you will be thankful.

124   And when you said to the believers,
            'Is it not enough for you that your Lord reinforced you
                with three thousand angels, sent down?'

125   Yes indeed! But if you are steadfast and have taqwa
            and they come upon you suddenly,
        your Lord will reinforce you with five thousand angels,
            clearly identified.

126   Allah only did this for it to be good news for you
            and so that your hearts might be set at rest by it
                (help comes from no one but Allah,
                    the Almighty, the All-Wise)
127   and so that He might cut off a group of those who disbelieve
            or crush them
        and they might be turned back in defeat.

128   You have no part in the affair.
            Either He will turn towards them
                or He will punish them,
        for they are wrongdoers.
129   Everything in the heavens
            and everything in the earth
                belongs to Allah.

---

* This and the rest of the sura refer to the Battle of 'Uhud which took place near Madina in 3 AH.

He forgives whoever He wills
    and punishes whoever He wills.
Allah is Ever-Forgiving, Most Merciful.

130   You who believe! do not feed on riba,
        multiplied and then remultiplied.
    Have taqwa of Allah
        so that hopefully you will be successful.

131   Have fear of the Fire
        which has been prepared for the unbelievers.

132   Obey Allah and the Messenger
        so that hopefully you will gain mercy.

133   Race each other to forgiveness from your Lord
        and a Garden as wide as the heavens and the earth,
            prepared for the godfearing:
134   those who give in times of both ease and hardship,
        those who control their rage and pardon other people –
            Allah loves good-doers –
135   those who, when they act indecently or wrong themselves,
        remember Allah and ask forgiveness for their bad actions
            (and who can forgive bad actions except Allah?)
        and do not knowingly persist in what they were doing.

136   Their recompense is forgiveness from their Lord,
        and Gardens with rivers flowing under them,
            remaining in them timelessly, for ever.
        How excellent is the reward of those who act!

137   Whole societies have passed away before your time,
        so travel about the earth
    and see the final fate of the deniers.

138   This is a clear explanation for all mankind,
        and guidance and admonition for the godfearing.

139   Do not give up and do not be downhearted.
        You shall be uppermost if you are believers.

140   If you have received a wound,
        they have already received a similar wound.
    We deal out such days to people turn by turn,

so that Allah will know those who believe
   and can gather martyrs from among you –
     Allah does not love wrongdoers –
141   and so that Allah can purge those who believe
     and wipe out the unbelievers.

142   Or did you imagine that you were going to enter the Garden
     without Allah knowing those among you who had struggled
      and knowing the steadfast?

143   You were longing for death before you met it.
     Now you have seen it with your own eyes.

144   Muhammad is only a Messenger
     and he has been preceded by other Messengers.
   If he were to die or be killed,
     would you turn on your heels?
   Those who turn on their heels
     do not harm Allah in any way.
   Allah will recompense the thankful.

145   No self can die except with Allah's permission,
     at a predetermined time.
   If anyone desires the reward in this world,
     We will give him some of it.
   If anyone desires the reward in the Next World,
     We will give him some of it.
   We will recompense the thankful.

146   Many a Prophet has been killed,
     when there were many thousands with him!
   They did not give up
     in the face of what assailed them
      in the Way of Allah,
     nor did they weaken,
      nor did they yield.
   Allah loves the steadfast.

147   All they said was, 'Our Lord, forgive us our wrong actions
     and any excesses we went to in what we did
      and make our feet firm
     and help us against these unbelieving people.'

148   So Allah gave them the reward in this world
        and the best reward in the Next World.
           Allah loves good-doers.

149   You who believe! if you obey those who disbelieve,
        they will turn you round on your heels
           and you will be transformed into losers.

150   No, Allah is your Protector.
        And He is the best of helpers.

151   We will cast terror into the hearts of those who disbelieve
        because they have associated others with Allah
           for which He has not sent down any authority.
        Their shelter will be the Fire.
    How evil is the abode of the wrongdoers!

152   Allah fulfilled His promise to you when you
        were slaughtering them by His permission.
    But then you faltered, disputing the command,
        and disobeyed after He showed you what you love.*
    Among you are those who want this world
        and among you are those who want the Next World.
    Then He turned you from them in order to test you –
        but He has pardoned you.
    Allah shows favour to the believers.

153   Remember when you were scrambling up the slope,
           refusing to turn back for anyone,
        and the Messenger was calling to you from the rear.
    Allah rewarded you with one distress in return for another
        so you would not feel grief for what escaped you
           or what assailed you.
    Allah is aware of what you do.

154   Then He sent down to you, after the distress, security,
        restful sleep overtaking a group of you,
    whereas another group became prey to anxious thoughts,
        thinking other than the truth about Allah –
           thoughts belonging to the Time of Ignorance** –
        saying, 'Do we have any say in the affair at all?'

---

* This refers to a group of archers who left their position in the Battle of Uhud to gather booty
allowing the enemy to regroup, counter-attack, and almost carry the day.
** The time before the coming of the Prophet and the revelation of the Qur'an.

Say, 'The affair belongs entirely to Allah.'
They are concealing within themselves things
     which they do not disclose to you,
saying, 'If we had only had a say in the affair,
     none of us would have been killed here in this place.'
Say, 'Even if you had been inside your homes,
     those people for whom bring killed was decreed
       would have gone out to their place of death.'
So that Allah might test what is in your breasts
     and purge what is in your hearts.
Allah knows what your hearts contain.

155   Those of you who turned their backs
     on the day the two armies clashed –
it was Shaytan who made them slip
     for what they had done.
But Allah has pardoned them.
     Allah is Ever-Forgiving, All-Forbearing.

156   You who believe! do not be like those who disbelieve
     and say of their brothers,
when they are going on journeys or military expeditions,
     'If they had only been with us,
       they would not have died or been killed,'
     so that Allah can make that anguish for them in their hearts.
It is Allah Who gives life and causes to die.
     Allah sees what you do.

157   If you are killed in the Way of Allah or if you die,
     forgiveness and mercy from Allah
are better than anything you can acquire.

158   If you die or you are killed,
     it is to Allah that you will be gathered.

159   It is a mercy from Allah that you were gentle with them.
     If you had been rough or hard of heart,
       they would have scattered from around you.
     So pardon them and ask forgiveness for them,
       and consult with them about the matter.
     Then when you have reached a firm decision,
       put your trust in Allah.
Allah loves those who put their trust in Him.

160   If Allah helps you, no one can vanquish you.
           If He forsakes you, who can help you after that?
       So the believers should put their trust in Allah.

161   No Prophet would ever be guilty of misappropriation.
           Those who misappropriate will arrive on the Day of Rising
               with what they have misappropriated.
           Then every self will be paid in full for what it earned.
               They will not be wronged.

162   Is someone who pursues the pleasure of Allah
           the same as someone who incurs displeasure from Allah
               and whose refuge is Hell?
       What an evil destination!

163   They have different ranks with Allah.
           Allah sees what they do.

164   Allah showed great kindness to the believers
           when He sent a Messenger to them from among themselves
               to recite His Signs to them and purify them
                   and teach them the Book and Wisdom,
               even though before that they were clearly misguided.

165   Why is it that when a calamity happens to you,
           when you have already inflicted twice as much,
       you say, 'How could this possibly happen?'
           Say, 'It has come from your own selves.'
       Allah has power over all things.

166   What assailed you on the day the two armies met
           was by Allah's permission,
       so that He would know the believers,

167   and so that He would know the hypocrites.
       They were told, 'Come and fight in the Way of Allah
           or at least help defend us.'
       They said, 'If we knew that there would be a fight,
           we would certainly follow you.'
       They were closer to unbelief that day than to faith,
           saying with their mouths what was not in their hearts.
               And Allah knows best what they are hiding.

168   They are those who said of their brothers,
           when they themselves had stayed behind,
       'If they had only obeyed us, they would not have been killed.'

Say, 'Then ward off death from yourselves
    if you are telling the truth.'

169   Do not suppose that those killed in the Way of Allah are dead.
    No indeed! They are alive and well provided for
        in the very presence of their Lord,
170   delighting in the favour Allah has bestowed on them,
rejoicing over those they left behind
    who have not yet joined them,
feeling no fear and knowing no sorrow,
171   rejoicing in blessings and favour from Allah
    and that Allah does not let the wage
        of the believers go to waste.

172   Those who did good and were godfearing
    among those who responded to Allah and the Messenger
        after the wound had been inflicted
    will have an immense reward:
173   those to whom people said,
    'The people have gathered against you, so fear them.'
But that merely increased their faith and they said,
    'Allah is enough for us and the Best of Guardians.'

174   So they returned with blessings and bounty from Allah
    and no evil touched them.
They pursued the pleasure of Allah.
    Allah's favour is indeed immense.

175   It was only Shaytan frightening you through his friends.
    But do not fear them – fear Me if you are believers.

176   Do not let those who rush headlong into unbelief sadden you.
    They do not harm Allah in any way.
Allah desires to assign no portion to them in the Next World.
    They will have a terrible punishment.

177   Those who sell faith for unbelief
    do not harm Allah in any way.
They will have a painful punishment.

178   Those who disbelieve should not imagine
    that the extra time We grant to them
        is good for them.

We only allow them more time
    so they will increase in evildoing.
They will have a humiliating punishment.

179   Allah will only leave the believers in the position you now are in
        until He can sift out the rotten from the good.
    Allah has not given you access to the Unseen.
But Allah chooses those of His Messengers whom He wills.
    So believe in Allah and His Messengers.
        If you believe and are godfearing
    you will have an immense reward.

180   Those who are tight-fisted with the bounty Allah has given them
        should not suppose that that is better for them.
        No indeed, it is worse for them!
What they were tight-fisted with
    will be hung around their necks
        on the Day of Rising.
Allah is the inheritor of the heavens and the earth
    and Allah is aware of what you do.

181   Allah has heard the words of those who say,
        'Allah is poor and we are rich.'
We will write down what they said
    and their killing of the Prophets
        without any right to do so
and We will say, 'Taste the punishment of the Burning.'

182   That is on account of what you did.
    Allah does not wrong His slaves.

183   Those who say, 'Allah has made a contract with us
        that we should not believe in any Messenger
            until he brings us a sacrifice consumed by fire.'
Say, 'Messengers came to you before me with the Clear Signs
        and with what you say.
So why did you kill them if you are telling the truth?'

184   If they deny you, Messengers before you were also denied,
        who brought the Clear Signs and written texts
            and the illuminating Book.

185   Every self will taste death.
    You will be paid your wages in full on the Day of Rising.

Anyone who is distanced from the Fire
    and admitted to the Garden
        has triumphed.
The life of this world is just the enjoyment of delusion.

186   You will be tested in your wealth and in yourselves
    and you will hear many abusive words
from those given the Book before you
    and from those who are idolators.
But if you are steadfast and are godfearing,
    that is the most resolute course to take.

187   Allah made a covenant with those given the Book:
    'You must make it clear to people and not conceal it.'
But they toss it in disdain behind their backs
    and sell it for a paltry price.
What an evil sale they make!

188   Those who exult in what they have done
    and love to be praised for what they have not done
should not suppose that they have escaped the punishment.
    They will have a painful punishment.

189   The kingdom of the heavens and earth belongs to Allah.
    Allah has power over all things.

190   In the creation of the heavens and the earth,
    and the alternation of night and day,
        there are Signs for people with intelligence:
191   those who remember Allah,
    standing, sitting and lying on their sides,
    and reflect on the creation of the heavens and the earth:
'Our Lord, You have not created this for nothing.
    Glory be to You!
So safeguard us from the punishment of the Fire.
192   Our Lord, those You cast into the Fire,
    You have indeed disgraced.
        The wrongdoers will have no helpers.
193   Our Lord, we heard a caller calling us to faith:
    "Believe in your Lord!"
        and we believed.
Our Lord, forgive us our wrong actions,
    erase our bad actions from us
        and take us back to You with those who are truly good.

194　Our Lord, give us what You promised us
　　　　through Your Messengers,
　　　and do not disgrace us on the Day of Rising.
　　　　You do not break Your promise.'

195　Their Lord responds to them:
　　　　'I will not let the deeds of any doer among you go to waste,
　　　　　male or female – you are both the same in that respect.
　　　Those who made hijra and were driven from their homes
　　　　and suffered harm in My Way and fought and were killed,
　　　I will erase their bad actions from them
　　　　and admit them into Gardens
　　　　　with rivers flowing under them,
　　　　　　as a reward from Allah.
　　　The best of all rewards is with Allah.'

196　Do not be deceived by the fact that
　　　　those who disbelieve move freely about the earth.
197　A brief enjoyment;
　　　　then their shelter will be Hell.
　　　What an evil resting-place!

198　But those who have taqwa of their Lord will have Gardens
　　　　with rivers flowing under them,
　　　　　remaining in them timelessly, for ever:
　　　　　　hospitality from Allah.
　　　What is with Allah is better for those who are truly good.

199　Among the people of the Book
　　　　there are some who believe in Allah
　　and in what has been sent down to you
　　　　and what was sent down to them,
　　　　　and who are humble before Allah.
　　　They do not sell Allah's Signs for a paltry price.
　　Such people will have their reward with their Lord.
　　　　And Allah is swift at reckoning.

200　You who believe, be steadfast;
　　　　be supreme in steadfastness;
　　　　　be firm on the battlefield;
　　　　　　and have taqwa of Allah;
　　　　so that hopefully you will be successful.

Sura 4

An-Nisa'
Women

In the name of Allah, All-Merciful, Most Merciful

1   O mankind!
     have taqwa of your Lord who created you
       from a single self
      and created its mate from it
     and then disseminated many men and women
      from the two of them.
     Have taqwa of Allah in whose name
      you make demands on one another
     and also in respect of your families.
      Allah watches over you continually.

2   Give orphans their property,
     and do not substitute bad things for good.
   Do not assimilate their property into your own.
     Doing that is a serious crime.

3   If you are afraid of not behaving justly towards orphans,
     then marry other permissible women,
      two, three or four.
   But if you are afraid of not treating them equally,
     then only one, or those you own as slaves.
   That makes it more likely that you will not be unfair.

4   Give women their dowry as an outright gift.
     But if they are happy to give you some of it,
      make use of it with pleasure and goodwill.

5   Do not hand over to the simple-minded any property of theirs
        for which Allah has made you responsible,
    but provide for them and clothe them out of it,
        and speak to them correctly and courteously.

6   Keep a close check on orphans
        until they reach a marriageable age,
        then if you perceive that they have sound judgement
        hand over their property to them.
    Do not consume it extravagantly and precipitately
        before they come of age.
    Those who are wealthy should abstain from it altogether.
        Those who are poor should use it sensibly and correctly.
    When you hand over their property to them
        ensure that there are witnesses on their behalf.
        Allah suffices as a Reckoner.

7   Men receive a share
        of what their parents and relatives leave
    and women receive a share
        of what their parents and relatives leave,
    a fixed share, no matter whether it is a little or a lot.

8   If other relatives or orphans or poor people
        attend the sharing-out,
        provide for them out of it
        and speak to them correctly and courteously.

9   People should show concern in the same way
        that they would fear for small children
        if they were to die leaving them behind.
    They should have taqwa of Allah
        and say words that are appropriate.

10   People who consume the property of orphans wrongfully
        consume nothing in their bellies except fire.
        They will roast in a Searing Blaze.

11   Allah instructs you regarding your children:
        A male receives the same as the share of two females.
    If there are more than two daughters
        they receive two-thirds of what you leave.
        If she is one on her own she receives a half.

Each of your parents receives a sixth of what you leave
    if you have children.
If you are childless and your heirs are your parents
    your mother receives a third.
If you have brothers or sisters your mother receives a sixth,
    after any bequest you make or any debts.
With regard to your fathers and your sons,
    you do not know which of them is going to benefit you more.
These are obligatory shares from Allah.
    Allah is All-Knowing, All-Wise.

12   You receive half of what your wives leave if they are childless.
    If they have children you receive a quarter of what they leave
        after any bequest they make or any debts.
They receive a quarter of what you leave if you are childless.
    If you have children they receive an eighth of what you leave
        after any bequest you make or any debts.
If a man or woman has no direct heirs,
    but has a brother or sister,
        each of them receives a sixth.
If there are more than that they share in a third
    after any bequest you make or any debts,
making sure that no one's rights are prejudiced.
This is an instruction from Allah.
    Allah is All-Knowing, All-Forbearing.

13   These are Allah's limits.
    As for those who obey Allah and His Messenger,
        We will admit them into Gardens
            with rivers flowing under them,
        remaining in them timelessly, for ever.
    That is the Great Victory.

14   As for him who disobeys Allah and His Messenger
    and oversteps His limits,
        We will admit him into a Fire,
            to remain in it timelessly, for ever.
    He will have a humiliating punishment.

15   If any of your women commit fornication,
        four of you must be witnesses against them.
If they bear witness, detain them in their homes
    until death releases them
or Allah ordains another procedure for their case.

16   If two men commit a like abomination, punish them.
          If they repent and reform, leave them alone.
              Allah is Ever-Returning, Most Merciful.

17   Allah only accepts the repentance
          of those who do evil in ignorance
      and then quickly repent after doing it.
          Allah turns towards such people.
              Allah is All-Knowing, All-Wise.

18   There is no repentance for people who persist in doing evil
          until death comes to them
      and who then say, 'Now I repent,'
          nor for people who die unbelievers.
      We have prepared for them a painful punishment.

19   You who believe! it is not halal for you
          to inherit women by force.
      Nor may you treat them harshly so that you can make off
          with part of what you have given them,
      unless they commit an act of flagrant indecency.
          Live together with them correctly and courteously.
      If you dislike them, it may well be that you dislike something
          in which Allah has placed a lot of good.

20   If you desire to exchange one wife for another
          and have given your original wife a large amount,
              do not take any of it.
      Would you take it by means of slander and outright crime?

21   How could you take it
          when you have been intimate with one another
              and they have made a binding contract with you?

22   Do not marry any women your fathers married –
          except for what may have already taken place.
      That is an indecent act, a loathsome thing and an evil path.

23   Haram for you are:
          your mothers and your daughters and your sisters,
          your maternal aunts and your paternal aunts,
          your brothers' daughters and your sisters' daughters,
          your foster mothers who have suckled you,
          your foster sisters by suckling,

your wives' mothers,
your stepdaughters who are under your protection:
    the daughters of your wives
        whom you have had sexual relations with
        (though if you have not had sexual relations with them
            there is nothing blameworthy for you in it then),
    the wives of your sons whom you have fathered,
    and marrying two sisters at the same time –
        except for what may have already taken place.
            Allah is Ever-Forgiving, Most Merciful.

24   And also married women,
            except for those you have taken in war as slaves.
        This is what Allah has prescribed for you.
    Apart from that He has made all other women halal for you
        provided you seek them with your wealth in marriage
            and not in fornication.
    When you consummate your marriage with them
        give them their prescribed dowry.
    There is nothing wrong
        in any further agreement you might come to
            after the dowry has been given.
        Allah is All-Knowing, All-Wise.

25   If any of you do not have the means
            to marry free women who are believers,
    you may marry slavegirls who are believers.
        Allah knows best about your faith;
            you are all the same in that respect.
    Marry them with their owners' permission
        and give them their dowries correctly and courteously
            as married women, not in fornication
                or taking them as lovers.
    When they are married, if they commit fornication
        they should receive half the punishment of free women.
    This is for those of you who are afraid of committing fornication.
            But being patient is better for you.
        Allah is Ever-Forgiving, Most Merciful.

26   Allah desires to make things clear to you
            and to guide you to the correct practices of those before you
                and to turn towards you.
        Allah is All-Knowing, All-Wise.

27   Allah desires to turn towards you,
            but those who pursue their lower appetites
            desire to make you deviate completely.
28   Allah desires to make things lighter for you.
            Man was created weak.

29   You who believe! do not consume one another's property
            by false means,
        but only by means of mutually agreed trade.
            And do not kill yourselves.
        Allah is Most Merciful to you.

30   As for anyone who does that out of enmity and wrongdoing,
            We will roast him in a Fire.
        That is an easy matter for Allah.

31   If you avoid the serious wrong actions you have been forbidden,
            We will erase your bad actions from you
                and admit you by a Gate of Honour.

32   Do not covet what Allah has given to some of you
            in preference to others –
                men have a portion of what they acquire
            and women have a portion of what they acquire;
                but ask Allah for His bounty.
        Allah has knowledge of all things.

33   We have appointed heirs for everything
            that parents and relatives leave.
        If you have a bond with people, give them their share.
            Allah is a witness of all things.

34   Men have charge of women
            because Allah has preferred the one above the other
        and because they spend their wealth on them.
            Right-acting women are obedient,
        safeguarding their husbands' interests in their absence
            as Allah has guarded them.
        If there are women whose disobedience you fear,
            you may admonish them,
                refuse to sleep with them,
                    and then beat them.
        But if they obey you, do not look for a way to punish them.
            Allah is All-High, Most Great.

35   If you fear a breach between a couple,
            send an arbiter from his people
                and an arbiter from her people.
            If the couple desire to put things right,
        Allah will bring about a reconciliation between them.
            Allah is All-Knowing, All-Aware.

36   Worship Allah and do not associate anything with Him.
            Be good to your parents and relatives
                and to orphans and the very poor,
            and to neighbours who are related to you
                and neighbours who are not related to you,
            and to companions and travellers and your slaves.
                Allah does not love anyone vain or boastful.

37   As for those who are tight-fisted
            and direct others to be tight-fisted,
                and hide the bounty Allah has given them,
        We have prepared a humiliating punishment
            for those who disbelieve,
38   and also for those who spend their wealth to show off to people,
            not believing in Allah and the Last Day.
        Anyone who has made Shaytan his comrade,
            what an evil comrade he is!

39   What harm would it have done them
            to have believed in Allah and the Last Day
        and to have given of what Allah has provided for them?
            Allah knows everything about them.

40   Allah does not wrong anyone by so much as the smallest speck.
            And if there is a good deed Allah will multiply it
                and pay out an immense reward direct from Him.

41   How will it be when We bring a witness from every nation
            and bring you as a witness against them?

42   On that day those who disbelieved and disobeyed the Messenger
            will wish that they were one with the level earth.
        They will not be able to hide a single circumstance from Allah.

43   You who believe!
            do not approach the prayer when you are drunk,
                so that you will know what you are saying,

nor in a state of major impurity – unless you are travelling –
until you have washed yourselves completely.
If you are ill or on a journey,
or any of you have come from the lavatory
or touched women,
and you cannot find any water,
then do tayammum with pure earth,
wiping your faces and your hands.
Allah is Ever-Pardoning, Ever-Forgiving.

44   Do you not see those who were given a portion of the Book
trading in misguidance
and wanting you to be misguided from the way?
45   Allah knows best who your enemies are.
Allah suffices as a Protector; Allah suffices as a Helper.

46   Some of the Jews distort the true meaning of words,
saying, 'We hear and disobey,'
and 'Listen without listening,'
and *'Ra'ina!'**
twisting them with their tongues,
disparaging the deen.
If they had said, 'We hear and we obey,'
and 'Listen,'
and, *'Undhurna!'**
that would have been better for them
and more upright.
But Allah has cursed them for their unbelief.
Very few of them believe.

47   You who have been given the Book!
believe in what We have sent down
confirming what is with you,
before We obliterate faces,
turning them inside out,
or We curse you as We cursed
the Companions of the Sabbath.
Allah's command is always carried out.

48   Allah does not forgive anything being associated with Him
but He forgives whoever He wills
for anything other than that.

* Two Arabic words meaning "Look at us." But the former can be ambiguously construed in a
derogatory way whereas the latter cannot.

Anyone who associates something with Allah
    has committed a terrible crime.

49   Do you not see those who claim to be purified?
        No, Allah purifies whoever He wills.
    They will not be wronged by so much as the smallest speck.

50   Look how they invent lies against Allah.
        That suffices as an outright felony.

51   Do you not see those who were given a portion of the Book
        believing in idols and false gods
            and saying to those who disbelieve,
    'These people are better guided on their path
        than the believers'?

52   Those are the ones Allah has cursed.
        And if someone is cursed by Allah
            you will not find any one to help him.

53   Or do they indeed really own a portion
        of Allah's kingdom?
    In that case they do not give so much as a scrap
        to other people!

54   Or do they in fact envy other people
        for the bounty Allah has granted them?
    We gave the family of Ibrahim the Book and Wisdom,
        and We gave them an immense kingdom.

55   Some of them believe in him,
        and some bar access to him.
    Hell will suffice as a Searing Blaze!

56   As for those who reject Our Signs,
        We will roast them in a Fire.
    Every time their skins are burned off,
        We will replace them with new skins
    so that they can taste the punishment.
        Allah is Almighty, All-Wise.

57   But as for those who believe and do right actions,
        We will admit them into Gardens
            with rivers flowing under them,

remaining in them timelessly, for ever and ever.
In them they will have spouses of perfect purity
and We will admit them into cool, refreshing shade.

58   Allah commands you to return to their owners
the things you hold on trust
and, when you judge between people, to judge with justice.
How excellent is what Allah exhorts you to do!
Allah is All-Hearing, All-Seeing.

59   You who believe! obey Allah and obey the Messenger
and those in command among you.
If you have a dispute about something,
refer it back to Allah and the Messenger,
if you believe in Allah and the Last Day.
That is the best thing to do and gives the best result.

60   Do you not see those who claim that they believe
in what has been sent down to you
and what was sent down before you,
still desiring to turn to a satanic source for judgement
in spite of being ordered to reject it?
Shaytan wants to misguide them far away.

61   When they are told, 'Come to what Allah has sent down
and to the Messenger,'
you see the hypocrites turning away from you completely.

62   How will it be when a disaster strikes them
because of what they have done,
and then they come to you swearing by Allah:
'We desired nothing but good and reconciliation'?

63   Allah knows what is in such people's hearts
so turn away from them and warn them
and speak to them with words that take effect.

64   We sent no Messenger except to be obeyed by Allah's permission.
If only when they wronged themselves they had come to you
and asked Allah's forgiveness
and the Messenger had asked forgiveness for them
they would have found Allah Ever-Relenting, Most Merciful.

65   No, by your Lord, they are not believers
            until they make you their judge
                in the disputes that break out between them,
        and then find no resistance within themselves to what you decide
            and submit themselves completely.

66   If We had directed them to kill themselves or leave their homes,
            they would not have done so, except for a very few.
        But if they had done what they were urged to do,
            it would have been better for them
                and far more strengthening.

67   In that case We would have given them
            an immense reward from Us
68   and We would have guided them on a straight path.

69   Whoever obeys Allah and the Messenger
            will be with those whom Allah has blessed:
        the Prophets and the truly sincere,
            the martyrs and the righteous.
        What excellent company such people are!

70   That is favour from Allah.
            Allah suffices as a Knower.

71   You who believe! take all necessary precautions,
            then go out to fight in separate groups
                or go out as one body.

72   Among you there are people who hang back
            and if you encounter a setback then they say,
        'Allah has blessed me in that I was not there with them.'

73   But if you meet with favour from Allah they say –
            as if there were no friendship between you and them –
        'Oh! If only I had been with them so that I too
            might have won a great victory.'

74   So let those who sell the life of this world for the Next World
            fight in the Way of Allah.
        If someone fights in the Way of Allah,
            whether he is killed or is victorious,
        We will pay him an immense reward.

75 What reason could you have
  for not fighting in the Way of Allah –
  for those men, women and children who are oppressed
  and say, 'Our Lord, take us out of this city
  whose inhabitants are wrongdoers!
  Give us a protector from You! Give us a helper from You!'?

76 Those who believe fight in the Way of Allah.
  Those who disbelieve fight in the way of false gods.
  So fight the friends of Shaytan!
  Shaytan's scheming is always feeble.

77 Do you not see those who were told:
  'Hold back from fighting
  but establish the prayer and pay zakat'?
  Then when fighting is prescribed for them,
  a group of them fear people as Allah should be feared,
  or even more than that.
  They say, 'Our Lord, why have you prescribed fighting for us?
  If only You would give us just a little more time!'
  Say, 'The enjoyment of this world is very brief.
  The Next World is better for the godfearing.
  You will not be wronged by so much as the smallest speck.'

78 Wherever you are, death will catch up with you,
  even if you are in impregnable fortresses.
  If a good thing happens to them, they say,
  'This has come from Allah.'
  But if a bad thing happens to them, they say,
  'This has come from you.'
  Say, 'Everything comes from Allah.'
  What is the matter with these people
  that they scarcely understand a single word?

79 Any good thing that happens to you comes from Allah.
  Any bad thing that happens to you comes from yourself.
  We have sent you to mankind as a Messenger.
  Allah suffices as a Witness.

80 Whoever obeys the Messenger has obeyed Allah.
  If anyone turns away,
  We did not send you to them as their keeper.

81   They have the word, 'Obedience!' on their tongues
          but when they leave your presence,
              a group of them spend the night
          plotting to do other than what you say.
      Allah is recording their nocturnal plotting.
          So let them be and put your trust in Allah.
              Allah suffices as a Guardian.

82   Will they not ponder the Qur'an?
          If it had been from other than Allah,
      they would have found many inconsistencies in it.

83   When news of any matter reaches them they spread it about,
          whether it is of a reassuring or disquieting nature.
      If they had only referred it to the Messenger
          and those in command among them,
      those among them able to discern the truth about it
          would have had proper knowledge of it.
      If it were not for Allah's favour to you and His mercy,
          all but a very few of you would have followed Shaytan.

84   So fight in the way of Allah –
          you are only answerable for yourself –
              and spur on the believers.
      It may well be that Allah will curb the force of the unbelievers.
          Allah has greater force and greater power to punish.

85   Those who join forces for good will receive a reward for it.
          Those who join forces for evil will be answerable for it.
              Allah gives all things what they deserve.

86   When you are greeted with a greeting,
          return the greeting or improve on it.
      Allah takes account of everything.

87   Allah, there is no god but Him.
          He will gather you to the Day of Rising
              about which there is no doubt.
      And whose speech could be truer than Allah's?

88   How is it that you have become two parties
          regarding the hypocrites,
              when Allah has returned them to unbelief for what they did?

Do you desire to guide people Allah has misguided?
  When Allah misguides someone, you will find no way for him.

89   They would like you to disbelieve as they disbelieve
        so that you will all be the same.
     Do not take any of them as friends
        until they have made hijra in the Way of Allah.
     But if they run away then seize them
        and kill them wherever you find them.
     Do not take any of them as either a friend or helper –
90   except for those who seek shelter with people
              with whom you have a treaty,
           or who come to you greatly perturbed at the prospect
              of fighting either you or their own people.
     If Allah had willed, He could have given them
           the upper hand over you
        and then they would have fought you.
     If they keep away from you
           and do not fight you and submit to you,
        Allah has not given you any way against such people.

91   You will find others who desire to be safe from you
           and safe from their own people.
        Each time they are returned to fitna
           they are overwhelmed by it.
     If they do not keep away from you or submit to you
           or refrain from fighting,
        seize them and kill them wherever you find them.
     Over such people We have given you clear authority.

92   A believer should never kill another believer
           unless it is by mistake.
     Anyone who kills a believer by mistake
           should free a believing slave
              and pay blood-money to his family
           unless they forgo it as a sadaqa.
     If he is from a people who are your enemies
           and is a believer,
              you should free a believing slave.
     If he is from a people you have a treaty with,
           blood money should be paid to his family
              and you should free a believing slave.
     Anyone who cannot find the means
           should fast two consecutive months.

This is a concession from Allah.
>   Allah is All-Knowing, All-Wise.

93 As for anyone who kills a believer deliberately,
>   his repayment is Hell,
>   remaining in it for ever.
>   Allah is angry with him and has cursed him,
>   and has prepared for him a terrible punishment.

94 You who believe!
>   when you go out to fight in the Way of Allah
>   verify things carefully.
>   Do not say, 'You are not a believer',
>   to someone who greets you as a Muslim,
>   simply out of desire for the goods of this world.
>   With Allah there is booty in abundance.
>   That is the way you were before
>   but Allah has been kind to you.
>   So verify things carefully.
>   Allah is aware of what you do.

95 Those believers who stay behind –
>   other than those forced to by necessity –
>   are not the same as those who do jihad in the Way of Allah,
>   sacrificing their wealth and themselves.
>   Allah has given those who do jihad
>   with their wealth and themselves
>   a higher rank than those who stay behind.
>   Allah has promised the Best to both,
>   but Allah has preferred those who do jihad
>   over those who stay behind
>   by an immense reward:

96   high ranks conferred by Him
>   as well as forgiveness and mercy.
>   Allah is Ever-Forgiving, Most Merciful.

97 The angels ask those they take
>   while they are wronging themselves,
>   'What were your circumstances?'
>   They reply, 'We were oppressed on earth.'
>   They say, 'Was Allah's earth not wide enough
>   for you to have made hijra elsewhere in it?'
>   The shelter of such people will be Hell.
>   What an evil destination!

98   Except for those men, women and children
       who really are oppressed
   and do not have any other possibility
       and are not guided to any way.

99   It may well be that Allah will pardon them.
       Allah is Ever-Pardoning, Ever-Forgiving.

100   Those who make hijra in the Way of Allah
       will find many places of refuge on the earth
          and ample sustenance.
   If anyone leaves his home,
       making hijra to Allah and His Messenger,
          and death catches up with him,
   it is Allah Who will reward him.
   Allah is Ever-Forgiving, Most Merciful.

101   When you are travelling in the land,
       there is nothing wrong in your shortening your prayer
   if you fear that those who disbelieve may harass you.
       The unbelievers are your clear-cut enemies.

102   When you are with them and leading them in the prayer,
       a group of them should stand with you,
          keeping hold of their weapons.
   When they prostrate, the others should guard your backs.
       Then the other group who have not yet prayed
          should come and pray with you.
   They too should be careful and keep hold of their weapons.
       Those who disbelieve would like you to be negligent
          of your arms and equipment
       so that they can swoop down on you once and for all.
   There is nothing wrong, if you are bothered by rain or you are ill,
       in laying your weapons down; but take every precaution.
   Allah has prepared a humiliating punishment
       for the unbelievers.

103   When you have finished the prayer, remember Allah
       standing, sitting and lying on your sides.
   When you are safe again perform the prayer in the normal way.
       The prayer is prescribed for the believers at specific times.

104   Do not relax in pursuit of the enemy.
       If you feel pain, they too are feeling it just as you are,

but you hope for something from Allah
which they cannot hope for.
Allah is All-Knowing, All-Wise.

105   We have sent down the Book to you with the truth
so that you can judge between people
according to what Allah has shown to you.
But do not be an advocate for the treacherous.

106   And ask Allah's forgiveness.
Allah is Ever-Forgiving, Most Merciful.

107   Do not argue on behalf of those who betray themselves.
Allah does not love any evildoing traitors.

108   They try to conceal themselves from people,
but they cannot conceal themselves from Allah.
He is with them when they spend the night
saying things which are not pleasing to Him.
Allah encompasses everything they do.

109   Here you are arguing on their behalf in this world,
but who will argue with Allah on their behalf
on the Day of Rising?
Who will act as guardian for them then?

110   Anyone who does evil or wrongs himself
and then asks Allah's forgiveness
will find Allah Ever-Forgiving, Most Merciful.

111   If anyone commits an evil action
the responsibility for it is his alone.
Allah is All-Knowing, All-Wise.

112   Anyone who commits an error or an evil action,
and then ascribes it to someone innocent,
bears the weight of slander and clear wrongdoing.

113   Were it not for Allah's favour to you and His mercy,
a group of them would almost have managed to mislead you.
But they mislead no one but themselves
and do not harm you in any way.
Allah has sent down the Book and Wisdom to you
and taught you what you did not know before.
Allah's favour to you is indeed immense.

114 There is no good in much of their secret talk,
   except in the case of those who enjoin sadaqa,
    or what is right,
   or putting things right between people.
  If anyone does that, seeking the pleasure of Allah,
   We will give him an immense reward.

115 But if anyone opposes the Messenger
   after the guidance has become clear to him,
  and follows other than the path of the believers,
   We will hand him over to whatever he has turned to,
    and We will roast him in Hell.
  What an evil destination!

116 Allah does not forgive anything being associated with Him
   but He forgives whoever He wills
    for anything other than that.
  Anyone who associates something with Allah
   has gone very far astray.

117 What they call on apart from Him are female idols.
   What they call on is an arrogant shaytan
118   whom Allah has cursed.
  He said, 'I will take a certain fixed proportion of Your slaves.
119   I will lead them astray and fill them with false hopes.
   I will command them and they will cut off cattle's ears.
   I will command them and they will change Allah's creation.'
  Anyone who takes Shaytan as his protector in place of Allah
   has clearly lost everything.
120 He makes promises to them and fills them with false hopes.
   But what Shaytan promises them is nothing but delusion.
121 The shelter of such people will be Hell.
   They will find no way to escape from it.

122 But as for those who believe and do right actions,
   We will admit them into Gardens
    with rivers flowing under them,
  remaining in them timelessly, for ever and ever.
   Allah's promise is true.
  Whose speech could be truer than Allah's?

123 It is not a matter of wishful thinking on your part
   nor of the wishful thinking of the People of the Book.

Anyone who does evil will be repaid for it.
He will not find any protector or helper besides Allah.

124   Anyone, male or female, who does right actions
                and is a believer,
            will enter the Garden.
        They will not be wronged by so much as the tiniest speck.

125   Who could have a better deen than someone
                who submits himself completely to Allah
                    and is a good-doer,
            and follows the religion of Ibrahim,
                a man of pure natural belief?
        Allah took Ibrahim as an intimate friend.

126   What is in the heavens and in the earth belongs to Allah.
            Allah encompasses all things.

127   They will ask you for a fatwa about women.
            Say, 'Allah gives you a fatwa about them;
            and also what is recited to you in the Book about orphan girls
                to whom you do not give the inheritance they are owed,
                    while at the same time desiring to marry them;
            and also about young children who are denied their rights:
                that you should act justly with respect to orphans.'
                    Whatever good you do, Allah knows it.

128   If a woman fears cruelty or aversion on her husband's part,
                there is nothing wrong in the couple becoming reconciled.
                    Reconciliation is better.
            But people are prone to selfish greed.
        If you do good and are godfearing,
            Allah is aware of what you do.

129   You will not be able to be completely fair between your wives,
                however hard you try.
            But do not be completely partial so as to leave a wife,
                as it were, suspended in mid-air.
            And if you make amends and are godfearing,
                Allah is Ever-Forgiving, Most Merciful.

130   If a couple do separate,
                Allah will enrich each of them

from His boundless wealth.
Allah is All-Encompassing, All-Wise.

131 What is in the heavens and in the earth belongs to Allah.
We have instructed those given the Book before you
and you yourselves, to have taqwa of Allah,
but if you disbelieve,
what is in the heavens and in the earth belongs to Allah.
Allah is Rich Beyond Need, Praiseworthy.

132 What is in the heavens and in the earth belongs to Allah.
Allah suffices as a Guardian.

133 Mankind! if He wanted, He could remove you altogether,
and produce others instead.
Allah certainly has the power to do that.

134 If anyone desires the reward of this world,
the reward of both this world and the Next World
is with Allah.
Allah is All-Hearing, All-Seeing.

135 You who believe! be upholders of justice,
bearing witness for Allah alone,
even against yourselves or your parents and relatives.
Whether they are rich or poor,
Allah is well able to look after them.
Do not follow your own desires and deviate from the truth.
If you twist or turn away, Allah is aware of what you do.

136 You who believe! Believe in Allah and His Messenger
and in the Book He sent down to His Messenger,
and the Books He sent down before.
Anyone who rejects Allah and His angels
and His Books and His Messengers and the Last Day
has gone very far astray.

137 As for those who believe and then return to unbelief,
and then again believe and then return to unbelief,
and then increase in unbelief,
Allah will not forgive them or guide them on any path.

138 Give news to the hypocrites
that they will have a painful punishment.

139   Do those who take the unbelievers as protectors,
              rather than the believers,
           hope to find power and strength with them?
       Power and strength belong entirely to Allah.

140   It has been sent down to you in the Book
              that when you hear Allah's Signs
                 being rejected and mocked at by people,
           you must not sit with them till they start talking of other things.
              If you do you are just the same as them.
       Allah will gather all the hypocrites and unbelievers into Hell.

141   Those who anticipate the worst for you say,
              'Were we not with you?'
                 whenever you gain a victory from Allah,
           but if the unbelievers have a success they say,
              'Did we not have the upper hand over you
           and yet in spite of that keep the believers away from you?'
              Allah will judge between you on the Day of Rising.
       Allah will not give the unbelievers any way against the believers.

142   The hypocrites think they deceive Allah,
              but He is deceiving them.
       When they get up to pray,
              they get up lazily,
                 showing off to people,
           and only remembering Allah a very little.

143   They vacillate between the two –
              not joining these or joining those.
       If Allah misguides someone,
              you will not find any way for him to go.

144   You who believe! do not take the unbelievers as friends
              rather than the believers.
       Do you want to give Allah clear proof against you?

145   The hypocrites are in the lowest level of the Fire.
              You will not find any one to help them,
146   except those who repent and put things right
              and hold fast to Allah
                 and dedicate their deen to Allah alone;
              they are with the believers.
       Allah will give the believers an immense reward.

147   Why should Allah punish you if you are thankful and believe?
        Allah is All-Thankful, All-Knowing.

148   Allah does not like evil words being voiced out loud,
                except in the case of someone who has been wronged.
        Allah is All-Hearing, All-Knowing.

149   Whether you reveal a good act or keep it hidden,
                or pardon an evil act,
        Allah is Ever-Pardoning, All-Powerful.

150   Those who reject Allah and His Messengers
                and desire to cause division
                between Allah and His Messengers,
        saying, 'We believe in some and reject the others,'
                wanting to take a pathway in between,
151   such people are the true unbelievers.
        We have prepared a humiliating punishment for the unbelievers.

152   Those who believe in Allah and His Messengers
                and do not differentiate between any of them,
                We will pay them their wages.
        Allah is Ever-Forgiving, Most Merciful.

153   The People of the Book will ask you to bring down
                a Book from heaven to them.
        They asked Musa for even more than that.
                They said, 'Let us see Allah with our own eyes.'
        So the lightning-bolt struck them down for their wrongdoing.
                Then they adopted the Calf
                        after the Clear Signs had come to them,
                but We pardoned them for that
                        and gave Musa clear authority.

154   We lifted up the Mount above their heads
                in accordance with the covenant they had made,
        and We said to them, 'Enter the gate prostrating,'
                and We said to them, 'Do not break the Sabbath,'
                        and We made a binding covenant with them.

155   Because of the fact that they broke their covenant,
                and rejected Allah's Signs,
        and killed the Prophets without any right to do so
                and said, 'Our hearts are uncircumcised,'

Allah has stamped them with unbelief,
so they do not believe except for very few.

156 And on account of their unbelief,
and their utterance of a monstrous slander against Maryam,

157 and their saying, 'We killed the Messiah,
'Isa son of Maryam, Messenger of Allah.'
They did not kill him and they did not crucify him
but it was made to seem so to them.
Those who argue about him are in doubt about it.
They have no real knowledge of it, just conjecture.
But they certainly did not kill him.

158 Allah raised him up to Himself.
Allah is Almighty, All-Wise.

159 There is not one of the People of the Book
who will not believe in him before he dies;
and on the Day of Rising
he will be a witness against them.

160 Because of wrongdoing on the part of the Jews,
We made haram for them some good things
which had previously been halal for them;
and because of their obstructing many people
from the Way of Allah,

161 and because of their practising riba
when they were forbidden to do it,
and because of their consuming people's wealth
by wrongful means,
We have prepared for the unbelievers among them
a painful punishment.

162 But those of them who are firmly rooted in knowledge,
and the believers,
believe in what has been sent down to you
and what was sent down before you:
those who establish the prayer and pay zakat,
and believe in Allah and the Last Day –
We will pay such people an immense wage.

163 We have revealed to you as We revealed to Nuh
and the Prophets who came after him.
And We revealed to Ibrahim
and Isma'il and Ishaq and Ya'qub and the Tribes,
and 'Isa and Ayyub and Yunus

and Harun and Sulayman.
And We gave Dawud the Zabur.

164   There are Messengers We have already told you about
           and Messengers We have not told you about;
               and Allah spoke directly to Musa –
165   Messengers bringing good news and giving warning,
           so that people will have no argument against Allah
               after the coming of the Messengers.
       Allah is Almighty, All-Wise.

166   But Allah bears witness to what He has sent down to you.
       He has sent it down with His knowledge.
           The angels bear witness as well.
       And Allah suffices as a Witness.

167   Those who disbelieve and bar access to the Way of Allah
           have gone very far astray.

168   Allah will not forgive those who disbelieve and do wrong
           or guide them on any path,
169   except the path of Hell,
           remaining in it timelessly,
               for ever and ever.
       That is easy for Allah.

170   Mankind! the Messenger has brought you
           the truth from your Lord,
               so it is better for you to believe.
       But if you disbelieve,
       everything in the heavens and the earth belongs to Allah.
       Allah is All-Knowing, All-Wise.

171   People of the Book! do not go to excess in your deen.
           Say nothing but the truth about Allah.
       The Messiah, 'Isa son of Maryam, was only the Messenger of Allah
           and His Word, which He cast into Maryam,
               and a Spirit from Him.
       So believe in Allah and His Messengers.
           Do not say, 'Three.'
               It is better that you stop.
       Allah is only One God.
           He is too Glorious to have a son!

Everything in the heavens and in the earth belongs to Him.
Allah suffices as a Guardian.

172 The Messiah would never disdain to be a slave to Allah
nor would the angels near to Him.
If any do disdain to worship Him, and grow arrogant,
He will in any case gather them all to Him.

173 As for those who believe and do right actions,
He will pay them their wages in full
and will give them increase from His favour.
As for those who show disdain and grow arrogant,
He will punish them with a painful punishment.
They will not find any protector or helper for themselves
besides Allah.

174 Mankind! a clear proof has come to you from your Lord.
We have sent down a Clear Light to you.

175 As for those who believe in Allah and hold fast to Him,
He will admit them into mercy and favour from Him
and will guide them to Him on a straight path.

176 They will ask you for a fatwa.
Say: 'Allah gives you a fatwa
about people who die without direct heirs:
If a man dies childless but has a sister
she receives half of what he leaves,
and he is her heir if she dies childless.
If there are two sisters
they receive two-thirds of what he leaves.
If there are brothers and sisters
the males receive the share of two females.
Allah makes things clear to you so you will not go astray.
Allah has knowledge of all things.'

Sura 5

Al-Ma'ida
The Table

In the name of Allah, All-Merciful, Most Merciful

1   You who believe! fulfil your contracts.
        All livestock animals are halal for you,
            except those that are recited to you now;
        but it is still not halal to hunt
            while you are in ihram.
    Allah makes whatever judgements He wills.

2   You who believe! do not profane
        the sacred rites of Allah
        or the sacred months,
        or the sacrificial animals,
        or the ritual garlands,
        or those heading for the Sacred House,
            desiring profit and good pleasure from their Lord.
    When you have come out of ihram, then hunt for game.
        Do not let hatred for a people who debar you
            from the Masjid al-Haram
        incite you into going beyond the limits.
    Help each other to goodness and taqwa.
        Do not help each other to wrongdoing and enmity.
    Have taqwa of Allah.
        Allah is severe in retribution.

3   Haram for you are
        carrion, blood and pork,
    and what has been consecrated to other than Allah,
    and animals which have been strangled,

and animals which have been killed by a blow,
and animals which have fallen to their death,
and animals which have been gored,
and animals which wild beasts have eaten –
    except those you are able to slaughter properly –
and animals which have been sacrificed on altars,
and deciding things by means of divining arrows –
    that is deviance.

    Today the unbelievers have despaired
        of overcoming your deen.
           So do not be afraid of them but be afraid of Me.
    Today I have perfected your deen for you
        and completed My blessing upon you
        and I am pleased with Islam as a deen for you.

But if anyone is forced by hunger,
    not intending any wrongdoing,
Allah is Ever-Forgiving, Most Merciful.

4   They will ask you what is halal for them.
        Say: 'All good things are halal for you,
and also what is caught for you by hunting animals
    which you have trained as Allah has taught you.
Eat what they catch for you,
    mentioning Allah's name over it.'
And have taqwa of Allah.
    Allah is swift at reckoning.

5   Today all good things have been made halal for you.
And the food of those given the Book is also halal for you
    and your food is halal for them.
So are free women from among the believers
    and free women of those given the Book before you,
        once you have given them their dowries in marriage,
    not in fornication or taking them as lovers.
But as for anyone who rejects faith,
    his actions will come to nothing
and in the Next World he will be among the losers.

6   You who believe! when you get up to do the prayer,
    wash your faces and your hands
        and your arms to the elbows,
    and wipe over your heads,

and wash your feet to the ankles.
If you are in a state of major impurity,
     then purify yourselves.
But if you are ill or on a journey,
     or have come from the lavatory,
          or have touched women,
     and cannot find any water,
then do tayammum with pure earth,
     and wipe your faces and your hands.
Allah does not want to make things difficult for you,
     but He does want to purify you
          and to perfect His blessing upon you
     so that hopefully you will be thankful.

7   Remember Allah's blessing to you
          and the covenant He made with you
               when you said, 'We hear and we obey.'
       Have taqwa of Allah.
          Allah knows what the heart contains.

8   You who believe! show integrity for the sake of Allah,
          bearing witness with justice.
       Do not let hatred for a people incite you into not being just.
          Be just.
       That is closer to taqwa.
          Have taqwa of Allah.
          Allah is aware of what you do.

9   Allah has promised those who believe and do right actions
          forgiveness and an immense reward.

10   But those who disbelieve and deny Our Signs,
          are the Companions of the Blazing Fire.

11   You who believe! remember Allah's blessing to you
          when certain people were on the verge
               of raising their hands against you
          and He held their hands back from you.
               Have taqwa of Allah.
       The believers should put their trust in Allah.

12   Allah made a covenant with the tribe of Israel
          and We raised up twelve leaders from among them.
       Allah said, 'I am with you.

If you establish the prayer and pay zakat,
   and believe in My Messengers
      and respect and support them,
   and make a generous loan to Allah,
I will erase your wrong actions from you
   and admit you into Gardens
      with rivers flowing under them.
Any of you who disbelieve after that
   have gone astray from the right way.'

13   But because of their breaking of their covenant,
   We have cursed them and hardened their hearts.
They distort the true meaning of words
   and have forgotten a good portion
      of what they were reminded of.
You will never cease to come upon
   some act of treachery on their part,
      except for a few of them.
Yet pardon them, and overlook.
   Allah loves good-doers.

14   We also made a covenant with those who say,
   'We are Christians,'
and they too forgot a good portion
   of what they were reminded of.
So We stirred up enmity and hatred between them
   until the Day of Rising
when Allah will inform them about what they did.

15   People of the Book! Our Messenger has come to you,
   making clear to you much of the Book
      that you have kept concealed,
         and passing over a lot.
A Light has come to you from Allah
   and a Clear Book.

16   By it, Allah guides
   those who follow what pleases Him
      to the ways of Peace.
He will bring them from the darkness to the light
   by His permission,
and guide them to a straight path.

17   Those who say, 'Allah is the Messiah, son of Maryam,'
          disbelieve.
      Say: 'Who possesses any power at all over Allah
          if He desires to destroy the Messiah, son of Maryam,
              and his mother, and everyone else on earth?'
      The kingdom of the heavens and the earth
          and everything between them
              belongs to Allah.
          He creates whatever He wills.
      Allah has power over all things.

18   The Jews and Christians say, 'We are Allah's children
          and His loved ones.'
      Say: 'Why, then, does He punish you for your wrong actions?
          No, you are merely human beings
              among those He has created.
      He forgives whoever He wills and He punishes whoever He wills.
          The kingdom of the heavens and the earth
              and everything between them
                  belongs to Allah.
              He is our final destination.'

19   People of the Book! Our Messenger has come to you,
          making things clear to you,
              after a period with no Messengers,
                  lest you should say,
          'No one came to us bringing good news or warning.'
      Someone has come to you bringing good news and a warning.
          Allah has power over all things.

20   Remember when Musa said to his people,
          'My people! remember Allah's blessing to you
      when He appointed Prophets among you
          and appointed kings for you,
      and gave you what He had not given
          to anyone else in all the worlds!
21   'My people! enter the Holy Land
          which Allah has ordained for you
      Do not turn back in your tracks
          and so become transformed into losers.'

22   They said, 'There are gigantic people in it, Musa.
          We will not enter it until they leave.
      If they leave it, then we will go in.'

23   Two men among those who were afraid,
          but whom Allah had blessed,
     said, 'Enter the gate against them!
          Once you have entered it, you will be victorious.
     Put your trust in Allah if you are believers.'

24   They said, 'We will never enter it, Musa,
          as long as they are there.
     So you and your Lord go and fight.
          We will stay sitting here.'

25   He said, 'My Lord, I have no control over anyone
          but myself and my brother,
     so make a clear distinction between us
          and this deviant people.'

26   He said, 'The land will be forbidden to them for forty years
          during which they will wander aimlessly about the earth.
          Do not waste grief on this deviant people.'

27   Recite to them the true report of Adam's two sons
          when they offered a sacrifice
     and it was accepted from one of them
          but not accepted from the other.
          The one said, 'I shall kill you.'
     The other said, 'Allah only accepts
          from people who are godfearing.
28   Even if you do raise your hand against me to kill me,
     I am not going to raise my hand against you to kill you.
          Truly I fear Allah, the Lord of all the worlds.
29   I want you to take on both my wrongdoing and your wrongdoing
          and so become one of the Companions of the Fire.
     That is the repayment of the wrongdoers.'

30   So his lower self persuaded him to kill his brother,
          and he killed him and became one of the lost.

31   Then Allah sent a crow which scratched at the earth
          to show him how to conceal his brother's corpse.
     He said, 'Woe is me! Can I not even be like this crow
          and conceal my brother's corpse?'
     And he became one of those who suffer bitter remorse
32   on account of that.
     So We decreed for the tribe of Israel

that if someone kills another person –
    unless it is in retaliation for someone else
        or for causing corruption in the earth –
    it is as if he had murdered all mankind.
And if anyone saves another person's life,
    it is as if he had given life to all mankind.
Our Messengers came to them with Clear Signs
    but even after that many of them
        committed outrages in the earth.

33   The reprisal against those who wage war
        on Allah and His Messenger,
and go about the earth corrupting it,
    is that they should be killed or crucified,
        or have their alternate hands and feet cut off,
        or be banished from the land.
That will be their degradation in this world
    and in the Next World they will have a terrible punishment,
34   except for those who repent
    before you gain power over them.
Know that Allah is Ever-Forgiving, Most Merciful.

35   You who believe! have taqwa of Allah
    and seek the means of drawing near to Him,
        and do jihad in His Way,
    so that hopefully you will be successful.

36   As for those who disbelieve,
    if they had everything on the earth
        and the same again with it
to ransom themselves from the punishment
    of the Day of Rising,
    it would not be accepted from them.
They will have a painful punishment.

37   They will want to get out of the Fire
    but they will not be able to.
They will have an everlasting punishment.

38   As for thieves, both male and female,
    cut off their hands in reprisal for what they have done:
an object lesson from Allah.
    Allah is Almighty, All-Wise.

39   But if anyone repents after his wrongdoing
          and puts things right,
      Allah will turn towards him.
          Allah is Ever-Forgiving, Most Merciful.

40   Do you not know that the kingdom of the heavens and earth
          belongs to Allah?
      He punishes whoever He wills
          and forgives whoever He wills.
      Allah has power over all things.

41   O Messenger! do not be grieved by those
          who rush headlong into unbelief
      among those who say 'We believe' with their tongues
          when their hearts contain no faith,
      nor by those among the Jews who listen to lies,
          listen to other people who have not come to you,
      distorting words from their proper meanings,
          saying, 'If you are given this, then take it.
              If you are not given it, then beware!'
      If Allah desires misguidance for someone,
          you cannot help him against Allah in any way.
      Those are the people whose hearts
          Allah does not want to purify.
      They will have disgrace in this world
          and in the Next World they will have a terrible punishment.

42   They are people who listen to lies
          and consume ill-gotten gains.
      If they come to you,
          you can either judge between them
              or turn away from them.
      If you turn away from them,
          they cannot harm you in any way.
      But if you do judge,
          judge between them justly.
              Allah loves the just.

43   How can they make you their judge
          when they have the Torah with them
              which contains the judgement of Allah?
      Then even after that they turn their backs!
          Such people are certainly not believers.

44   We sent down the Torah containing guidance and light,
         and the Prophets who had submitted themselves
             gave judgement by it for the Jews –
         as did their scholars and their rabbis –
     by what they had been allowed to preserve of Allah's Book
         to which they were witnesses.
     Do not be afraid of people, be afraid of Me.
         And do not sell My Signs for a paltry price.
     Those who do not judge by what Allah has sent down,
         such people are unbelievers.

45   We prescribed for them in it:
         a life for a life,
         an eye for an eye,
         a nose for a nose,
         an ear for an ear,
         a tooth for a tooth,
         and retaliation for wounds.
     But if anyone forgoes that as a sadaqa,
         it will act as expiation for him.
     Those who do not judge by what Allah has sent down,
         such people are wrongdoers.

46   And We sent 'Isa son of Maryam following in their footsteps,
         confirming the Torah that came before him.
     We gave him the Injil containing guidance and light,
         confirming the Torah that came before it,
     and as guidance and admonition for the godfearing.

47   The people of the Injil should judge
         by what Allah sent down in it.
     Those who do not judge by what Allah has sent down,
         such people are deviators.

48   And We have sent down the Book to you with truth,
         confirming and conserving the previous Books.
     So judge between them by what Allah has sent down
         and do not follow their whims and desires
             deviating from the Truth that has come to you.
     We have appointed a law and a practice for every one of you.
     Had Allah willed, He would have made you a single community,
         but He wanted to test you regarding what has come to you.
     So compete with each other in doing good.

Every one of you will return to Allah
   and He will inform you regarding the things
      about which you differed.

49   Judge between them by what Allah has sent down
         and do not follow their whims and desires.
      And beware of them lest they lure you away
         from some of what Allah has sent down to you.
      If they turn their backs, then know that Allah
         wants to afflict them with some of their wrong actions.
            Many of mankind are deviators.

50   Do they then seek the judgement of the Time of Ignorance?*
         Who could be better at giving judgement than Allah
            for people with certainty?

51   You who believe! do not take the Jews and Christians
            as your friends;
         they are the friends of one another.
      Any of you who takes them as friends is one of them.
         Allah does not guide wrongdoing people.

52   Yet you see those with sickness in their hearts rushing to them,
         saying, 'We fear the wheel of fate may turn against us.'
      But it may well be that Allah will bring about victory
         or some other contingency from Him.
      Then they will deeply regret their secret thoughts.

53   Those who believe say,
         'Are these the people who swore by Allah,
            with their most earnest oaths, that they were with you?'
      Their actions have come to nothing and they now are losers.

54   You who believe! if any of you renounce your deen,
         Allah will bring forward a people
      whom He loves and who love Him,
         humble to the believers,
            fierce to the unbelievers,
      who strive in the Way of Allah
         and do not fear the blame of any censurer.
      That is the unbounded favour of Allah
         which He gives to whoever He wills.
      Allah is Boundless, All-Knowing.

---

* The time before the coming of the Prophet and the revelation of the Qur'an.

55   Your friend is only Allah and His Messenger
        and those who believe:
    those who establish the prayer
        and pay zakat, and bow.

56   As for those who make Allah their friend,
        and His Messenger and those who believe:
    it is the party of Allah who are victorious!

57   You who believe! do not take as friends
        any of those given the Book before you or the unbelievers
            who make a mockery and a game out of your deen.
    Have taqwa of Allah if you are believers.

58   When you call to the prayer,
        they make a mockery and a game of it.
    That is because they are people who do not use their intellect.

59   Say: 'People of the Book! do you resent us for any other reason
        than that we believe in Allah
            and what was sent down to us,
                and what was sent down before,
            and because most of you are deviators?'

60   Say: 'Shall I tell you of a reward with Allah far worse than that:
        that of those whom Allah has cursed
            and with whom He is angry –
    turning some of them into monkeys and into pigs –
        and who worshipped false gods?
    Such people are in a worse situation
        and further from the right way.'

61   When they come to you, they say, 'We believe.'
        But they entered with unbelief and left with it.
    Allah knows best what they were hiding.

62   You see many of them rushing to wrongdoing and enmity
        and acquiring ill-gotten gains.
        What an evil thing they do!

63   Why do their scholars and rabbis not prohibit them
        from evil speech and acquiring ill-gotten gains?
        What an evil thing they invent!

64   The Jews say, 'Allah's hand is chained.'
         Their hands are chained
            and they are cursed for what they say!
       No! Both His hands are open wide
         and He gives however He wills.
       What has been sent down to you from your Lord
         increases many of them in insolence and unbelief.
       We have incited enmity and hatred between them
         until the Day of Rising.
       Each time they kindle the fire of war,
         Allah extinguishes it.
       They rush about the earth corrupting it.
         Allah does not love corrupters.

65   If only the People of the Book had believed and been godfearing,
         We would have erased their evil deeds from them
            and admitted them into Gardens of Delight.

66   If only they had implemented the Torah and the Injil
         and what was sent down to them from their Lord,
       they would have been fed from above their heads
         and beneath their feet.
       Among them there is a moderate group
         but what most of them do is evil.

67   O Messenger! transmit what has been sent down to you
         from your Lord.
       If you do not do it you will not have transmitted His Message.
         Allah will protect you from people.
       Allah does not guide the people of the unbelievers.

68   Say: 'People of the Book! you have nothing to stand on
         until you implement the Torah and the Injil
       and what has been sent down to you from your Lord.'
         What has been sent down to you from your Lord
            increases many of them in insolence and unbelief.
         So do not waste your grief on the people of the unbelievers.

69   Those who believe and those who are Jews
         and the Sabaeans and the Christians,
       all who believe in Allah and the Last Day and act rightly
         will feel no fear and know no sorrow.

70   We made a covenant with the tribe of Israel
            and We sent Messengers to them.
        Each time a Messenger came to them
            with something their lower selves did not desire,
        they denied some and they murdered others.

71   They thought there would be no fitna.
            They were blind and deaf.
        Then Allah turned towards them.
            Then many of them went blind and deaf again.
                Allah sees what they do.

72   Those who say that the Messiah, son of Maryam, is Allah
            are unbelievers.
        The Messiah said, 'Tribe of Israel! worship Allah,
            my Lord and your Lord.
        If anyone associates anything with Allah,
            Allah has forbidden him the Garden
                and his refuge will be the Fire.'
        The wrongdoers will have no helpers.

73   Those who say that Allah is the third of three
            are unbelievers.
        There is no god but One God.
        If they do not stop saying what they say,
            a painful punishment will afflict
                those among them who disbelieve.

74   Why do they not turn to Allah and ask for His forgiveness?
            Allah is Ever-Forgiving, Most Merciful.

75   The Messiah, the son of Maryam, was only a Messenger,
            before whom other Messengers came and went.
        His mother was a woman of truth.
            Both of them ate food.
        See how We make the Signs clear to them!
            Then see how they are perverted!

76   Say: 'Do you worship, besides Allah,
            something which has no power to harm or help you
                when Allah is the All-Hearing, the All-Knowing?'

77   Say: 'People of the Book! do not go to extremes in your deen,
            asserting other than the truth,

and do not follow the whims and desires of people
    who were misguided previously
and have misguided many others,
    and are far from the right way.'

78   Those among the tribe of Israel who disbelieve
    were cursed on the tongue of Dawud
        and that of 'Isa, son of Maryam.
    That is because they rebelled
        and overstepped the limits.

79   They would not restrain one another
    from any of the wrong things that they did.
How evil were the things they used to do!

80   You see many of them taking those who disbelieve
        as their friends.
    What their lower selves have advanced for them is evil indeed,
        bringing Allah's anger down upon them.
    They will suffer punishment timelessly, for ever.

81   If they had believed in Allah and the Prophet
    and what has been sent down to him,
they would not have taken them as friends.
    But most of them are deviators.

82   You will find that the people most hostile
    to those who believe
        are the Jews and the idolators.
You will find the people most affectionate
    to those who believe
        are those who say, 'We are Christians.'
That is because some of them are priests and monks
    and because they are not arrogant.

83   When they listen to what has been sent down to the Messenger,
    you see their eyes overflowing with tears
        because of what they recognise of the truth.
They say, 'Our Lord, we believe!
    So write us down among the witnesses.

84   How could we not believe in Allah,
    and the truth that has come to us,
when we long for our Lord to include us among the righteous?'

85   Allah will reward them for what they say
          with Gardens with rivers flowing under them,
              remaining in them timelessly, for ever.
      That is the recompense of the good-doers.

86   As for those who disbelieve and deny Our Signs,
          they are the Companions of the Blazing Fire.

87   You who believe! do not make haram
          the good things Allah has made halal for you,
              and do not overstep the limits.
      Allah does not love people who overstep the limits.

88   Eat the halal and good things Allah has provided for you,
          and have taqwa of Allah,
              Him in Whom you believe.

89   Allah does not take you to task for your inadvertent oaths,
          but He will take you to task for oaths you make intentionally.
      The expiation in that case is to feed ten poor people
          with the average amount you feed your family,
              or clothe them, or free a slave.
          Anyone without the means to do so should fast three days.
      That is the expiation for breaking oaths
          when you have sworn them.
          Keep your oaths.
      In this way Allah makes His Signs clear to you,
          so that hopefully you will be thankful.

90   You who believe! wine and gambling,
          stone altars and divining arrows
              are filth from the handiwork of Shaytan.
      Avoid them completely
          so that hopefully you will be successful.

91   Shaytan wants to stir up enmity and hatred between you
          by means of wine and gambling,
      and to debar you from remembrance of Allah
          and from the prayer.
      Will you not then give them up?

92   Obey Allah and obey the Messenger and beware!
          If you turn your backs, know that Our Messenger
              is only responsible for clear transmission.

93   Those who believe and do right actions
            are not to blame for anything they have consumed
        provided they are godfearing and believe and do right actions,
            and then again are godfearing and believe,
                and then are godfearing and do good.
                    Allah loves good-doers.

94   You who believe! Allah will test you with game animals
            which come within the reach of your hands and spears,
        so that Allah will know those who fear Him in the Unseen.
            Anyone who oversteps the limits after this
                will have a painful punishment.

95   You who believe! do not kill game while you are in ihram.
            If one of you kills any deliberately,
        the reprisal for it is a livestock animal
            equivalent to what he killed,
                as judged by two just men among you,
            a sacrifice to reach the Ka'ba,
        or expiation by feeding the poor,
            or fasting commensurate with that,
        so that he may taste the evil consequences of what he did.
            Allah has pardoned all that took place in the past;
        but if anyone does it again Allah will take revenge on him.
            Allah is Almighty, Exactor of Revenge.

96   Anything you catch in the sea is halal for you,
            and all food from it,
        for your enjoyment and that of travellers,
            but land game is haram for you
                while you are in ihram.
            So have taqwa of Allah,
        Him to whom you will be gathered.

97   Allah has made the Ka'ba, the Sacred House,
            a special institution for mankind,
                and also the sacred months
                and the sacrificial animals
                and the ritual garlands.
        That is so you will know that Allah knows
            what is in the heavens and in the earth
        and that Allah has knowledge of all things.

98   Know that Allah is fierce in retribution
       and that Allah is Ever-Forgiving, Most Merciful.

99   The Messenger is only responsible for transmission.
       Allah knows what you divulge and what you hide.

100   Say: 'Bad things and good things are not the same,
       even though the abundance of the bad things
          may seem attractive to you.'
    Have taqwa of Allah, people of intelligence,
       so that hopefully you will be successful.

101   You who believe! do not ask about matters which,
       if they were made known to you,
          would make things difficult for you.
    If you do ask about them
       when the Qur'an is being sent down,
          they will be made known to you.
    Allah has ignored them.
    Allah is Ever-Forgiving, All-Forbearing.

102   People before you asked about them
       and then later came to reject them.

103   Allah did not institute any such thing
       as *bahira* or *sa'iba* or *wasila* or *hami*.*
    Those who disbelieved invented lies against Allah.
       Most of them do not use their intellect.

104   When they are told, 'Come to what Allah has sent down
       and to the Messenger,'
    they say, 'What we found our fathers doing
       is enough for us.'
    What! Even if their fathers did not know anything
       and were not guided!

105   You who believe! you are only responsible for yourselves.
       The misguided cannot harm you as long as you are guided.
          All of you will return to Allah
       and He will inform you about what you were doing.

106   You who believe! when one of you is near to death
       and makes a will,

---

* Certain pre-Islamic taboos and superstitions connected with camels.

two just men from among you should act as witnesses;
or, if you are travelling when the misfortune of death occurs,
    two men who are strangers to you.
You should detain them after the prayer
    and, if you are doubtful, they should swear by Allah:
'We will not sell it for any price, even to a near relative,
    and we will not conceal the testimony of Allah.
        If we did we would indeed be wrongdoers.'

107   If it then comes to light that the two of them
    have merited the allegation of wrongdoing,
two others who have the most right to do so
    should take their place and swear by Allah:
'Our testimony is truer than their testimony.
    We have not committed perjury.
If we had we would indeed be wrongdoers.'

108   That makes it more likely
that they will give their evidence properly
    or be afraid that their oaths will be refuted
        by subsequent oaths.
Have taqwa of Allah and listen carefully.
    Allah does not guide deviant people.

109   On the day Allah gathers the Messengers together
    and says, 'What response did you receive?'
they will say, 'We do not know.
    You are the Knower of unseen things.'

110   Remember when Allah will say, ''Isa, son of Maryam,
    remember My blessing to you and to your mother
when I reinforced you with the Purest Ruh
    so that you could speak to people in the cradle
        and when you were fully grown;
and when I taught you the Book and Wisdom,
    and the Torah and the Injil;
and when you created a bird-shape out of clay
    by My permission,
and then breathed into it and it became a bird
    by My permission;
and healed the blind and the leper
    by My permission;
and when you brought forth the dead
    by My permission;
and when I held back the tribe of Israel from you,
    when you brought them the Clear Signs

and those of them who disbelieved said,
   "This is nothing but downright magic";
111   and when I inspired the Disciples to believe
   in Me and in My Messenger,
they said, "We belelieve.
   Bear witness that we are Muslims."'

112   And when the Disciples said, ''Isa son of Maryam!
   Can your Lord send down a table to us out of heaven?'
He said, 'Have taqwa of Allah if you are believers!'

113   They said, 'We want to eat from it
   and for our hearts to be at peace
and to know that you have told us the truth
   and to be among those who witness it.'

114   'Isa son of Maryam said, 'Allah, our Lord,
   send down a table to us out of heaven
     to be a feast for us,
       for the first and last of us,
     and as a Sign from You.
   Provide for us!
     You are the Best of Providers!'

115   Allah said, 'I will send it down to you
   but if anyone among you disbelieves after that,
I will punish him with a punishment the like of which
   I will not inflict on anyone else in all the worlds!'

116   And when Allah says, ''Isa son of Maryam!
   Did you say to people, "Take me and my mother
     as gods besides Allah?"'
he will say, 'Glory be to You!
   It is not for me to say what I have no right to say!
If I had said it, then You would have known it.
   You know what is in my self
     but I do not know what is in Your Self.
   You are the Knower of all unseen things.
117   I said to them nothing but what You ordered me to say:
   "Worship Allah, my Lord and your Lord."
I was a witness against them
   as long as I remained among them,
but when You took me back to You,

You were the One watching over them.
    You are Witness of all things.
118   If You punish them,
        they are Your slaves.
    If you forgive them,
You are the Almighty, the All-Wise.'

119   Allah will say, 'This is the Day
        when the sincerity of the sincere
            will benefit them.
    They will have Gardens
        with rivers flowing under them,
    remaining in them timelessly,
        for ever and ever.
    Allah is pleased with them
        and they are pleased with Him.
    That is the Great Victory.'

120   The kingdom of the heavens and the earth
        and everything in them
            belongs to Allah.
        He has power over all things.

Sura 6

Al-An'am
Livestock

In the name of Allah, All-Merciful, Most Merciful

1   Praise belongs to Allah
  who created the heavens and the earth
   and appointed darkness and light.
 Then those who disbelieve
  make others equal to their Lord!

2   It is He who created you from clay
  and then decreed a fixed term,
 and another fixed term is specified with Him.
  Yet you still have doubts!

3   He is Allah in the heavens and in the earth.
  He knows what you keep secret
   and what you make public
  and He knows what you earn.

4   Not one of their Lord's Signs comes to them
  without their turning away from it.
5   They deny the truth each time it comes to them
  but news of what they were mocking
   will certainly reach them.

6   Have they not seen how many generations
  We destroyed before them
 which We had established on the earth
  far more firmly than We have established you?
 We sent down heaven upon them in abundant rain
  and made rivers flow under them.

But We destroyed them for their wrong actions
and raised up further generations after them.

7   Even if We were to send down a book to you on parchment pages
and they were actually to touch it with their own hands,
those who disbelieve would still say,
'This is nothing but downright magic.'

8   They say, 'Why has an angel not been sent down to him?'
If We were to send down an angel,
that would be the end of the affair
and they would have no reprieve.
9   And if We had made him an angel
We would still have made him a man,
and further confused for them
the very thing they are confused about!

10   Messengers before you were also mocked,
but those who jeered were engulfed
by what they mocked.

11   Say: 'Travel about the earth
and see the final fate of the deniers.'

12   Say: 'To whom does everything in the heavens and earth belong?'
Say: 'To Allah.'
He has made mercy incumbent on Himself.
He will gather you to the Day of Rising
about which there is no doubt.
As for those who have lost their own selves,
they do not believe.

13   All that inhabits the night and the day belongs to Him.
He is the All-Hearing, the All-Knowing.

14   Say: 'Am I to take anyone other than Allah as my protector,
the Bringer into Being of the heavens and the earth,
He who feeds and is not fed?'
Say: 'I am commanded to be the first of the Muslims,'
and, 'Do not be among the idolators.'

15   Say: 'I fear, were I to disobey my Lord,
the punishment of a dreadful Day.'

16   Anyone from whom punishment is averted on that Day
        has been shown great mercy by Allah.
            That is the Clear Victory.

17   If Allah touches you with harm,
        none can remove it but Him.
    If He touches you with good,
        He has power over all things.
18   He is the Absolute Master over His slaves.
        He is the All-Wise, the All-Aware.

19   Say: 'What thing is greatest as a witness?'
        Say: 'Allah.
    He is Witness between me and you.
        This Qur'an has been revealed to me
            so that I may warn you by it,
        and anyone else it reaches.
    Do you then bear witness
        that there are other gods
            together with Allah?'
    Say: 'I do not bear witness.'
        Say: 'He is only One God,
    and I am free of all you associate with Him.'

20   Those We have given the Book recognise it
        as they recognise their own children.
    As for those who have lost their own selves,
        they do not believe.

21   Who could do greater wrong
        than someone who invents lies against Allah
            or denies His Signs?
        The wrongdoers are certainly not successful.

22   On the Day We gather them all together,
        We will say to those who associated others with Allah,
    'Where are the partner-gods, for whom you made such claims?'

23   Then they will have no recourse except to say,
        'By Allah, our Lord, we were not idolaters.'
24   See how they lie against themselves
        and how what they invented
            has forsaken them!

25   Some of them listen to you
         but We have placed covers on their hearts,
     preventing them from understanding it,
         and heaviness in their ears.
     Though they see every Sign, they still do not believe,
         so that when they come to you, disputing with you,
             those who disbelieve say,
     'This is nothing but the myths of previous peoples!'

26   They keep others from it
         and avoid it themselves.
     They are only destroying themselves
         but they are not aware of it.

27   If only you could see when they are standing before the Fire
         and saying, 'Oh! If only we could be sent back again,
     we would not deny the Signs of our Lord
         and we would be among the believers.'

28   No, it is simply that what they were concealing before
         has been shown to them;
     and if they were sent back they would merely return
         to what they were forbidden to do.
             Truly they are liars.

29   They say, 'There is nothing but this life
         and we will not be raised again.'

30   If only you could see when they are standing before their Lord.
         He will say, 'Is this not the Truth?'
     They will say, 'Yes indeed, by our Lord!'
         He will say, 'Then taste the punishment for your unbelief.'

31   Those who deny the meeting with Allah have lost,
         so that, when the Last Hour comes upon them suddenly,
     they will say, 'Alas for how we neglected it!'
         They will bear their burdens on their backs.
         How evil is what they bear!

32   The life of this world is nothing but a game and a diversion.
         The Next World is better for the godfearing.
         So will you not use your intellect?

33   We know that what they say distresses you.
          It is not that they are calling you a liar;
      the wrongdoers are just denying Allah's Signs.

34   Messengers before you were also denied
          but they were steadfast
      in the face of the denial and injury they suffered
          until Our help arrived.
      There is no changing the Words of Allah.
          And news of other Messengers has come to you.

35   If their turning away is hard on you,
          then go down a tunnel deep into the earth,
              if you can,
          or climb up a ladder into heaven,
              and bring them a Sign.
      If Allah had wanted to
          He would have gathered them all to guidance.
      So do not be among the ignorant.

36   Only those who can hear respond.
          As for the dead,
              Allah will raise them up,
      then to Him they will be returned.

37   They ask, 'Why has no Sign been sent down to him
          from his Lord?'
          Say, 'Allah has the power to send down a Sign.'
              But most of them do not know it.

38   There is no creature crawling on the earth
          or flying creature, flying on its wings,
              who are not communities just like yourselves –
      We have not omitted anything from the Book –
          then they will be gathered to their Lord.

39   Those who deny Our Signs
          are deaf and dumb in utter darkness.
      Allah misguides whomever He wills,
          and puts whomever He wills on a straight path.

40   Say: 'What do you think?
          If Allah's punishment were to come upon you
              or the Hour,

would you call on other than Allah
if you are being truthful?'

41   It is Him you call on
and, if He wills, He will deliver you
from whatever it was that made you call on Him;
and you will forget what you associated with Him.

42   We sent Messengers to nations before you,
and afflicted those nations with hardship and distress
so that hopefully they would humble themselves.

43   If only they had humbled themselves
when Our violent force came upon them!
However, their hearts were hard
and Shaytan made what they were doing
seem attractive to them.

44   When they forgot what they had been reminded of,
We opened up for them the doors to everything, until,
when they were exulting in what they had been given,
We suddenly seized them and at once they were in despair.

45   So the last remnant of the people who did wrong was cut off.
Praise belongs to Allah, the Lord of all the worlds!

46   Say: 'What do you think?
If Allah took away your hearing and your sight
and sealed up your hearts,
what god is there, other than Allah,
who could give them back to you?'
Look how We vary the Signs, yet still they turn away!

47   Say: 'What do you think?
If Allah's punishment were to come upon you
suddenly by night or openly by day,
would any but the wrongdoing people be destroyed?'

48   We do not send the Messengers except to bring good news
and to give warning.
As for those who believe and put things right,
they will feel no fear and they will know no sorrow.

49   The punishment will fall on those who deny Our Signs
because they were deviators.

50   Say: 'I do not say to you that I possess the treasuries of Allah,
     nor do I know the Unseen,
       nor do I say to you that I am an angel.
     I only follow what has been revealed to me.'
   Say: 'Are the blind the same as those who see?
     So will you not reflect?'

51   Warn by it those who fear they will be gathered to their Lord,
     having no protector or intercessor apart from Him,
       so that hopefully they will be godfearing.

52   Do not chase away those who call on their Lord
     morning and evening, seeking His Face.
   Their reckoning is in no way your responsibility
     and your reckoning is in no way their responsibility.
   Indeed if you did chase them away,
     you would be among the wrongdoers.

53   In this way We try some of them by means of others
     so that they say, 'Are these the people among us
       to whom Allah has shown His favour?'
   Does not Allah know best those who are thankful?

54   When those who believe in Our Signs come to you,
     say, 'Peace be upon you!'
   Your Lord has made mercy incumbent on Himself.
     If anyone among you does evil out of ignorance
   and then afterwards repents and puts things right,
     He is Ever-Forgiving, Most Merciful.

55   In that way We make the Signs plain
     so that you may clearly see
       the path of the evildoers.

56   Say: 'I am forbidden to worship
     those you call upon besides Allah.'
   Say: 'I do not follow your whims and desires.
     If I did I would go astray
       and not be among the guided.'

57   Say: 'I stand on a Clear Sign from my Lord
     and yet you have denied it.
   I do not have in my possession
     what you are in such haste to bring about.

Jurisdiction belongs to Allah alone.
    He tells the truth
and He is the Best of Deciders.'

58   Say: 'If I did have in my possession
        what you are in such haste to bring about,
    the affair between me and you would have been decided.
        Allah has greatest knowledge of the wrongdoers.'

59   The keys of the Unseen are in His possession.
        No one knows them but Him.
    He knows everything in the land and sea.
        No leaf falls without His knowing it.
    There is no seed in the darkness of the earth,
        and nothing moist or dry
    which is not in a Clear Book.

60   It is He who takes you back to Himself at night,
        while knowing the things you perpetrate by day,
            and then wakes you up again,
    so that a specified term may be fulfilled.
        Then you will return to Him.
    Then He will inform you about what you did.

61   He is the Absolute Master of His slaves.
        He sends angels to watch over you.
    Then when death comes to one of you,
        Our messengers take him,
    and they do not fail in their task.

62   Then they are returned to Allah,
        their Master, the Real.
    Jurisdiction belongs to Him alone
        and He is the Swiftest of Reckoners.

63   Say: 'Who rescues you from the darkness of the land and sea?
        You call on Him humbly and secretly:
    "If you rescue us from this,
        we will truly be among the thankful."'

64   Say: 'Allah rescues you from it,
        and from every plight.
    Then you associate others with Him.'

65   Say: 'He possesses the power to send you punishment
            from above your heads
                or from beneath your feet,
        or to confuse you in sects
            and make you taste one another's violence.'
        Look how We vary the Signs
            so that hopefully they will understand.

66   Your people deny it and yet it is the Truth.
            Say: 'I am not here as your guardian.
67   Every communication has its time,
            and you will certainly come to know.'

68   When you see people engrossed in mockery of Our Signs,
            turn from them until they start to talk of other things.
        And if Shaytan should ever cause you to forget,
            once you remember, do not stay sitting with the wrongdoers.

69   Their reckoning is in no way the responsibility
            of those who are godfearing.
        But remind them so that hopefully
            they themselves will be godfearing.

70   Abandon those who have turned their deen
                into a game and a diversion
            and who have been deluded by the life of this world.
        Remind by it lest a person be delivered up to destruction
                for what he has earned
            with no protector or intercessor besides Allah.
        Were he to offer every kind of compensation,
            it would not be accepted from him.
        Such people are delivered up to destruction
            for what they have earned.
        They will have scalding water to drink
            and a painful punishment
                because they disbelieved.

71   Say: 'Are we to call on something besides Allah
            which can neither help nor harm us,
        and to turn on our heels after Allah has guided us,
            like someone the shaytans have lured away in the earth,
                leaving him confused and stupefied,
            despite the fact that he has companions
                calling him to guidance,

saying, "Come with us!"?'
Say: 'Allah's guidance, that is true guidance.
   We are commanded to submit as Muslims
      to the Lord of all the worlds,

72   and to establish the prayer and have taqwa of Him.
   It is He to Whom you will be gathered.'

73   It is He Who created the heavens and the earth with truth.
   The day He says 'Be!' it is.
      His speech is Truth.
  The Kingdom will be His on the Day the Trumpet is blown,
   the Knower of the Unseen and the Visible.
      He is the All-Wise, the All-Aware.

74   Remember when Ibrahim said to his father, Azar,
    'Do you take idols as gods?
  I see that you and your people are clearly misguided.'

75   Because of that We showed Ibrahim
    the dominions of the heavens and the earth
  so that he might be one of the people of certainty.

76   When night covered him he saw a star and said,
    'This is my Lord!'
  Then when it set he said,
    'I do not love what sets.'

77   Then when he saw the moon come up he said,
    'This is my Lord!'
  Then when it set he said,
    'If my Lord does not guide me,
      I will be one of the misguided people.'

78   Then when he saw the sun come up he said,
    'This is my Lord! This is greater!'
  Then when it set he said,
    'My people, I am free of what
      you associate with Allah!

79   I have turned my face to Him
  Who brought the heavens and earth into being,
    a pure natural believer.
  I am not one of the idolators.'

80   His people argued with him.
    He said, 'Are you arguing with me about Allah
      when He has guided me?

I have no fear of any partner you ascribe to Him
    unless my Lord should will such a thing to happen.
My Lord encompasses all things in His knowledge
    so will you not pay heed?

81   Why should I fear what you have associated with Him
    when you yourselves apparently have no fear
        of associating partners with Allah
    for which He has sent down no authority to you?
Which of the two parties is more entitled to feel safe,
    if you have any knowledge?

82   Those who believe
and do not mix up their faith with any wrongdoing,
    they are the ones who are safe;
        it is they who are guided.'

83   This is the argument We gave to Ibrahim
    against his people.
We raise in rank anyone We will.
    Your Lord is All-Wise, All-Knowing.

84   We gave him Ishaq and Ya'qub,
    each of whom We guided.
        And before him We had guided Nuh.
And among his descendants were Dawud and Sulayman,
    and Ayyub, Yusuf, Musa and Harun.
That is how We recompense the good-doers.

85   And Zakariyya, Yahya, 'Isa and Ilyas.
    All of them were among the righteous.
86   And Isma'il, al-Yasa', Yunus and Lut.
    All of them We favoured over all beings.
87   And some of their forebears, descendants and brothers;
    We chose them and guided them to a straight path.

88   That is Allah's guidance.
    He guides by it those of His slaves He wills.
If they had associated others with Him,
    nothing they did would have been of any use.

89   They are the ones to whom We gave
    the Book, Judgement and Prophethood.
        If these people reject it
We have already entrusted it to a people who did not.

90   They are the ones Allah has guided,
            so be guided by their guidance.
       Say, 'I do not ask you for any wage for it.
            It is simply a reminder to all beings.'

91   They do not measure Allah with His true measure
            when they say, 'Allah would not send down anything
                 to a mere human being.'
       Say: 'Who, then, sent down the Book which Musa brought
            as a Light and Guidance for the people?'
       You put it down on sheets of paper to display it
            while concealing much.
       You were taught things you did not know,
            neither you nor your forefathers.
       Say: 'Allah!'
            Then leave them engrossed
                 in playing their games.

92   This is a Book We have sent down and blessed,
            confirming what came before it,
       so that you can warn the Mother of Cities*
            and the people around it.
       Those who believe in the Next World
            believe in it and safeguard their prayer.

93   Who could do greater wrong than someone
            who invents lies against Allah
       or who says, 'It has been revealed to me,'
            when nothing has been revealed to him,
       or someone who says, 'I will send down
            the same as Allah has sent down'?
       If you could only see the wrongdoers in the throes of death
            when the angels are stretching out their hands, saying,
                 'Disgorge your own selves!
       Today you will be repaid with the punishment of humiliation
            for saying something other than the truth about Allah,
                 and being arrogant about His Signs.'

94   'You have come to Us all alone just as We created you at first,
            leaving behind you everything We bestowed on you.
       We do not see your intercessors accompanying you,

---

* Makka.

those you claimed were your partners with Allah.
The link between you is cut.
Those you made such claims for have forsaken you.'

95   Allah is He Who splits the seed and kernel.
He brings forth the living from the dead,
and produces the dead out of the living.
That is Allah, so how are you perverted?

96   It is He Who splits the sky at dawn,
and appoints the night as a time of stillness
and the sun and moon as a means of reckoning.
That is what the Almighty, the All-Knowing has ordained.

97   It is He Who has appointed the stars for you
so you might be guided by them
in the darkness of the land and sea.
We have made the Signs clear for people who have knowledge.

98   It is He Who first produced you from a single self,
then from a resting-place and a repository.
We have made the Signs clear for people who understand.

99   It is He Who sends down water from the sky
from which We bring forth growth of every kind,
and from that We bring forth the green shoots
and from them We bring forth close-packed seeds,
and from the spathes of the date palm
date clusters hanging down,
and gardens of grapes and olives and pomegranates,
both similar and dissimilar.
Look at their fruits as they bear fruit and ripen.
There are Signs in that for people who believe.

100   Yet they make the jinn co-partners with Allah
when He created them!
And they attribute sons and daughters to Him
without any knowledge.
Glory be to Him!
He is far above what they describe!

101   He is the Originator of the heavens and the earth.
How could He have a son when He has no wife?

He created all things
and He has knowledge of all things.

102   That is Allah, your Lord.
       There is no god but Him,
          the Creator of everything.
       So worship Him.
    He is responsible for everything.

103   Eyesight cannot perceive Him
       but He perceives eyesight.
    He is the All-Penetrating, the All-Aware.

104   'Clear insights have come to you from your Lord.
       Whoever sees clearly, does so to his own benefit.
          Whoever is blind, it is to his own detriment.
    I am not here as your keeper.'

105   That is how We vary the Signs,
       so that they say, 'You have been studying,'
    and so We can make it clear to people who know.

106   Follow what has been revealed to you from your Lord –
       there is no god but Him –
    and turn away from the idolators.

107   If Allah had willed,
       they would not have associated anything with Him.
    We did not appoint you over them as their keeper
       and you are not set over them as their guardian.

108   Do not curse those they call upon besides Allah,
       in case that makes them curse Allah
          in animosity, without knowledge.
    In this way We make the actions of every nation
       seem attractive to them.
    Then they will return to their Lord,
       and He will inform them about what they did.

109   They have sworn by Allah with their most earnest oaths
       that if a Sign comes to them they will believe in it.
    Say: 'The Signs are in Allah's control alone.'
       What will make you realise

that even if a Sign did come,
they would still would not believe?

110   We will overturn their hearts and sight,
just as when they did not believe in it at first,
and We will abandon them
to wander blindly in their excessive insolence.

111   Even if We sent down angels to them,
and the dead spoke to them,
and We gathered together everything in front of them
right before their eyes,
they would still not believe unless Allah willed.
The truth is that most of them are ignorant.

112   In this way We have appointed as enemies to every Prophet
shaytans from both mankind and from the jinn,
who inspire each other with delusions
by means of specious words –
if your Lord had willed, they would not have done it,
so abandon them and all they fabricate –
113   so that the hearts of those who do not believe in the Next World
incline towards them and are pleased with them
and perpetrate whatever they perpetrate.

114   'Am I to desire someone other than Allah as a judge
when it is He who has sent down the Book to you
clarifying everything?'
Those We have given the Book
know it has been sent down from your Lord with truth,
so on no account be among the doubters.

115   The Words of your Lord are perfect in truthfulness and justice.
No one can change His Words.
He is the All-Hearing, the All-Knowing.

116   If you obeyed most of those on earth,
they would misguide you from Allah's Way.
They follow nothing but conjecture.
They are only guessing.

117   Your Lord knows best who is misguided from His Way
and He knows best those who are guided.

118   Eat that over which the name of Allah has been mentioned,
             if you believe in His Signs.

119   What is the matter with you that you do not eat
             that over which the name of Allah has been mentioned,
         when He has made clear to you what He has made haram for you
             except when you are forced to eat it?
         Many people lead others astray through their whims and desires
             without having any knowledge.
         Your Lord knows best those who overstep the limits.

120   Abandon wrong action, outward and inward.
             Those who commit wrong action
         will be repaid for what they perpetrated.

121   Do not eat anything over which
             the name of Allah has not been mentioned.
                 To do so is sheer deviance.
         The shaytans inspire their friends to dispute with you.
             If you obeyed them you would then be idolators.

122   Is someone who was dead and whom We brought to life,
             supplying him with a light
                 by which to walk among people,
         the same as someone who is in utter darkness,
             unable to emerge from it?
         That is how what they were doing
             is made to seem attractive to the unbelievers.

123   And likewise in every city
             We set up its greatest wrongdoers to plot in it.
         They plot against themselves alone,
             but they are not aware of it.

124   When a Sign comes to them, they say,
             'We will not believe until we have been given
                 the same as the Messengers of Allah were given.'
         Allah knows best where to place His Message.
             Debasement in the sight of Allah
                 and a severe punishment
             will strike those who did wrong
                 for the plots that they concocted.

125 When Allah desires to guide someone,
        He expands his breast to Islam.
    When He desires to misguide someone,
        He makes his breast narrow and constricted
            as if he were climbing up into the sky.
    That is how Allah defiles those who do not believe.

126 This is the path of your Lord – straight.
        We have made the Signs clear for people who remember.

127 They will have the Abode of Peace with their Lord.
        He is their Protector because of what they have done.

128 On the Day We gather them all together:
        'Company of jinn, you gained many followers
            among mankind.'
    And their friends among mankind will say,
        'Our Lord, we benefited from one another,
            and now we have reached the term
                which You determined for us.'
    He will say, 'The Fire is your home.
        You will be in it timelessly, for ever,
            except as Allah wills.
        Your Lord is All-Wise, All-Knowing.'

129 In that way We make the wrongdoers friends of one another
        because of what they have done.

130 Company of jinn and men!
        did not Messengers come to you from among yourselves
            relating My Signs to you
        and warning you of the encounter of this Day of yours?
    They will say, 'We testify against ourselves.'
        The life of this world deluded them
            and they will testify against themselves
                that they were unbelievers.

131 That was because their Lord
        would never have destroyed the cities unjustly
            while their people were unaware.

132 All have ranks according to what they did.
        Your Lord is not unaware of what they do.

133   Your Lord is the Rich Beyond Need, the Possessor of Mercy.
        If He wanted, He could remove you
           and replace you with anything else He wanted to,
   just as He produced you from the descendants of another people.

134   What you are promised will come about
        and you can do nothing to prevent it.

135   Say: 'My people, do as you are doing,
        just as I am doing.
   You will certainly come to know
        who will have the best home in the end.
   The wrongdoers will certainly not be successful.'

136   They assign to Allah
        a share of the crops and livestock
           He has created,
   saying, 'This is for Allah,' –
        as they allege –
        'and this is for our idols.'
   Their idols' share does not reach Allah
        whereas Allah's share reaches their idols!
   What an evil judgement they make!

137   In the same way their idols have made killing their children
        appear good to many of the idolaters,
   in order to destroy them and confuse them in their deen.
        If Allah had willed, they would not have done it;
           so abandon them and what they fabricate.

138   They say, 'These animals and crops are sacrosanct.
        No one may eat them except those we wish', –
           as they allege –
        and animals on whose backs it is forbidden to ride,
      and animals over which they do not mention Allah's name,
        inventing falsehood against Him.
   He will repay them for the things they have invented.

139   They say, 'What is in the wombs of these animals
        is exclusively for our men and haram for our wives.
           But if it is stillborn, they can share in it.'
   He will repay them for their false depiction.
        He is All-Wise, All-Knowing.

140 Those who kill their children foolishly
without any knowledge
and make what Allah has provided for them haram,
inventing lies against Allah,
such people are lost.
They are misguided.
They are not guided.

141 It is He who produces gardens,
both cultivated and wild,
and palm-trees
and crops of diverse kinds,
and olives and pomegranates,
both similar and dissimilar.
Eat of their fruits when they bear fruit
and pay their due on the day of their harvest,
and do not be profligate.
He does not love the profligate.

142 And also animals for riding and for haulage
and animals for slaughtering and for wool.
Eat what Allah has provided for you
and do not follow in the footsteps of Shaytan.
He is an outright enemy to you.

143 There are eight in pairs:
A pair of sheep and a pair of goats –
Say: 'Is it the two males He has made haram,
or the two females,
or what the wombs of the two females contain?
Tell me with knowledge if you are being truthful.'

144 And a pair of camels and a pair of cattle –
Say: 'Is it the two males He has made haram,
or the two females,
or what the wombs of the two females contain?
Were you then witnesses
when Allah gave you this instruction?'
Who could do greater wrong
than someone who invents lies against Allah
thus leading people astray without any knowledge?
Allah does not guide the people of the wrongdoers.

145 Say: 'I do not find, in what has been revealed to me,
any food it is haram to eat

except for carrion, flowing blood, and pork –
> for that is unclean –
or some deviance consecrated to other than Allah.
But if anyone is forced to eat it,
> without desiring to or going to excess in it,
your Lord is Ever-Forgiving, Most Merciful.'

146   We made haram for the Jews
>> every animal with an undivided hoof,
> and in respect of cattle and sheep,
>> We made their fat haram for them,
> except what is attached to their backs or guts
>> or mixed up with bone.
That is how We repaid them for their insolence.
> And We certainly speak the truth.

147   If they call you a liar, say:
> 'Your Lord possesses boundless mercy,
but His violent force cannot be averted
> from the people of the evildoers.'

148   Those who associate others with Allah will say,
> 'If Allah had willed
we would not have associated anything with Him,
>> nor would our fathers;
> nor would we have made anything haram.'
In the same way the people before them also lied
> until they felt Our violent force.
Say: 'Do you have some knowledge you can produce for us?
> You are following nothing but conjecture.
>> You are only guessing.'

149   Say: 'Allah's is the conclusive argument.
> If He had willed He could have guided every one of you.'

150   Say: 'Produce your witnesses to testify
> that Allah made this haram.'
If they do testify, do not testify with them
> and do not follow the whims and desires
>> of people who deny Our Signs,
> and who do not believe in the Next World
>> and make others equal to their Lord.

151   Say: 'Come and I will recite to you
            what your Lord has commanded you':
       that you do not associate anything with Him;
       that you are good to your parents;
       that you do not kill your children because of poverty –
            We will provide for you and them;
       that you do not approach indecency –
                outward or inward;
       that you do not kill any person Allah has made inviolate –
            except with the right to do so.
       That is what He instructs you to do
            so that hopefully you will use your intellect.

152   And that you do not go near the property of orphans
            before they reach maturity –
                except in a good way;
       that you give full measure and full weight with justice –
            We impose on no self any more than it can bear;
       that you are equitable when you speak –
                even if a near relative is concerned;
            and that you fulfil Allah's contract.
       That is what He instructs you to do,
            so that hopefully you will pay heed.

153   This is my Path and it is straight, so follow it.
            Do not follow other ways
                or you will become cut off from His Way.
       That is what He instructs you to do,
            so that hopefully you will be godfearing.

154   Then We gave Musa the Book,
            complete and perfect for him who does good,
                elucidating everything,
            and a guidance and a mercy,
       so that hopefully they will believe
            in their encounter with their Lord.

155   And this is a Book We have sent down and blessed,
            so follow it and be godfearing
       so that hopefully you will receive mercy.

156   So you cannot say:
            'The Book was only sent down to the two groups before us
                and we were ignorant of their studies.'

157   Nor can you say:
           'If the Book had been sent down to us,
     We would have been better guided than they were.'
           For a Clear Sign has come to you from your Lord,
              and guidance and mercy.
     Who could do greater wrong than someone
           who denies Allah's Signs
              and turns away from them?
     We will repay those who turn away from Our Signs
           with the worst kind of punishment
              because they turned away.

158   What are they waiting for but for the angels to come to them
              or for your Lord Himself to come,
           or for one of your Lord's Signs to come?
     On the day that one of your Lord's Signs does come,
           no faith which a self professes will be of any use to it
     if it did not believe before and earn good in its faith.
           Say: 'Wait, then; We too are waiting.'

159   As for those who divide up their deen and form into sects,
           you have nothing whatsoever to do with them.
              Their case will go back to Allah
           and then He will inform them about what they did.

160   Those who produce a good action
           will receive ten like it.
     But those who produce a bad action
           will only be repaid with its equivalent
              and they will not be wronged.

161   Say: 'My Lord has guided me to a straight path,
              a well-founded deen,
           the religion of Ibrahim,
              a man of pure natural belief.
     He was not one of the idolators.'

162   Say: 'My prayer and my rites,
              my living and my dying,
              are for Allah alone,
           the Lord of all the worlds,
163   Who has no partner.
     I am commanded to be like that
     and I am the first of the Muslims.'

164   Say: 'Am I to desire other than Allah as Lord
            when He is the Lord of all things?'
        What each self earns is for itself alone.
            No burden-bearer can bear another's burden.
        Then you will return to your Lord,
            and He will inform you
        regarding the things about which you differed.

165   It is He who appointed you khalifs on the earth
            and raised some of you above others in rank
        so He could test you regarding what He has given you.
            Your Lord is Swift in Retribution;
        and He is Ever-Forgiving, Most Merciful.

Sura 7

Al-A'raf
The Ramparts

In the name of Allah, All-Merciful, Most Merciful

1   Alif Lam Mim Sad

2   It is a Book sent down to you –
so let there be no constriction in your breast because of it –
     so that you can give warning by it
and as a reminder to the believers.

3   Follow what has been sent down to you from your Lord
     and do not follow any protectors apart from Him.
       How little you remember!

4   How many cities We have destroyed!
     Our violent force came down on them during the night,
       or while they were asleep during the day.

5   And their only utterance,
     when Our violent force came down upon them,
was the cry: 'Truly we have been wrongdoers!'

6   We will question those to whom the Messengers were sent,
     and We will question the Messengers.

7   We will tell them about it with knowledge.
     We are never absent.

8   The weighing that Day will be the truth.
     As for those whose scales are heavy,
       they are the successful.

9   As for those whose scales are light,

they are the ones who have lost their own selves
because they wrongfully rejected Our Signs.

10   We have established you firmly on the earth
and granted you your livelihood in it.
What little thanks you show!

11   We created you and then formed you
and then We said to the angels,
'Prostrate before Adam,'
and they prostrated – except for Iblis.
He was not among those who prostrated.

12   He said, 'What prevented you from prostrating
when I commanded you to?'
He replied, 'I am better than him.
You created me from fire
and You created him from clay.'

13   He said, 'Descend from Heaven.
It is not for you to be arrogant in it.
So get out!
You are one of the abased.'

14   He said, 'Grant me a reprieve
until the day they are raised up.'

15   He said, 'You are one of the reprieved.'

16   He said, 'By Your misguidance of me,
I will lie in ambush for them
on your straight path.

17   Then I will come at them,
from in front of them and behind them,
from their right and from their left.
You will not find most of them thankful.'

18   He said, 'Get out of it,
reviled and driven out.
As for those of them who follow you,
I will fill up Hell
with every one of you.'

19   'Adam, live in the Garden, you and your wife,
and eat of it wherever you like.
But do not go near this tree
lest you become wrongdoers.'

20   Then Shaytan whispered to them,
          disclosing to them their private parts
              that had been concealed from them.
      He said, 'Your Lord has only forbidden you this tree
          lest you become angels
              or among those who live for ever.'
21   He swore to them,
          'I am one of those who give you good advice.'

22   So he enticed them to do it by means of trickery.
          Then when they tasted the tree,
              their private parts were disclosed to them
      and they started stitching together the leaves of the Garden
          in order to cover themselves.
      Their Lord called out to them, 'Did I not forbid you this tree
          and tell you, "Shaytan is an outright enemy to you"?'

23   They said, 'Our Lord, we have wronged ourselves.
          If You do not forgive us and have mercy on us,
              we will be among the lost.'

24   He said, 'Go down from here as enemies to each other!
          You will have residence on the earth
              and enjoyment for a time.'
25   He said, 'On it you will live and on it die
          and from it you will be brought forth.'

26   Children of Adam! We have sent down clothing to you
          to conceal your private parts,
              and fine apparel,
          but the garment of taqwa –
              that is best!
      That is one of Allah's Signs,
          so that hopefully you will pay heed.

27   Children of Adam! do not let Shaytan tempt you into trouble
          as He expelled your parents from the Garden,
              stripping them of their covering
      and disclosing to them their private parts.
      He and his tribe see you from where you do not see them.
          We have made the shaytans friends
              of those who do not believe.

28 Whenever they commit an indecent act,
   they say, 'We found our fathers doing it
     and Allah commanded us to do it too.'
   Say: 'Allah does not command indecency.
   Do you say things about Allah you do not know?'

29 Say: 'My Lord has commanded justice.
   Stand and face Him in every mosque
   and call on Him, making your deen sincerely His.
   As He originated you, so you will return.'

30 One group He guided; but another group
   got the misguidance they deserved.
   They took the shaytans as friends instead of Allah
   and thought that they were guided.

31 Children of Adam! wear fine clothing in every mosque
   and eat and drink but do not be profligate.
     He does not love the profligate.

32 Say: 'Who has forbidden the fine clothing
   Allah has produced for His slaves
     and the good kinds of provision?'
   Say: 'On the Day of Rising such things will be exclusively
     for those who believed during their life in this world.'
   In this way We make the Signs clear for people who know.

33 Say: 'My Lord has forbidden indecency,
     both open and hidden,
   and wrong action,
   and wrongful tyranny,
   and associating anything with Allah
     for which He has sent down no authority,
   and saying things about Allah you do not know.'

34 Every nation has an appointed time.
   When their time comes,
   they cannot delay it a single hour
     or bring it forward.

35 Children of Adam! if Messengers come to you
     from among yourselves,
       recounting My Signs to you,
   those who are godfearing and put things right,
     will feel no fear and they will know no sorrow.

36　　　But as for those who reject Our Signs
　　　　　　and are arrogant regarding them,
　　　　they are the Companions of the Fire,
　　　　　　remaining in it timelessly, for ever.

37　　　Who could do greater wrong
　　　　　　than someone who invents lies against Allah
　　　　　　　　or denies His Signs?
　　　　Such people's portion of the Book will catch up with them
　　　　　　so that when Our messengers come to them
　　　　　　　　to take them in death,
　　　　saying, 'Where are those you called upon besides Allah?'
　　　　　　they will say, 'They have forsaken us,'
　　　　testifying against themselves that they were unbelievers.

38　　　He will say, 'Enter the Fire
　　　　　　together with the nations of jinn and men
　　　　　　　　who have passed away before you.'
　　　　Each time a nation enters, it will curse its sister nation, until,
　　　　　　when they are all gathered together in it,
　　　　　　　　the last of them will say to the first,
　　　　'Our Lord, those are the ones who misguided us,
　　　　　　so give them a double punishment in the Fire.'
　　　　He will say, 'Each will receive double.
　　　　　　But you do not know it.'

39　　　The first of them will say to the last,
　　　　　　'You are in no way superior to us
　　　　so taste the punishment for what you earned.'

40　　　As for those who deny Our Signs
　　　　　　and are arrogant regarding them,
　　　　the Gates of Heaven will not be opened for them,
　　　　　　and they will not enter the Garden
　　　　until a camel goes through a needle's eye.
　　　　　　That is how We repay the evildoers.

41　　　They will have Hell as a resting-place
　　　　　　and covering layers on top of them.
　　　　That is how We repay wrongdoers.

42　　　As for those who believe and do right actions –
　　　　　　We impose on no self any more than it can bear –

they are the Companions of the Garden,
    remaining in it timelessly, for ever.

43   We will strip away any rancour in their hearts.
      Rivers will flow under them and they will say,
    'Praise be to Allah who has guided us to this!
      We would not have been guided,
        had Allah not guided us.
    The Messengers of our Lord came with the Truth.'
      It will be proclaimed to them:
        'This is your Garden
    which you have inherited for what you did.'

44   The Companions of the Garden will call out
      to the Companions of the Fire,
    'We have found that what our Lord promised us is true.
      Have you found that what your Lord promised you is true?'
    They will say, 'Yes, we have!'
      Between them a herald will proclaim:
    'May the curse of Allah be on the wrongdoers
45   those who bar access to the Way of Allah,
          desiring to make it crooked,
            and reject the Next World.'

46   There will be a dividing wall between them
      and on the ramparts there will be men
        who recognise everyone by their mark.
    They will call out to the people of the Garden:
      'Peace be upon you!'
        They have not entered it
      for all their ardent desire to do so.

47   When they turn their eyes
      towards the Companions of the Fire,
    they will say, 'Our Lord, do not place us
      with the people of the wrongdoers!'

48   The Companions of the Ramparts will call out
      to men they recognise by their mark,
    saying, 'What you amassed was of no use to you,
      nor was your arrogance.
49   Are these the people you swore
      that Allah's mercy would never reach?'
    'Enter the Garden. You will feel no fear and know no sorrow.'

50   The Companions of the Fire will call out
           to the Companions of the Garden,
                'Pour down some water to us
           or some of what Allah has given you as provision.'
      They will say, 'Allah has forbidden them to the unbelievers:
51   those who took their deen as a diversion and a game,
                and were deluded by the life of this world.'
           Today We will forget them
      just as they forgot the encounter of this Day
           and denied Our Signs.

52   We have brought them a Book
           elucidating everything with knowledge,
      as guidance and a mercy for people who believe.

53   What are they waiting for but its fulfilment?
           The Day its fulfilment occurs,
                those who forgot it before will say,
           'The Messengers of our Lord came with the Truth.
           Are there any intercessors to intercede for us,
                or can we be sent back so that we may do
           something other than what we did?'
      They have lost their own selves
           and what they invented has forsaken them.

54   Your Lord is Allah,
      Who created the heavens and the earth in six days
           and then settled Himself firmly on the Throne.
      He covers the day with the night,
           each pursuing the other urgently;
      and the sun and moon and stars
           are subservient to His command.
      Both creation and command belong to Him.
           Blessed be Allah, the Lord of all the worlds.

55   Call on your Lord humbly and secretly.
           He does not love those who overstep the limits.

56   Do not corrupt the earth after it has been put right.
           Call on Him fearfully and eagerly.
      Allah's mercy is close to the good-doers.

57   It is He who sends out the winds,
           bringing advance news of His mercy,

so that when they have lifted up the heavy clouds,
    We dispatch them to a dead land
        and send down water to it,
    by means of which We bring forth all kinds of fruit.
In the same way We will bring forth the dead,
    so that hopefully you will pay heed.

58   Good land yields up its plants by its Lord's permission,
        but that which is bad only yields up scantily.
    In this way We vary the Signs for people who are thankful.

59   We sent Nuh to his people
        and he said, 'My people, worship Allah!
            You have no other god than Him.
        I fear for you the punishment of a dreadful Day.'

60   The ruling circle of his people said, 'We see you in flagrant error.'

61   He said, 'My people, I am not in error at all
        but rather am a Messenger from the Lord of all the worlds,
62   transmitting my Lord's Message to you
                and giving you good counsel,
            and I know from Allah what you do not know.
63   Or are you astonished that a reminder
            should come to you from your Lord
                by way of a man among you,
            to warn you and make you godfearing
                so that perhaps you will may gain mercy?'

64   But they denied him so We rescued him
        and those with him in the Ark.
    And We drowned the people who denied Our Signs.
        They were a blind people.

65   And to 'Ad We sent their brother Hud, who said,
        'My people, worship Allah!
    You have no other god than Him.
        So will you not be godfearing?'

66   The ruling circle of those of his people who disbelieved said,
        'We consider you a fool and think you are a liar.'

67   He said, 'My people, I am by no means a fool,
        but rather am a Messenger from the Lord of all the worlds,

68   transmitting my Lord's Message to you,
            and I am a faithful counsellor to you.

69   Or are you astonished that a reminder
         should come to you from your Lord
           by way of a man among you
         in order to warn you?
       Remember when He appointed you successors
         to the people of Nuh,
           and increased you greatly in stature.
       Remember Allah's blessings,
         so that hopefully you will be successful.'

70   They said, 'Have you come to us to make us worship Allah alone
         and abandon what our fathers used to worship?
    Then bring us what you have promised us
         if you are telling the truth.'

71   He said, 'Punishment and anger
         have come down on you from your Lord.
    Do you argue with me regarding names
         which you and your forefathers invented
    and for which Allah has sent down no authority?
         Wait, then; I am waiting with you.'

72   So We rescued him and those with him by mercy from Us,
         and We cut off the last remnant
           of those who denied Our Signs
             and were not believers.

73   And to Thamud We sent their brother Salih, who said,
         'My people, worship Allah!
           You have no other god than Him.
        A Clear Sign has come to you from your Lord.
           This is the She-Camel of Allah as a Sign for you.
       Leave her alone to eat on Allah's earth
         and do not harm her in any way
           or a painful punishment will afflict you.

74   Remember when He appointed you successors to 'Ad
         and settled you in the land.
    You built palaces on its plains
         and carved out houses from the mountains.
       Remember Allah's blessings
         and do not go about the earth, corrupting it.'

75   The ruling circle of those of his people who were arrogant
          said to those who were oppressed –
             those among them who believed –
          'Do you know that Salih has been sent from his Lord?'
       They said, 'We believe in what he has been sent with.'

76   Those who were arrogant said,
          'We reject Him in whom you believe.'

77   And they hamstrung the She-Camel,
          spurning their Lord's command,
       and said, 'Salih! Bring us what you have promised us
          if you are one of the Messengers.'

78   So the earthquake seized them
          and morning found them
             lying flattened in their homes.

79   He turned away from them and said,
          'My people, I transmitted my Lord's message to you
             and gave you good counsel.
          However, you do not like good counsellors!'

80   And Lut, when he said to his people,
          'Do you commit an obscenity
             not perpetrated before you
                by anyone in all the worlds?
81   You come with lust to men instead of women.
             You are indeed a depraved people.'

82   The only answer of his people was to say,
          'Expel them from your city!
       They are people who keep themselves pure!'

83   So We rescued him and his family –
          except for his wife.
       She was one of those who stayed behind.

84   We rained down a rain upon them.
          See the final fate of the evildoers!

85   And to Madyan We sent their brother Shu'ayb who said,
          'My people, worship Allah!
             You have no other god than Him.

A Clear Sign has come to you from your Lord.
>> Give full measure and full weight.
>>> Do not diminish people's goods.
>> Do not cause corruption in the land
>>> after it has been put right.
>> That is better for you if you are believers.

86 Do not lie in wait on every pathway, threatening people,
>> barring those who believe from the Way of Allah,
>>> desiring to make it crooked.
>> Remember when you were few
>>> and He increased your number:
>>>> see the final fate of the corrupters!

87 There is a group of you who believe
>> in what I have been sent with
>>> and a group who do not,
>> so be steadfast until Allah judges between us.
>>> He is the best of judges.'

88 The ruling circle of those of his people who were arrogant said,
>> 'We will drive you out of our city, Shu'ayb,
>>> you and those who believe along with you,
>>>> unless you return to our religion.'
> He said, 'What, even though we detest it?

89 We would be inventing lies against Allah
>> if we returned to your religion
>>> after Allah has saved us from it.
>> We could never return to it
>>> unless Allah our Lord so willed.
>> Our Lord encompasses everything in His knowledge.
>>> We have put our trust in Allah.
>> Our Lord, judge between us and our people with truth.
>>> You are the best of judges.'

90 The ruling circle of those of his people who disbelieved said,
>> 'If you follow Shu'ayb, you will definitely be lost.'

91 So the earthquake seized them
>> and morning found them
> lying flattened in their homes.

92 As for those who denied Shu'ayb,
>> it was as if they had never lived there.
> It was the people who denied Shu'ayb
>> who were the lost.

93 So he turned away from them and said,
 'My people, I transmitted My Lord's message to you
  and gave you good counsel.
 Why should I grieve for a people who disbelieve?'

94 We have never sent a Prophet to any city
 without seizing its people with hardship and distress
  so that hopefully they would be humble.

95 Then We gave them good in exchange for evil
 until they increased in number and said,
'Our forefathers too underwent both hardship and ease.'
 Then We seized them suddenly
  when they were not expecting it.

96 If only the people of the cities had believed and been godfearing,
 We would have opened up to them
  blessings from heaven and earth.
 But they denied the truth
  so We seized them for what they earned.

97 Do the people of the cities feel secure
 against Our violent force coming down on them
  in the night while they are asleep?
98 Or do the people of the cities feel secure
 against Our violent force coming down on them
  in the day while they are playing games?
99 Do they feel secure against Allah's devising?
 No one feels secure against Allah's devising
  except for those who are lost.

100 Is it not clear to those who have inherited the earth
 after these people
that, if We wanted to, We could strike them
 for their wrong actions,
sealing up their hearts so that they cannot hear?

101 These cities – We have given you news of them.
 Their Messengers came to them with Clear Signs,
  but they were never going to believe
   in what they had previously rejected.
 That is how Allah seals up the hearts of the unbelievers.
102 We did not find many of them worthy of their contract.
 We found most of them deviators.

103   And then, after them, We sent Musa with Our Signs
           to Pharaoh and his ruling circle
               but they wrongfully rejected them.
           See the final fate of the corrupters!

104   Musa said, 'Pharaoh! I am truly a Messenger
           from the Lord of all the worlds,
105   duty bound to say nothing about Allah except the truth.
           I have come to you with a Clear Sign from your Lord.
       So send the tribe of Israel away with me.'

106   He said, 'If you have come with a Clear Sign
           produce it if you are telling the truth.'

107   So he threw down his staff and there it was,
           unmistakably a snake.
108   And he drew out his hand and there it was,
           pure white to those who looked.

109   The ruling circle of Pharaoh's people said,
           'This is certainly a skilled magician
110   who desires to expel you from your land,
           so what do you recommend?'

111   They said, 'Detain him and his brother
           and send out marshals to the cities,
112   to bring you all the skilled magicians.'

113   The magicians came to Pharaoh and they asked,
           'Will we receive a reward if we are the winners?'
114   He said, 'Yes, and you will be among those brought near.'

115   They said, 'Musa, will you throw first
           or shall we be the ones to throw?'
116   He said, 'You throw.' And when they threw,
           they cast a spell on the people's eyes
               and caused them to feel great fear of them.
           They produced an extremely powerful magic.

117   We revealed to Musa, 'Throw down your staff.'
           And it immediately swallowed up what they had forged.
118   So the Truth took place
           and what they did was shown to be false.

119   They were defeated then and there,
              transformed into humbled men.

120   The magicians threw themselves down in prostration.
121   They said, 'We believe in the Lord of all the worlds,
122   the Lord of Musa and Harun.'

123   Pharaoh said, 'Have you believed in him
              before I authorised you to do so?
       This is just some plot you have concocted
              in the city to drive its people from it.
                   You will soon know!
124   I will cut off your opposite hands and feet
              and then I will crucify every one of you.'

125   They said, 'We are returning to our Lord.
126   You are only avenging yourself on us
       because we believed in our Lord's Signs
              when they came to us.
       Our Lord, pour down steadfastness upon us
              and take us back to You as Muslims.'

127   The ruling circle of Pharaoh's people said,
              'Are you going to leave Musa and his people
                   to cause corruption in the earth
                        and abandon you and your gods?'
       He said, 'We will kill their sons and let their women live.
              We have absolute power over them!'

128   Musa said to his people, 'Seek help in Allah
              and be steadfast.
       The earth belongs to Allah.
              He bequeathes it to any of His slaves He wills.
       The successful outcome is for those who are godfearing.'

129   They said, 'We suffered harm before you came to us
              and after you came to us.'
       He said, 'It may well be that your Lord
              is going to destroy your enemy
       and make you the successors in the land
              so that He can see how you behave.'

130   We seized Pharaoh's people
              with years of drought and scarcity of fruits
        so that hopefully they would pay heed.

131   Whenever a good thing came to them,
              they said, 'This is our due.'
        But if anything bad happened to them,
              they would blame their ill fortune
                    on Musa and those with him.
        No indeed! Their ill fortune will be with Allah.
              But most of them did not know.

132   They said, 'No matter what kind of Sign
              you bring us to bewitch us,
                    we will not believe in you.'

133   So We sent down on them
              floods, locusts, lice, frogs and blood,
                    Signs, clear and distinct,
              but they proved arrogant
                    and were an evildoing people.

134   Whenever the plague came down on them they said,
              'Musa, pray to your Lord for us
                    by the contract He has with you.
              If you remove the plague from us,
                    we will definitely believe in you
              and send the tribe of Israel away with you.'
135   But when We removed the plague from them –
              for a fixed term which they fulfilled –
                    they broke their word.

136   Then We took revenge on them
              and drowned them in the sea
        because they denied Our Signs
              and paid no attention to them.

137   And We bequeathed to the people who had been oppressed
              the easternmost part of the land We had blessed,
                    and its westernmost part as well.
              The most excellent Word of your Lord
                    was fulfilled for the tribe of Israel
              on account of their steadfastness.
                    And We utterly destroyed

what Pharaoh and his people made
and the buildings they constructed.

138 We conveyed the tribe of Israel across the sea
and they came upon some people
who were devoting themselves
to some idols which they had.
They said, 'Musa, give us a god
just as these people have gods.'
He said, 'You are indeed an ignorant people.
139 What these people are doing
is destined for destruction.
What they are doing is purposeless.'

140 He said, 'Should I seek something other than Allah
as a god for you
when He has favoured you over all other beings?'

141 Remember when We rescued you from Pharaoh's people
who were inflicting an evil punishment on you,
killing your sons and letting your women live.
In that there was a terrible trial from your Lord.

142 We set aside thirty nights for Musa
and then completed them with ten,
so the appointed time of his Lord
was forty nights in all.
Musa said to his brother Harun,
'Be my khalif among my people.
Keep order and do not follow the way of the corrupters.'

143 When Musa came to Our appointed time
and his Lord spoke to him,
he said, 'My Lord, show Yourself to me
so that I may look at You!'
He said, 'You will not see Me,
but look at the mountain.
If it remains firm in its place,
then you will see Me.'
But when His Lord manifested Himself to the mountain,
He crushed it flat
and Musa fell unconscious to the ground.
When he regained consciousness he said,

'Glory be to You! I turn in repentance to You
and I am the first of the believers!'

144   He said, 'Musa, I have chosen you over all mankind
for My Message and My Word.
Take what I have given you and be among the thankful.'

145   We wrote about everything for him on the Tablets
as an admonition and making all things clear.
'Seize hold of it vigorously
and command your people to adopt the best in it.
I will show you the home of the deviators!'

146   I will divert from My Signs all those
who are arrogant in the earth
without any right.
Even if they see every Sign,
they will not believe in it.
If they see the way of right guidance,
they will not take it as a way.
But if they see the way of error,
they will take that as a way.
That is because they denied Our Signs
and paid no attention to them.

147   As for those who denied Our Signs
and the encounter of the Next World,
their actions will come to nothing.
Will they be repaid except for what they did?

148   After he left, Musa's people adopted a calf
made from their ornaments,
a form which made a lowing sound.
Did they not see that it could not speak to them
or guide them to any way?
They adopted it and so they were wrongdoers.

149   When they took full stock of what they had done
and saw they had been misled, they said,
'If our Lord does not have mercy on us and forgive us,
we will certainly be among the lost.'

150   When Musa returned to his people in anger and great sorrow,
he said, 'What an evil thing you did

in my absence after I left!
>Did you want to hasten your Lord's command?'
He threw down the Tablets
>and seized hold of his brother's head,
>>dragging him towards him.
Harun said, 'Son of my mother,
>The people oppressed me and almost killed me.
Do not give my enemies cause to gloat over me.
>Do not include me with the wrongdoing people.'

151   He said, 'My Lord, forgive me and my brother
>and admit us into Your mercy.
You are the Most Merciful of the merciful.'

152   As for those who adopted the Calf,
>anger from their Lord will overtake them
together with abasement in the life of this world.
>That is how We repay the purveyors of falsehood.

153   But as for those who do evil actions
>and then subsequently repent and believe,
in that case your Lord is Ever-Forgiving, Most Merciful.

154   When Musa's anger abated he picked up the Tablets
>and in their inscription was guidance and mercy
>>for all of them who feared their Lord.

155   Musa chose seventy men from his people for Our appointed time
>and when the earthquake seized them he said,
'My Lord, if You had willed,
>You could have destroyed them previously
>>and me as well.
Would You destroy us for what the fools among us did?
>It was only a trial from You by which
>>You misguided those You willed
>>>and guided those You willed.
You are our Protector so forgive us and have mercy on us.
>You are the Best of Forgivers.

156   Prescribe good for us in this world and the Next World.
>We have truly turned to You.'

He said, 'As for My punishment, I strike with it anyone I will.
>My mercy extends to all things

but I will prescribe it for those who are godfearing and pay zakat,
    and those who believe in Our Signs:

157   those who follow the Messenger,
      the Unlettered Prophet,
whom they find written down with them
    in the Torah and the Injil,
commanding them to do right
    and forbidding them to do wrong,
making good things halal for them
    and bad things haram for them,
relieving them of their heavy loads
    and the chains which were around them.
Those who believe in him
    and honour him and help him,
and follow the Light that has been sent down with him,
    they are the ones who are successful.'

158   Say: 'Mankind! I am the Messenger of Allah to you all,
      of Him to whom the kingdom of the heavens
        and earth belongs.
There is no god but Him.
    He gives life and causes to die.'
So believe in Allah and His Messenger,
    the Unlettered Prophet,
who believes in Allah and His words,
    and follow him
so that hopefully you will be guided.'

159   Among the people of Musa
      there is a group who guide by the truth
        and act justly in accordance with it.

160   We divided them up into twelve tribes – communities.
      We revealed to Musa,
        when his people asked him for water:
    'Strike the rock with your staff.'
Twelve fountains flowed out from it
    and all the people knew their drinking place.
And We shaded them with clouds
    and sent down manna and quails to them:
'Eat of the good things We have provided you with.'
    They did not wrong Us;
rather it was themselves they wronged.

161   When they were told: 'Live in this town
        and eat of it wherever you like
    and say, "Relieve us of our burdens!"
        and enter the gate prostrating.
    Your mistakes will be forgiven you.
        We will grant increase to good-doers.'

162   But those of them who did wrong substituted words
        other than those they had been given.
    So We sent a plague on them from heaven
        for their wrongdoing.

163   Ask them about the town which was by the sea
        when they broke the Sabbath –
    when their fish came to them near the surface
        on their Sabbath day
    but did not come on the days
        which were not their Sabbath.
    In this way We put them to the test
        because they were deviators.

164   When a group of them said, 'Why do you rebuke a people
        whom Allah is going to destroy or severely punish?'
    they said, 'So that we have an excuse to present to your Lord,
        and so that hopefully they will be godfearing.'

165   Then when they forgot what they had been reminded of,
        We rescued those who had forbidden the evil
    and seized those who did wrong with a harsh punishment
        because they were deviators.

166   When they were insolent
        about what they had been forbidden to do,
    We said to them, 'Be apes, despised, cast out!'

167   Then your Lord announced that He would send against them
        until the Day of Rising
    people who would inflict an evil punishment on them.
        Your Lord is Swift in Retribution.
    And He is Ever-Forgiving, Most Merciful.

168   And We divided them into nations in the earth.
        Some of them are righteous
            and some are other than that.

We tried them with good and evil
> so that hopefully they would return.

169   An evil generation has succeeded them,
> inheriting the Book,

taking the goods of this lower world,
> and saying, 'We will be forgiven.'

But if similar goods come to them again
> they still take them.

Has not a covenant been made with them in the Book,
> that they should only say the truth about Allah
>> and have they not studied what is in it?

The Final Abode is better for the godfearing.
> Will you not use your intellect?

170   As for those who hold fast to the Book and establish the prayer,
> We will not let the wage of the righteous go to waste.

171   When We uprooted the mountain,
> lifting it above them like a canopy,

and they thought it was about to fall on them:
> 'Seize hold vigorously of what We have given you
>> and remember what is in it,
> so that hopefully you will be godfearing.'

172   When your Lord took out all their descendants
> from the loins of the children of Adam

and made them testify against themselves
> 'Am I not your Lord?'

they said, 'We testify that indeed You are!'
> Lest you say on the Day of Rising,
>> 'We knew nothing of this.'

173   Or lest you say,
> 'Our forefathers associated others with Allah
>> before our time,

and we are merely descendants coming after them.

So are You going to destroy us
> for what those purveyors of falsehood did?'

174   That is how We make the Signs clear
> so that hopefully they will return.

175   Recite to them the tale of him to whom We gave Our Signs,
> but who then cast them to one side

and Shaytan caught up with him.
He was one of those lured into error.

176   If We had wanted to, We would have raised him up by them.
But he gravitated towards the earth
and pursued his whims and base desires.
His metaphor is that of a dog:
if you chase it away,
it lolls out its tongue and pants,
and if you leave it alone,
it lolls out its tongue and pants.
That is the metaphor of those who deny Our Signs.
So tell the story so that hopefully they will reflect.

177   How evil is the metaphor of those who deny Our Signs.
It is themselves that they have badly wronged.

178   Whoever Allah guides is truly guided;
but those He misguides are the lost.

179   We created many of the jinn and mankind for Hell.
They have hearts they do not understand with.
They have eyes they do not see with.
They have ears they do not hear with.
Such people are like cattle.
No, they are even further astray!
They are the unaware.

180   To Allah belong the Most Beautiful Names,
so call on Him by them
and abandon those who desecrate His Names.
They will be repaid for what they did.

181   Among those We have created
there is a community who guide by the Truth
and act justly according to it.

182   But as for those who deny Our Signs,
We will lead them, step by step, into destruction
from where they do not know.

183   I will give them more time.
My strategy is sure.

184   Have they not reflected?
         Their companion is not mad.
         He is only a clear warner.

185   Have they not looked into
         the dominions of the heavens and the earth
            and what Allah has created,
    and seen that it may well be
         that their appointed time is near?
    In what discourse after this will they believe?

186   If Allah misguides people, no one can guide them.
         We will abandon them to wander blindly
            in their excessive insolence.

187   They will ask you about the Hour: when is it due?
         Say: 'Knowledge of it rests with my Lord alone.
            He alone will reveal it at its proper time.
         It hangs heavy in the heavens and the earth.
            It will not come upon you except suddenly.'
    They will ask you as if you had full knowledge of it.
         Say: 'Knowledge of it rests with Allah alone.
            But most people do not know that.'

188   Say: 'I possess no power to help or harm myself,
         except as Allah wills.
    If I had had knowledge of the Unseen,
         I would have sought to gain much good
            and no evil would have touched me.
    I am only a warner and a bringer of good news
         to people who believe.'

189   It is He who created you from a single self
         and made from him his spouse
            so that he might find repose in her.
    Then when he covered her she bore a light load
         and carried it around.
    Then when it became heavy
         they called on Allah, their Lord,
    'If You grant us a healthy child,
         we will be among the thankful!'

190   Then when He granted them a healthy, upright child,
              they associated what He had given them with Him.
       But Allah is far above what they associate with Him!

191   Do they make things into partner-gods
              which cannot create anything
                  and are themselves created;
192   which are not capable of helping them
              and cannot even help themselves?
193   If you call them to guidance they will not follow you.
              It makes no difference if you call them or stay silent.
194   Those you call on besides Allah
              are slaves just like yourselves.
       Call on them and let them respond to you
              if you are telling the truth.
195   Do they have legs they can walk with?
              Do they have hands they can grasp with?
       Do they have eyes they can see with?
              Do they have ears they can hear with?
       Say: 'Call on your partner-gods
              and try all your wiles against me
                  and grant me no reprieve.
196   My Protector is Allah who sent down the Book.
              He takes care of the righteous.'

197   Those you call on besides Him are not capable of helping you.
              They cannot even help themselves.

198   If you call them to guidance, they do not hear.
              You see them looking at you, yet they do not see.

199   Make allowances for people,
              command what is right,
       and turn away from the ignorant.

200   If an evil impulse from Shaytan provokes you,
              seek refuge in Allah.
       He is All-Hearing, All-Seeing.

201   As for those who are godfearing,
              when they are bothered by visitors from Shaytan,
       they remember and immediately see clearly.

202 But as for their brothers,
    the visitors lead them further into error.
      And they do not stop at that!

203 If you do not bring them a Sign,
    they say, 'Why have you not come up with one?'
Say, 'I follow only what has been revealed to me from my Lord.'
    This is clear insight from your Lord,
      and guidance and mercy,
        for people who believe.

204 When the Qur'an is recited listen to it and be quiet
    so that hopefully you will gain mercy.

205 Remember your Lord in yourself
    humbly and fearfully,
without loudness of voice,
    morning and evening.
Do not be one of the unaware.

206 Those who are in the presence of your Lord
    do not consider themselves too great to worship Him.
They glorify His praise and they prostrate to Him.

Sura 8

Al-Anfal
Booty

In the name of Allah, All-Merciful, Most Merciful

1 They will ask you about booty.
   Say: 'Booty belongs to Allah and the Messenger.
   So have taqwa of Allah and put things right between you.
   Obey Allah and His Messenger if you are believers.'

2 The believers are those whose hearts tremble
      when Allah is mentioned,
   whose faith is increased
      when His Signs are recited to them,
   and who put their trust in their Lord;
3   those who establish the prayer
   and give of what We have provided for them.
4   They are in truth the believers.
   They have high ranks with their Lord
      and forgiveness
   and generous provision.

5 Just as your Lord brought you out from your house with truth,
      even though a group of the believers disliked it,
6 arguing with you about the Truth after it had been made clear
      as though they were being driven to their death
         with open eyes.*

7 When Allah promised you
      that one of the two parties would be yours
   and you would have liked it to have been the unarmed one,

---

* This ayat and almost the whole of this sura refer directly to the expedition and battle of Badr
when the Muslims won their first great victory over the idolators of Makka.

whereas Allah desired to verify the Truth by His words
　　and to cut off the last remnant of the unbelievers.

8　This was so that He might verify the Truth
　　and nullify the false,
　even though the evildoers hate that.

9　Remember when you called on your Lord for help
　　and He responded to you:
　'I will reinforce you with a thousand angels
　　riding rank after rank.'

10　Allah only did this to give you good news
　　and that so your hearts would be at rest.
　Victory comes from no one but Allah.
　　Allah is Almighty, All-Wise.

11　And when He overcame you with sleep, making you feel secure,
　　and sent you down water from heaven
　to purify you and remove the taint of Shaytan from you,
　　and to fortify your hearts and make your feet firm.

12　And when your Lord revealed to the angels,
　　'I am with you so make those who believe firm.
　I will cast terror into the hearts of those who disbelieve,
　　so strike their necks and strike all their finger joints!'
13　This was because they were hostile to Allah and His Messenger.
　　If anyone is hostile to Allah and His Messenger,
　　　Allah is severe in retribution.

14　That is your reward, so taste it.
　　The unbelievers will also have
　　　the punishment of the Fire.

15　You who believe!
　　when you encounter those who disbelieve
　advancing in massed ranks into battle,
　　do not turn your backs on them.
16　Anyone who turns his back on them that day,
　　unless he is withdrawing to rejoin the fight
　　　or withdrawing to support another group,
　　brings Allah's anger down upon himself.
　　　His refuge is Hell.
　What an evil destination!

17   You did not kill them;
          it was Allah who killed them;
      and you did not throw,
          when you threw;
      it was Allah who threw:
          so He might test the believers
      with this excellent trial from Him.
          Allah is All-Hearing, All-Knowing.

18   That is your reward.
          Allah always confounds
      the schemes of the unbelievers.

19   If it was a decisive victory you were seeking,
          that victory has clearly been won.
      If you desist, it will better for you;
          but if you return, We also will return.
      Your troops will not help you at all,
          however many they are.
      Allah is with the believers.

20   You who believe! obey Allah and His Messenger.
          And do not turn away from him when you are able to hear.

21   Do not be like those who say, 'We hear,'
          when they do not hear.

22   The worst of beasts in Allah's sight
          are those who are deaf and dumb and have no intellect.

23   If Allah knew of any good in them,
          He would have made them able to hear.
      But even if He had made them able to hear,
          they would still have turned away.

24   You who believe! respond to Allah and to the Messenger
          when He calls you to what will bring you to life!
      Know that Allah intervenes between a man and his heart
          and that you will be gathered to Him.

25   Be fearful of trials which will not afflict
          solely those among you who do wrong.
      Know that Allah is severe in retribution.

26   When you were few and oppressed in the land,
          afraid that the people would snatch you away,
      He gave you refuge and supported you with His help

and provided you with good things
so that hopefully you would be thankful.

27   You who believe! do not betray Allah and His Messenger,
            and do not knowingly betray your trusts.
28   Know that your wealth and children are a trial
            and that there is an immense reward with Allah.

29   You who believe! if you have taqwa of Allah,
            He will give you discrimination
        and erase your bad actions from you
            and forgive you.
        Allah's favour is indeed immense.

30   When those who disbelieve were plotting against you
            to imprison you or kill you or expel you:
        they were plotting and Allah was plotting,
            but Allah is the Best of Plotters.

31   When Our Signs are recited to them,
            they say, 'We have already heard all this.
        If we wanted, we could say the same thing.
            This is nothing but the myths of previous peoples.'
32   And they say, 'Allah, if this is really the truth from You,
            rain down stones on us out of heaven
        or send a painful punishment down on us.'

33   Allah would not punish them
            while you were among them.
        Allah would not punish them
            as long as they sought forgiveness.
34   But why should Allah not punish them now
            when they bar access to the Masjid al-Haram?
        They are not its guardians.
            Only people who are godfearing can be its guardians.
        But most of them do not know that.

35   Their prayer at the House is nothing but whistling and clapping.
            So taste the punishment because you disbelieved!

36   Those who disbelieve spend their wealth
            barring access to the Way of Allah.
        They will spend it;
            then they will regret it;

then they will be overthrown.
Those who disbelieve will be gathered into Hell,

37   so that Allah may sift the bad out from the good,
        and pile the bad on top of one another,
           heaping them all together,
        and tip them into Hell.
           They are the lost.

38   Say to those who disbelieve that if they stop,
        they will be forgiven what is past;
    but if they return to it, they have the pattern
        of previous peoples in the past.

39   Fight them until there is no more fitna
        and the deen is Allah's alone.
    If they stop, Allah sees what they do,

40   but if they turn away,
    know that Allah is your Master,
        the Best of Masters,
           and the Best of Helpers!

41   Know that when you take any booty
        a fifth of it belongs to Allah, and to the Messenger,
    and to close relatives, orphans, the very poor and travellers,
        if you believe in Allah
    and in what We have sent down to Our slave
        on the Day of Discrimination,
           the day the two groups met –
        Allah has power over all things –

42   when you were on the nearer slope,
        and they were on the further slope
           and the caravan was lower down than you.
    If you had made an appointment with them
        you would have broken the appointment.
    However, it happened so that Allah might settle
        a matter whose result was preordained:
    so that those who died
        would die with clear proof,
    and those who lived
        would live with clear proof.
    Allah is All-Hearing, All-Knowing.

43   Remember when Allah showed them to you
        in your dream as only a few.
    If He had shown you them as many,

you would have lost heart
and quarrelled about the matter;
 but Allah saved you.
He knows what your hearts contain.

44 Remember when Allah made you see them as few
  when you met them,
and also made you seem few in their eyes.
  This was so that Allah could settle
a matter whose result was preordained.
  All matters return to Allah.

45 You who believe! when you meet a troop,
   stand firm
 and remember Allah repeatedly
so that hopefully you will be successful.

46 Obey Allah and His Messenger
and do not quarrel among yourselves
  lest you lose heart
   and your momentum disappear.
And be steadfast.
  Allah is with the steadfast.

47 Do not be like those who left their homes in arrogance,
  showing off to people
and barring them from the way of Allah –
  Allah encompasses what they do –

48 when Shaytan made their actions appear good to them,
  saying, 'No one will overcome you today
   for I am at your side.'
But when the two parties came in sight of one another,
  he turned round on his heels
saying, 'I wash my hands of you.
  I see what you do not see.
   I fear Allah.
Allah is severe in retribution.'

49 And when the hypocrites
  and those with sickness in their hearts
said, 'These people have been deluded by their deen.'
  But those who put their trust in Allah
will find Allah to be Almighty, All-Wise.

50   If only you could see when the angels take back
          those who disbelieved at their death,
              beating their faces and their backs:
      'Taste the punishment of the Burning!
51   That is for what you did.
      Allah does not wrong His slaves.'

52   Such was the case with Pharaoh's people
          and those before them.
      They rejected Allah's Signs
          so Allah seized them for their wrong actions.
      Allah is Strong, Severe in Retribution.

53   That is because Allah would never change
          a blessing He has conferred on a people
      until they have changed what was in themselves.
          Allah is All-Hearing, All-Knowing.

54   Such was the case with Pharaoh's people
          and those before them.
      They denied their Lord's Signs
          so We destroyed them for their wrong actions.
      We drowned Pharaoh's people.
          All of them were wrongdoers.

55   The worst of animals in the sight of Allah
          are those who disbelieve and do not believe,
56   those with whom you make a treaty
          and who then break it every time.
              They are not godfearing.

57   So if you come upon such people in war,
          make a harsh example of them
      to deter those coming after them
          so that hopefully they will pay heed.

58   If you fear treachery on the part of a people,
          revoke your treaty with them mutually.
      Allah does not love treacherous people.

59   Do not imagine that those who disbelieve have got ahead.
          They are quite powerless.

60   Arm yourselves against them
        with all the firepower and cavalry you can muster,
to terrify the enemies of Allah and your enemies,
        and others besides them whom you do not know.
           Allah knows them.
Anything you spend in the Way of Allah
        will be repaid to you in full.
           You will not be wronged.

61   If they incline to peace,
        you too incline to it,
           and put your trust in Allah.
He is the All-Hearing, the All-Knowing.

62   If they intend to deceive you,
        Allah is enough for you.
It is He who supported you with His help
        and with the believers,
63   and unified their hearts.
Even if you had spent everything on the earth,
        you could not have unified their hearts.
But Allah has unified them.
        He is Almighty, All-Wise.

64   O Prophet! Allah is enough for you,
        and for the believers who follow you.

65   O Prophet! spur on the believers to fight.
        If there are twenty of you who are steadfast,
           they will overcome two hundred;
        and if there are a hundred of you,
           they will overcome a thousand of those who disbelieve,
        because they are people who do not understand.

66   Now Allah has made it lighter on you,
        knowing there is weakness in you.
If there are a hundred of you who are steadfast,
        they will overcome two hundred;
and if there are a thousand of you,
        they will overcome two thousand
           with Allah's permission.
Allah is with the steadfast.

67 It is not fitting for a Prophet to take captives
        until he has let much blood in the land.
    You desire the goods of this world,
        whereas Allah desires the Next World.
    Allah is Almighty, All-Wise.

68 Were it not for a prior decree
        which had already proceeded from Allah,
    a terrible punishment would have afflicted you
        on account of what you took.

69 So make full use of any booty you have taken
        which is halal and good;
            and have taqwa of Allah.
    Allah is Ever-Forgiving, Most Merciful.

70 O Prophet! say to those you are holding prisoner,
        'If Allah knows of any good in your hearts,
    He will give you something better than what
        has been taken from you
            and forgive you.'
    Allah is Ever-Forgiving, Most Merciful.

71 But if they mean to betray you,
        they have already previously betrayed Allah,
            so He has given you power over them.
    Allah is All-Knowing, All-Wise.

72 Those who believe and have made hijra
        and done jihad with their wealth and themselves
            in the Way of Allah,
    and those who have given refuge and help,
        they are the friends and protectors of one another.
    But as for those who believe but have not made hijra,
        you are not in any way responsible for their protection
            until they make hijra.
    But if they ask you for help in respect of the deen,
        it is your duty to help them,
    except against people you have a treaty with.
        Allah sees what you do.

73 Those who disbelieve
        are the friends and protectors of one another.

If you do not act in this way there will be turmoil in the land
and great corruption.

74   Those who believe and have made hijra
and done jihad in the Way of Allah
and those who have given refuge and help,
they are the true believers.
They will have forgiveness and generous provision.

75   Those who believe and make hijra later on
and accompany you in doing jihad,
they also are of your number.
But blood relations are closer to one another
in the Book of Allah.
Allah has knowledge of all things.

Sura 9

At-Tawba
Repentance

1   An announcement to those idolators
        you have a general treaty with
that Allah and His Messenger are free of them:
2   'You may travel about in the land for four months
           and know that you cannot thwart Allah
        and that Allah will humiliate the unbelievers.'

3   A proclamation from Allah and His Messenger to mankind
        on the day of the greater pilgrimage:
'Allah is free of the idolators,
    as is His Messenger.
If you repent,
    it will be better for you.
But if you turn your backs,
    know that you cannot thwart Allah.'
Give the unbelievers the news of a painful punishment –
4   except those among the idolators
        you have treaties with,
who have not then broken their treaties with you in any way,
    or granted assistance to anyone against you.
Honour their treaties until their time runs out.
    Allah loves the godfearing.

5   Then, when the sacred months are over,
        kill the idolators wherever you find them,
          and seize them and besiege them
        and lie in wait for them on every road.
If they repent and establish the prayer and pay zakat,
    let them go on their way.
    Allah is Ever-Forgiving, Most Merciful.

6   If any of the idolators ask you for protection,
              give them protection
          until they have heard the words of Allah.
      Then convey them to a place where they are safe.
          That is because they are a people who do not know.

7   How could any of the idolators possibly have a treaty
              with Allah and with His Messenger,
          except for those you made a treaty with at the Masjid al-Haram?
              As long as they are straight with you, be straight with them.
              Allah loves the godfearing.

8   How indeed! For if they get the upper hand over you,
              they will respect neither kinship nor treaty.
          They please you with their mouths
              but their hearts belie their words.
                  Most of them are deviators.

9   They have sold Allah's Signs for a paltry price,
              and they have barred access to His Way.
          What they have done is truly evil.

10   They respect neither kinship nor treaty
              where a believer is concerned.
          They are people who overstep the limits.

11   But if they repent and establish the prayer and pay zakat,
              they are your brothers in the deen.
          We make the Signs clear for people who have knowledge.

12   If they break their oaths after making their treaty
              and defame your deen,
          then fight the leaders of unbelief –
              their oaths mean nothing –
          so that hopefully they will stop.

13   Will you not fight a people
              who have broken their oaths
                  and resolved to expel the Messenger,
          and who initiated hostilities against you in the first place?
              Is it them you fear?
          Allah has more right to your fear if you are believers.

14   Fight them!
>>> Allah will punish them at your hands,
>>>> and disgrace them
>>> and help you against them,
>> and heal the hearts of those who believe.

15   He will remove the rage from their hearts.
>>> Allah turns to anyone He wills.
>> Allah is All-Knowing, All-Wise.

16   Or did you suppose that you would be left
>>> without Allah knowing those of you who have done jihad
>> and who have not taken anyone as their intimate friends
>>> besides Allah and His Messenger and the believers?
>> Allah is aware of what you do.

17   It is not for the idolators to frequent the mosques of Allah,
>>> bearing witness against themselves of their unbelief.
>> They are the ones whose actions will come to nothing.
>>> They will be in the Fire timelessly, for ever.

18   The mosques of Allah should only be frequented
>>> by those who believe in Allah and the Last Day
>>>> and establish the prayer and pay zakat,
>>>>> and fear no one but Allah.
>>> They are the ones most likely to be guided.

19   Do you make the giving of water to the pilgrims
>>> and looking after the Masjid al-Haram
>> the same as believing in Allah and the Last Day
>>> and doing jihad in the Way of Allah?
>> They are not equal in the sight of Allah.
>>> Allah does not guide wrongdoing people.

20   Those who believe and make hijra
>>> and do jihad in the Way of Allah
>>>> with their wealth and themselves
>>> have a higher rank with Allah.
>> They are the ones who are victorious.

21   Their Lord gives them the good news
>>> of His mercy and good pleasure
>> and Gardens where they will enjoy everlasting delight,

22   remaining in them timelessly, for ever and ever.
            Truly there is an immense reward with Allah.

23   You who believe, do not befriend your fathers and brothers
                if they prefer unbelief to faith.
            Those among you who do befriend them are wrongdoers.

24   Say: 'If your fathers or your sons
                or your brothers or your wives or your tribe,
                or any wealth you have acquired,
                or any business you fear may slump,
                or any house which pleases you,
            are dearer to you than Allah and His Messenger
                and doing jihad in His Way,
            then wait until Allah brings about His command.
                Allah does not guide people who are deviators.'

25   Allah has helped you on many occasions,
                including the Day of Hunayn*
            when your great numbers delighted you
                but did not help you in any way,
            and the earth seemed narrow to you
                for all its great breadth,
            and you turned your backs.

26   Then Allah sent down His serenity
                on His Messenger and on the believers,
            and sent down troops you could not see,
                and punished those who disbelieved.
            That is how the unbelievers are repaid.

27   Then after that Allah will turn to anyone He wills.
                Allah is Ever-Forgiving, Most Merciful.

28   You who believe! the idolaters are unclean,
                so after this year they should not come near
                    the Masjid al-Haram.
                If you fear impoverishment,
            Allah will enrich you from His bounty if He wills.
                Allah is All-Knowing, All-Wise.

---

* A battle against Thaqif, the main tribe of the city of Ta'if, which took place shortly after the conquest of Makka. The large Muslim army was at first almost defeated in an early surprise attack by
the enemy.

29   Fight those of the people who were given the Book
       who do not believe in Allah and the Last Day
          and who do not make haram
      what Allah and His Messenger have made haram
          and do not take as their deen the deen of Truth,
   until they pay the jizya with their own hands
      in a state of complete abasement.

30   The Jews say, ''Uzayr is the son of Allah,'
      and the Christians say, 'The Messiah is the son of Allah.'
   That is what they say with their mouths,
      copying the words of those who disbelieved before.
   Allah fight them! How perverted they are!

31   They have taken their rabbis and monks as lords besides Allah,
      and also the Messiah, son of Maryam.
   Yet they were commanded to worship only one God.
      There is no god but Him!
   Glory be to Him above anything they associate with Him!

32   They desire to extinguish Allah's Light with their mouths.
      But Allah refuses to do other than perfect His Light,
          even though the unbelievers detest it.

33   It is He who sent His Messenger
      with guidance and the Deen of Truth
          to exalt it over every other deen,
      even though the idolators detest it.

34   You who believe! many of the rabbis and monks
      devour people's property under false pretences
          and bar people from access to the Way of Allah.
   As for those who hoard up gold and silver
      and do not spend it in the Way of Allah,
   give them the news of a painful punishment
35   on the Day it is heated up in the fire of Hell
   and their foreheads, sides and backs are branded with it:
      'This is what you hoarded for yourselves,
          so taste what you were hoarding!'

36   There have been twelve months with Allah in the Book of Allah,
      from the day He first created the heavens and earth.
   Four of them are haram.
      That is the True Deen.

So do not wrong one another during them.
However, fight the idolators totally
    just as they fight you totally,
and know that Allah is with the godfearing.

37   Deferring a sacred month is an increase in unbelief
          by which the unbelievers lead many people astray.
      One year they make it profane and another sacred
          to tally with the number Allah has made sacred.
      In that way they profane what Allah has made sacred.
          Their bad actions are made to seem good to them.
          Allah does not guide unbelieving people.

38   You who believe! what is the matter with you
          that when you are told,
      'Go out and fight in the way of Allah,'
          you sink down heavily to the earth?
      Are you happier with this world than the Next World?
          Yet the enjoyment of this world is very small
              compared to that of the Next World.

39   If you do not go out to fight,
          He will punish you with a painful punishment
              and substitute another people in your place.
      You will not harm Him in any way.
          Allah has power over all things.

40   If you do not help him, Allah did help him
          when the unbelievers drove him out
              and there were two of them in the Cave.*
      He said to his companion,
          'Do not be despondent, Allah is with us.'
      Then Allah sent down His serenity upon him
          and reinforced him with troops you could not see.
      He made the word of the unbelievers undermost.
          It is the word of Allah which is uppermost.
              Allah is Almighty, All-Wise.

41   Go out to fight, whatever your circumstances or desires,
          and do jihad with your wealth and yourselves
              in the Way of Allah.
          That is better for you if you only knew.

---

* Referring to the time when the Prophet did hijra from Makka to Madina with Abu Bakr and they took refuge in a cave.

42   If it had been a case of easy gains and a short journey,
         they would have followed you,
but the distance was too great for them.
         They will swear by Allah:
'Had we been able to, we would have gone out with you.'
         They are destroying their own selves.
Allah knows that they are lying.

43   Allah pardon you!
         Why did you excuse them until it was clear to you
            which of them were telling the truth
            and until you knew the liars?

44   Those who believe in Allah and the Last Day
         do not ask you to excuse them from doing jihad
            with their wealth and themselves.
         Allah knows the people who are godfearing.

45   Only those who do not believe in Allah and the Last Day
         ask you to excuse them.
Their hearts are full of doubt
         and in their doubt they waver to and fro.

46   If they had really desired to go out,
         they would have made proper preparations for it,
but Allah was averse to their setting out
         so He held them back and they were told:
'Stay behind with those who stay behind.'

47   If they had gone out among you,
         they would have added nothing to you but confusion.
They would have scurried about amongst you
         seeking to cause conflict between you,
and among you there are some who would have listened to them.
         Allah knows the wrongdoers.

48   They have already tried to cause conflict before,
         and turned things completely upside down for you,
until the truth came and Allah's command prevailed
         even though they detested it.

49   Among them are there some who say,
         'Give me permission to stay.
            Do not put temptation in my way.'

Have they not fallen into that very temptation?
     Hell hems in the unbelievers.

50   If good happens to you it galls them.
     If a mishap occurs to you, they say,
'We made our preparations in advance,'
     and they turn away rejoicing.

51   Say: 'Nothing can happen to us
except what Allah has ordained for us.
     He is Our Master.
It is in Allah that the believers should put their trust.'

52   Say: 'What do you await for us
     except for one of the two best things?*
But what we await for you
     is for Allah to inflict a punishment on you
either directly from Himself or at our hands.
     So wait, we are waiting with you!'

53   Say: 'Whether you give readily or reluctantly,
     it will not be accepted from you.
You are people who are deviators.'

54   Nothing prevents what they give from being accepted from them
     but the fact that they have rejected Allah and His Messenger,
and that they only come to the prayer lethargically,
     and that they only give reluctantly.

55   Do not let their wealth and children impress you.
     Allah merely wants to punish them by them
       during their life in this world
and for them to expire while they are unbelievers.

56   They swear by Allah that they are of your number,
     but they are not of your number.
Rather, they are people who are scared.

57   If they could find a bolt-hole, cave or burrow,
     they would turn and scurry away into it.

58   Among them there are some who find fault with you
     concerning the zakat.

---

* Martyrdom or victory.

If they are given some of it, they are pleased
    but if they are not given any, they are angry.

59   If only they had been pleased with what
    Allah and His Messenger had given them
and had said, 'Allah is enough for us.
    Allah will give us of His bounty
        as will His Messenger.
    It is to Allah that we make our plea.'

60   Zakat is for:
    the poor,
    the destitute,
    those who collect it,
    reconciling people's hearts,
    freeing slaves,
    those in debt,
    spending in the Way of Allah,
    and travellers.
It is a legal obligation from Allah.
    Allah is All-Knowing, All-Wise.

61   Among them are some who insult the Prophet,
    saying he is only an ear.
Say, 'An ear of good for you,
    believing in Allah and believing in the believers,
        and a mercy for those among you who believe.'
As for those who insult the Messenger of Allah,
    they will have a painful punishment.

62   They swear to you by Allah in order to please you,
    but it would be more fitting for them
to please Allah and His Messenger
    if they are believers.

63   Do they not know that whoever opposes
    Allah and His Messenger,
        will have the Fire of Hell,
    remaining in it timelessly, for ever?
        That is the great disgrace.

64   The hypocrites are afraid that a sura
    may be sent down about them,
        informing them of what is in their hearts.

Say: 'Go on mocking! Allah will expose
    everything you are afraid of.'

65   If you ask them they will say,
        'We were only joking and playing around.'
    Say: 'Would you make a mockery of Allah
        and of His Signs and of His Messenger?
66   Do not try to excuse yourselves.
        You have disbelieved after having believed.
    If one group of you is pardoned,
        another group will be punished
            for being evildoers.'

67   The men and women of the hypocrites
        are as bad as one another.
    They command what is wrong and forbid what is right
        and keep their fists tightly closed.
    They have forgotten Allah, so He has forgotten them.
        The hypocrites are deviators.

68   Allah has promised the men and women
        of the hypocrites and unbelievers
            the Fire of Hell,
        remaining in it timelessly, for ever.
    It will suffice them.
        Allah has cursed them.
    They will have everlasting punishment.

69   Like those before you who had greater strength than you
        and more wealth and children.
    They enjoyed their portion;
        so enjoy your portion as those before you enjoyed theirs.
    You have plunged into defamation as they plunged into it.
        The actions of such people come to nothing
            in this world or the Next World.
                They are the lost.

70   Has the news of those who came before them not reached them
        the people of Nuh and 'Ad and Thamud,
            and the people of Ibrahim
        and the inhabitants of Madyan and the Upturned Cities?
    Their Messengers brought them the Clear Signs.
        Allah did not wrong them;
            rather they wronged themselves.

71 The men and women of the believers
   are friends of one another.
   They command what is right and forbid what is wrong,
   and establish the prayer and pay zakat,
   and obey Allah and His Messenger.
   They are the people on whom Allah will have mercy.
   Allah is Almighty, All-Wise.

72 Allah has promised the men and women of the believers
   Gardens with rivers flowing under them,
   remaining in them timelessly, for ever,
   and fine dwellings in the Gardens of Eden.
   And Allah's good pleasure is even greater.
   That is the great victory.

73 O Prophet, do jihad against the unbelievers and hypocrites
   and be harsh with them.
   Their shelter will be Hell.
   What an evil destination!

74 They swear by Allah that they said nothing,
   but they definitely spoke the word of unbelief
   and returned to unbelief after their Islam.
   They planned something which they did not achieve
   and they were vindictive for no other reason
   than that Allah and His Messenger had enriched them
   from His bounty.
   If they were to repent, it would be better for them.
   But if they turn away, Allah will punish them
   with a painful punishment in this world and the Next World,
   and they will not find any protector or helper on the earth.

75 Among them there were some
   who made an agreement with Allah:
   'If He gives us of His bounty we will definitely give sadaqa
   and be among the righteous.'
76 But when He does give them of His bounty
   they are tight-fisted with it and turn away,
77 so He has punished them by putting hypocrisy in their hearts
   until the day they meet Him
   because they failed Allah in what they promised Him
   and because they lied.

78   Do they not know that Allah knows
          their secrets and their private talk,
     and that Allah is the Knower of all unseen things?

79   As for the people who find fault with those believers
          who give sadaqa spontaneously,
     and with those who can find nothing to give
          but their own effort,
             and deride them,
          Allah derides them.
     They will have a painful punishment.

80   You can ask forgiveness for them,
          or not ask forgiveness for them.
     Even if you asked forgiveness for them seventy times,
          Allah still would not forgive them.
     That is because they have rejected Allah and His Messenger.
          Allah does not guide deviant people.

81   Those who were left behind
          were glad to stay behind the Messenger of Allah.
     They did not want to do jihad
          with their wealth and themselves
             in the Way of Allah.
     They said, 'Do not go out to fight in the heat.'
          Say: 'The Fire of Hell is much hotter,
             if they only understood.'

82   Let them laugh little and weep much,
          in repayment for what they have earned.

83   If Allah returns you to a group of them,
          and they ask you for permission to go out,
     say, 'You will never go out with me,
          nor will you ever fight an enemy with me.
     You were happy to stay behind the first time,
          so stay behind with those who are left behind.'

84   Never pray over any of them who die
          or stand at their graves.
     They rejected Allah and His Messenger
          and died as deviators.

85   Do not let their wealth and their children impress you.
         Allah merely wants to punish them by them in this world,
            and for them to expire while they are unbelievers.

86   When a sura is sent down saying:
         'Believe in Allah
         and do jihad together with His Messenger,'
      those among them with wealth will ask you to excuse them,
         saying, 'Let us remain with those who stay behind.'

87   They are pleased to be with those who stay behind.
         Their hearts have been stamped
            so they do not understand.

88   But the Messenger and those who believe along with him
         have done jihad with their wealth and with themselves.
      They are the people who will have the good things.
         They are the ones who are successful.

89   Allah has prepared Gardens for them
         with rivers flowing under them,
      remaining in them timelessly, for ever.
         That is the great victory.

90   The desert arabs came with their excuses
         asking for permission to stay,
      and those who lied to Allah and His Messenger
         stayed behind.
      A painful punishment will afflict
         those among them who disbelieve.

91   Nothing is held against the weak and sick
         or against those who find nothing to spend,
      provided they are true to Allah and His Messenger –
         there is no way open against good-doers,
            Allah is Ever-Forgiving, Most Merciful –
92   nor is anything held against those who,
         when they came to you
      for you to provide them with mounts
         and you said, 'I cannot find anything
            on which to mount you,'
      turned away with their eyes overflowing with tears,
         overcome by grief at having nothing to give.

93   There are only grounds against those
        who ask you for permission to stay when they are rich.
    They were pleased to be among those who were left behind.
        Allah has sealed up their hearts so they do not know.

94   They will make excuses to you when you return to them.
        Say: 'Do not make excuses, we will not believe you.
           Allah has already informed us about you.
        Allah will see your actions, as will His Messenger.
    Then you will be returned
           to the Knower of the Unseen and the Visible,
        and He will inform you regarding what you did.'

95   They will swear to you by Allah when you return to them,
        so that you leave them alone.
    Leave them alone, then! They are filth.
        Their shelter will be Hell
           as repayment for what they did.

96   They will swear to you to make you pleased with them,
        but even if you are pleased with them,
    Allah is certainly not pleased with deviant people.

97   The desert arabs are more obdurate in unbelief and hypocrisy
        and more likely not to know the limits
    which Allah has sent down to His Messenger.
        Allah is All-Knowing, All-Wise.

98   Among the desert arabs there are some
        who regard what they give as an imposition
           and are waiting for your fortunes to change.
        The evil turn of fortune will be theirs!
           Allah is All-Hearing, All-Knowing.

99   And among the desert arabs there are some
        who believe in Allah and the Last Day
    and regard what they give as something
        which will bring them nearer to Allah
           and to the prayers of the Messenger.
        It does indeed bring them near.
    Allah will admit them into His mercy.
        Allah is Ever-Forgiving, Most Merciful.

100   The forerunners – the first of the Muhajirun and the Ansar –
        and those who have followed them in doing good:
    Allah is pleased with them and they are pleased with Him.
        He has prepared Gardens for them

with rivers flowing under them,
remaining in them timelessly, for ever and ever.
That is the great victory.

101 Some of the desert Arabs around you are hypocrites
and some of the people of Madina
are obdurate in their hypocrisy.
You do not know them but We know them.
We will punish them twice over
and then they will be returned to a terrible punishment.

102 But others have acknowledged their wrong actions
and mixed a right action with another which is wrong.
It may well be that Allah will turn towards them.
Allah is Ever-Forgiving, Most Merciful.

103 Take zakat from their wealth
to purify and cleanse them
and pray for them.
Your prayers bring relief to them.
Allah is All-Hearing, All-Knowing.

104 Do they not know that Allah accepts repentance from His slaves
and acknowledges their zakat,
and that Allah is the Ever-Relenting, the Most Merciful?

105 Say: 'Act, for Allah will see your actions,
and so will His Messenger and the believers.
You will be returned to the Knower of the Unseen and the Visible
and He will inform you regarding what you did.'

106 And others are left awaiting Allah's command
as to whether He will punish them or turn to them.
Allah is All-Knowing, All-Wise.

107 As for those who have set up a mosque,
causing harm and out of unbelief,
to create division between the believers,
and in readiness for those who previously
made war on Allah and His Messenger,
they will swear, 'We only desired the best.'
But Allah bears witness that they are truly liars.

108   Do not ever stand in it.
        A mosque founded on taqwa from the first day
            has a greater right for you to stand in it.
        In it there are men who love to purify themselves.
            Allah loves those who purify themselves.

109   Who is better:
            someone who founds his building
                on taqwa of Allah and His good pleasure,
            or someone who founds his building
                on the brink of a crumbling precipice
                    so that it collapses with him
                        into the Fire of Hell?
            Allah does not love wrongdoers.

110   The buildings they have built will not cease
            to be a bone of contention in their hearts,
                until their hearts are cut to shreds.
            Allah is All-Knowing, All-Wise.

111   Allah has bought from the believers
            their selves and their wealth
                in return for the Garden.
        They fight in the Way of Allah
            and they kill and are killed.
        It is a promise binding on Him
            in the Torah, the Injil and the Qur'an
        and who is truer to his contract than Allah?
            Rejoice then in the bargain you have made.
                That is the great victory.

112   Those who repent,
            those who worship,
            those who praise,
            those who fast,
            those who bow,
            those who prostrate,
            those who command the right,
            those who forbid the wrong,
            those who preserve the limits of Allah:
        give good news to the believers.

113   It is not right for the Prophet and those who believe
            to ask forgiveness for the idolators –

even if they are close relatives –
after it has become clear to them
that they are the Companions of the Blazing Fire.

114   Ibrahim would not have asked forgiveness for his father
but for a promise he made to him,
and when it became clear to him
that he was an enemy of Allah,
he renounced him.
Ibrahim was tender-hearted and forbearing.

115   Allah would never misguide a people after guiding them
until He had made it clear to them how to be godfearing.
Allah has knowledge of all things.

116   Allah is He to whom the kingdom
of the heavens and earth belongs.
He gives life and causes to die.
You have no protector or helper besides Allah.

117   Allah has turned towards the Prophet,
and the Muhajirun and the Ansar,
those who followed him at the 'time of difficulty',*
after the hearts of a group of them had almost deviated.
Then He turned towards them –
He is All-Gentle, Most Merciful to them –
118   and also towards the three who were left behind,*
so that when the earth became narrow for them,
for all its great breadth,
and their own selves became constricted for them
and they realised that there was no refuge from Allah
except in Him,
He turned to them so that they might turn to Him.
Allah is the Ever-Relenting, the Most Merciful.

119   You who believe! have taqwa of Allah
and be with the truly sincere.

120   It was not for people of Madina,
and the desert arabs around them,
to remain behind the Messenger of Allah
nor to prefer themselves to him.

---

* This ayat refers to the Expedition of Tabuk when three believers wrongfully excused themselves
from taking part.

That is because no thirst or weariness or hunger
    will afflict them in the Way of Allah,
nor will they take a single step to infuriate the unbelievers,
    nor secure any gain from the enemy,
without a right action being written down for them because of it.
    Allah does not let the wage of the good-doers go to waste.

121   Nor will they give away any amount,
    whether large or small,
nor will they cross any valley,
    without it being written down for them
so that Allah can recompense them
    for the best of what they did.

122   It is not necessary for the believers to go out all together.
    If a party from each group of them were to go out
        so they could increase their knowledge of the deen
    they would be able to notify their people
        when they returned to them
    so that hopefully they would take warning!

123   You who believe! fight those of the unbelievers
        who are near to you
    and let them find you implacable.
Know that Allah is with the godfearing.

124   Each time a sura is sent down
    there are some among them who say,
'Which of you has this increased in faith?'
    As for those who believe,
        it increases them in faith
        and they rejoice at it.

125   But as for those with sickness in their hearts,
    it adds defilement to their defilement,
        and they die unbelievers.

126   Do they not see that they are tried
    once or twice in every year?
But still they do not turn back.
    They do not pay heed.

127   Each time a sura is sent down,
    they look at one another,
implying, 'Can anyone see you?'

Then they turn away.
Allah has turned their hearts away
　　because they are people who do not understand.

128　A Messenger has come to you from among yourselves.
　　Your suffering is distressing to him;
he is deeply concerned for you;
　　he is gentle and merciful to the believers.

129　But if they turn away, say,
　　'Allah is enough for me.
There is no god but Him.
　　I have put my trust in Him.
He is the Lord of the Mighty Throne.'

Sura 10

Yunus
Jonah

1   Alif Lam Ra
Those are the Signs of the Wise Book.

2   Do people find it so surprising
        that We should reveal to a man among them:
            'Warn mankind
        and give good news to those who believe
    that they are on a sure footing with their Lord'?
        The unbelievers say, 'This is downright magic!'

3   Your Lord is Allah,
    Who created the heavens and the earth in six days
        and then established Himself firmly on the Throne.
    He directs the whole affair.
        No one can intercede except with His permission.
    That is Allah your Lord, so worship Him.
        Will you not pay heed?

4   Each and every one of you will return to Him.
        Allah's promise is true.
    He brings creation out of nothing
        and then regenerates it
    so that he can repay with justice
        those who believed and did right actions.
    Those who disbelieved will have scalding water to drink
        and a painful punishment because of their unbelief.

5   It is He who appointed the sun to give radiance,
           and the moon to give light,
                 assigning it phases
     so you would know the number of years
           and the reckoning of time.
     Allah did not create these things except with truth.
           We make the Signs clear for people who know.

6   In the alternation of night and day
           and what Allah has created in the heavens and the earth
                 there are Signs for people who are godfearing.

7   As for those who do not expect to meet Us
           and are content with the life of this world
                 and at rest in it,
           and those who are heedless of Our Signs,
8   their shelter will be the Fire
     because of what they earned.

9   But as for those who believe and do right actions,
           their Lord will guide them by their faith.
     Rivers will flow under them in Gardens of Delight.
10   Their call there is:
                 'Glory be to You, O Allah!'
           Their greeting there is:
                 'Peace!'
           The end of their call is:
     'Praise be to Allah, the Lord of all the worlds!'

11   If Allah were to hasten evil for people
           the way they try to hasten good,
     their term would already have been completed for them.
           We abandon those who do not expect to meet Us
     to wander blindly in their excessive insolence.

12   When harm touches man, he calls on Us,
           lying on his side or sitting down or standing up.
     Then when We remove the harm from him
           he carries on as if he had never called on Us
                 when the harm first touched him.
     In that way We make what they have done
           appear good to the profligate.

13   We destroyed generations before you when they did wrong.
        Their Messengers brought them the Clear Signs,
            but they were never going to believe.
        That is how We repay evildoers.

14   Then We appointed you after them to be khalifs on the earth
        so We might observe how you would act.

15   When Our Clear Signs are recited to them,
        those who do not expect to meet Us say,
    'Bring a Qur'an other than this one or change it.'
        Say: 'It is not for me to change it of my own accord.
    I follow nothing except what is revealed to me.
        I fear, were I to disobey my Lord,
            the punishment of a Dreadful Day.'

16   Say: 'Had Allah so wished,
        I would not have recited it to you
    nor would He have made it known to you.
        I lived among you for many years before it came.
            Will you not use your intellect?'

17   Who could do greater wrong than someone
        who invents lies against Allah
            or denies His Signs?
    Evildoers are certainly not successful.

18   They worship, instead of Allah,
        what can neither harm them nor help them,
    saying, 'These are our intercessors with Allah.'
        Say: 'Would you inform Allah of something
            about which He does not know
        either in the heavens or on the earth?'
    May He be glorified and exalted
        above what they associate with Him!

19   Mankind was only one community but then they differed,
        and had it not been for a prior Word from your Lord,
    they would already have been judged
        regarding the differences between them.

20   They say, 'Why has a Sign not been sent down to him
        from his Lord?'

Say: 'The Unseen belongs to Allah alone.
  So wait, I am waiting with you.'

21   When We let people taste mercy
  after hardship has afflicted them,
immediately they plot against Our Signs.
  Say: 'Allah is swifter at plotting.'
Your plotting is recorded by Our messengers.

22   It is He who conveys you on both land and sea
  so that when some of you are on a boat,
    running before a fair wind, rejoicing at it,
and then a violent squall comes upon them
    and the waves come at them from every side
      and they realise there is no way of escape,
they call on Allah, making their deen sincerely His:
  'If You rescue us from this,
    we will truly be among the thankful.'

23   But then, when He does rescue them,
  they become rebellious in the earth
    without any right to do so.
Mankind, your rebelliousness is only against yourselves.
  There is the enjoyment of the life of this world
    and then you will return to Us
  and We will inform you about what you did.

24   The likeness of the life of this world
  is that of water which We send down from the sky,
and which then mingles with the plants of the earth
  to provide food for both people and animals.
Then, when the earth is at its loveliest
  and takes on its fairest guise
and its people think they have it under their control,
  Our command comes upon it by night or day
    and We reduce it to dried-out stubble,
  as though it had not been flourishing just the day before!
In this way We make Our Signs clear for people who reflect.

25   Allah calls to the Abode of Peace
  and He guides whom He wills to a straight path.

26   Those who do good will have the best and more!
  Neither dust nor debasement

will darken their faces.
They are the Companions of the Garden,
remaining in it timelessly, for ever.

27   But as for those who have earned bad actions –
a bad action will be repaid with one the like of it.
Debasement will darken them.
They will have no one to protect them from Allah.
It is as if their faces were covered
by dark patches of the night.
Those are the Companions of the Fire,
remaining in it timelessly, for ever.

28   On the Day We gather them all together,
We will say then to those who associated others with Allah,
'To your place, you and your partner-gods!'
Then We will sift them out and their partner-gods will say,
'It was not us you worshipped.
29   Allah is a sufficient witness between us and you.
We were unaware of your worship.'

30   Then and there every self will be tried for what it did before.
They will be returned to Allah, their Master, the Real,
and what they invented will abandon them.

31   Say: 'Who provides for you out of heaven and earth?
Who controls hearing and sight?
Who brings forth the living from the dead
and the dead from the living?
Who directs the whole affair?'
They will say, 'Allah.'
Say, 'So will you not be godfearing?'

32   That is Allah, your Lord, the Truth,
and what is there after truth except misguidance?
So how have you been distracted?

33   In that way the Word of your Lord is realised
against those who are deviators,
in that they do not believe.

34   Say: 'Can any of your partner-gods
bring creation out of nothing
and then regenerate it?'

Say: 'Allah brings creation out of nothing
       and then regenerates it.
    So how have you been perverted?'

35   Say: 'Can any of your partner-gods guide to the truth?'
       Say: 'Allah guides to the truth.
    Who has more right to be followed –
       He who guides to the truth,
          or he who cannot guide unless he is guided?
    What is the matter with you?
       How do you reach your judgement?'

36   Most of them follow nothing but conjecture.
       Conjecture is of no avail at all against the truth.
    Allah most certainly knows what they are doing.

37   This Qur'an could never have been devised by any besides Allah.
       Rather it is confirmation of what came before it
    and an elucidation of the Book which contains no doubt
       from the Lord of all the worlds.

38   Do they say, 'He has invented it'?
       Say: 'Then produce a sura like it
    and call on anyone you can besides Allah
       if you are telling the truth.'

39   No, the fact is that they have denied something
       which their knowledge does not embrace
    and the meaning of which has not yet reached them.
       In the same way those before them also denied the truth.
          See the final fate of the wrongdoers!

40   Among them there are some who believe in it
       and some who do not.
    Your Lord best knows the corrupters.

41   If they deny you, say,
       'I have my actions
          and you have your actions.
    You are not responsible for what I do
       and I am not responsible for what you do.'

42   Among them there are some who listen to you.
                But can you make the deaf hear
            even though they cannot understand?

43   Among them there are some who look at you.
                But can you guide the blind,
            even though they cannot see?

44   Allah does not wrong people in any way;
                rather it is people who wrong themselves.

45   On the day We gather them together –
                when it will seem as if they had tarried
                    no more than an hour of a single day –
                they will recognise one another.
            Those who denied the meeting with Allah will have lost.
                They were not guided.

46   Whether We show you something
                of what We have promised them
            or take you back to Us,
                they will still return to Us.
            Then Allah will be witness
                against what they are doing.

47   Every nation has a Messenger
                and when their Messenger comes
            everything is decided between them justly.
                They are not wronged.

48   They say, 'When will this promise be kept
                if you are telling the truth?'

49   Say: 'I possess no power to harm or help myself
                except as Allah wills.
            Every nation has an appointed time.
                When their appointed time comes,
                    they cannot delay it a single hour
                        or bring it forward.'

50   Say: 'What do you think?
                If His punishment came upon you by night or day,
            what part of it would the evildoers then try to hasten?'

51   And then, when it actually comes about:
           'Now do you believe in it?
       It was this that you were trying to hasten!'

52   Then it will be said to those who did wrong,
           'Taste the punishment of eternity!
       Have you been repaid for anything
           other than what you earned?'

53   They will ask you to tell them if this is true.
           Say: 'Yes indeed, by my Lord, it certainly is true
               and you can do nothing to prevent it.'

54   If every self that did wrong
           possessed everything on earth,
               it would offer it as a ransom.
       They will show remorse
           when they see the punishment.
       Everything will be decided between them justly.
           They will not be wronged.

55   Yes, everything in the heavens and earth
           belongs to Allah.
       Yes, Allah's promise is true
           but most of them do not know it.

56   He gives life and causes to die
           and you will be returned to Him.

57   Mankind!
           admonition has come to you from your Lord
               and also healing for what is in the breasts
           and guidance and mercy for the believers.

58   Say: 'It is the favour of Allah and His mercy
           that should be the cause of their rejoicing.
       That is better than anything they accumulate.'

59   Say: 'What do you think about the things
           Allah has sent down to you as provision
       which you have then designated as halal and haram?'
           Say: 'Has Allah given you authority to do this
               or are you inventing lies against Allah?'

60   What will those who invent lies against Allah
         think on the Day of Rising?
     Allah shows favour to mankind
         but most of them are not thankful.

61   You do not engage in any matter
         or recite any of the Qur'an
           or do any action
     without Our witnessing you
         while you are occupied with it.
     Not even the smallest speck eludes your Lord,
         either on earth or in heaven.
     Nor is there anything smaller than that,
         or larger,
     which is not in a Clear Book.

62   Yes, the friends of Allah
         will feel no fear and know no sorrow:
63   those who believe and are godfearing,
64   there is good news for them
     in the life of this world and in the Next World.
         There is no changing the words of Allah.
           That is the great victory!

65   Do not be grieved by what they say.
         All might belongs to Allah.
     He is the All-Hearing, the All-Knowing.

66   Yes, indeed!
         Everyone in the heavens
           and everyone on the earth
             belongs to Allah.
     Those who call on something other than Allah
         are not really following their partner-gods.
     They are only following conjecture.
         They are only guessing.

67   It is He who appointed the night for you,
         so that you could rest in it,
           and the day for seeing.
     There are certainly Signs in that
         for people who listen.

68   They say, 'Allah has a son.'
      Glory be to Him!
    He is the Rich Beyond Need.
      Everything in the heavens
        and everything on the earth
        belongs to Him.
    Have you authority to say this
      or are you saying about Allah
        what you do not know?

69   Say: 'People who invent lies against Allah
      will not be successful.'
70   There is the enjoyment of this world.
      Then they will return to Us.
    Then We will let them taste
      the terrible punishment
        because they disbelieved.

71   Recite to them the story of Nuh when he said to his people,
      'My people, if my standing here
        and reminding you of Allah's Signs
      has become too much for you to bear,
        know that I have put my trust in Allah.
    So decide, you and your gods, on what you want to do
      and be open about it.
    Do with me whatever you decide
      and do not keep me waiting.
72   If you turn your backs,
      I have not asked you for any wage.
    My wage is the responsibility of Allah alone.
      I am commanded to be one of the Muslims.'

73   But they denied him so We rescued him,
      and all those with him, in the Ark
        and We made them the successors
        and We drowned the people who denied Our Signs.
    See the final fate of those who were warned!

74   Then after him We sent Messengers to their people,
      and they brought them the Clear Signs,
    but they were never going to believe in something
      which they had previously denied.
    That is how We seal up the hearts
      of those who overstep the limits.

75   Then after them We sent Musa and Harun with Our Signs
        to Pharaoh and his ruling circle,
   but they were arrogant and were a people of evildoers.

76   When the truth came to them from Us,
        they said, 'This is downright magic!'

77   Musa said, 'Do you say to the truth
        when it comes to you, "This is magic"?
          Magicians are not successful.'

78   They said, 'Have you come to us to turn us
        from what we found our fathers doing,
          and to gain greatness in the land?
   We do not believe you.'

79   Pharaoh said, 'Bring me every knowledgeable magician.'

80   When the magicians came, Musa said to them,
        'Throw whatever you have to throw!'

81   When they had thrown, Musa said,
        'What you have brought is magic.
          Allah will certainly prove it false.
        Allah does not uphold the actions of corrupters.'

82   Allah confirms the Truth by His words,
        even though the evildoers hate it.

83   No one believed in Musa except for a few of his people
        out of fear that Pharaoh, and the elders,
          would persecute them.
   Pharaoh was high and mighty in the land.
        He was one of the profligate.

84   Musa said, 'My people! if you believe in Allah,
        then put your trust in Him, if you are Muslims.'

85   They said, 'We have put our trust in Allah.
        Our Lord, Do not make us a target
          for this wrongdoing people,

86   and rescue us, by Your mercy,
          from this unbelieving people!'

87   We revealed to Musa and his brother:
           'Settle your people in houses in Egypt
       and make your houses places of worship
               and establish the prayer
       and give good news to the believers.'

88   Musa said, 'Our Lord,
           You have given Pharaoh and his ruling circle
               finery and wealth in the life of this world,
           Our Lord, so that they may be misguided from Your Way.
           Our Lord, obliterate their wealth and harden their hearts
               so that they do not believe
       until they see the painful punishment.'

89   He said, 'Your request is answered,
           so go straight and do not follow
       the way of those who have no knowledge.'

90   We brought the tribe of Israel across the sea
           and Pharaoh and his troops pursued them
               out of tyranny and enmity.
       Then, when he was on the point of drowning,
           he said, 'I believe that there is no god
       but Him in whom the tribe of Israel believe.
           I am one of the Muslims.'
91   'What, now! When previously you rebelled
           and were one of the corrupters?
92   Today We will preserve your body
           so you can be a Sign for people who come after you.
       Surely many people are heedless of Our Signs.'

93   We settled the tribe of Israel in a noble place
           and gave them good things as provision.
       They did not differ until knowledge came to them.
           Your Lord will decide between them on the Day of Rising
       regarding the things about which they differed.

94   If you are in any doubt about what We have sent down to you,
           then ask those who were reciting the Book before you.
       The truth has come to you from your Lord,
           so on no account be one of the doubters.
95   And on no account be among those who deny Allah's Signs
           and so become one of the lost.

96   Those against whom the words of your Lord are justly carried out
             will never believe –

97   not even if every Sign were to come to them –
             until they see the painful punishment.

98   How is it that there has never been a city that believed,
             whose faith then brought it benefit,
                 except the people of Yunus?
        When they believed We removed from them
             the punishment of disgrace in the life of this world
        and We let them have enjoyment for a time.

99   If your Lord had willed, all the people on the earth
             would have believed.
        Do you think you can force people to be believers?

100   No self can believe except with Allah's permission.
             He places a blight on those who do not use their intellect.

101   Say: 'Look at what there is in the heavens and on the earth.'
             But Signs and warnings are of no avail
                 to people who do not believe.

102   What are they waiting for but the same fate
             as those who passed away before them?
      Say: 'Wait, I will be among the people waiting with you.'

103   Then We will rescue Our Messengers
             and those who believe as well.
      It is incumbent upon Us to rescue the believers.

104   Say: 'Mankind! if you are in any doubt about my deen,
             I do not worship those you worship besides Allah.
      Rather I worship Allah who will take you back to Him
             and I am commanded to be one of the believers:

105   Turn your face towards the deen in pure natural faith,
             and on no account be among the idolators.

106   Do not call on something besides Allah
             which can neither help nor harm you.
      If you do, you will then be wrongdoers.'

107   If Allah afflicts you with harm,
             no one can remove it except Him.
      If He desires good for you,

no one can avert His favour.
He bestows it on whichever of His slaves He wills.
He is Ever-Forgiving, Most Merciful.

108　Say: 'Mankind! the truth has come to you from your Lord.
Whoever is guided is only guided for his own good.
Whoever is misguided is only misguided to his detriment.
I have not been set over you as a guardian.'

109　Follow what has been revealed to you
and be steadfast until Allah's judgement comes.
He is the Best of Judges.

Sura 11

Hud

In the name of Allah, All-Merciful, Most Merciful

1   Alif Lam Ra
A Book whose ayats are perfectly constructed,
        and then demarcated,
        coming directly from One who is All-Wise, All-Aware.

2   'Do not worship anyone but Allah!
        I am a warner and bringer of good news to you from Him.
3   Ask your Lord for forgiveness
        and then repent to Him.
He will let you enjoy a good life until a specified time,
        and will give His favour to all who merit it.
But if you turn your backs,
        I fear for you the punishment of a Mighty Day.
4   You will return to Allah.
        He has power over all things.'

5   See how they wrap themselves round
        trying to conceal their feelings from Him!
No, indeed! When they wrap their garments round themselves,
        He knows what they keep secret
            and what they make public.
        He knows what their hearts contain.

6   There is no creature on the earth
        which is not dependent upon Allah for its provision.
He knows where it lives and where it dies.
        They are all in a Clear Book.

7   It is He who created the heavens and the earth in six days
            when His Throne was on the water,
        in order to test which of you has the best actions.
            If you say, 'You will be raised up after death,'
        those who disbelieve will say,
            'This is nothing but downright magic.'

8   If We postpone the punishment for them for a limited time,
            they will say, 'What is holding it back?'
        No, indeed! The day it reaches them
            it will not be averted from them
        and the things they mocked at will encompass them.

9   If We let man taste mercy from Us,
            and then take it away from him,
                he is despairing, ungrateful;
10   but if We let him taste blessings
            after hardship has afflicted him,
        he says, 'My troubles have gone away,'
            and he is overjoyed, boastful –
11   except for those who are steadfast and do right actions.
            They will receive forgiveness and a large reward.

12   Perhaps you are leaving aside
            part of what has been revealed to you
        and your breast is constricted by this because they say,
            'Why has treasure not been sent down to him
                or an angel not accompanied him?'
        You are only a warner
            and Allah is Guardian over all things.

13   Or do they say, 'He has invented it?'
            Say, 'Then produce ten invented suras like this,
        and call on anyone you can besides Allah
            if you are telling the truth.'

14   If they do not respond to you
            then know that it has been sent down
                with Allah's knowledge
            and that there is no god but Him.
        So will you not become Muslims?

15   As for those who desire the life of this world and its finery,
            We will give them full payment in it for their actions.

They will not be deprived here of their due.

16   But such people will have nothing in the Next World but the Fire.
      What they achieved here will come to nothing.
          What they did will prove to be null and void.

17   But as for those who have clear evidence from their Lord
          followed up by a witness from Him –
              and before it the Book of Musa came
                  as a model and a mercy –
          such people believe in it.
      Any faction which rejects it is promised the Fire.
          Be in no doubt about it.
      It is the Truth from your Lord.
          But most people do not believe.

18   Who could do greater wrong
          than those who invent lies against Allah?
      Such people will be arrayed before their Lord
          and the witnesses will say,
      'Those are the ones who lied against their Lord.'
          Yes indeed! Allah's curse is on the wrongdoers,
19   those who bar access to the way of Allah
          desiring to make it crooked
              and reject the Next World.

20   They were not able to thwart Allah on earth,
          and had no protectors besides Allah.
      The punishment will be doubled for them.
          They were unable to hear and could not see.

21   Those are the people who have lost their own selves.
          What they invented has abandoned them.
22   Without question they will be the greatest losers in the Hereafter.

23   As for those who believe and do right actions
          and humble themselves before their Lord,
      they are the Companions of the Garden,
          remaining in it timelessly, for ever.

24   The likeness of the two groups
          is that of the blind and deaf
              and the seeing and hearing.
      Are they the same as one another?
          So will you not pay heed?

25   We sent Nuh to his people:
       'I am a clear warner to you.
26   Worship none but Allah.
    I fear for you the punishment of a painful day.'

27   The ruling circle of those of his people who disbelieved said,
       'We do not see you as anything
            but a human being like ourselves.
    We do not see anyone following you
            but the lowest of us, unthinkingly.
    We do not see you as superior to us.
    On the contrary, we consider you to be liars.'

28   He said, 'My people!
       What do you think?
    If I were to have clear evidence from my Lord
       and He had given me a mercy direct from Him,
            but you were blind to it,
    could we force it on you if you were unwilling?
29   My people!
    I do not ask you for any wealth for it.
       My wage is the responsibility of Allah alone.
    I will not chase away those who believe.
       They are surely going to meet their Lord.
    However, I see you as ignorant people.
30   My people!
    Who would help me against Allah
       if I did drive them away?
            So will you not pay heed?
31   I do not say to you that I possess the treasuries of Allah;
       nor do I know the Unseen;
            nor do I say that I am an angel;
       nor do I say to those who are vile in your eyes
            that Allah will not give them any good.
    Allah knows best what is in their hearts.
    If I did, I would certainly be one of the wrongdoers.'

32   They said, 'Nuh, you have argued with us
       and argued much
    so bring us what you have promised us
       if you are telling the truth.'
33   He said, 'Allah will bring it to you if He wills
       and you will not be able to prevent it.

34 My counsel will not benefit you,
  for all my desire to counsel you,
 if Allah desires to lead you into error.
  He is your Lord
 and you will return to Him.'

35 Or do they say, 'He has invented it'?
  Say: 'If I have invented it the crime will be laid at my door,
   but I am innocent of the crimes which you commit.'

36 It was revealed to Nuh:
  'None of your people are going to believe
   except for those who have already believed,
  so do not be distressed at what they do.
37 Build the Ark under Our supervision and as We reveal
  and do not address Me concerning the wrongdoers.
   They shall be drowned.'

38 He began to build the Ark and every time
  some nobles of his people passed him by,
   they ridiculed him.
 He said, 'Though you ridicule us now,
  we will certainly ridicule you as you do us.
39 You will soon know who will receive
  a punishment which disgraces him
 and find unleashed against himself
  an everlasting punishment.'

40 So when Our command came,
  and water bubbled up from the earth,
 We said, 'Load into it a pair of every species,
  and your family –
   except for those against whom
    the Word was preordained –
  and all who believe.'
 But those who believed with him were only few.

41 He said, 'Embark in it.
  In the name of Allah be its voyage and its landing!
   Truly my Lord is Ever-Forgiving, Most Merciful.'

42 It sailed with them through mountainous waves,
  and Nuh called out to his son, who had kept himself apart,
 'My son! Come on board with us.

Do not stay with the unbelievers!'

43 He said, 'I will take refuge on a mountain;
It will protect me from the flood.'
He said, 'There is no protection
from Allah's command today
except for those He has mercy on.'
The waves surged in between them
and he was among the drowned.

44 It was said, 'Earth, swallow up your water!'
and, 'Heaven, hold back your rain!'
And the water subsided
and the affair was concluded
and the Ark came to land on al-Judi.
And it was said, 'Away with the people of the wrongdoers!'

45 Nuh called out to his Lord and said,
'My Lord, my son is one of my family
and Your promise is surely the truth
and You are the Justest of Judges.'

46 He said, 'Nuh, he is definitely not of your family.
He is someone whose action was not righteous.
Do not, therefore, ask Me for something
about which you have no knowledge.
I admonish you lest you should be among the ignorant.'

47 He said, 'My Lord, I seek refuge with You
from asking You for anything
about which I have no knowledge.
If You do not forgive me
and have mercy on me,
I will be among the lost.'

48 It was said, 'Nuh, descend with peace from Us
and with blessings on you and on the nations
which will issue from those who are with you.
But there are nations to whom We will give enjoyment
and then a painful punishment from Us will afflict them.'

49 That is some of the news of the Unseen which We reveal to you.
Neither you nor your people knew it before this time.
So be steadfast.
The best end result is for the godfearing.

50 And to 'Ad We sent their brother Hud.
He said, 'My people! worship Allah.
You have no god apart from Him.
You are merely fabricators.
51 My people!
I do not ask you for any wage for it.
My wage is the responsibility of Him who brought me into being.
So will you not use your intellect?
52 My people!
Ask forgiveness of your Lord
and then repent to Him.
He will send heaven down to you in abundant rain,
and increase you with strength upon strength.
Do not turn away as evildoers.'

53 They said, 'Hud, you have not brought us any clear sign.
We will not forsake our gods for what you say.
We do not believe you.
54 We only say that one of our gods
has driven you mad.'
He said, 'I call on Allah to be my witness,
and you also bear witness,
that I am free of all the gods you have
55 apart from Him.
So scheme against me, all of you together,
and then grant me no respite.
56 I have put my trust in Allah,
my Lord and your Lord.
There is no creature He does not hold by the forelock.
My Lord is on a Straight Path.
57 If you turn your backs,
I have transmitted to you what I was sent to you with,
and my Lord will replace you with another people,
and you will not harm Him at all.
My Lord is the Preserver of everything.'

58 When Our command came,
We rescued Hud and those who believed along with him
by a mercy from Us.
We rescued them from a harsh punishment.

59 That was 'Ad.
They denied the Signs of their Lord
and disobeyed His Messengers

and followed the command
of every obdurate tyrant.

60 They were pursued by a curse in this world
and on the Day of Rising.
Yes indeed! 'Ad rejected their Lord,
so away with 'Ad, the people of Hud!

61 To Thamud We sent their brother Salih.
He said, 'My people, worship Allah!
You have no god apart from Him.
He brought you into being from the earth
and made you its inhabitants.
So ask His forgiveness
and then turn in repentance to Him.
My Lord is Close and Quick to Respond.'

62 They said, 'Salih, we had great hopes in you
before this happened.
Do you forbid us to worship
what our fathers worshipped?
We have grave doubts
about what you are calling us to.'

63 He said, 'My people!
What do you think?
If I were to possess a Clear Sign from my Lord
and He had given me mercy from Him:
who would help me against Allah if I disobeyed Him?
You would not increase me in anything but loss.

64 My people!
Here is the she-camel of Allah as a Sign for you.
So leave her alone to eat on Allah's earth
and do not inflict any harm on her
or you will be overcome by an imminent punishment.'

65 But they hamstrung her, so he said,
'Enjoy yourselves in your land for three more days.
That is a promise which will not be belied.'

66 Then when Our command came
We rescued Salih and those who believed along with him
by a mercy from Us from the disgrace of that day.
Your Lord is the All-Strong, the Almighty.

67   The Great Blast seized hold of those who did wrong
           and morning found them lying flattened in their homes.
68   It was as if they had never lived there at all.
           Yes indeed! Thamud rejected their Lord.
               So away with Thamud!

69   Our messengers brought the good news to Ibrahim.
           They said, 'Peace!' and he too said, 'Peace!'
       and brought in a roasted calf without delay.

70   When he saw that their hands were not reaching for it,
           he suspected them and felt afraid of them.
               They said, 'Have no fear!
           We have been sent to the people of Lut.'

71   His wife was standing there and she laughed out loud.
           So We gave her the good news of Ishaq,
               and beyond Ishaq, Ya'qub.

72   She said, 'Woe is me!
           How can I give birth when I am an old woman
               and my husband here is an aged man?
           This is indeed an astonishing thing!'

73   They said, 'Are you astonished at Allah's command?
           May Allah's mercy and His blessings be upon you,
               People of the House!
           He is Praiseworthy, All-Glorious.'

74   When the feeling of fear left Ibrahim,
           and the good news reached him,
       he disputed with Us about the people of Lut.

75   Ibrahim was forbearing, compassionate, penitent.

76   'Ibrahim, turn away from this!
           Your Lord's command has come.
       A punishment is coming to them
           which cannot be repelled.'

77   When Our messengers came to Lut,
           he was distressed for them,
       and very concerned for them,
           and said, 'This is a dreadful day.'

78   His people came running to him excitedly –
         they were long used to committing evil acts.
      He said, 'My people, here are my daughters.
         They are purer for you.
      So have taqwa of Allah and do not shame me with my guests.
         Is there not one rightly-guided man among you?'
79   They said, 'You know we have no claim on your daughters.
         You know very well what it is we want.'
80   He said, 'If only I had the strength to combat you
         or could take refuge in some powerful support!'

81   They said, 'Lut, we are messengers from your Lord.
         They will not be able to get at you.
      Set out with your family – except for your wife –
            in the middle of the night
      and none of you should look back.
      What strikes them will strike her as well.
            Their promised appointment is the morning.
               Is the morning not close at hand?'

82   When Our command came,
         We turned their cities upside down
      and rained down on them stones of hard baked clay,
            piled on top of one another in layers,
83   each one earmarked by your Lord.
         And they are never far from the wrongdoers.

84   And to Madyan their brother Shu'ayb.
         He said, 'My people, worship Allah!
            You have no god apart from Him.
      Do not give short measure and short weight.
         I see you prospering and I fear for you
      the punishment of an all-encompassing Day.
85   My people!
      Give full measure and full weight with justice;
            do not diminish people's goods;
         and do not go about the earth, corrupting it.
86   What endures with Allah is better for you
               if you are believers.
         I am not set over you as your keeper.'

87   They said, 'Shu'ayb, do your prayers instruct you
         that we should abandon what our fathers worshipped

or stop doing whatever we want to with our wealth?
You are clearly the forbearing, the rightly-guided!'

88   He said, 'My people!
            What do you think?
        If I do possess a Clear Sign from my Lord
            and He has given me His good provision,
        I would clearly not want to go behind your backs
            and do something I have forbidden you to do.
        I only want to put things right as far as I can.
            My success is with Allah alone.
        I have put my trust in Him and I turn to Him.
89   My people!
        Do not let your breach with me
            provoke you into doing wrong
        so that the same thing happens to you
            as happened to the people of Nuh
        and the people of Hud and the people of Salih;
            and the people of Lut are not far distant from you.
90   Ask your Lord for forgiveness
            and then turn in repetance to Him.
        My Lord is Most Merciful, Most Loving.'

91   They said, 'Shu'ayb, We do not understand much of what you say
            and we see you are weak among us.
        Were it not for your clan, we would have stoned you.
            We do not hold you in high esteem!'

92   He said, 'My people!
            Do you esteem my clan more than you do Allah?
        You have made Him into something
            to cast disdainfully behind your backs!
        But my Lord encompasses everything that you do!
93   My people!
            Do as you think best.
        That is what I am doing.
            You will certainly come to know
        who will receive a punishment to disgrace him,
            and who is a liar.
                So look out.
        I will be on the lookout with you.'

94   When Our command came, We rescued Shu'ayb
            and those who believed along with him

by a mercy from Us.
The Great Blast seized hold of those who did wrong
  and morning found them lying flattened in their homes
95   as if they had never lived there at all.
Yes indeed! Away with Madyan just like Thamud!

96   We sent Musa with Our Signs and clear authority
97   to Pharaoh and his ruling circle.
They followed Pharaoh's command
  but Pharaoh's command was not rightly guided.

98   He will go ahead of his people on the Day of Rising
  and lead them down into the Fire.
What an evil watering-hole to be led to!

99   They are pursued by a curse in this world
  and on the Day of Rising.
What an evil gift to be given!

100 That is some of the news of the cities
  which We relate to you.
Some of them are still standing,
  while others are now just stubble.

101 We did not wrong them;
  rather they wronged themselves.
The gods they called upon besides Allah
      did not help them at all
  when Allah's command came upon them.
They did nothing but increase their ruin.

102 Such is the iron grip of your Lord
  when He seizes the cities which do wrong.
      His grip is painful, violent.

103 There is certainly a Sign in that
  for anyone who fears the punishment of the Next World.
That is a Day to which mankind will all be gathered.
  That is a Day which will be witnessed by everyone.

104 We will only postpone it
  until a predetermined time.

105   On the Day it comes, no self will speak
             except by His permission.
        Some of them will be wretched
             and others glad.

106   As for those who are wretched,
             they will be in the Fire,
                 where they will sigh and gasp,
107   remaining in it timelessly, for ever,
             as long as the heavens and earth endure,
                 except as your Lord wills.
        Your Lord is the Doer of what He wills.

108   As for those who are glad,
             they will be in the Garden,
        remaining in it timelessly, for ever,
             as long as the heavens and earth endure,
                 except as your Lord wills:
             an uninterrupted gift.

109   So be in no doubt about what these people worship.
             They only worship as their forebears worshipped previously.
        We will pay them their portion in full, with no rebate!

110   We gave Musa the Book and people differed concerning it
             and had it not been for a prior Word from your Lord,
        it would already have been decided between them.
             They are indeed in grave doubt about it.

111   Your Lord will pay each one of them
             for his actions in full.
        He is aware of what they do.

112   Go straight as you have been commanded,
             and also those who turn with you to Allah,
                 and do not exceed the bounds.
             He sees what you do.

113   Do not rely on those who do wrong
             thus causing the Fire to afflict you,
        for you have no protector besides Allah;
             then you will not be helped.

114 Establish the prayer at each end of the day
and in the first part of the night.
Good actions eradicate bad actions.
This is a reminder for people who pay heed.

115 And be steadfast.
Allah does not let the wage
of good-doers go to waste.

116 Would that there had been more people with a vestige of good
among the generations of those who came before you,
who forbade corruption in the earth,
other than the few among them whom We saved.
Those who did wrong gladly pursued
the life of luxury that they were given
and were evildoers.

117 Your Lord would never have destroyed the cities wrongfully
as long as their inhabitants were putting things right.

118 If your Lord had wanted to,
He would have made mankind into one community
but they persist in their differences,

119 except for those whom your Lord has mercy on.
That is what He created them for –
so that the Word of your Lord would be fulfilled:
'I will fill up Hell with the jinn and mankind all together.'

120 We have given you all this news about the Messengers
so We can make your heart firm by means of it.
The truth has come to you in this
and an admonishment and reminder to the believers.

121 Say to those who disbelieve:
'Do as you think best.
That is what we are doing.

122 And wait.
We too are waiting.'

123 The Unseen of the heavens and the earth belongs to Allah
and the whole affair is returned to Him.
So worship Him and put your trust in Him.
Your Lord is not unaware of what you do.

Sura 12

Yusuf

In the name of Allah, All-Merciful, Most Merciful

1   Alif Lam Ra
     Those are the Signs of the Clear Book.

2   We have sent it down as an Arabic Qur'an
         so that hopefully you will use your intellect.

3   We tell you the best of stories in revealing this Qur'an to you,
         even though you were unaware of it before it came.

4   When Yusuf told his father, 'Father! I saw
     eleven bright stars, and the sun and moon as well.
     I saw them all prostrate in front of me.'
5   He said, 'My son, don't tell your brothers your dream
     lest they devise some scheme to injure you,
     Shaytan is a clear-cut enemy to man.
6   Accordingly your Lord will pick you out
     and teach you the true meaning of events
     and perfectly fulfil His blessing on you
     as well as on the family of Ya'qub
     as He fulfilled it perfectly before
     upon your forebears, Ibrahim and Ishaq.
     Most certainly your Lord is Knowing, Wise.'

7   In Yusuf and his brothers there are Signs
     for every one of those who wants to ask.
8   When they declared, 'Why! Yusuf and his brother
     are dearer to our father than we are

although we constitute a powerful group.
Our father is clearly making a mistake.

9   Kill Yusuf or expel him to some land
so that your father will look to you alone
and then you can be people who do right.'

10 One of them said, 'Do not take Yusuf's life
but throw him to the bottom of the well,
so that some travellers may discover him,
if this is something that you have to do.'

11 They said, 'Our father! What is wrong with you
that you refuse to trust us with Yusuf
when in truth we only wish him well?

12 Why don't you send him out with us tomorrow
so he can enjoy himself and play about?
All of us will make sure that he is safe.'

13 He said, 'It grieves me to let him go with you
I fear a wolf might come and eat him up
while you are heedless, not attending him.'

14 They said, 'If a wolf does come and eat him up
when together we make up a powerful group
in that case we would truly be in loss!'

15 But when, in fact, they did go out with him
and gathered all together and agreed
to put him at the bottom of the well,
We then revealed to him that: 'You will
inform them of this deed they perpetrate
at a time when they are totally unaware.'

16 That night they came back to their father in tears,

17 saying, 'Father, we went out to run a race
and left Yusuf together with our things
and then a wolf appeared and ate him up
but you are never going to believe us now,
not even though we really tell the truth.'

18 They then produced his shirt with false blood on it.
He said, 'It is merely that your lower selves
have suggested something to you which you did;
but beauty lies in showing steadfastness.
It is Allah alone who is my Help
in face of the event that you describe.'

19 Some travellers came that way and then dispatched
their water-drawer who let his bucket down.
He said, 'Good news for me, I've found a boy!'

They then hid him away among their goods.
Allah knew very well what they were doing.

20   They sold him for a pittance, a few small coins,
considering him to be of little worth.

21   The Egyptian who had bought him told his wife,
'Look after him with honour and respect.
It's possible he will be of use to us
or perhaps we might adopt him as a son.'
And thus We established Yusuf in the land
to teach him the true meaning of events.
Allah is in control of His affair.
However, most of mankind do not know.

22   And then when he became a full-grown man,
We gave him knowledge and right judgement too.
That is how We reward all doers of good.

23   The woman whose house it was solicited him.
She barred the doors and said, 'Come over here!'
He said, 'Allah is my refuge! He is my lord
and has been good to me with where I live.
Those who do wrong will surely not succeed.'

24   She wanted him and he would have wanted her,
had he not seen the Clear Proof of his Lord.
That happened so We might avert from him
all evil and lust. He was Our chosen slave.

25   They raced to the door. She tore his shirt at the back.
They met her husband by the door. She said,
'How should a man whose intention was to harm
your family be punished for what he did
except with prison or painful punishment?'

26   He said, 'It was she who tried to seduce me.'
A witness from her people then declared,
'If his shirt is torn in front, she speaks the truth
and he has clearly told a shameless lie.

27   If his shirt is torn at the back, then she has lied
and he has clearly told the simple truth.'

28   He saw the shirt torn at the back and said,
'The source of this is women's deviousness.
Without a doubt your guile is very great.

29   Yusuf, ignore all this, and you, my wife,
should ask forgiveness for your evil act.
There is no doubt that you are in the wrong.'

30   Some city women said, 'The governor's wife
      solicited her slave. He's fired her heart
      with love. We see that she's the one to blame.'

31   But when she heard of their malicious talk,
      she sent for them and made a sumptuous meal
      and then she gave a knife to each of them.
      She said, 'Go out to them.' When they saw him,
      they were amazed by him and cut their hands.
      They said, 'Allah preserve us! This is no man.
      What can this be but a noble angel here!'

32   She said, 'You see! It's him you blamed me for.
      I tried seducing him but he refused.
      If he does not do what I order him,
      he will be put in prison and brought low.'

33   He said, 'My Lord, the prison is preferable
      to me than what they call on me to do.
      Unless You turn their guile away from me,
      it may well be that I will fall for them
      and so become a man of ignorance.'

34   His Lord replied to him and turned away
      from him their female guile and deviousness.
      He is the One Who Hears, the One Who Knows.

35   Then, after they had seen the Signs, they thought
      that they should still imprison him for a time.

36   Two servants entered prison along with him.
      One said, 'I dreamt that I was pressing grapes.'
      The other said, 'I dreamt I carried bread
      upon my head and birds were eating it.
      Tell us the true meaning of these dreams.
      We see that you are one of the righteous.'

37   He said, 'No meal to feed you will arrive
      before I have informed you what they mean.
      That is part of what my Lord taught me.
      For I have left the religion of a people
      who clearly do not believe in Allah
      nor do they have faith in the Next World.

38   I hold fast to the creed of my forebears
      Ibrahim and Ishaq and Ya'qub.
      We don't associate anything with Allah.
      And that is how Allah has favoured us
      and all mankind, but most do not give thanks.

39   My fellow-prisoners, are many lords better,
      or Allah, the only One, the Conqueror?

40   What you serve apart from Him are only names
which you and your forefathers have made up
There is no mandate for them from Allah.
Allah alone is qualified to judge.
His order is to worship none but Him.
That is in truth the straight and upright deen,
but most of mankind simply do not know.

41   My fellow-captives, one of you will serve
his lord with wine, the other of you will
be crucified and birds will eat his head.
The thing you asked about is foreordained.'

42   He said to the one of them he knew was saved,
'Please mention me when you are with your lord,'
but Shaytan made him forget to remind his lord,
and so he stayed in prison for several years.

43   The King declared, 'I dreamt of seven fat cows
which seven thin ones ate and seven green ears
of wheat and seven others which were dry.
O counsellors! Explain my dream to me
if you are those who can interpret visions!'

44   They said, 'A jumbled mass of mixed-up dreams!
We do not know the meaning of such things.'

45   The one of them who had been saved then said,
remembering after a period, 'I will tell
you what it signifies, so send me out.'

46   'O truthful Yusuf, tell us of seven fat cows
which seven thin ones ate and seven green ears
of wheat and seven others which were dry
so that I can return to them and let them know.'

47   He said, 'Sow for seven years in the normal way
and leave that which you harvest in the ear
except for a small amount from which you eat.

48   Then after that seven hard years will arrive
in which you can eat from what you set aside
for them, except for a little which you store.

49   Then after that another year will come
in which the people will be helped by rain
in plenty and when they once more will press.'

50   The King said, 'Bring him to me straight away!'
but when the envoy came to him, he said,
'Go back to your master and enquire of him

what happened about the women who cut their hands.
My Lord has knowledge of their cunning guile.'

51   He said, 'What was this past affair of yours
when you solicited Yusuf?' Then they said
'Allah forbid! We know no bad of him.'
The governor's wife then said, 'The truth has now
emerged. Indeed I tried to seduce him then
and he has simply told the honest truth.

52   In this way he may know at last that I
did not dishonour him behind his back
and that Allah most surely does not guide
the deviousness of the dishonourable.

53   I do not say my self was free from blame.
The self indeed commands to evil acts –
except for those my Lord has mercy on.
My Lord, He is Forgiving, Merciful.'

54   The King said, 'Bring him to me straight away!
so I may draw him very close to me.'
When he had spoken with him, he declared,
'Today you are trusted, established in our sight.'

55   He said, 'Entrust the country's stores to me.
In truth I am a knowing guardian.'

56   And thus We established Yusuf in the land
so he could live in any place he pleased.
We grant Our grace to anyone We will
and We do not allow to go to waste
the wage of any people who do good.

57   But the wages of the Hereafter are the best
for people who believe and fear their Lord.

58   The brothers of Yusuf came into his presence
and he knew them but they did not know him.

59   Then, having supplied their needs, he said to them,
'Bring me your brother, your father's youngest son.
Do you not see that I dispense full measure
and am the most hospitable of hosts?

60   But if you do not bring him here to me,
your measure from me then will be denied
and you will not come near to me at all.'

61   They said, 'We will request our father for him.
That is something we will surely do.'

62   He told his serving men, 'Put back their goods
into their saddlebags for them to find

when they arrive back to their families
so that perhaps they will return again.'

63   Then when they got back to their father's house,
they said, 'Father! Our measure will be denied.
Please send our brother with us so we may
obtain our measure. We will take care of him.'

64   He said, 'How will my trusting him to your care
be different from entrusting his brother before?
However, the Best of Guardians is Allah.
He is the Most Merciful of the merciful.'

65   Then when they opened up their saddlebags
and found their merchandise returned to them,
they said, 'Our father! What more could we ask!
Here is our merchandise returned to us.
We can provide our families with food,
and guard our brother and get an extra load.
That is an easy measure to obtain.'

66   He said, 'I will not send him out with you
until you make a covenant with Allah
to bring him home unless you are overwhelmed.'
When they had made their covenant, he said,
'Allah is Guardian over what we say.'

67   He said, 'My sons! You must not enter through
a single gate. Go in through different gates.
But I cannot save you from Allah at all,
for judgement comes from no one but Allah.
In Him I put my trust, and let all those
who put their trust, put it in Him alone.'

68   But when they entered as their father said,
it did not save them from Allah at all,
yet a need in Ya'qub's soul was satisfied.
He had knowledge which We had taught him,
but most of mankind simply do not know.

69   Then when they entered into Yusuf's presence,
he drew his brother close to him and said,
'I am your brother. Do not be distressed
concerning all the things they used to do.'

70   Then when he had supplied them with their needs,
he put the goblet in his brother's bag.
A herald called out, 'Caravan! You are thieves!'

71   They turned to them and said, 'What are you missing?'

72   They said, 'We're missing the goblet of the king.

The man who brings it will get a camel's load.
Regarding that I stand as guarantor.'

73 They said, 'By Allah, you know we did not come
to corrupt the land and that we are not thieves.'

74 They said, 'What is the reparation for it
if it in fact transpires that you are liars?'

75 They said, 'Its reparation shall be him
in the saddlebags of whom it is discovered.
With us that is how wrongdoers are repaid.'

76 He started with their bags before his brother's.
and then produced it from his brother's bag.
In that way We devised a cunning scheme
for Yusuf. He could not have held his brother
according to the statutes of the King –
only because Allah had willed it so.
We raise the rank of anyone We will.
Over everyone with knowledge is a Knower.

77 They said, 'If he steals now, his brother stole
before.' But Yusuf kept it to himself
and still did not disclose it to them, saying,
'The plight that you are in is worse than that.
Allah knows best the matter you describe.'

78 They said, 'Your Eminence! He has an old
and venerable father, so take one of us
instead of him. We see without a doubt
that you are of the people who do good.'

79 He said, 'Allah forbid that we should take
any but him with whom our goods were found.
In that case we would clearly be wrongdoers.'

80 When they despaired of him, they went apart
to talk alone. The eldest of them said,
'You know full well your father had you make
a covenant with Allah concerning this,
and how before you failed him with Yusuf.
I will not leave this land until I have
permission from my father, or Allah
decides about the case on my behalf.
Truly He is the justest Judge of all.

81 Return now to your father and say to him,
"Your son stole, father. We can do no more
than testify to what we know and we
are not the guardians of the Unseen.

82   Ask questions of the town in which we were
        and of the caravan in which we came
        for we are surely telling you the truth."'

83   He said, 'It's merely that your lower selves
        suggested something to you which you did.
        But beauty lies in having steadfastness.
        Perhaps Allah will bring them all together.
        He is indeed All-Knowing and All-Wise.'

84   He turned himself away from them and said,
        'What anguish is my sorrow for Yusuf!'
        And then his eyes turned white from hidden grief.

85   They said, 'By Allah, you will not ever cease
        to mention Yusuf, till you waste away
        or are among the people of the grave!'

86   He said, 'I make complaint about my grief
        and sorrow to Allah alone because
        I know things from Allah you do not know.

87   My sons! Seek news of Yusuf and his brother.
        Do not despair of solace from Allah.
        No one despairs of solace from Allah
        except for people who are unbelievers.'

88   So when they came into his presence, they said,
        'Your Eminence! Hardship has hit us and
        our families. We bring scant merchandise,
        but fill the measure for us generously.
        Allah always rewards a generous giver.'

89   He said, 'Are you aware of what you did
        to Yusuf and his brother in ignorance?'

90   They said, 'Are you Yusuf?' He said, 'I am
        indeed Yusuf, and this here is my brother.
        Allah has acted graciously to us.
        As for those who fear Allah and are steadfast,
        Allah does not allow to go to waste
        the wage of any people who do good.'

91   They said, 'By Allah, Allah has favoured you
        above us. Clearly we were in the wrong.'

92   He said, 'No blame at all will fall on you.
        Today you have forgiveness from Allah.
        He is the Most Merciful of the merciful.

93   Go with this shirt of mine and cast it on
        my father's face and he will see again.
        Then come to me with all your families.'

94   And when the caravan went on its way,
      their father said, 'I can smell Yusuf's scent!
      You probably think I have become senile.'

95   They said, 'By Allah! Your mind is still astray.'

96   But when the bringer of the good news came,
      he cast it on his face and sight returned.
      He said, 'Did I not say to you before,
      I know things from Allah you do not know?'

97   They said, 'Our father, may we be forgiven
      for all the many wrongs that we have done.
      We were indeed greatly mistaken men.'

98   He said, 'I will ask my Lord to pardon you.
      He is Ever-Forgiving, Most Merciful.'

99   Then when they entered into Yusuf's presence,
      he drew his parents close to him and said,
      'Enter Egypt safe and sound, if Allah wills.'

100   He raised his parents up onto the throne.
      The others fell prostrate in front of him.
      He said, 'My father, truly this is now
      the interpretation of the dream I had.
      My Lord has made it all come true; and He
      was kind to me by letting me out of prison
      and brought you from the desert when Shaytan
      had caused dissent between me and my brothers.
      My Lord is kind to anyone He wills.
      He is indeed All-Knowing and All-Wise.

101   My Lord, You have granted power to me on earth
      and taught me the true meaning of events.
      Originator of the heavens and earth,
      You are my Friend in this world and the Next.
      So take me as a Muslim at my death
      and join me to the people who are righteous.'

102   This is news of the Unseen which We reveal to you.
      You were not with them when they decided what to do
      and devised their scheme.

103   But most people,
      for all your eagerness,
      are not believers.

104   You do not ask them for any wage for it.
      It is only a reminder to all beings.

105   How many Signs there are in the heavens and earth!
          Yet they pass them by, turning away from them.
106   Most of them do not believe in Allah
          without associating others with Him.

107   Do they feel secure that
          the all-enveloping punishment of Allah
             will not come upon them,
          or that the Last Hour
             will not come upon them
          all of a sudden
      when they least expect it?

108   Say: 'This is my way.
          I call to Allah with inner sight,
             I and all who follow me.
          Glory be to Allah!
      I am not one of the idolators!'

109   We sent none before you but men inspired with revelation
          from among the people of the cities.
      Have they not travelled in the land
          and seen the final fate of those before them?
      The abode of the Next World is better
          for those who are godfearing.
      So will you not use your intellect?

110   Then when the Messengers despaired
          and thought themselves denied,
      Our help came to them,
          and those We willed were saved.
      Our violent force cannot be averted
          from people who are evildoers.

111   There is instruction in their stories
          for people of intelligence.
      This is not a narration which has been invented
          but confirmation of all that came before,
      a clarification of everything,
          and a guidance and a mercy
             for people who believe.

Sura 13

Ar-Ra'd
Thunder

In the name of Allah, All-Merciful, Most Merciful

1   Alif Lam Mim Ra
    Those are the Signs of the Book.
And what has been sent down
    to you from your Lord
        is the Truth.
But most people do not believe.

2   Allah is He who raised up the heavens
    without any support –
      you can see that –
and then established Himself firmly on the Throne.
    He made the sun and moon subservient,
      each running for a specified term.
    He directs the whole affair.
He makes the Signs clear
    so that hopefully you will be certain
      about the meeting with your Lord.

3   It is He who stretched out the earth
    and placed firmly embedded mountains and rivers in it
      and made two types of every kind of fruit.
    He covers over day with night.
There are Signs in that for people who reflect.

4   In the earth there are diverse regions side by side
    and gardens of grapes and cultivated fields,
      and palm-trees sharing one root

and others with individual roots,
    all watered with the same water.
    And We make some things better to eat than others.
There are Signs in that for people who use their intellect.

5   If you are surprised at their blindness,
    what could be more surprising than their words:
'What, when we are turned to dust,
    shall we then be created all anew?'
These are the people who reject their Lord.
    Such people have iron collars round their necks.
Such people are the Companions of the Fire,
    remaining in it timelessly, for ever.

6   They want you to hasten the bad rather than the good
    when examples of punishment
      are there before them in the past.
Your Lord has forgiveness for people for their wrongdoing;
    but your Lord is also severe in retribution.

7   Those who disbelieve say, 'If only a Sign could
    be sent down to him from his Lord!'
      You are only a warner.
    Every people has a guide.

8   Allah knows what every female bears
    and every shrinking of the womb
    and every swelling.
Everything has its measure with Him,
9   the Knower of the Unseen and the Visible,
    the Most Great, the High-Exalted.

10   It makes no difference
    whether you keep secret what you say
      or voice it out loud,
    whether you hide in the night
      or go out in the day.

11   Everyone has a succession of angels
    in front of him and behind him,
      guarding him by Allah's command.
Allah never changes a people's state
    until they change what is in themselves.
When Allah desires evil for a people,

there is no averting it.
They have no protector apart from Him.

12 It is He Who shows you the lightning,
striking fear and bringing hope;
it is He Who heaps up the heavy clouds.

13 The thunder glorifies His praise,
as do the angels,
out of fear of Him.
He discharges the thunderbolts,
striking with them anyone He wills.
Yet still they argue about Allah
when He is inexorable in His power!

14 The call of truth is made to Him alone.
Those they call upon apart from Him
do not respond to them at all.
It is like someone stretching out
his cupped hands towards water
to convey it to his mouth:
it will never get there.
The call of the unbelievers only goes astray.

15 Everyone in heaven and earth prostrates to Allah
willingly or unwillingly,
as do their shadows in the morning and the evening.

16 Say: 'Who is the Lord of the heavens and the earth?'
Say: 'Allah.'
Say: 'So why have you taken protectors apart from Him
who possess no power to help or harm themselves?'
Say: 'Are the blind and the seeing equal?
Or are darkness and light the same?
Or have they assigned partners to Allah
who create as He creates,
so that all creating seems the same to them?'
Say: 'Allah is the Creator of everything.
He is the One, the All-Conquering.'

17 He sends down water from the sky
and river-beds fill up and flow
according to their size,
and the floodwater carries with it

          an increasing layer of scum;
     a similar kind of scum comes
          from what you heat up in the fire,
     when you desire to make jewellery or other things.
          That is how Allah depicts the true and the false.
     As for the scum, it is quickly swept away.
          But as for that which is of use to people,
               it remains behind in the ground.
     That is a metaphor which Allah has made

18   Those who respond to their Lord will receive the best.
          But as for those who do not respond to Him,
     even if they owned everything on the earth
          and the same again with it,
               they would offer it as a ransom.
     They will receive an evil Reckoning.
          Their shelter will be Hell.
               What an evil resting-place!

19   Is he who knows that what has been sent down to you
          from your Lord is the truth like him who is blind?
     It is only people of intelligence who pay heed:
20   those who fulfil Allah's contract
               and do not break their agreement;
21   those who join what Allah has commanded to be joined
               and are afraid of their Lord
                    and fear an evil Reckoning;
22   those who are steadfast in seeking the face of their Lord,
               and establish the prayer
          and give from the provision We have given them,
               secretly and openly,
          and stave off evil with good,
     it is they who will have the Ultimate Abode –
23   Gardens of Eden which they will enter,
     and all of their parents, wives and children who were righteous.
          Angels will enter in to welcome them from every gate:
24   'Peace be upon you because of your steadfastness!
          How wonderful is the Ultimate Abode!'

25   But as for those who break Allah's contract
          after it has been agreed
     and sever what Allah has commanded to be joined,
          and cause corruption in the earth,

the curse will be upon them.
  They will have the Evil Abode.

26 Allah expands provision to anyone He wills
      and restricts it.
    They rejoice in the life of this world.
      Yet the life of this world,
        compared to the Next World,
      is only fleeting enjoyment.

27 Those who disbelieve say, 'Why has a Sign
      not been sent down to him from his Lord?'
    Say: 'Allah misguides whoever He wills
      and guides to Himself all who turn to Him:
28 those who believe and whose hearts find peace
      in the remembrance of Allah.
    Only in the remembrance of Allah
      can the heart find peace.'

29 Those who believe and do right actions,
      happiness will be theirs
    and a wonderful Homecoming.

30 In the same way We have sent you among a nation
      before which other nations passed away,
    to recite to them what We have revealed to you.
      Yet they still reject the All-Merciful.
    Say: 'He is my Lord; there is no god but Him.
      I put my trust in Him and I turn to Him.'

31 Even if there was a Qur'an which moved mountains,
      or split the earth open or spoke to the dead . . .!
        On the contrary! The affair is Allah's altogether.
    Do those who believe not know that if Allah had wanted to
      He could have guided all mankind?
    Those who disbelieve will not cease to be struck by disaster
      for what they have done –
        or a disaster will happen close to their homes –
      until Allah's promise is fulfilled.
    Allah will not fail to keep His promise.

32 Messengers before you were mocked.
      I gave those who disbelieved a little more time

and then I seized them.
How terrible was My retribution!

33 What then of Him who is standing over every self
seeing everything it does?
Yet still they associate others with Allah!
Say: 'Name them!
Or would you inform Him of something in the earth
He does not know,
or are they words that are simply guesswork
on your part?'
However, the plotting of those who disbelieved
seems good to them
and they bar the way.
Anyone misguided by Allah has no guide.

34 They will receive punishment in the life of this world
and the punishment of the Next World is harsher still.
They have no defender against Allah.

35 What is the Garden promised to the godfearing like?
It has rivers flowing under it
and its foodstuffs and cool shade never fail.
That is the final fate of the godfearing.
But the final fate of the unbelievers is the Fire.

36 Those to whom We gave the Book
rejoice at what has been sent down to you
but some of the parties refuse to acknowledge part of it.
Say: 'I have only been ordered to worship Allah
and not to associate anything with Him.
I summon to Him and I will return to Him.'

37 Accordingly We have sent it down as a judgement in Arabic.
If you followed their whims and desires
after the knowledge that has come to you,
you would have no protector or defender against Allah.

38 We sent Messengers before you
and gave them wives and children.
Nor was any Messenger able to bring a Sign
except by Allah's permission.
There is a prescribed limit to every term.

39   Allah erases whatever He wills
        or endorses it.
    The Master Copy of the Book is in His Hands.

40   Whether We show you something
        of what We have promised them
            or We take you back to Us,
        your responsibility is transmission
            and the Reckoning is Ours.

41   Do they not see how We come to the land
        eroding it at its extremities.
            Allah judges
    and there is no reversing His judgement.
        He is swift at reckoning.

42   Those before them plotted
        but all plotting belongs to Allah.
    He knows what each self earns,
        and the unbeliever will soon know
    who has the Ultimate Abode.

43   Those who disbelieve say, 'You are not a Messenger.'
        Say: 'Allah is a sufficient witness between you and me,
            and anyone else who has knowledge of the Book.'

Sura 14

Ibrahim
Abraham

In the name of Allah, All-Merciful, Most Merciful

1   Alif Lam Ra
This is a Book We have sent down to you
    so that you can bring mankind
        from the darkness to the light,
    by the permission of their Lord,
to the Path of the Almighty, the Praiseworthy.

2   Allah is He to Whom everything in the heavens
    and everything in the earth belongs.
Woe to the unbelievers because of a terrible punishment –
3   those who prefer the life of this world to the Next World,
      and bar access to the way of Allah,
        wanting to make it crooked;
      they are greatly misguided.

4   We have not sent any Messenger
    except with the language of his people
      so he can make things clear to them.
Allah misguides anyone He wills
    and guides anyone He wills.
He is the Almighty, the All-Wise.

5   We sent Musa with Our Signs:
    'Bring your people from the darkness to the light.
    and remind them of the Days of Allah.'
There are certainly Signs in that
    for everyone who is steadfast, thankful.

6   Remember when Musa said to his people,
       'Remember Allah's blessing upon you
    when He rescued you from the people of Pharaoh.
       They were inflicting an evil punishment on you,
    slaughtering your sons and letting your women live.
       In that there was a terrible trial from your Lord.
7   And when your Lord announced:
       "If you are grateful, I will certainly give you increase,
    but if you are ungrateful, My punishment is severe."'

8   Musa said, 'If you were to be ungrateful,
       you and everyone on the earth,
    Allah is Rich Beyond Need, Praiseworthy.'

9   Has news not reached you of those who came before you,
       the peoples of Nuh and 'Ad and Thamud,
         and those who came after them
       who are known to no one but Allah?
    Their Messengers came to them with Clear Signs,
       but they put their hands to their mouths, saying,
         'We reject what you have been sent with.
       We have grave doubts about what you are calling us to.'

10   Their Messengers said, 'Is there any doubt about Allah,
       the Bringer into Being of the heavens and the earth?
    He summons you to forgive you for your wrong actions
       and to defer you until a specified time.'
    They said, 'You are nothing but human beings like ourselves
       who want to debar us from what our fathers worshipped;
         so bring us a clear authority.'

11   Their Messengers said to them,
       'We are nothing but human beings like yourselves.
    But Allah shows favour to any of His slaves He wills.
       It is not for us to bring you an authority
         except by Allah's permission.
       So let the believers put their trust in Allah.
12   And why indeed should we not put our trust in Allah
       when He has guided us to our ways?
    We will be steadfast however much you harm us.
       Those who trust put their trust in Allah.'

13   Those who disbelieved said to their Messengers,
       'We will drive you from our land

    unless you return to our religion.'
    Their Lord revealed to them,
    'We will destroy those who do wrong.

14   We will leave you the land to live in after them.
    That is the reward of those who fear My station
        and fear My threat.'

15   They asked for Allah's victory,
        and every obdurate tyrant failed.

16   And beyond him is Hell
        where he will be given pus to drink.

17   He gulps at it but can hardly swallow it down.
        Death comes at him from every side
            but he does not die.
    And beyond him is relentless punishment.

18   The metaphor of those who reject their Lord
        is that their actions are like ashes
            scattered by strong winds
                on a stormy day.
    They have no power at all
        over anything they have earned.
    That is extreme misguidance.

19   Do you not see that Allah has created
        the heavens and the earth with truth?
    If He wished He could eliminate you
        and bring about a new creation.

20   That is not difficult for Allah.

21   They will all parade before Allah
        and the weak will say to those who were arrogant,
    'We followed you, so can you help us at all
        against the punishment of Allah?'
    They will say, 'If Allah had guided us,
        we would have guided you.
    It makes no difference
        whether we cannot stand it
            or bear it patiently.
    We have no way of escape.'

22   When the affair is decided Shaytan will say,
        'Allah made you a promise,
            a promise of truth,

and I made you a promise
  but broke my promise.
I had no authority over you,
  except that I called you
    and you responded to me.
Do not, therefore, blame me but blame yourselves.
  I cannot come to your aid nor you to mine.
I reject the way you associated me with Allah before.'
  The wrongdoers will have a painful punishment.

23   Those who believed and did right actions
        will be admitted into Gardens
      with rivers flowing under them,
        remaining in them timelessly, for ever
          by the permission of their Lord.
        Their greeting there is 'Peace!'

24   Do you do not see how Allah
        makes a metaphor of a good word:
      a good tree whose roots are firm
        and whose branches are in heaven?
25   It bears fruit regularly
        by its Lord's permission.
      Allah makes metaphors for people
        so that hopefully they will pay heed.

26   The metaphor of a corrupt word
        is that of a rotten tree,
      uprooted on the surface of the earth.
        It has no staying-power.

27   Allah makes those who believe firm
        with the Firm Word
      in the life of this world and the Next World.
        But Allah misguides the wrongdoers.
      Allah does whatever He wills.

28   Do you not see those who have exchanged
        Allah's blessing for unbelief,
      and moved their people to the abode of ruin:
29   Hell, where they will roast?
          What an evil place to stay!

30   They have made others equal to Allah
         to misguide people from His Way.
     Say: 'Enjoy yourselves!
         Your destination is the Fire!'

31   Tell My slaves who believe
         that they should establish the prayer
     and give from what We have provided for them,
         secretly and openly,
     before a Day arrives on which there will be
         no trading and no friendship.

32   Allah is He who created the heavens and the earth
         and sends down water from the sky
             and by it brings forth fruits as provision for you.
     He has made the ships subservient to you
             to run upon the sea by His command,
         and He has made the rivers subservient to you,
33   and He has made the sun and moon subservient to you
         holding steady to their courses,
     and He has made the night and day subservient to you.

34   He has given you everything you have asked Him for.
         If you tried to number Allah's blessings,
             you could never count them.
         Man is indeed wrongdoing, ungrateful.

35   When Ibrahim said,
     'My Lord! Make this land a place of safety
         and keep me and my sons from worshipping idols.
36   My Lord! They have misguided many of mankind.
         If anyone follows me, he is with me
             but if anyone disobeys me,
         You are Ever-Forgiving, Most Merciful.
37   Our Lord! I have settled some of my offspring
         by Your Sacred House in an uncultivated valley.
     Our Lord! Let them establish the prayer!
         Make the hearts of mankind incline towards them
             and provide them with fruits,
         so that hopefully they will be thankful.
38   Our Lord! You know what we keep hidden
         and what we divulge.
     Nothing is hidden from Allah
         either on the earth or in heaven.

39 Praise be to Allah Who, despite my old age,
          has given me Isma'il and Ishaq.
             My Lord is the Hearer of Prayer.
40 My Lord! Make me and my descendants
          people who establish the prayer.
             My Lord! Accept my supplication.
41 Our Lord! Forgive me and my parents and the believers
          on the Day the Reckoning takes place.'

42 Do not consider Allah to be unaware
          of what the wrongdoers perpetrate.
    He is merely deferring them to a Day
          on which their sight will be transfixed,
43   rushing headlong –
    heads back, eyes vacant, hearts hollow.

44 Warn mankind of the Day
          when the punishment will reach them.
             Those who did wrong will say,
    'Our Lord, reprieve us for a short time.
          We will respond to Your call
             and follow the Messengers.'
    'But did you not swear to Me before
          that you would never meet your downfall,
45 even though you inhabited the houses
          of those who had wronged themselves
    and it was made clear to you
          how We had dealt with them
    and We gave you many examples?'

46 They concocted their plots,
          but their plots were with Allah,
             even if they were such
    as to make the mountains vanish.

47 Do not imagine that Allah will break
          His promise to His Messengers.
    Allah is Almighty, Exactor of Revenge.

48 On the Day the earth is changed to other than the earth,
          and the heavens likewise,
    and they parade before Allah, the One, the All-Conquering,
49   that Day you will see the evildoers yoked together in chains,

50   wearing shirts of tar, their faces enveloped in the Fire.

51   So that Allah may repay every self for what it earned.
                   Allah is swift at reckoning.

52   This is a communication to be transmitted to mankind
                   so that they may be warned by it
            and so that they will know that He is One God
                   and so that people of intelligence will pay heed.

Sura 15

Al-Hijr

In the name of Allah, All-Merciful, Most Merciful

1   Alif Lam Ra
Those are the Signs of the Book
    and a clear Qur'an.

2   It may be that those who disbelieve
    will wish that they had been Muslims.

3   Leave them to eat and enjoy themselves.
    Let false hope divert them.
      They will soon know.

4   We did not destroy any city
    without it having a set time.

5   No nation can advance its appointed time
    nor can they delay it.

6   They say, 'You, to whom the Reminder has been sent down,
    are clearly mad.
7   Why do you not bring angels to us
    if you are telling the truth?'

8   The angels only descend with the truth
    and then they would be granted no reprieve.

9   It is We Who have sent down the Reminder
    and We Who will preserve it.

10   We sent Messengers before you
           among the disparate groups of previous peoples.

11   No Messenger came to them
           without their mocking him.

12   In that way We insert it into
           the evildoers' hearts.

13   They do not believe in it,
           even though the example
     of the previous peoples
           has gone before.

14   Even if We opened up to them a door into heaven,
           and they spent the day ascending through it,

15   they would only say, 'Our eyesight is befuddled!
           Or rather we have been put under a spell!'

16   We have placed constellations in heaven
           and made them beautiful for those who look.

17   We have guarded them from every cursed Shaytan –

18   except for the one who listens stealthily,
           and he is followed by an open flame.

19   As for the earth, We stretched it out
           and cast firmly embedded mountains in it
    and made everything grow in due proportion on it.

20   And We put livelihoods in it both for you
           and for those you do not provide for.

21   There is nothing that does not have its stores with Us
           and We only send it down in a known measure.

22   We send forth the pollinating winds
           and send down water from the sky
           and give it to you to drink.
           And it is not you who keep its stores.

23   It is We who give life and cause to die
           and We are the Inheritor.

24   We know those of you who have gone ahead
           and those who are still to come.

25   It is your Lord who will gather them.
        He is All-Wise, All-Knowing.

26   We created mankind out of dried clay
        formed from fetid black mud.

27   We created the jinn before
        out of the fire of a searing wind.

28   When your Lord said to the angels,
        'I am creating a human being out of dried clay
          formed from fetid black mud
29   When I have formed him
        and breathed My Ruh into him,
    fall down in prostration in front of him!'

30   Then the angels prostrated all together,
        every one of them –
31   except Iblis.
    He disdained to be one of the prostrators.

32   He said, 'Iblis, what is it that prevents you
        being among the prostrators?'

33   He said, 'I will not prostrate to a human being
        whom You have created out of dried clay
          formed from fetid black mud.'

34   He said, 'Get out from here,
        you are accursed.
35   The curse will be on you
        till the Day of Reckoning.'

36   He said, 'My Lord, grant me a reprieve
        until the Day they are raised again.'

37   He said, 'You are among the reprieved
38   until the Day whose time is known.'

39   He said, 'My Lord, because You misled me,
        I will make things on the earth seem good to them
        and I will mislead them all, every one of them,
40   except Your slaves among them who are sincere.'

41   He said, 'This is a Straight Path to Me.
42   You have no authority over any of My slaves
           except for the misled who follow you.'
43   Hell is the promised meeting-place for all of them.
44   It has seven gates and each gate has its allotted share.

45   Those who have taqwa will be amid Gardens and Springs:
46   'Enter them in peace, in complete security!'
47   We will strip away any rancour in their hearts –
           brothers, resting on couches face-to-face.
48   They will not be affected by any tiredness there
           and they will never be made to leave.

49   Tell My slaves that I am the Ever-Forgiving, the Most Merciful,
50   but also that My punishment is the Painful Punishment.

51   And tell them about the guests of Ibrahim.
52   When they came in to him, they said, 'Peace!'
           He said, 'Truly we are afraid of you.'
53   They said, 'Do not be afraid.
           We bring you the good news of a boy of great knowledge.'
54   He said, 'Do you bring me this good news
           despite the fact of old age having reached me?
               What kind of good news are you bringing me?'
55   They said, 'We bring you good news of the truth,
           so do not be among those who despair.'
56   He said, 'Who despairs of the mercy of his Lord
           except for misguided people?'
57   He added, 'What is your business, messengers?'
58   They said, 'We have been sent to a people who are evildoers –
59   with the exception of the family of Lut,
           all of whom We will save,
60   except for his wife.
     We have decreed her to be
           one of those who stay behind.'

61   When the Messengers came to the family of Lut,
62   he said, 'You are people we do not know.'
63   They said, 'We have come to you
           with what they had doubts about.
64   We have brought you the truth
           and we are certainly truthful men.
65   Travel with your family in the dead of night,
           following behind with them in front of you.

None of you must look back.
Go where you are ordered.'

66   We revealed to him the command We had decreed:
that on the following morning
the last remnant of those people would be cut off.

67   The people of the city came, exulting at the news.

68   He said, 'These are my guests so do not put me to shame.
69   Have taqwa of Allah and do not dishonour me.'
70   They said, 'Did we not forbid you to play host to anyone at all?'
71   He said, 'Here are my daughters
if you are determined to do something.'

72   By your life! They were wandering blindly in their drunkenness!

73   So the Great Blast seized hold of them at the break of day.

74   We turned the place completely upside down
and rained down on them stones of hard-baked clay.
75   There are certainly Signs in that for the discerning.

76   They were beside a road which still exists.
77   There is certainly a Sign in that for the believers.

78   The people of the Thicket* were also wrongdoers.
79   We took revenge on them as well.
They are both beside a well-beaten track.

80   The people of al-Hijr denied the Messengers.

81   We brought them Our Signs
but they turned away from them.
82   They carved out houses from the mountains, feeling safe,
83   but the Great Blast seized hold of them in the morning,
84   so all that they earned was of no use to them.

85   We did not create the heavens and earth
and everything between them,
except with truth.

---

* The 'Thicket' may be a description or the name of an actual place. It may be another name for
the people of Madyan.

The Hour is certainly coming,
so turn away graciously.

86   Your Lord, He is the Creator, the All-Knowing.

87   We have given you the Seven Oft-repeated*
and the Magnificent Qur'an.

88   Do not direct your eyes longingly to what
We have given certain of them to enjoy.
Do not feel sad concerning them.
And take the believers under your wing.

89   Say: 'I am indeed a clear warner.'

90   Just as We sent down punishment on the dissectors,
91   those who divide the Qur'an into little pieces.

92   By your Lord, We will question them all,
every one of them,
93   about what they did!

94   Proclaim what you have been ordered to
and turn away from the idolators.

95   We are enough for you against the mockers,
96   those who set up another god besides Allah.
They will soon know!

97   We know that your breast is constricted by what they say.

98   So glorify your Lord with praise and be one of the prostrators.

99   And worship your Lord until what is Certain comes to you.

---

* This is generally considered to refer to Sura al-Fatiha.

Sura 16

An-Nahl
The Bee

In the name of Allah, All-Merciful, Most Merciful

1   Allah's command is coming, so do not try to hasten it.
 Glory be to Him!
He is exalted above anything they associate with Him.

2   He sends down angels with the Ruh of His command
  to any of His slaves He wills:
 'Give warning that there is no god but Me,
  so have taqwa of Me!'

3   He created the heavens and the earth with truth.
 He is exalted above anything they associate with Him.

4   He created man from a drop of sperm
 and yet he is an open challenger!

5   And He created livestock.
 There is warmth for you in them,
  and various uses
 and some you eat.

6   And there is beauty in them for you
  in the evening
 when you bring them home
  and in the morning
 when you drive them out to graze.

7   They carry your loads to lands
 you would never reach
  except with great difficulty.
 Your Lord is All-Gentle, Most Merciful.

8   And horses, mules and donkeys
          both to ride and for adornment.
     And He creates other things you do not know.

9   The Way should lead to Allah,
          but there are those who deviate from it.
     If He had wished He could have guided every one of you.

10   It is He who sends down water from the sky.
               From it you drink and from it come the shrubs
                    among which you graze your herds.
11   And by it He makes crops grow for you
               and olives and dates and grapes
                    and fruit of every kind.
     There is certainly a Sign in that
          for people who reflect.

12   He has made night and day subservient to you,
               and the sun and moon and stars,
                    all subject to His command.
     There are certainly Signs in that
          for people who use their intellect.

13   And also the things of varying colours
          He has created for you in the earth.
     There is certainly a Sign in that
          for people who pay heed.

14   It is He who made the sea subservient to you
               so that you can eat fresh flesh from it
                    and bring out from it ornaments to wear.
     And you see the ships cleaving through it
          so that you may seek His bounty,
     and so that hopefully you will show thanks.

15   He cast firmly embedded mountains on the earth
               so it would not move under you,
                    and rivers and pathways
               so that hopefully you would be guided,
16   and landmarks.
     And they are guided by the stars.

17   Is He who creates like him who does not create?
          So will you not pay heed?

18   If you tried to number Allah's blessings,
       you could never count them.
    Allah is Ever-Forgiving, Most Merciful.

19   Allah knows what you keep secret
       and what you make public.

20   Those you call on besides Allah
       do not create anything.
    They are themselves created.

21   They are dead, not alive,
       and they are not aware
    of when they will be raised.

22   Your God is One God.
    As for those who do not believe in the Next World,
       their hearts are in denial
    and they are puffed up with pride.

23   There is no doubt that Allah knows
       what they keep secret
          and what they make public.
    He does not love people puffed up with pride.

24   When they are asked, 'What has your Lord sent down?'
       they say, 'Myths and legends of previous peoples.'

25   So on the Day of Rising they will carry
       the full weight of their own burdens
    and some of the burdens of those
       they misguided without knowledge.
          What an evil load they bear!

26   Those before them also plotted,
       and Allah came at their building
          from the foundations
       and the roof caved in on top of them.
    The punishment came at them
       from where they did not expect.

27   Then on the Day of Rising He will disgrace them,
       and say, 'Where are My partner gods
          for whose sake you became so hostile?'

Those given knowledge will say,
    'Today there is disgrace and evil for the unbelievers.'

28   As for those the angels take in death
        while they are wronging themselves,
    they will offer their submission:
        'We did not do any evil.'
           Oh yes you did!
    Allah knows what you were doing.

29   'Enter the gates of Hell,
        remaining in it timelessly, for ever.
    How evil is the abode of the arrogant!'

30   When those who have taqwa of Allah are asked,
        'What has your Lord sent down?'
           their reply is, 'Good!'
    There is good in this world for those who do good,
        and the abode of the Next World is even better.
    How wonderful is the abode of the godfearing:
31   Gardens of Eden which they enter,
           with rivers flowing under them,
        where they have whatever they desire.
    That is how Allah repays the godfearing:
32   those the angels take in a virtuous state.
    They say, 'Peace be upon you!
        Enter the Garden for what you did.'

33   What are they waiting for but the angels to come to them
        or your Lord's command to come?
    That is like what those before them did.
        Allah did not wrong them;
           rather they wronged themselves.

34   The evil actions they did assailed them.
        They were engulfed by what they mocked.

35   The idolaters say, 'If Allah had willed
        we would not have worshipped anything apart from Him,
           neither we nor our fathers,
         nor would we have forbidden anything without His say.'
           Those before them said the same.
    Are the Messengers responsible for anything
        but clear transmission?

36   We sent a Messenger among every people saying:
        'Worship Allah and keep clear of all false gods.'
    Among them were some whom Allah guided
        but others received the misguidance they deserved.
    Travel about the earth and see the final fate of the deniers.

37   However eager you are for them to be guided,
        Allah will not guide those whom He misguides.
            They will have no helpers.

38   They swear by Allah with their most earnest oaths
        that Allah will not raise up those who die,
    when, on the contrary, it is a binding promise on Him;
        but most people do not know it.

39   It is so that He can make clear to them
        the things they differed about
    and so that those who disbelieved
        will know that they were liars.

40   Our Word to a thing when We desire it
        is just to say to it 'Be!' and it is.

41   As for those who make hijra for Allah's sake after being wronged,
        We shall give them good lodging in this world,
            and the reward of the Next World is greater still
                if they only knew –
42   those who are steadfast and put their trust in their Lord.

43   We have only ever sent before you
        men who were given Revelation –
    ask the People of the Reminder if you do not know –
44   who brought Clear Signs and Revealed Books.
    And We have sent down the Reminder to you
        so that you can make clear to mankind
            what has been sent down to them
        so that hopefully they will reflect.

45   Do those who plot evil actions feel secure
        that Allah will not cause the earth to swallow them up
    or that a punishment will not come upon them
        from where they least expect?
46   Or that He will not seize them on their travels,
        something they are powerless to prevent?

47   Or that He will not seize them little by little?
         For your Lord is All-Compassionate, Most Merciful.

48   Do they not see the things Allah has created,
         casting their shadows to the right and to the left,
             prostrating themselves before Allah
                 in complete humility?

49   Everything in the heavens
         and every creature on the earth
             prostrates to Allah,
         as do the angels.
      They are not puffed up with pride.

50   They fear their Lord above them
         and do everything they are ordered to do.

51   Allah says, 'Do not take two gods.
         He is only One God.
             So dread Me alone.'

52   Everything in the heavens and earth belongs to Him,
         and the deen belongs to Him, firmly and for ever.
      So why do you fear anyone other than Allah?

53   Any blessing you have is from Allah.
         Then when harm touches you,
             it is to Him you cry for help.

54   But when He removes the harm from you,
         a group of you associate others with their Lord,

55   ungrateful for what We have given them.
         Enjoy yourselves. You will soon know!

56   They allot a portion of the provision We have given them
         to things they have no knowledge of at all.
      By Allah, you will be asked about what you invented!

57   They allot daughters to Allah –
         glory be to Him! –
      while they have what they want!

58   When one of them is given the good news of a baby girl,
         his face darkens and he is furious.

59   He hides away from people because of the evil
         of the good news he has been given.
      Should he keep her ignominiously
         or bury her in the earth?
      What an evil judgement they make!

60   Those who do not believe in the Next World
         have an evil likeness.
      Allah's is the Highest Likeness.
         He is the Almighty, the All-Wise.

61   If Allah were to punish people for their wrong actions,
         not a single creature would be left upon the earth,
            but He defers them till a predetermined time.
      When their specified time arrives,
         they cannot delay it for a single hour
            nor can they bring it forward.

62   They allot to Allah what they themselves dislike
         and their tongues frame the lie
            that they will receive the Best.
      There is no doubt at all that they will receive the Fire
         and that they are people who go to excess.

63   By Allah, We sent Messengers to communities before your time,
         but Shaytan made their actions seem good to them.
            Therefore today he is their protector.
      They will have a painful punishment.

64   We have only sent down the Book to you
         so that you can make clear to them
            the things about which they differ,
      and as a guidance and a mercy to people who believe.

65   Allah sends down water from the sky
         and by it brings the dead earth back to life.
      There is certainly a Sign in that for people who hear.

66   There is instruction for you in cattle.
         From the contents of their bellies,
            from between the dung and blood,
         We give you pure milk to drink,
            easy for drinkers to swallow.

67   And from the fruit of the date-palm and the grape-vine
         you derive both intoxicants and wholesome provision.
      There is certainly a Sign in that for people who use their intellect.

68   Your Lord revealed to the bees:
         'Build dwellings in the mountains and the trees,
            and also in the structures which men erect.
69   Then eat from every kind of fruit
            and travel the paths of your Lord,
         which have been made easy for you to follow.'
      From inside them comes a drink of varying colours,
         containing healing for mankind.
      There is certainly a Sign in that for people who reflect.

70   Allah created you and then will take you back again.
         And some of you revert to the lowest form of life
            so that after having knowledge,
               you know nothing at all.
         Allah is All-Knowing, All-Powerful.

71   Allah has favoured some of you over others in provision,
         but those who have been favoured
            do not give their provision to their slaves
         so they become the same in respect of it.
      So why do they renounce the blessings of Allah?

72   Allah has given you wives from among yourselves,
         and given you children and grandchildren
            from your wives,
         and provided good things for you.
      So why do they believe in falsehood
         and reject the blessings of Allah,
73   and worship, instead of Allah,
         things that have no control over their provision
            from the heavens or earth in any way,
         and are themselves completely impotent?

74   Do not try to make metaphors for Allah.
         Allah knows and you do not know.

75   Allah does make a metaphor:
         an owned slave possessing no power over anything,
      and someone We have given plentiful provision
         who gives out from it secretly and openly.

Are they the same?
Praise be to Allah! They are not!
But most people do not know it.

76 Allah makes another metaphor:
two men, one of them deaf and dumb,
unable to do anything,
a burden on his master,
no matter where he directs him
he brings no good,
is he the same as someone
who commands justice
and is on a straight path?

77 The Unseen of the heavens and earth belongs to Allah.
The matter of the Hour is only the blink of an eye away,
or even nearer.
Allah has power over all things.

78 Allah brought you out of your mothers' wombs
knowing nothing at all,
and gave you hearing, sight and hearts
so that perhaps you would show thanks.

79 Do they not see the birds suspended in mid-air up in the sky?
Nothing holds them there except Allah.
There are certainly Signs in that for people who believe.

80 Allah has made your houses places of rest for you
and made houses for you out of cattle hides
which are light for you to carry
both when you are travelling
and when you are staying in one place.
And from their wool and fur and hair
you obtain clothing and carpets
and household utensils for a time.

81 Allah has made shaded places for you in what He has created
and He has made shelters for you in the mountains
and He has made shirts for you to protect you from the heat
and shirts to protect you from each other's violence.
In that way He perfects His blessing on you
so that hopefully you will become Muslims.

82   But if they turn their backs,
        you are only responsible
           for clear transmission.

83   They acknowledge Allah's blessing
        and then deny it.
     Most of them are unbelievers.

84   On the Day We raise up a witness from every nation,
        those who disbelieved will not be excused
           nor will they be able to appease Allah.

85   When those who did wrong see the punishment,
        it will not be lightened for them.
     They will be granted no reprieve.

86   When those who associated others with Allah
        see those they associated, they will say,
     'Our Lord, these are our partner gods,
        the ones we called upon apart from You.'
     But they will fling their words back in their faces:
        'You are truly liars!'

87   On that Day they will offer their submission to Allah
        and the things they invented will abandon them.

88   As for those who disbelieve
        and barred access to the way of Allah,
     We will heap punishment on top of their punishment
        because of the corruption they brought about.

89   On that Day We will raise up among every community
        a witness against them from amongst themselves,
           and bring you as a witness against them.
     We have sent down the Book to you making all things clear
        and as guidance and mercy and good news for the Muslims.

90   Allah commands justice
        and doing good
           and giving to relatives.
     And He forbids indecency
        and doing wrong
           and tyranny.
     He warns you so that hopefully you will pay heed.

91 Be true to Allah's contract when you have agreed to it,
and do not break your oaths once they are confirmed
and you have made Allah your guarantee.
Allah knows what you do.

92 Do not be like a woman who spoils the thread she has spun
by unravelling it after it is strong,
by making your oaths a means of deceiving one another,
merely because one community is bigger than another.
Allah is only testing you by this.
He will make clear to you on the Day of Rising
the things about which you differed.

93 If Allah had willed He would have made you one community.
However, He misguides anyone He wills
and guides anyone He wills.
You will be questioned about what you did.

94 Do not make your oaths a means of deceiving one another
or your foot will slip after it was firmly placed
and you will taste evil for barring access to the Way of Allah
and you will have a terrible punishment.

95 Do not sell Allah's contract for a paltry price.
What is with Allah is better for you
if you only knew.

96 What is with you runs out
but what is with Allah goes on for ever.
Those who were steadfast will be recompensed
according to the best of what they did.

97 Anyone who acts rightly,
male or female,
being a believer,
We will give them a good life
and We will recompense them
according to the best of what they did.

98 Whenever you recite the Qur'an,
seek refuge with Allah from the accursed Shaytan.

99 He has no authority over those who believe
and put their trust in their Lord.

100   He only has authority over those who take him as a friend
            and associate others with Allah.

101   If We replace one ayat with another one –
            and Allah knows best what He is sending down –
        they say, 'You are just inventing this!'
            No indeed! Most of them have no knowledge.

102   Say: 'The Purest Ruh has brought it down
                from your Lord with truth,
            to make those who believe firm,
        and as guidance and good news for the Muslims.'

103   We know that they say,
            'It is only a human being who is teaching him.'
        The language of him they allude to is a foreign one
            whereas this is in clear and lucid Arabic.

104   As for those who do not believe in Allah's Signs,
            Allah will not guide them
        and they will have a painful punishment.

105   Those who do not believe in Allah's Signs
            are merely inventing lies.
        It is they who are the liars.

106   Those who reject Allah after having believed –
            except for someone forced to do it
                whose heart remains at rest in its faith –
        but as for those whose breasts become dilated with unbelief,
            anger from Allah will come down on them.
                They will have a terrible punishment.

107   That is because they prefer
            the life of this world to the Next World
        and because Allah does not guide unbelieving people.

108   Those are the people whose hearts, hearing and sight
            Allah has sealed up.
                They are the unaware.

109   There is no doubt
            that in the Next World
                they will be the losers.

110   But to those who made hijra after they were persecuted
            and then did jihad and remained steadfast,
        to them your Lord is Ever-Forgiving, Most Merciful.

111   On that Day every self will come to argue for itself
            and every self will be paid in full for what it did.
                They will not be wronged.

112   Allah makes an example of a city which was safe and at peace,
            its provision coming to it plentifully from every side.
        Then it showed ingratitude for Allah's blessings
            so Allah made it wear the robes of hunger and fear
                for what it did.
113   A Messenger from among them came to them
                but they denied him.
        So the punishment seized them and they were wrongdoers.

114   So eat from what Allah has provided for you,
            halal and good,
        and be thankful for the blessing of Allah
            if it is Him you worship.

115   He has forbidden you carrion, blood and pork
            and anything consecrated to other than Allah.
        But if someone is forced to eat it,
            without desiring to or going to excess in it,
        your Lord is Ever-Forgiving, Most Merciful.

116   Do not say about what your lying tongues describe:
            'This is halal and this is haram,'
                inventing lies against Allah.
        Those who invent lies against Allah are not successful –
117   a brief enjoyment,
        then they will have a painful punishment.

118   We forbade the Jews
            those things We told you about before.
        We did not wrong them;
            rather they wronged themselves.

119   But to those who do evil in ignorance
            and then after that repent and put things right,
        to them your Lord is Ever-Forgiving, Most Merciful.

120   Ibrahim was a community in himself,
           exemplary, obedient to Allah,
               a man of pure natural belief.
           He was not one of the idolators.

121   He was thankful for His blessings.
           Allah chose him
       and guided him to a straight path.

122   We gave him good in this world
           and in the Next World he will be one of the righteous.

123   Then We revealed to you:
           'Follow the religion of Ibrahim,
               a man of pure natural faith.
           He was not one of the idolators.'

124   The Sabbath was only enjoined on those who differed about it.
           Your Lord will judge between them on the Day of Rising
               regarding the things about which they differed.

125   Call to the way of your Lord with wisdom and fair admonition,
           and argue with them in the kindest way.
       Your Lord knows best who is misguided from His way.
           And He knows best who are guided.

126   If you want to retaliate,
           retaliate to the same degree
               as the injury done to you.
           But if you are patient,
               it is better to be patient.

127   Be patient.
           But your patience is only by Allah.
               Do not be grieved by them
       and do not be constricted by the plots they hatch.

128   Allah is with those who have taqwa of Him
           and with the good-doers.

Sura 17

Al-Isra'
The Night Journey

In the name of Allah, All-Merciful, Most Merciful

1   Glory be to Him who took His slave on a journey by night
        from the Masjid al-Haram to the Masjid al-Aqsa,*
           whose surroundings We have blessed,
        in order to show him some of Our Signs.
    He is the All-Hearing, the All-Seeing.

2   We gave Musa the Book and made it
        guidance for the tribe of Israel:
    'Do not take anyone besides Me as a guardian.'

3   Descendants of those We carried with Nuh.
        He was a grateful slave.

4   We decreed in the Book for the tribe of Israel:
        'You will twice cause corruption on the earth
           and you will rise to a great height.
5   When the promised first time came,
        We sent against you slaves of Ours
           possessing great force,
        and they ransacked your houses,
           rampaging right through them.
    It was a promise which was fulfilled.
6   Then once again We gave you the upper hand over them
        and supplied you with more wealth and children
           and made you the most numerous group.
7   If you do good, you do it to yourselves.
        If you do evil, you do it to your detriment.

---

* In Jerusalem.

When the next promised time arrived,
>it was so that they could injure you and enter the Temple
>>as they had entered it the first time,
>and in order to completely destroy what they had conquered.

8   It may well be that your Lord will have mercy on you.
>But if you revert to what you did, We also will revert.
>>We have made Hell a prison for the unbelievers.'

9   This Qur'an guides to the most upright Way
>and gives good news to the believers
>>who do right actions
>that they will have a large reward.

10   But as for those who do not believe in the Next World,
>We have prepared for them a painful punishment.

11   Man prays for evil just as he prays for good.
>Man is prone to be impetuous.

12   We made the night and day two Signs.
>We blotted out the Sign of the night
and made the Sign of the day a time for seeing
>so that you can seek favour from your Lord
and will know the number of years
>and the reckoning of time.
We have made all things very clear.

13   We have fastened the destiny of every man about his neck
>and on the Day of Rising We will bring out a Book for him
>>which he will find spread open in front of him.

14   'Read your Book! Today your own self
>is reckoner enough against you!'

15   Whoever is guided is only guided to his own good.
>Whoever is misguided is only misguided to his detriment.
No burden-bearer can bear another's burden.
>We never punish until We have sent a Messenger.

16   When We desire to destroy a city,
>We send a command to the affluent in it
>>and they become deviant in it
>and the Word is justly carried out against it
>>and We annihilate it completely.

17 How many generations We destroyed after Nuh!
Your Lord is well able to be aware of
and see the wrong actions of His slaves!

18 As for anyone who desires this fleeting existence,
We hasten in it whatever We will
to whoever We want.
Then We will consign him to Hell
where he will roast, reviled and driven out.

19 But as for anyone who desires the Next World,
and strives for it with the striving it deserves,
being a believer,
the striving of such people will be gratefully acknowledged.

20 We sustain each one,
the former and the latter,
through the generous giving of your Lord;
and the giving of your Lord is not restricted.

21 Look how We favour some of them over others.
But the Next World has higher ranks and greater favours.

22 Do not set up any other god together with Allah
and so sit there reviled and forsaken.

23 Your Lord has decreed
that you should worship none but Him,
and that you should show kindness to your parents.
Whether one or both of them reach old age with you,
do not say 'Ugh!' to them out of irritation
and do not be harsh with them
but speak to them with gentleness and generosity.

24 Take them under your wing, out of mercy, with due humility
and say: 'Lord, show mercy to them
as they did in looking after me when I was small.'

25 Your Lord knows best what is in your selves.
If you are righteous,
He is Ever-Forgiving to the remorseful.

26 Give your relatives their due,
and the very poor and travellers
but do not squander what you have.

27   Squanderers are brothers to the shaytans,
                   and Shaytan was ungrateful to his Lord.

28   But if you do turn away from them,
                   seeking the mercy you hope for from your Lord,
            then speak to them with words that bring them ease.

29   Do not keep your hand chained to your neck
                   but do not extend it either to its full extent
            so that you sit there blamed and destitute.

30   Your Lord expands the provision of anyone He wills
                   and restricts it.
            He is aware of and sees His slaves.

31   Do not kill your children out of fear of being poor.
                   We will provide for them and you.
            Killing them is a terrible mistake.

32   And do not go near to fornication.
                   It is an indecent act, an evil way.

33   Do not kill any person Allah has made inviolate,
                   except with the right to do so.
            If someone is wrongly killed
                   We have given authority to his next of kin.
            But he should not be excessive in taking life.
                   He will be helped.

34   Do not go near the property of orphans
                   before they reach maturity,
                       except in a good way.
                   Fulfil your contracts.
                       Contracts will be asked about.

35   Give full measure when you measure
                   and weigh with a level balance.
            That is better and gives the best result.

36   Do not pursue what you have no knowledge of.
                   Hearing, sight and hearts will all be questioned.

37   Do not strut arrogantly about the earth.
           You will certainly never split the earth apart
       nor will you ever rival the mountains in height.

38   All of that is evil action and hateful in the sight of your Lord.

39   That is part of the wisdom your Lord has revealed to you.
           Do not set up another god together with Allah
               and so be thrown into Hell,
                   blamed and driven out.

40   Has your Lord honoured you with sons
           and Himself taken the angels as daughters?
       It is truly something terrible that you say!

41   We have made things clear in this Qur'an
           so that they might pay heed,
       but it only makes them run away the more!

42   Say: 'If there had, as you say, been other gods together with Him,
           they would have sought a way to the Master of the Throne.'

43   Glory be to Him!
           He is exalted above what they say
               in Greatness and Sublimity!

44   The seven heavens and the earth and everyone in them
           glorify Him.
       There is nothing which does not glorify Him with praise
           but you do not understand their glorification.
               He is All-Forbearing, Ever-Forgiving.

45   When you recite the Qur'an,
           We place an obscuring veil between you
               and those who do not believe in the Next World.
46   We have placed covers on their hearts,
           preventing them from understanding it,
               and heaviness in their ears.
       When you mention your Lord alone in the Qur'an,
           they turn their backs and run away.

47   We know how they listen when they listen to you,
           and when they confer together secretly,

and when the wrongdoers say,
'You are only following a man who is bewitched!'

48   Look how they make likenesses of you and go astray.
       They are unable to find their way.

49   They say, 'What! When we are bones and crumbled dust,
       will we then be raised up as a new creation!'

50   Say: 'It would not matter if you were rock or iron
51   or indeed any created thing that you think is harder still!'
         They will say, 'Who will bring us back again?'
       Say: 'He who brought you into being in the first place.'
     They will shake their heads at you and ask, 'When will it happen?'
       Say: 'It may well be that it is very near.'

52   On the Day He calls you, you will respond by praising Him
       and think that you have only tarried a very short time.

53   Say to My slaves that they should only say the best.
       Shaytan wants to stir up trouble between them.
         Shaytan is an outright enemy to man.

54   Your Lord knows you best.
       If He wills, He will have mercy on you,
         and, if He wills, He will punish you.
       We did not send you to be their guardian.

55   My Lord knows best everyone in the heavens and earth.
       We favoured some of the Prophets over others.
         And We gave Dawud the Zabur.

56   Say: 'Call on those you make claims for apart from Him.
       They possess no power to remove any harm from you
         or to change anything.'

57   Those they call on are themselves seeking
       the means by which they might approach their Lord –
         even those who are the closest to Him –
     and are hoping for His mercy and fearing his punishment.
     The punishment of your Lord is truly something to be feared.

58   There is no city We will not destroy before the Day of Rising,
          or punish with a terrible punishment.
             That is inscribed in the Book.

59   Nothing has prevented Us sending you Signs
          except the fact that the previous peoples denied them.
      We gave Thamud the she-camel as a visible Sign,
          and then they mistreated her.
      We do not send Signs except to frighten people.

60   When We said to you, 'Surely your Lord
          encompasses the people with His knowledge.'
      We only appointed the vision We showed you
             and the Accursed Tree in the Qur'an
          as a trial and temptation for the people.
      We frighten them,
          but it only increases them
             in their excessive insolence.

61   When We said to the angels,
          'Prostrate yourselves to Adam!'
             they prostrated, except for Iblis.
      He said 'What! Am I to prostrate
          to one You have created out of clay?'

62   He said, 'Do You see this creature
          You have honoured over me?
      If You reprieve me till the Day of Rising,
          I will be the master of his descendants
             except for a very few.'

63   He said, 'Go! And as for any who follow you,
          your repayment is Hell,
             repayment in full!

64   Stir up any of them you can with your voice
          and rally against them your cavalry and your infantry
      and share with them in their children and their wealth
          and make them promises!
      The promise of Shaytan is nothing but delusion.

65   But as for My slaves,
      you will not have any authority over them.'
          Your Lord suffices as a guardian.

66   Your Lord is He who propels the ships on the sea for you
          so that you may seek His bounty.
     He is indeed Most Merciful to you.

67   When harm occurs to you at sea,
          those you call on vanish –
              except for Him alone!
     But when He delivers you to dry land,
          you turn away.
     Man truly is ungrateful.

68   Do you feel secure against Him
          causing the shore to swallow you up
              or sending against you a sudden squall of stones?
     Then you will find no one to be your guardian.
69   Or do you feel secure against Him
          taking you back into it another time
              and sending a violent storm against you
                  and drowning you for your ingratitude?
     Then you will find no one to defend you against Us.

70   We have honoured the sons of Adam
          and conveyed them on land and sea
     and provided them with good things
          and favoured them greatly
              over many We have created.

71   On the Day We summon every people with their records,
          those who are given their Book in their right hand
     will read their Book and they will not be wronged
          by even the smallest speck.

72   Those who are blind in this world
          will be blind in the Next World
              and even further off the Path.

73   They were very near to enticing you away
          from some of what We have revealed to you,
     hoping that you would invent something against Us.
          Then they would have taken you as their intimate.
74   If We had not made you firm,
          you would have leaned towards them
              a little.

75   Then We would have let you taste
          a double punishment in life
              and a double punishment in death.
          You would not have found any helper against Us.
76   They were very near to scaring you from the land
          with the object of expelling you from it.
      But had they done so they would only
          have remained there a short time after you.

77   That was the pattern with those We sent before you
          as Our Messengers.
      You will not find any changing of Our pattern.

78   Establish the prayer
          from the time the sun declines
              until the darkening of the night,
          and also the recitation at dawn.
      The dawn recitation is certainly witnessed.

79   And stay awake for prayer during part of the night
          as a supererogatory action for yourself.
      It may well be that your Lord
          will raise you to a Praiseworthy Station.

80   Say: 'My Lord, make my entry sincere
          and make my leaving sincere
      and grant me supporting authority
          direct from Your Presence.'

81   Say: 'Truth has come and falsehood has vanished.
          Falsehood is always bound to vanish.'

82   We send down in the Qur'an that which
          is a healing and a mercy to the believers,
              but it only increases the wrongdoers in loss.

83   When We bless man, he turns away and draws aside.
          When evil touches him, he despairs.

84   Say: 'Each man acts according to his nature,
          but your Lord knows best
              who is best guided on the Path.'

85   They will ask you about the Ruh.
                 Say: 'The Ruh is my Lord's concern.
            You have only been given a little knowledge.'

86   If We wished We could take away what We have revealed to you
                 and then you would not find any to guard you from Us –
87   but for a mercy from your Lord.
            His favour to you is indeed immense.

88   Say: 'If both men and jinn banded together
                 to produce the like of this Qur'an,
            they could never produce anything like it,
                 even if they backed each other up.'

89   We have variegated throughout this Qur'an
                 all kinds of examples for people,
            but most people spurn anything but unbelief.

90   They say, 'We will not believe you
                 until you make a spring gush out from the earth for us;
91   or have a garden of dates and grapes
                 which you make rivers come pouring through;
92   or make the sky, as you claim, fall down on us in lumps;
                 or bring Allah and the angels here as a guarantee;
93   or possess a house built out of gleaming gold;
                 or ascend up into heaven –
            and even then we will not believe in your ascent
                 unless you bring us down a book to read!'
            Say: 'Glory be to my Lord!
                 Am I anything but a human messenger?'

94   Nothing prevents people from believing
                 when guidance comes to them
                       but the fact that they say,
            'Has Allah sent a human being as Messenger?'

95   Say: 'If there had been angels on the earth
                 going about in peace,
            We would have sent down to them
                 an angel from heaven as Messenger.'

96   Say: 'Allah is a sufficient witness between me and you.
                 He is certainly aware of and sees His slaves.'

97   Whoever Allah guides
             is truly guided.
        But as for those He leads astray,
             you will not find any protectors for them
                  apart from Him.
        We will gather them on the Day of Rising,
             flat on their faces,
                  blind, dumb and deaf.
        Their shelter will be Hell.
             Whenever the Blaze dies down,
                  We will increase it for them.

98   That is their repayment for rejecting Our Signs
             and saying, 'What, when we are bones and crumbled dust,
                  will we then be raised up as a new creation?'

99   Do they not see that Allah,
             Who created the heavens and earth,
                  has the power to create the like of them,
             and has appointed fixed terms for them
                  of which there is no doubt?
        But the wrongdoers still spurn anything but unbelief.

100   Say: 'Even if you possessed the vast storehouses
             of my Lord's mercy,
        you would still hold back, out of the fear that they would run out.'
             Truly man is niggardly!

101   We gave Musa nine Clear Signs.
             Ask the tribe of Israel about when he came to them
                  and Pharaoh said to him,
             'Musa, I think you are bewitched.'

102   He said, 'You know that no one sent these down
             but the Lord of the heavens and earth
                  to be clear proofs.
             Pharaoh, I think you are destroyed.'

103   He wanted to scare them from the land
             but We drowned him
        and every one of those with him.

104   We said to the tribe of Israel after that,
             'Inhabit the land and, when the promise

of the Next World comes,
We will produce you as a motley crowd.'

105   We have sent it down with truth
and with truth it has come down.
We only sent you to bring good news
and to give warning.

106   We have divided up the Qur'an,
so you can recite it to mankind at intervals,
and We have sent it down little by little.

107   Say: 'Believe in it or do not believe in it.'
Certainly, when it is recited to them,
those who were given knowledge before it
fall on their faces in prostration,
108   saying, 'Glory be to our Lord!
The promise of our Lord is truly fulfilled!'
109   Weeping, they fall to the ground in prostration,
and it increases them in humility.

110   Say: 'Call on Allah or call on the All-Merciful,
whichever you call upon,
the Most Beautiful Names are His.'
Do not be too loud in your prayer or too quiet in it,
but try to find a way between the two.
111   And say: 'Praise be to Allah Who has had no son
and Who has no partner in His Kingdom
and Who needs no one to protect Him from abasement.'
And proclaim His Greatness repeatedly!

Sura 18

Al-Kahf
The Cave

In the name of Allah, All-Merciful, Most Merciful

1   Praise belongs to Allah
        Who has sent down the Book to His slave
           and has put no crookedness in it.
2   It is straight, to warn of violent force direct from Him,
        and to give the good news to the believers,
           those who do right actions,
        that for them there is an excellent reward,
3   a place in which they will remain for ever,
4   and to warn those who say 'Allah has a son.'
5   They have no knowledge of this,
        neither they nor their fathers.
    It is a monstrous utterance
        which has issued from their mouths.
    What they say is nothing but a lie.

6   Perhaps you may destroy yourself with grief,
        chasing after them,
    if they do not believe in these words.

7   We made everything on the earth adornment for it
        so that We could test them to see
           whose actions are the best.

8   We will certainly make everything on it a barren wasteland.

9   Do you consider that the Companions of the Cave and Ar-Raqim
        were one of the most remarkable of Our Signs?

10   When the young men took refuge in the cave and said,
            'Our Lord, give us mercy directly from You
        and open the way for us to right guidance in our situation.'

11   So We sealed their ears with sleep
            in the cave for a number of years.
12   Then We woke them up again
            so that We might see which of the two groups
        would better calculate the time they had stayed there.

13   We will relate their story to you with truth.
            They were young men who believed in their Lord
                and We increased them in guidance.
14   We fortified their hearts when they stood up and said,
            'Our Lord is the Lord of the heavens and the earth
                and We will not call on any god apart from Him.
            We would in that case have uttered an abomination.
15   These people of ours have taken gods apart from Him.
            Why do they not produce a clear authority concerning them?
                Who could do greater wrong than someone
                    who invents a lie against Allah?
16   When you have separated yourselves from them
            and everything they worship except Allah,
                take refuge in the cave
            and your Lord will unfold His mercy to you
        and open the way to the best for you in your situation.'

17   You would have seen the sun, when it rose,
            inclining away from their cave towards the right,
        and, when it set, leaving them behind on the left,
            while they were lying in an open part of it.
                That was one of Allah's Signs.
            Whoever Allah guides is truly guided.
        But if He misguides someone,
            you will find no protector for them
                to guide them rightly.
18   You would have supposed them to be awake
            whereas in fact they were asleep.
        We turned them to the right and to the left,
            and, at the entrance, their dog stretched out its paws.
        If you had looked down and seen them,
            you would have turned from them and run
        and have been filled with terror at the sight of them.

19   That was the situation when we woke them up
        so they could question one another.
    One of them asked, 'How long have you been here?'
        They replied, 'We have been here for a day or part of a day.'
    They said, 'Your Lord knows best how long you have been here.
        Send one of your number into the city
            with this silver you have,
    so he can see which food is purest and bring you some of it to eat.
        But he should go about with caution
            so that no one is aware of you,

20   for if they find out about you they will stone you
                or make you revert to their religion
            and then you will never have success.'

21   Accordingly We made them chance upon them unexpectedly
        so they might know that Allah's promise is true
            and that there is no doubt about the Hour.
    When they were arguing among themselves about the matter,
        they said, 'Wall up their cave,
            their Lord knows best about them.'
    But those who got the better of the argument concerning them
        said, 'We will build a place of worship over them.'

22   They will say, 'There were three of them,
        their dog being the fourth.'
    They will say, 'There were five of them,
        their dog being the sixth,'
            guessing at the Unseen.
    And they will say, 'There were seven of them,
        their dog being the eighth.'
    Say: 'My Lord knows best their number.
        Those who know about them are very few.'

23   So do not enter into any argument concerning them,
        except in relation to what is clearly known.
    And do not seek the opinion of any of them regarding them.

24   Never say about anything,
        'I will do that tomorrow,'
            without adding 'If Allah wills.'
    Remember your Lord when you forget,
        and say, 'Hopefully my Lord will guide me
    to something closer to right guidance than this.'

25   They stayed in their Cave for three hundred years
        and added nine.

26   Say: 'Allah knows best how long they stayed.
        The Unseen of the heavens and the earth belongs to Him.
            How perfectly He sees, how well He hears!
        They have no protector apart from Him.
            Nor does He share His rule with anyone.'

27   Recite what has been revealed to you of your Lord's Book.
        No one can change His Words.
    You will never find any safe haven apart from Him.

28   Restrain yourself patiently with those
        who call on their Lord morning and evening,
            desiring His face.
    Do not turn your eyes from them,
        desiring the attractions of this world.
    And do not obey someone whose heart
        We have made neglectful of Our remembrance
    and who follows his own whims and desires
        and whose life has transgressed all bounds.

29   Say: 'It is the truth from your Lord;
        so let whoever wishes believe
            and whoever wishes disbelieve.'
    We have prepared for the wrongdoers a Fire
        whose billowing walls of smoke will hem them in.
    If they call for help, they will be helped with water
        like seething molten brass, frying their faces.
    What a noxious drink! What an evil repose!

30   But as for those who believe and do right actions,
        We will not let the wage of good-doers go to waste.

31   They will have Gardens of Eden
        with rivers flowing under them.
    They will be adorned in them with bracelets made of gold
        and wear green garments made of the finest silk
            and rich brocade,
        reclining there on couches under canopies.
    What an excellent reward! What a wonderful repose!

32   Make an example for them of two men.
        To one of them We gave two gardens of grape-vines
            and surrounded them with date-palms,
            putting between them some cultivated land.

33　　　　Both gardens yielded their crops and did not suffer any loss,
　　　　　　and We made a river flow right through the middle of them.

34　　　　He was a man of wealth and property
　　　　　　and he said to his companion, debating with him,
　　　　'I have more wealth than you and more people under me.'

35　　　　He entered his garden and wronged himself by saying,
　　　　'I do not think that this will ever end.

36　　　　I do not think the Hour will ever come.
　　　　But if I should be sent back to my Lord,
　　　　　　I will definitely get something better in return.'

37　　　　His companion, with whom he was debating, said to him,
　　　　　　'Do you then disbelieve in Him who created you from dust,
　　　　then from a drop of sperm, and then formed you as a man?

38　　　　　　He is, however, Allah, my Lord,
　　　　　　and I will not associate anyone with my Lord.

39　　　　Why, when you entered your garden, did you not say,
　　　　　　"It is as Allah wills, there is no strength but in Allah"?
　　　　Though you see me with less wealth and children
　　　　　　than you possess,

40　　　　it may well be that my Lord will give me
　　　　　　something better than your garden
　　　　and send down on it a fireball from the sky
　　　　　　so that morning finds it a shifting heap of dust,

41　　　　or morning finds its water drained into the earth
　　　　　　so that you cannot get at it.'

42　　　　The fruits of his labour were completely destroyed
　　　　　　and he woke up wringing his hands in grief,
　　　　　　　　rueing everything that he had spent on it.
　　　　It was a ruin with all its trellises fallen in.
　　　　　　He said, 'Oh, if only I had not associated
　　　　　　　　anyone with my Lord!'

43　　　　There was no group to come to his aid, besides Allah,
　　　　　　and he was not given any help.

44　　　　In that situation the only protection is with Allah, the Real.
　　　　　　He gives the best reward and the best outcome.

45　　　　Make a metaphor for them of the life of this world.
　　　　　　It is like water which We send down from the sky
　　　　　　　　and the plants of the earth combine with it
　　　　　　but then become dry chaff scattered by the winds.
　　　　Allah has absolute power over everything.

46   Wealth and sons are an embellishment of the life of this world.
               But, in your Lord's sight, right actions which are lasting
                   bring a better reward and are a better basis for hope.

47   On the Day We make the mountains move
               and you see the earth laid bare
       and We gather them together,
               not leaving out a single one of them,
48   they will be paraded before your Lord in ranks:
               'You have come to Us just as We created you at first.
                   Yes indeed! Even though you claimed
                   that We would not fix a time with you.'

49   The Book will be set in place and you will see
               the evildoers fearful of what is in it.
       They will say, 'Alas for us! What is this Book
               which does not pass over any action,
                   small or great,
               without recording it?'
       They will find there everything they did
               and your Lord will not wrong anyone at all.

50   When We said to the angels,
               'Prostrate yourselves to Adam,'
       they prostrated with the exception of Iblis.
               He was one of the jinn
       and wantonly deviated from his Lord's command.
               Do you take him and his offspring
                   as protectors apart from Me
                       when they are your enemy?
               How evil is the exchange the wrongdoers make!

51   I did not make them witnesses
               of the creation of the heavens and the earth
                   nor of their own creation.
       I would not take as assistants those who lead astray!

52   On the Day He says, 'Call My partner-gods,
               those for whom you made such claims,'
       they will call on them but they will not respond to them.
               We will place between them an unbridgeable gulf.

53　The evildoers will see the Fire
　　　　and realise they are going to fall into it
　　　　　　and find no way of escaping from it.

54　We have variegated throughout this Qur'an
　　　　all kinds of examples for people,
　　but, more than anything else, man is argumentative!

55　When guidance came to the people
　　　　nothing prevented them from believing
　　　　　　and asking for forgiveness from their Lord
　　but the fact that the pattern of previous peoples
　　　　　　did not happen to them
　　or that the punishment did not appear before their eyes.

56　We only send the Messengers
　　　　to bring good news
　　　　　　and to give warning.
　　Those who disbelieve use fallacious arguments
　　　　to deny the truth.
　　They make a mockery of My Signs
　　　　and also of the warning they were given.

57　Who could do greater wrong than someone
　　　　who is reminded of the Signs of his Lord
　　and then turns away from them,
　　　　forgetting all that he has done before?
　　We have placed covers on their hearts,
　　　　preventing them from understanding it,
　　　　　　and heaviness in their ears.
　　Though you call them to guidance,
　　　　they will nonetheless never be guided.

58　Your Lord is the Ever-Forgiving, the Possessor of Mercy.
　　　　If He had taken them to task
　　　　　　for what they have earned,
　　　　He would have hastened their punishment.
　　Instead, they have a promised appointment
　　　　and they will not find any refuge from it.

59　Those cities: We destroyed them when they did wrong
　　　　and fixed a promised time for their destruction.

60   Remember when Musa said to his servant, 'I will not give up
          until I reach the meeting-place of the two seas,
            even if I must press on for many years.'

61   But when they reached their meeting-place,
          they forgot their fish
        which quickly burrowed its way into the sea.

62   When they had gone a distance further on,
          he said to his servant, 'Bring us our morning meal.
            Truly this journey of ours has made us tired.'

63   He said, 'Do you see what has happened?
          When we went to find shelter at the rock,
            I forgot the fish.
     No one made me forget to remember it except Shaytan.
          It found its way into the sea in an amazing way.'

64   He said, 'That is the very thing that we were looking for!'
          So, following their footsteps, they retraced their route.

65   They found a slave of Ours whom We had granted mercy from Us
          and whom We had also given knowledge direct from Us.

66   Musa said to him, 'May I follow you
          on condition that you teach me
          some of the right guidance you have been taught?'

67   He said, 'You will not be able to bear with me.

68   How indeed could you bear with patience
          something you have not encompassed in your knowledge?'

69   Musa said, 'You will find me patient, if Allah wills,
          and I will not disobey you in any matter.'

70   He said, 'Then if you follow me,
          do not question me about anything
        until I myself make mention of it to you.'

71   They continued until they boarded a boat and he scuttled it.
         Then Musa said, 'Did you scuttle it
          so that its owners might be drowned?
        This is truly a dreadful thing that you have done!'

72   He said, 'Did I not say
         that you would not be able to bear with me?'

73   Musa said, 'Do not take me to task because I forgot.
        Do not demand of me something which is too difficult.'

74   So they went on until they met a youngster whom he killed.
         Musa said, 'Have you killed a boy who has done no wrong,
            without it being in retaliation for someone else?
        This is truly an appalling thing that you have done!'

75   He said, 'Did I not tell you
         that you would not be able to bear with me?'

76   Musa said, 'If I ask you about anything after this,
              then you should no longer keep me company.
              I will have given you excuse enough.'
77   So they went on until they reached the inhabitants of a town.
              They asked them for food but they refused them hospitality.
              They found there a wall about to fall down
                    and he built it up.
              Musa said, 'If you had wanted, you could have taken a wage
              for doing that.'
78   He said, 'This is where you and I part company.
              I will let you know the explanation of those things
                    about which you were not able to restrain yourself.
79   As for the boat,
              it belonged to some poor people who worked on the sea.
              I wanted to damage it
                    because a king was coming behind them,
                         commandeering every boat.
80   As for the boy, his parents were believers
              and we feared that he would darken their days
                    with excessive insolence and unbelief.
81   We wanted their Lord to give them in exchange
              a purer son than him, one more compassionate.
82   As for the wall, it belonged to two young orphans in the town
              and there was a treasure underneath it,
                    belonging to them.
              Their father was one of the righteous
                    and your Lord wanted them to come of age
              and then to unearth their treasure as a mercy from your Lord.
                    I did not do it of my own volition.
              That is the explanation of the things
                    about which you were not able to restrain yourself.'

83   They will ask you about Dhu'l-Qarnayn.
              Say: 'I will tell you something about him.'
84   We gave him power and authority on the earth
              and granted him a way to everything.
85   So he followed a way
86   until he reached the setting of the sun
                    and found it setting in a muddy spring
                         and found a people by it.
              We said, 'Dhu'l-Qarnayn! You can either punish them
                    or else you can treat them with gentleness.'

87   He said, 'As for those who do wrong, we will punish them
         and then they will be returned to their Lord
     and He will punish them with a dreadful punishment.

88   But as for him who believes and acts rightly,
         he will receive the best of rewards
     and we will issue a command, making things easy for him.'

89   Then he followed a way
90   until he reached the rising of the sun
         and found it rising on a people to whom
            We had not given any shelter from it.
91   Our knowledge encompasses all that happened to him.

92   Then he followed a path
93   until he arrived between the two mountains
         where he found a people scarcely able to understand speech.
94   They said, 'Dhu'l-Qarnayn!
         Yajuj and Majuj are causing corruption in the land.
            Can we, therefore, pay tribute to you
         in return for your constructing
            a barrier between us and them?'
95   He said, 'The power my Lord has granted me is better than that.
         Just give me a strong helping hand
            and I will build a solid barrier between you and them.
96   Bring me ingots of iron!'
         Then, when he had made it level between
            the two high mountain-sides, he said, 'Blow!'
         and when he had made it a red hot fire,
            he said, 'Bring me molten brass to pour over it.'
97   They were, therefore, unable to climb over it
         nor were they able to make a breach in it.
98   He said, 'This is a mercy from my Lord.
         But when my Lord's promise comes about,
            He will crush it flat.
         The promise of my Lord is surely true.'

99   We will abandon them, that Day,
         to pound against each other in surging waves
     and the Trumpet will be blown
         and We will gather them all together.

100   That Day We will display Hell in its totality to the unbelievers,

101   those whose eyes were blind to My remembrance
        and whose ears were unable to hear.

102   Do those who disbelieve imagine
        that they can take My slaves
            as protectors instead of Me?
    We have prepared Hell
        as hospitality for the unbelievers!

103   Say: 'Shall I inform you of the greatest losers in their actions?
104   People whose efforts in the life of this world are misguided
            while they suppose that they are doing good.'
105   Those are the people who reject their Lord's Signs
        and the meeting with Him.
    Their actions will come to nothing
        and, on the Day of Rising,
    We will not assign them any weight.

106   That is their repayment – Hell –
        because they disbelieved and made a mockery
            of My Signs and of My Messengers.

107   Those who believe and do right actions
        will have the Gardens of Firdaws as hospitality,
108   remaining in them timelessly, for ever,
        with no desire to move away from them.

109   Say: 'If all the sea were ink to write down the Words of my Lord,
        it would run out long before the Words of my Lord ran out,'
    even if We were to bring the same amount of ink again.

110   Say: 'I am only a human being like yourselves
        who has received revelation.
            Your god is One God.
    So let him who hopes to meet his Lord act rightly
        and not associate anyone in the worship of his Lord.'

Sura 19

Maryam
Mary

In the name of Allah, All-Merciful, Most Merciful

1   Kaf Ha Ya 'Ayn Sad

2   Remembering your Lord's mercy to His slave Zakariyya,

3   when he called on his Lord in secret

4   and said, 'My Lord,
    my bones have lost their strength
    and my head is crowned with white,
    but in calling on You, My Lord,
    I have never been disappointed.

5   I fear my relatives when I am gone
    and my wife is barren,
    so give me an heir from You

6   to be my inheritor
    and the inheritor of the family of Ya'qub,
    and make him, my Lord, pleasing to You.'

7   'Zakariyya! We give you the good news
    of a boy named Yahya,
    a name We have given to no one else before.'

8   He said, 'My Lord! How can I have a boy
    when my wife is barren
    and I have reached advanced old age?'

9   He said, 'It will be so!
    Your Lord says, "That is easy for Me to do.
    I created you before, when you were not anything."'

10   He said, 'My Lord, give me a Sign.'
         He said, 'Your Sign is not to speak to people for three nights
             despite the fact that you are perfectly able to.'

11   He came out to his people from the Upper Room
         and gestured to them to glorify Allah
             in the morning and the evening.

12   'Yahya, take hold of the Book with vigour.'
         We gave him judgement while still a child,
13   and tenderness and purity from Us –
                 he was godfearing –
14   and devotion to his parents –
         he was not insolent or disobedient.

15   Peace be upon him the day he was born,
         and the day he dies,
     and the day he is raised up again alive.

16   Mention Maryam in the Book,
         how she withdrew from her people
             to an eastern place,
17   and veiled herself from them.
     Then We sent Our Ruh to her
         and it took on for her the form
             of a handsome, well-built man.
18   She said, 'I seek refuge from you with the All-Merciful
         if you are godfearing.'
19   He said, 'I am only your Lord's messenger
         so that He may give you a pure boy.'
20   She said, 'How can I have a boy
             when no man has touched me
         and I am not an unchaste woman?'
21   He said, 'It will be so!
         Your Lord says, "That is easy for Me.
     It is so that We can make him a Sign for mankind
         and a mercy from Us."
     It is a matter already decreed.'

22   So she conceived him and withdrew with him
         to a distant place.
23   The pains of labour drove her to the trunk of a date-palm.
         She said, 'Oh if only I had died before this time
             and were something discarded and forgotten!'

24   A voice called out to her from under her,
         'Do not grieve! Your Lord has placed
            a small stream at your feet.
25   Shake the trunk of the palm towards you
         and fresh, ripe dates will drop down onto you.
26   Eat and drink and delight your eyes.
         If you should see anyone at all, just say,
         "I have made a vow of silence to the All-Merciful
            and today I will not speak to any human being."'

27   She brought him to her people, carrying him.
         They said, 'Maryam! You have done an unthinkable thing!
28   Sister of Harun, your father was not an evil man
         nor was your mother an unchaste woman!'
29   She pointed towards him.
         They said, 'How can a baby in the cradle speak?'
30   He said, 'I am the slave of Allah,
         He has given me the Book and made me a Prophet.
31   He has made me blessed wherever I am
         and directed me to pray and pay zakat as long as I live,
32   and to show devotion to my mother.
         He has not made me insolent or arrogant.
33   Peace be upon me the day I was born,
            and the day I die
         and the day I am raised up again alive.'

34   That is 'Isa, son of Maryam,
         the word of truth
     about which they are in doubt.

35   It is not fitting for Allah to have a son.
         Glory be to Him!
     When He decides on something,
         He just says to it, 'Be!' and it is.

36   'Allah is my Lord and your Lord
         so worship Him.
     This is a straight path.'

37   The parties differed among themselves.
         Woe to those who disbelieve
     when they are present on a terrible Day!

38   How clear will be their hearing,
            how perfect their sight,
                on the Day they come to Us;
            whereas today the wrongdoers
                are clearly misguided.

39   Warn them of the Day of Bitter Regret
            when the affair will be resolved.
        But they take no notice.
            They do not believe.

40   It is We who will inherit the earth
            and all those on it.
        They will be returned to Us.

41   Mention Ibrahim in the Book.
            He was a true man and a Prophet.
42   Remember when he said to his father,
            'Father, why do you worship
                what can neither hear nor see
            and is not of any use to you at all?
43   Father, knowledge which never reached you
            has come to me, so follow me
                and I will guide you to the right path.
44   Father, do not worship Shaytan.
            Shaytan was disobedient to the All-Merciful.
45   Father, I am afraid that a punishment
            from the All-Merciful will afflict you,
                and turn you into a comrade of Shaytan.'

46   He said, 'Do you forsake my gods, Ibrahim?
            If you do not stop, I will stone you.
        Keep away from me for a good long time.'

47   He said, 'Peace be upon you.
            I will ask my Lord to forgive you.
        He has always honoured me.
48   I will separate myself from you
        and all you call upon besides Allah
            and I will call upon my Lord.
        It may well be that, in calling on my Lord,
            I will not be disappointed.'

49   When he had separated himself from them,
        and what they worshipped besides Allah,
    We gave him Ishaq and Ya'qub,
        making each of them a Prophet.
50   We endowed them with Our mercy
        and made them highly honoured.

51   Mention Musa in the Book.
        He was truly sincere
        and was a Messenger and a Prophet.
52   We called out to him from the right hand side of the Mount
        and We brought him near in close communication.
53   We endowed him with Our mercy,
        making his brother Harun a Prophet.

54   Mention Isma'il in the Book.
        He was true to his promise
        and was a Messenger and a Prophet.
55   He used to command his people
        to perform the prayer and give zakat
    and he was pleasing to his Lord.

56   Mention Idris in the Book.
        He was a true man and a Prophet.
57   We raised him up to a high place.

58   Those are some of the Prophets Allah has blessed,
        from the descendants of Adam
    and from those We carried with Nuh,
        and from the descendants of Ibrahim and Isra'il
          and from those We guided and chose.
    When the Signs of the All-Merciful were recited to them
        they fell on their faces, weeping, in prostration.

59   An evil generation succeeded them
        who neglected the prayer
          and followed their appetites.
    They will plunge into the Valley of Evil –
60   except for those who repent
          and believe and act rightly.
        They will enter the Garden
    and they will not be wronged in any way:

61   Gardens of Eden which the All-Merciful
          has promised to His slaves in the Unseen.
      His promise is always kept.
62   They will not hear any prattling there –
          nothing but 'Peace'.
      They will receive their provision there
          morning and night.

63   That is the Garden which We will bequeath
          to those of Our slaves who are godfearing.
64   'We only descend at your Lord's command.
          Everything in front of us,
              and everything behind us,
          and everything in between
              belongs to Him.
      Your Lord does not forget.'

65   He is Lord of the heavens and the earth
          and everything in between them,
              so worship Him
          and persevere in His worship.
      Do you know of any other with His Name?

66   Man says, 'When I am dead,
          will I then be brought out again alive?'
67   Does not man recall that We created him before
          when he was not anything?

68   By your Lord, We will collect them and the shaytans together.
          Then We will assemble them around Hell on their knees.
69   Then We will drag out from every sect
          the one among them most insolent towards the All-Merciful.
70   Then it is We who will know best
          those most deserving to roast in it.
71   There is not one of you who will not come to it.
          That is the final decision of your Lord.
72   Then We will rescue those who are godfearing
          and We will leave the wrongdoers in it on their knees.

73   When Our Clear Signs are recited to them,
          those who disbelieve say to those who believe,
      'Which of the two parties has the better position
          and the more illustrious gathering?'

74   How many generations We have destroyed before them
        who had finer furnishings and a better outward show!

75   Say: 'As for those who are astray,
        let the All-Merciful prolong their term
           until they see what they were promised,
        whether it be the punishment or the Hour.
    Then they will know who is in the worse position
        and has the weaker troops.'

76   Allah augments those who are guided
        by giving them greater guidance.
    In your Lord's sight, right actions which are lasting
        are better both in reward and end result.

77   Have you seen him who rejects Our Signs and says,
        'I will certainly be given wealth and children there'?

78   Has he surveyed the Unseen
        or has he a contract with the All-Merciful?

79   No indeed! We will write down what he says
        and prolong the punishment for him.

80   We will inherit from him the things he is talking about
        and he will come to Us all alone.

81   They have taken other gods besides Allah
        to be a source of power and strength for them!

82   No indeed! They will reject their worship
        and will be opposed to them.

83   Do you not see that We send the shaytans
        against those who disbelieve
           to goad them on?

84   So do not try to hasten their punishment.
        We are simply counting out
           the number of their days.

85   On that Day We will gather the godfearing
        to the All-Merciful with due ceremony.

86   But We will drive the evildoers to Hell,
        like cattle to a watering hole.

87   They have no right of intercession.
        None do but those who have a contract
           with the All-Merciful.

88	They say, 'The All-Merciful has a son.'
89	They have devised a monstrous thing.
90	The heavens are all but rent apart
	and the earth split open
	and the mountains brought crashing down,
91	at their ascription of a son to the All-Merciful!
92	It is not fitting for the All-Merciful to have a son.
93	There is no one in the heavens and earth
	who will not come to the All-Merciful as a slave.
94	He has counted them and numbered them precisely.
95	Each of them will come to Him on the Day of Rising
	all alone.
96	As for those who believe and do right actions,
	the All-Merciful will bestow His love on them.
97	We have made it easy on your tongue
	so that you may give good news to the godfearing
	and warn stubbornly hostile people by it.
98	How many generations We have destroyed before them!
	Do you see a trace of any one of them
	or hear even a whisper?

Sura 20

Ta Ha

In the name of Allah, the All-Merciful, the Most Merciful

1	Ta Ha
2	We did not send down the Qur'an to you 　　to make you miserable,
3	but only as a reminder for those who have fear,
4	a Revelation from Him who created 　　　　the earth and the high heavens,
5	the All-Merciful, 　　established firmly upon the Throne.

6	Everything in the heavens 　　and everything on the earth and everything in between them 　　and everything under the ground 　　　　belongs to Him.

7	Though you speak out loud, 　　He knows your secrets and what is even more concealed.

8	Allah, there is no god but Him. 　　The Most Beautiful Names are His.

9	Has the story of Musa not reached you?

10	When he saw a fire and said to his family, 　　'Wait here. I can make out a fire. Maybe I will bring you a brand from it, 　　or will find guidance there.'

11   Then when he reached it,
        a voice called out,
    'Musa!

12   I am your Lord.
    Take off your sandals.
        You are in the holy valley of Tuwa.

13   I have chosen you,
    so listen well to what is revealed.

14   I am Allah.
        There is no god but Me,
           so worship Me
        and establish the prayer
           to remember Me.

15   The Hour is coming
        but I have concealed it
           so that every self
        may be repaid for its efforts.

16   Do not let those who do not believe in it
        and follow their whims and desires
           debar you from it
        or you will be destroyed.

17   What is that in your right hand, Musa?'

18   He said, 'It is my staff.
        I lean on it
    and beat down leaves for my sheep with it
        and I have other uses for it.'

19   He said, 'Throw it down, Musa.'

20   He threw it down
           and suddenly it was
    a slithering snake.

21   He said, 'Take hold of it and have no fear.
        We will return it to its original form.

22   Put your hand under your arm
        and press it to your side.
    It will emerge pure white
        yet quite unharmed,
           another Sign.

23   In this way We show you
        some of Our greatest Signs.

24   Go to Pharaoh.
    He has overstepped the bounds.'

25	He said, 'O Lord, expand my breast for me
26	and make my task easy for me.
27	Loosen the knot in my tongue
28	so that they will understand my words.
29	Assign me a helper from my family,
30	my brother Harun.
31	Strengthen my back by him
32	and let him share in my task,
33	so that we may glorify You much
34	and remember You much,
35	for You are watching us.'

36	He said, 'Your request has been granted, Musa.
37	We were gracious to you another time
38	when We revealed to your mother:
39	"Place him in the box
	and throw it into the sea
	and the sea will wash it up on the shore,
	where an enemy of Mine and his will pick it up."
	I showered you with love from Me
40	so that you would be brought up under My supervision.
41	When your sister went and said,
	"Shall I direct you to someone
	who will take care of him?"
	that was how We returned you to your mother
	so that she might delight her eyes
	and not be grieved.
	You killed a man and We rescued you from trouble
	and tested you with many trials.
	You stayed some years among the people of Madyan.
	Then you arrived at the pre-ordained time, Musa!
42	I have chosen you for Myself.
	Go, you and your brother, with My Signs
	and do not slacken in remembering Me.
43	Go to Pharaoh; he has overstepped the bounds.
44	But speak to him with gentle words
	so that hopefully he will pay heed
	or show some fear.'

45	They said, 'Our Lord, we are afraid
	that he might persecute us
	or overstep the bounds.'

46 He said, 'Have no fear.
I will be with you,
All-Hearing and All-Seeing.
47 Go to him and say,
"We are your Lord's Messengers
so send the tribe of Israel away with us
and do not punish them.
We have brought you
a Sign from your Lord.
Peace be upon those who follow the guidance.
48 It has been revealed to us
that punishment is for him who denies the truth
and turns away."'

49 Pharaoh said, 'Who then is your Lord, Musa?'
50 He said, 'Our Lord is He who gives each thing
its created form and then guides it.'
51 He said, 'What about the previous generations?'
52 He said, 'Knowledge of them is with my Lord in a Book.
My Lord does not misplace nor does He forget.'

53 It is He who made the earth a cradle for you
and threaded pathways for you through it
and sent down water from the sky
by which We have brought forth
various different types of plants.
54 Eat and pasture your cattle.
Certainly there are Signs in that
for people of sound intellect.
55 From it We created you,
to it We will return you,
and from it We will bring you forth
a second time.

56 We showed him all of Our Signs,
but he denied and spurned them.
57 He said, 'Have you come to us
to expel us from our land
by means of your magic, Musa?
58 We will bring you magic to match it.
So fix a time between us and you
which neither we nor you will fail to keep
at a place where we can meet halfway.'

59   He said, 'Your time is the day of the Festival.
                The people should gather in the morning.'

60   So Pharaoh went away and concocted his scheme
                and then he arrived.
61   Musa said to them, 'Woe to you!
                Do not fabricate lies against Allah
          or He will annihilate you with His punishment.
                Fabricators of lies are bound to fail.'
62   They argued among themselves about the matter
                and had a secret conference.
63   They said, 'These two magicians desire by their magic
                to expel you from your land
          and abolish your most excellent way of life,
64   so decide on your scheme
          and then arrive together in force.
                He who gains the upper hand today
                    will definitely prosper.'

65   They said, 'Musa, will you throw
                or shall we be the first to throw?'
66   He said, 'No, you throw!'
                And suddenly their ropes and staffs
          appeared to him, by their magic,
                to be slithering about.
67   Musa experienced in himself a feeling of alarm.

68   We said, 'Have no fear.
                You will have the upper hand.
69   Throw down what is in your right hand.
                It will swallow up their handiwork.
          Their handiwork is just a magician's trick.
                Magicians do not prosper wherever they go.'

70   The magicians threw themselves down in prostration.
                They said, 'We believe in the Lord of Harun and Musa.'
71   Pharaoh said, 'Do you believe in him
                before I have authorised you?
          He is your chief, the one who taught you magic.
                I will cut off your hands and feet alternately
                    and have you crucified on palm trunks.
                Then you will know for certain which of us
                    has the harsher and longer lasting punishment.'

72 They said, 'We will never prefer you
to the Clear Signs which have come to us
nor to Him who brought us into being.
Decide on any judgment you like.
Your jurisdiction only covers the life of this world.

73 We have put our faith in our Lord
so that He may forgive us for our mistakes
and for the magic which you forced us to perform.
Allah is better and longer lasting.'

74 As for those who come to their Lord as evildoers,
they will have Hell
where they will neither die
nor stay alive.

75 But as for those who come to Him as believers,
having done right actions,
they will have the highest ranks:

76 Gardens of Eden with rivers flowing under them,
remaining in them timelessly, for ever.
That is the reward of those who purify themselves.

77 We revealed to Musa,
'Travel with My slaves by night.
Strike a dry path for them through the sea.
Have no fear of being overtaken
and do not be afraid.'

78 Pharaoh pursued them with his troops
and the sea overwhelmed them utterly.

79 Pharoah misguided his people.
He was no guide.

80 Tribe of Israel!
We rescued you from your enemy
and made an appointment with you
on the right hand side of the Mount
and sent down manna and quails for you.

81 Eat of the good things We have provided for you
but do not go to excess in it
or My anger will be unleashed on you.
Anyone who has My anger unleashed on him
has plunged to his ruin.

82   But I am Ever-Forgiving to anyone who repents
         and believes and acts rightly
            and then is guided.

83   'Why have you hurried on ahead of your people, Musa?'
84   He said, 'They are following in my tracks.
         I have hurried on ahead to you, My Lord,
            to gain Your good pleasure.'
85   He said, 'We tried your people after you left
         and the Samiri has misguided them.'

86   Musa returned to his people in anger and great sorrow.
         He said, 'My people, did not your Lord
            make you a handsome promise?
     Did the fulfilment of the contract seem too long to you
         or did you want to unleash your Lord's anger upon yourselves,
            so you broke your promise to me?'
87   They said, 'We did not break our promise to you
         of our own volition.
     But we were weighed down with the heavy loads
         of the people's jewelry and we threw them in,
            for that is what the Samiri did.'
88   Then he produced a calf for them,
         a physical form which made a lowing sound.
     So they said, 'This is your god –
         and Musa's god as well, but he forgot.'
89   Could they not see that it did not reply to them
         and that it possessed no power
            to either harm or benefit them?

90   Harun had earlier said to them,
         'My people! It is just a trial for you.
            Your Lord is the All-Merciful,
         so follow me and obey my command!'
91   They said, 'We will not stop devoting ourselves to it
         until Musa returns to us.'

92   He said, 'What prevented you following me, Harun,
         when you saw that they had gone astray?
93   Did you too, then, disobey my command?'
94   He said, 'Son of my mother!
         Do not seize me by the beard or by the hair.
         I was afraid that you would say,

"You have caused division in the tribe of Israel
and taken no notice of anything I said."'

95 He said, 'What do you think you were doing, Samiri?'
96 He said, 'I saw what they did not see.
So I gathered up a handful
from the Messenger's footprints
and threw it in.
That is what my inner self urged me to do.'
97 He said, 'Go! In this world you will have to say,
"Untouchable!"
And you have an appointment
which you will not fail to keep.
Look at your god to which
you devoted so much time.
We will burn it up and then scatter it
as dust into the sea.
98 Your god is Allah alone,
there is no god but Him.
He encompasses all things in His knowledge.'

99 In this way We give you news of what has gone before
and We have given you a reminder direct from Us.
100 Those who turn away from it
will bear a heavy burden on the Day of Rising,
101 remaining in it timelessly, for ever.
What an evil load they will bear on the Day of Rising!

102 On the Day the Trumpet is blown –
and We gather the evildoers sightless on that Day –
103 they will whisper secretly to one other,
'You only stayed for ten.'
104 We know best what they will say
when the most correct of them will say,
'You only stayed one day.'

105 They will ask you about the mountains.
Say: 'My Lord will scatter them as dust.
106 He will leave them as a barren, level plain
107 on which you will see no dip or gradient.'

108 On that day they will follow the Summoner
who has no crookedness in him at all.

Voices will be humbled before the All-Merciful
and nothing but a whisper will be heard.

109   On that Day intercession will be of no avail
except for him whom the All-Merciful has authorised
and with whose speech He is well-pleased.

110   He knows what is in front of them and behind them.
But their knowledge does not encompass Him.

111   Faces will be humbled to the Living, the All-Sustaining.
and anyone weighed down with wrongdoing will have failed.

112   But anyone who does right actions, being a believer,
need fear no wrong or any belittlement.

113   In this way We have sent it down as an Arabic Qur'an
and We have made various threats in it
so that hopefully they will be godfearing
or it will spur them into remembrance.

114   High exalted be Allah, the King, the Real!
Do not rush ahead with the Qur'an
before its revelation to you is complete,
and say: 'My Lord, increase me in knowledge.'

115   We made a contract with Adam before, but he forgot.
We did not find that he had a firm resolve.

116   When We said to the angels,
'Prostrate yourselves to Adam!'
they prostrated, with the exception of Iblis
who disdained to do it.

117   We said, 'Adam, this is an enemy for you and your wife,
so do not let him expel you from the Garden
and thus make you miserable.

118   You will not go hungry in it or suffer from nakedness.

119   You will not go thirsty in it or burn in the sun.'

120   But Shaytan whispered to him, saying,
'Adam, shall I show you the way
to the Tree of Everlasting Life
and to a kingdom which will never fade away?'

121   So the two of them ate from it
and their private parts were disclosed to them
and they started stitching together the leaves of the Garden
to cover themselves.
Adam disobeyed his Lord and became misled.

122 But then his Lord chose him
   and turned to him and guided him.

123 He said, 'Go down from it, all of you,
   as enemies to one another!
   But when guidance comes to you from Me,
   all those who follow My guidance
   will not go astray and will not be miserable.

124 But if anyone turns away from My reminder,
   his life will be a dark and narrow one
   and on the Day of Rising
   We will gather him blind.'

125 He will say, 'My Lord, why have you gathered me blind
   when before I was able to see?'

126 He will say, 'Just as Our Signs came to you and you forgot them,
   in the same way you too are forgotten today.'

127 That is how We repay anyone who is profligate
   and does not believe in the Signs of his Lord.
   And punishment in the Next World
   is much harsher and longer lasting.

128 Are they not guided
   by the many generations We have destroyed before them,
   among whose dwelling places they walk about?
   There are Signs in that for people of sound intellect.

129 And were it not for a prior word from your Lord,
   and a specified term,
   it would inevitably have already taken place.

130 So be steadfast in the face of what they say
   and glorify your Lord with praise
   before the rising of the sun
   and before its setting.
   And glorify Him during part of the night
   and at both ends of the day,
   so that hopefully you will be pleased.

131 Do not direct your eyes longingly to what
   We have given certain of them to enjoy,
   the flower of the life of this world,
   so that We may test them by it.
   Your Lord's provision is better and longer lasting.

132   Instruct your family to do the prayer,
          and be constant in it.
      We do not ask you for provision.
          We provide for you.
      And the best end result
          is gained by taqwa.

133   They say, 'If only he would bring us a Sign from his Lord!'
          Have they not received the Clear Sign
             of what is written in the earlier texts?

134   If We had destroyed them
          with a punishment before this,
      they would have said, 'Our Lord,
          why did You not send us a Messenger,
      so we could follow Your Signs
          before we were humbled and disgraced?'

135   Say: 'Everyone is waiting expectantly
          so wait expectantly.
          You will soon know
      who are the Companions of the Right Path
          and who is is guided.'

Sura 21

Al-Anbiya'
The Prophets

In the name of Allah, All-Merciful, Most Merciful

1   Mankind's Reckoning has drawn very close to them,
    yet they heedlessly turn away.

2   No fresh reminder comes to them from their Lord
    without their listening to it as if it were a game.

3   Their hearts are distracted.
    Those who do wrong confer together secretly, saying,
    'Is this man anything but a human being like yourselves?
    Do you succumb to magic with your eyes wide open?'

4   Say: 'My Lord knows what is said in heaven and earth.
    He is the All-Hearing, the All-Knowing.'

5   Furthermore they say, 'A muddled jumble of dreams!'
    and, 'He has invented it!'
        and, 'He is a poet!'
    and, 'Let him bring us a Sign
        like those sent to previous peoples.'

6   None of the cities which We destroyed before them believed.
    So will they?

7   We have only ever sent before you
        men who were given Revelation.
    Ask the People of the Reminder if you do not know.

8   We did not give them bodies which did not eat food,
            nor were they immortal.

9   But We kept Our promise to them
            and rescued them and those We willed,
                and destroyed the profligate.

10   We have sent down to you a Book containing your Reminder.
            So will you not use your intellect?

11   How many cities which did wrong have We utterly destroyed,
            raising up other people after them!

12   When they perceived Our violent force
            they ran away from it.

13   'Do not run away!
            Return to the life of luxury you enjoyed
                and to the places where you lived,
            so that you can be interrogated!'

14   They said, 'Alas for us!
            We were indeed wrongdoers!'

15   That cry of theirs went on
            until We made them stubble,
                silent,
                stamped out.

16   We did not create heaven and earth
            and everything in between them
                as a game.

17   If We had desired to have some amusement,
            We would have derived it from Our Presence,
                but We did not do that.

18   Rather We hurl the truth against falsehood
            and it cuts right through it
                and it vanishes clean away!
            Woe without end to you
                for what you portray!

19   Everyone in the heavens and the earth belongs to Him.
            Those in His presence do not consider themselves
                too great to worship Him
            and do not grow tired of it.

20   They glorify Him by night and day,
            without ever flagging.

21   Or have they taken gods out of the earth
            who can bring the dead to life?

22   If there had been any gods besides Allah in heaven or on earth,
        they would both have been ruined.
    Glory be to Allah, Lord of the Throne,
        beyond what they describe!

23   He will not be questioned about what He does,
        but they will be questioned.

24   Or have they taken other gods besides Him?
        Say: 'Produce your proof!
    This is the message of those with me
        and the message of those before me.'
    But most of them do not know the truth,
        so they turn away.

25   We sent no Messenger before you
        without revealing to him:
    'There is no god but Me, so worship Me.'

26   They say, 'The All-Merciful has a son.'
        Glory be to Him!
    No, they are honoured slaves!
27   They do not precede Him in speech
            and they act on His command.

28   He knows what is in front of them and what is behind them.
        They only intercede on behalf of those
            with whom He is pleased,
        and even they are apprehensive out of fear of Him.
29   Were any of them to say,
        'I am a god apart from Him,'
    We would repay him with Hell.
        That is how We repay wrongdoers.

30   Do those who disbelieve not see
        that the heavens and the earth were sewn together
            and then We unstitched them
    and that We made from water every living thing?
        So will they not believe?

31   We placed firmly embedded mountains on the earth,
        so it would not move under them,
    and We put broad valleys as roadways in it,
        so that perhaps they might be guided.

32   We made the sky a preserved and protected roof
        yet still they turn away from Our Signs.

33   It is He who created night and day
        and the sun and moon,
   each one swimming in a sphere.

34   We did not give any human being before you immortality.
        And if you die, will they then be immortal?

35   Every self will taste death.
        We test you with both good and evil as a trial.
        And you will be returned to Us.

36   When those who disbelieve see you,
        they only make a mockery out of you:
   'Is this the one who makes mention of your gods?'
        Yet they reject mention of the All-Merciful.

37   Man was created hasty.
        I will show you My Signs
           so do not try to hasten Me.

38   They say, 'When will this promise come about
        if you are telling the truth?'

39   If those who disbelieve only knew of the time
        when they will not be able to keep the Fire away
           from their faces or their backs!
   And they will receive no help!

40   No, it will come upon them suddenly,
        confounding them,
   taking them completely by surprise,
        and they will not be able to ward it off.
   They will be granted no reprieve.

41   Messengers before you were also mocked,
        but those who jeered were engulfed
           by what they mocked.

42   Say: 'Who will protect you night and day from the All-Merciful?'
        Yet they turn away from the remembrance of their Lord.

43   Or do they have gods besides Us who will protect them?
          They cannot even help themselves!
               They will not be safe from Us.

44   No indeed! We have given these people enjoyment,
          as We did their fathers,
               until life seemed long and good to them.
     Do they not see how We come to the land
          eroding it from its extremities?
               Or are they the victors?

45   Say: 'I can only warn you through the Revelation.'
          But the deaf cannot hear the call when they are warned.

46   If even a single waft of the punishment were to touch them,
          they would say, 'Alas for us! We were indeed wrongdoers.'

47   We will set up the Just Balance on the Day of Rising
          and no self will be wronged in any way.
     Even if it be no more than the weight
          of a grain of mustard-seed,
               We will produce it.
     We are sufficient as a Reckoner.

48   We gave to Musa and Harun
          the Discrimination and a Shining Light
               and a Reminder for those who are godfearung:
49   those who fear their Lord in the Unseen
               and are apprehensive about the Hour.

50   This is a blessed Reminder which We have sent down.
          So are you going to ignore it?

51   We gave Ibrahim his right guidance early on,
          and We had complete knowledge of him.
52   When he said to his father and his people,
               'What are these statues you are clinging to?'
53   they said, 'We found our fathers worshipping them.'
54   He said, 'You and your fathers are clearly misguided.'
55   They said, 'Have you brought us the truth
               or are you playing games?'
56   He said, 'Far from it! Your Lord
          is the Lord of the heavens and the earth,

He who brought them into being.
I am one of those who bear witness to that.

57   By Allah, I will devise some scheme against your idols
when your backs are turned.'

58   He broke them in pieces, except for the biggest one,
so that they would have it to consult!

59   They said, 'Who has done this to our gods?
He is definitely one of the wrongdoers!'

60   They said, 'We heard a young man mentioning them.
They call him Ibrahim.'

61   They said, 'Bring him before the people's eyes
so they can be witnesses.'

62   They asked, 'Did you do this to our gods, Ibrahim?'

63   He said, 'No, this one, the biggest of them, did it.
Ask them if they are able to speak!'

64   They consulted among themselves and said,
'It is you yourselves who are wrongdoers.'

65   But then they relapsed back into their unbelief:
'You know full well these idols cannot talk.'

66   He said, 'Do you then worship, instead of Allah,
what cannot help or harm you in any way?

67   Shame on you and what you worship besides Allah!
Will you not use your intellect?'

68   They said, 'Burn him and support your gods
if you are resolved to do something.'

69   We said, 'Fire, be coolness and peace for Ibrahim!'

70   They desired to trap him
but We made them the losers.

71   We delivered both him and Lut
to the land which We had blessed for all beings.

72   And in addition to that We gave him Ishaq and Ya'qub
and made both of them righteous.

73   We made them leaders, guiding by Our command,
and revealed to them how to do good actions
and establish the prayer and pay zakat,
and they worshipped Us.

74   We gave right judgement and knowledge to Lut
and rescued him from the city
which committed disgusting acts.
They were evil people who were deviators.

75   We admitted him into Our mercy.
            He was one of the righteous.

76   And Nuh, when he called out before
            and We responded to him
        and rescued him and his family
            from the terrible plight.
77   We helped him against the people
            who rejected Our Signs.
        They were an evil people
            and We drowned them, every one.

78   And Dawud and Sulayman
            when they gave judgement about the field,
                when the people's sheep strayed into it at night.
            We were Witness to their judgement.
79   We gave Sulayman understanding of it.
            We gave each of them judgement and knowledge.
        We subjected the mountains to Dawud, glorifying,
                and the birds as well.
            This is something We are well able to do.
80   We taught him the art of making garments for you
            to protect you against each others' violence,
                But do you show any thanks?

81   And to Sulayman We gave the fiercely blowing wind,
            speeding at his command towards the land
                which We had blessed.
            And We had full knowledge of everything.
82   And some of the shaytans dived for him
            and did other things apart from that.
        And We were watching over them.

83   And Ayyub when he called out to his Lord,
                'Great harm has afflicted me,
            but You are the Most Merciful of the merciful,'
84   We responded to him and removed from him
            the harm which was afflicting him
        and restored his family to him,
            and the same again with them,
        as a mercy direct from Us
            and a Reminder to all worshippers.

85   And Isma'il and Idris and Dhu'l-Kifl –
      each one was among the steadfast.
86   We admitted them into Our mercy.
      They were among the righteous.

87   And Dhu'n-Nun when he left in anger
      and thought We would not punish him.
    He called out in the pitch darkness:
      'There is no god but You!
        Glory be to You!
      Truly I have been one of the wrongdoers.'
88   We responded to him and rescued him from his grief.
      That is how We rescue the believers.

89   And Zakariyya when he called out to his Lord,
      'My Lord, do not leave me on my own,
        though You are the Best of Inheritors.'
90   We responded to him and gave him Yahya,
      restoring for him his wife's fertility.
    They outdid one another in good actions,
      calling out to Us in yearning and in awe,
        and humbling themselves to Us.

91   And she who protected her private parts.
      We breathed into her some of Our Ruh
    and made her and her son a Sign for all the worlds.

92   This nation of yours is one nation
      and I am your Lord, so worship Me.
93   But they disagreed and split into different sects.
      Each one will return to Us.

94   As for anyone who does right actions and is a believer,
      his striving certainly does not go unthanked.
      We are writing it down on his behalf.

95   There is a ban on any city We have destroyed;
      they will not return.

96   When Yajuj and Majuj are let loose
      and rush down from every slope,
97   and the True Promise is very close,
    the eyes of those who disbelieved will be transfixed:

'Alas for us! We were unmindful of this!
No, rather we were certainly wrongdoers.'

98   You and what you worship besides Allah
       are fuel for Hell.
    You will go down into it.

99   If those had really been gods,
       they would not have gone down into it.
    Each one will be in it timelessly, for ever.

100   There will be sighing for them in it
       and they will not be able to hear.

101   Those for whom the Best from Us was pre-ordained,
       will be far away from it.

102   They will not hear the slightest hint of it
       and they will remain there timelessly, for ever,
         among everything their selves desire.

103   The greatest terror will not upset them
       and the angels will welcome them:
    'This is your Day, the one that you were promised.'

104   That Day We will fold up heaven
       like folding up the pages of a book.
    As We originated the first creation
       so We will regenerate it.
    It is a promise binding on Us.
       That is what We will do.

105   We wrote down in the Zabur,
       after the Reminder came:
    'It is My slaves who are righteous
       who will inherit the earth.'

106   Certainly there is a transmission in this
       for people who worship.

107   We have only sent you as a mercy to all the worlds.

108   Say: 'It is revealed to me
       that your god is One God.
         So are you Muslims?'

109   If they turn their backs, then say:
               'I have informed all of you equally
                   and I do not know
               if what you have been promised
                   is near or far.
110   He knows what is said openly
               and He knows what you hide.
111   For all I know it might be a trial for you
               and you will have enjoyment for a time.'

112   Say: 'Lord, judge with truth!
               Our Lord is the All-Merciful,
                   the One Whose help is sought
               in the face of what you describe.'

Sura 22

Al-Hajj
The Pilgrimage

In the name of Allah, All-Merciful, Most Merciful

1   Mankind, have taqwa of your Lord!
         The quaking of the Hour is a terrible thing.

2   On the day they see it,
          every nursing woman will be oblivious
             of the baby at her breast,
      and every pregnant woman
          will abort the contents of her womb,
      and you will think people drunk
          though they are not drunk;
      it is just that the punishment of Allah is so severe.

3   Among people there is one who argues about Allah
          without knowledge,
      and follows every rebellious shaytan.

4   It is written of him that if anyone takes him as a friend,
          he will mislead him
      and guide him to the punishment of the Searing Blaze.

5   Mankind! if you are in any doubt about the Rising,
          know that We created you from dust,
             then from a drop of sperm
          then from a clot of blood
             then from a lump of flesh,
                formed yet unformed,
      so We may make things clear to you.

We make whatever We will stay in the womb
    until a specified time
and then We bring you out as children
    so that you may reach your full maturity.
Some of you die
    and some of you revert to the lowest form of life
so that, after having knowledge,
    they then know nothing at all.
And you see the earth dead and barren;
    then when We send down water onto it
        it quivers and swells
and sprouts with luxuriant plants of every kind.

6   That is because Allah is the Real
        and gives life to the dead
            and has power over all things
7   and the Hour is coming without any doubt
        and Allah will raise up all those in the graves.

8   Among people there is one who argues about Allah
        without knowledge or guidance or any light-giving Book,
9   turning away arrogantly,
        to misguide people from the Way of Allah.
He will be disgraced in this world
        and on the Day of Rising
We will make him taste
        the punishment of the Burning:
10   'That is for what you did before.
        Allah does not wrong His slaves.'

11   Among the people there is one who worships Allah
        right on the edge.
    If good befalls him, he is content with it,
but if a trial befalls him, he reverts to his former ways,
    losing both this world and the Next World.
        That is indeed sheer loss.

12   Instead of Allah, he calls on something
        which cannot harm him or help him.
    That is extreme misguidance.

13   He calls on what is far more likely to harm than help.
        What an evil protector!
            What an evil associate!

14   Allah will admit those who believe and do right actions
         into Gardens with rivers flowing under them.
         Allah does whatever He wishes.

15   Anyone who thinks that Allah will not help him
         in this world and the Next World
     should stretch a rope up to the ceiling
         and then hang himself.
     Let him see whether his stratagem
         gets rid of what enrages him!

16   In this way We have sent it down as Clear Signs.
         Allah guides anyone He wills.

17   As for those who believe
         and those who are Jews and the Sabaeans
             and the Christians, Magians and idolators,
     Allah will distinguish between them on the Day of Rising.
         Allah is witness of all things.

18   Do you not see that everyone in the heavens
         and everyone on the earth
             prostrates to Allah,
     and the sun and moon and stars
         and the mountains, trees and beasts
             and many of mankind?
     But many of them inevitably merit punishment.
     Those Allah humiliates will have no one to honour them.
         Allah does whatever He wills.

19   Here are two rival groups who disputed concerning their Lord.
         Those who disbelieve
             will have garments of fire cut out for them,
                 and boiling water poured over their heads,
20   which will melt the contents of their bellies as well as their skin,
21   and they will be beaten with cudgels made of iron.
22   Every time they want to come out of it, because of their suffering,
         they will be driven back into it:
     'Taste the punishment of the Burning!'

23   But Allah will admit those who believe and do right actions
         into Gardens with rivers flowing under them
     where they will be adorned with gold bracelets and pearls,
         and where their clothing will be of silk.

24   They have been guided to speak good words
                 and guided to the Praiseworthy Path.

25   Those who disbelieve and bar access to the Way of Allah
                 and to the Masjid al-Haram
            which We have appointed for all mankind –
                 equally for those who live near it
                      and those who come from far away –
            those who desire to profane it with wrongdoing,
                 We will let them taste a painful punishment.

26   And We located the position of the House for Ibrahim:
                 'Do not associate anything with Me
            and purify My House for those who circle it,
                 and those who stand and bow and prostrate.
27   Announce the Hajj to mankind.
                 They will come to you on foot
                      and on every sort of lean animal,
                 coming by every distant road
28   so that they can be present at what will profit them
                 and invoke Allah's name on specific days
                      over livestock He has provided for them.
                 Eat of them and feed those who are poor and in need.
29   Then they should end their state of self-neglect
                 and fufil their vows and circle the Ancient House.'

30   That is it.
            If someone honours Allah's sacred things,
                 that is better for him in his Lord's sight.
            All livestock are permitted to you
                 except what has already been recited to you.
            Have done with the defilement of idols
                 and have done with telling lies.

31   Be people of pure natural faith in Allah,
                 not associating anything else with Him.
            As for anyone who associates others with Allah,
                 it is as though he had fallen from the sky
            and the birds had seized him and carried him away
                 or the wind had dropped him in a distant place.

32   That is it.
            As for those who honour Allah's sacred rites,
                 that comes from the taqwa in their hearts.

33   You can make use of the sacrificial animals until a specified time,
        and then their place of sacrifice is by the Ancient House.

34   We have appointed a rite of sacrifice for every nation
        so that they may invoke Allah's Name
            over the livestock He has given them.
    Your God is One God so submit to Him.
        Give good news to the humble-hearted,

35   whose hearts quake at the mention of Allah,
        and who are steadfast in the face of all that happens to them,
    those who establish the prayer
        and give of what We have provided for them.

36   We have appointed the sacrificial animals for you
        as one of the sacred rites of Allah.
    There is good in them for you,
        so invoke Allah's name over them,
            as they stand in rows.
    And then when they collapse on their sides,
        eat of them and feed both those who ask
            and those who are too shy to ask.
    In this way We have subjected them to you
        so that hopefully you will be thankful.

37   Their flesh and blood does not reach Allah
        but your taqwa does reach Him.
    In this way He has subjected them to you
        so that you may proclaim Allah's greatness
            for the way that He has guided you.
        Give good news to the good-doers.

38   Allah will defend those who believe.
        Allah does not love any thankless traitor.

39   Permission to fight is given to those who are fought against
        because they have been wronged –
    truly Allah has the power to come to their support –

40   those who were expelled from their homes without any right,
        merely for saying, 'Our Lord is Allah'
        (if Allah had not driven some people back
            by means of others,
        monasteries, churches, synagogues and mosques,
            where Allah's name is mentioned much,
        would have been pulled down and destroyed.
            Allah will certainly help those who help Him –
                Allah is All-Strong, Almighty),

41   those who, if We establish them firmly on the earth,
         will establish the prayer and pay zakat,
     and command what is right and forbid what is wrong.
         The end result of all affairs is with Allah.

42   If they deny you, the people of Nuh before them denied him
         and those of 'Ad and of Thamud
43   and the people of Ibrahim and the people of Lut
44   and the companions of Madyan;
           and Musa was denied as well.
     I allowed time to the unbelievers
         but then I seized them.
     How terrible was My denial!

45   How many wrongdoing cities We destroyed,
         and now all their roofs and walls are fallen in;
     how many abandoned wells and stuccoed palaces!

46   Have they not travelled about the earth
         and do they not have hearts to understand with
           or ears to hear with?
     It is not eyes that are blind
         but hearts in breasts that are blind.

47   They ask you to hasten the punishment.
         Allah will not break His promise.
     A day with your Lord is equivalent to
         a thousand years in the way you count.

48   How many wrongdoing cities I allowed time to
         and then I seized them.
     I am their final destination!

49   Say: 'Mankind, I am only a clear warner to you.'

50   As for those who believe and do right actions,
         they will have forgiveness and generous provision.

51   But as for those who strive against My Signs
         and try to thwart them,
     they will be the Companions of the Blazing Fire.

52   We did not send any Messenger or any Prophet before you
         without Shaytan insinuating something into his recitation

while he was reciting.
But Allah revokes whatever Shaytan insinuates
and then Allah confirms His Signs –
Allah is All-Knowing, All-Wise –

53   so that He can make what Shaytan insinuates
a trial for those with sickness in their hearts
and for those whose hearts are hard –
the wrongdoers are entrenched in hostility –

54   and so that those who have been given knowledge
will know it is the truth from their Lord
and believe in it
and their hearts will be humbled to Him.
Allah guides those who believe to a straight path.

55   But those who disbelieve will not cease to be in doubt of it
until the Hour comes on them suddenly
or the punishment of a desolate Day arrives.

56   Sovereignty on that Day will be Allah's.
He will judge between them.
Those who believe and do right actions
will be in Gardens of Delight.

57   But those who disbelieve and deny Our Signs
will have a humiliating punishment.

58   Those who make hijra in the Way of Allah
and then are killed or die,
Allah will provide for them handsomely.
Truly Allah is the best Provider.

59   He will admit them by an entrance
which is pleasing to them.
Allah is All-Knowing, All-Forbearing.

60   That is so.
And if anyone inflicts an injury
the same as the one done to him
and then is again oppressed,
Allah will come to his aid.
Allah is All-Pardoning, Ever-Forgiving.

61   That is because Allah merges night into day
and merges day into night
and because Allah is All-Hearing, All-Seeing.

62   That is because Allah is the Real
and what you call on apart from Him is false.
Allah is the All-High, the Most Great.

63   Do you not see that Allah sends down water from the sky
           and then in the morning the earth is covered in green?
      Allah is All-Subtle, All-Aware.
64   Everything in the heavens
                and everything in the earth
                     belongs to Him.
           Allah is the Rich Beyond Need, the Praiseworthy.

65   Do you not see that Allah has made everything on the earth
           subservient to you
           and the ships running upon the sea by His command?
      He holds back the heaven,
           preventing it from falling to the earth –
                except by His permission.
      Allah is All-Compassionate to mankind, Most Merciful.

66   It is He who gave you life
           and then will cause you to die
      and then will give you life again.
           Man is truly ungrateful.

67   We have appointed for every nation a rite that they observe,
           so let them not dispute with you about the matter.
                Call the people to your Lord.
                You are guided straight.

68   If they do argue with you, say:
           'Allah knows best what you are doing.'
69   Allah will judge between you on the Day of Rising
           regarding everything about which you differed.
70   Do you not know that Allah knows
           everything in heaven and earth?
      That is in a Book.
           That is easy for Allah.

71   They worship besides Allah
           something for which no authority has come down,
                something about which they have no knowledge.
           There is no helper for the wrongdoers.
72   When Our Signs are recited to them – Clear Signs –
           you can detect denial in the faces of those who disbelieve.
      They all but assault those who recite Our Signs to them!
           Say: 'Shall I inform you of something worse than that?

The Fire which Allah has promised those who disbelieve.
What an evil destination!'

73   Mankind! an example has been made,
    so listen to it carefully.
Those whom you call upon besides Allah
    are not even able to create a single fly,
        even if they were to join together to do it.
And if a fly steals something from them,
    they cannot get it back.
How feeble are both the seeker and the sought!

74   They do not measure Allah with His true measure.
    Allah is All-Strong, Almighty.

75   Allah chooses Messengers from the angels and from mankind.
    Allah is All-Hearing, All-Seeing.
76   He knows what is before them and what is behind them.
    All matters return to Allah.

77   You who believe! bow and prostrate and worship your Lord,
    and do good, so that hopefully you will be successful.
78   Do jihad for Allah with the jihad due to Him.
    He has selected you and not placed
        any constraint upon you in the deen –
    the religion of your forefather Ibrahim.
    He named you Muslims before and also in this,
        so that the Messenger could be witness against you
            and you could be witnesses against all mankind.
    So establish the prayer and pay zakat
        and hold fast to Allah.
    He is your Protector –
the Best Protector, the Best Helper.

Sura 23

Al-Muminun
The Believers

In the name of Allah, All-Merciful, Most Merciful

1	It is the believers who are successful:
2	those who are humble in their prayer;
3	those who turn away from worthless talk;
4	those who pay zakat;
5	those who guard their private parts –
6	except from their wives or those they own as slaves, in which case they are not blameworthy;
7	but those who desire anything more than that are people who have gone beyond the limits –
8	those who honour their trusts and their contracts;
9	those who safeguard their prayers:
10	such people are the inheritors
11	who will inherit Firdaws, remaining in it timelessly, for ever.
12	We created man from the purest kind of clay;
13	then made him a drop in a secure receptacle;
14	then formed the drop into a clot and formed the clot into a lump and formed the lump into bones and clothed the bones in flesh; and then brought him into being as another creature. Blessed be Allah, the Best of Creators!
15	Then subsequently you will certainly die.
16	Then on the Day of Rising you will be raised again.
17	We created above you seven levels and We were not unaware of the creation.

18	We sent down a measured amount of water from heaven
	and lodged it firmly in the earth;
	and We are well able to remove it.
19	By means of it We produce gardens of dates and grapes for you,
	in which there are many fruits for you
	and from which you eat,
20	and a tree springing forth from Mount Sinai
	yielding oil and a seasoning to those who eat.

18 We sent down a measured amount of water from heaven
  and lodged it firmly in the earth;
    and We are well able to remove it.
19 By means of it We produce gardens of dates and grapes for you,
  in which there are many fruits for you
    and from which you eat,
20 and a tree springing forth from Mount Sinai
  yielding oil and a seasoning to those who eat.

21 And there is certainly a lesson for you in your livestock.
  We give you to drink from what is in their bellies
and there are many ways in which you benefit from them,
  and some of them you eat;
22 and you are conveyed on them and on ships as well.

23 We sent Nuh to his people and he said,
  'My people, worship Allah.
You have no god other than Him.
  So will you not be godfearing?'
24 The ruling circle of those of his people who disbelieved said,
  'This is nothing but a human being like yourselves
    who simply wants to gain ascendancy over you.
If Allah had wished He would have sent angels down.
  We never heard of anything like this
    among our ancestors, the earlier peoples.
25 He is nothing but a man possessed
  so wait a while and see what happens to him.'
26 He said, 'My Lord, help me
  because of their calling me a liar!'

27 We revealed to him: 'Build the Ship
  under Our supervision and as We reveal.
When Our command comes
  and water bubbles up from the earth,
load into it a pair of every species,
  and your family – except for those among them
    against whom the word has already gone ahead.
And do not address Me concerning those who do wrong.
  They shall be drowned.
28 When you and those with you
  are settled in the Ship,
then say: "Praise be to Allah who has rescued us
  from the people of the wrongdoers!"

29   And say: "My Lord, land me in a blessed landing-place.
         You are the best Bringer to Land."'

30   There are Signs in that.
         We are always putting people to the test.

31   Then We raised up another generation after them
32   and sent a Messenger to them from themselves:
         'Worship Allah. You have no god other than Him!
         So will you not be godfearing?'
33   The ruling circle of his people – those who disbelieved
         and denied the encounter of the Next World
             and whom We had given opulence in this world –
         said, 'This is nothing but a human being like yourselves.
         who eats what you eat and drinks what you drink.
34   If you were to obey a human being like yourselves,
         you would, in that case, definitely be the losers.
35   Does he promise you that when you have died
         and become dust and bones
            you will be brought forth again?
36   What you have been promised is sheer nonsense!
37   What is there but our life in this world?
            We die and we live
               and we will not be raised again.
38   What is he but a man who
            has invented a lie against Allah?
         We do not believe in him.'
39   He said, 'My Lord, help me
         because of their calling me a liar!'
40   He said, 'In a short while they will be full of regret.'
41   The Great Blast seized hold of them inexorably
            and We turned them into dirty scum.
         Away with the people of the wrongdoers!

42   Then We raised up other generations after them.
43   No nation can advance its appointed time
            nor can they delay it.

44   Then We sent Our Messengers one after another, at intervals.
         Each time its Messenger came to a community
            they called him a liar
         so We made them follow one another too
            and turned them into myths and legends.
         Away with the people who do not believe!

45 Then We sent Musa and his brother Harun
with Our Signs and clear authority
46 to Pharaoh and his ruling circle.
But they were proud and were a haughty people.
47 They said, 'What! Should we believe
in two human beings like ourselves
when their people are our slaves?'
48 They denied them and so they were destroyed.

49 We gave Musa the Book
so that perhaps they would be guided.
50 And We made the son of Maryam and his mother a Sign
and gave them shelter on a mountainside
where there was a meadow and a flowing spring.

51 Messengers, eat of the good things and act rightly.
I most certainly know what you do.

52 This faith of yours is a single faith
and I am your Lord,
so have taqwa of Me.
53 But they disagreed and split up,
dividing into sects,
each party exulting in what it had.
54 So leave them in their glut of ignorance for a while.

55 Do they imagine that,
in the wealth and children We extend to them,
56 We are hastening to them with good things?
No indeed, but they have no awareness!

57 Those who are filled with the fear of their Lord,
58 those who believe in the Signs of their Lord,
59 those who do not associate anything with their Lord,
60 those who give what they have given,
their hearts fearful of their return to their Lord,
61 such people are truly racing towards good things,
and they are the first to reach them.

62 We do not impose on any self any more than it can stand.
With Us there is a Book that speaks the truth.
They will not be wronged.

63   However, their hearts are overwhelmed
            by ignorance about this matter
      and they do other things as well.

64   But then when We seize the affluent among them
            with the punishment,
      they will suddenly start praying fervently.
65   'Do not pray fervently today.
            You will not get any help from Us.
66   My Signs were recited to you
            and you turned round on your heels,
67   arrogant towards it,
      talking arrant nonsense all night long.'

68   Do they not ponder these words?
            Has anything come to them
      that did not come to their ancestors,
            the previous peoples?
69   Or is it that they do not recognise their Messenger
            and therefore do not acknowledge him?
70   Or do they say, 'He is a man possessed,'
            when he has brought the truth to them?
      But most of them hate the truth.

71   If the truth were to follow their whims and desires,
            the heavens and the earth and everyone in them
                  would have been brought to ruin.
      No indeed! We have given them their Reminder,
            but they have turned away from it.

72   Are you asking them for payment?
            Your Lord's payment is better.
      He is the Best of Providers.

73   You are calling them to a straight path.
74   But those who do not believe in the Next World
                  recoil from the path.

75   If We did have mercy on them
            and removed the harm afflicting them,
      they would still obstinately persist
            in wandering blindly in their excessive insolence.
76   We seized them with the punishment,

but they did not go low before their Lord;
nor will they humble themselves
77   until We open to them a gate to a harsh punishment
in which they will at once be crushed by despair.

78   It is He who has created hearing, sight and hearts for you.
What little thanks you show!
79   It is He who dispersed you about the earth
and you will be gathered to Him.
80   It is He who gives life and causes to die
and His is the alternation of night and day.
So will you not use your intellect?

81   And yet they say the same as previous peoples said.
82   They say, 'When we are dead and turned to dust and bones,
shall we then be raised again?
83   We and our forefathers were promised this before.
This is nothing but the myths of previous peoples!'

84   Say: 'To whom does the earth belong, and everyone in it,
if you have any knowledge?'
85   They will say: 'To Allah.'
Say: 'So will you not pay heed?'

86   Say: 'Who is the Lord of the Seven Heavens
and the Lord of the Mighty Throne?'
87   They will say: 'Allah.'
Say: 'So will you not be godfearing?'

88   Say: 'In whose hand is the dominion over everything,
He who gives protection and from whom
no protection can be given,
if you have any knowledge?'
89   They will say: 'Allah's.'
Say: 'So how have you been bewitched?'

90   The fact is that We have given them the truth
and they are liars.

91   Allah has no son and there is no other god accompanying Him,
for then each god would have gone off with what he created
and one of them would have been exalted above the other.
Glory be to Allah above what they describe,

92   Knower of the Unseen and the Visible!
            May He be exalted above all they associate with Him!

93   Say: 'My Lord, if You let me see what they have been promised,
94   do not then, my Lord,
            put me among the wrongdoing people!'
95   We are certainly capable of letting you see
            what We have promised them.

96   Ward off evil with what is better.
            We know very well what they express.

97   Say: 'My Lord, I seek refuge with You
            from the goadings of the shaytans,
98   and I seek refuge with You, my Lord,
            from their presence.'

99   When death comes to one of them,
            he says, 'My Lord, send me back again.
100   so that perhaps I may act rightly
            regarding the things I failed to do!'
      No indeed! They are merely words he utters.
            Before them there is an interspace
                until the Day they are raised up.

101   Then when the Trumpet is blown,
            that Day there will be no family ties between them;
      they will not be able to question one another.

102   Those whose scales are heavy,
            they are the successful.
103   Those whose scales are light,
            they are the losers of their selves,
      remaining in Hell timelessly, for ever.

104   The Fire will sear their faces,
            making them grimace horribly in it,
      their lips drawn back from their teeth.

105   'Were My Signs not recited to you
            and did you not deny them?'
106   They will say, 'Our Lord,
            our miserable destiny overpowered us.
                We were misguided people.

107   Our Lord, remove us from it!
            Then if we revert again,
        we will definitely be wrongdoers.'

108   He will say, 'Slink away into it
            and do not speak to Me.
109   There was a group of My slaves who said,
            "Our Lord, we believe,
        so forgive us and have mercy on us.
            You are the Best of the Merciful."
110   But you made a mockery of them
            so that they made you forget to remember Me
                while you were laughing at them.
111   Today I have rewarded them for being steadfast.
            They are the ones who are victorious.'

112   He will say, 'How many years did you tarry on the earth?'
113   They will say, 'We tarried there for a day or part of a day.
            Ask those able to count!'
114   He will say, 'You only tarried there for a little while
            if you did but know!
115   Did you suppose that We created you for amusement
            and that you would not be returned to Us?'

116   Exalted be Allah,
            the King, the Real.
        There is no god but Him,
            Lord of the Noble Throne.

117   Whoever calls on another god
            together with Allah,
        has no grounds for doing so at all
            and his reckoning is with his Lord.
        Truly the unbelievers have no success.

118   Say: 'My Lord, forgive and be merciful!
            You are the Best of the Merciful.'

Sura 24

An-Nur
Light

1   A sura We have sent down and imposed.
      We have sent down Clear Signs in it
        so that hopefully you will pay heed.

2   A woman and a man who commit fornication:
      flog both of them with one hundred lashes
    and do not let compassion for either of them possess you
        where Allah's deen is concerned,
      if you believe in Allah and the Last Day.
    A number of believers should witness their punishment.

3   A man who has fornicated may only marry
      a woman who has fornicated
        or a woman of the idolators.
    A woman who has fornicated may only marry
      a man who has fornicated
        or a man of the idolators.
    Doing such a thing is haram for the believers.

4   But those who make accusations against chaste women
      and then do not produce four witnesses:
        flog them with eighty lashes
    and never again accept them as witnesses.
      Such people are deviators –
5   except for those who after that repent
      and put things right.
    Allah is Ever-Forgiving, Most Merciful.

6   Those who make an accusation against their wives
            and have no witnesses except themselves,
        such people should testify four times by Allah
            that they are telling the truth
7   and a fifth time that Allah's curse
            will be upon them if they are lying.

8   And the punishment is removed from her
            if she testifies four times by Allah
                that he is lying
9   and a fifth time that Allah's anger
        will be upon her if he is telling the truth.

10   Were it not for Allah's favour to you and His mercy . . .
            and that Allah is Ever-Returning, All-Wise.

11   There is a group of you who propagated the lie.*
            Do not suppose it to be bad for you;
                rather it is good for you.
        Every one of them will incur the evil he has earned
            and the one who took it on himself to amplify it
                will receive a terrible punishment.

12   Why, when you heard it, did you not,
            as men and women of the believers,
        instinctively think good thoughts
            and say, 'This is obviously a lie'?

13   Why did they not produce four witnesses to it?
            Since they did not bring four witnesses,
                in Allah's sight, they are liars.

14   Were it not for Allah's favour to you and His mercy,
            both in this world and the Next World,
        a terrible punishment would have afflicted you
            for your plunging headlong into it.

15   You were bandying it about on your tongues,
            your mouths uttering something about which
                you had no knowledge.
        You considered it to be a trivial matter,
            but, in Allah's sight, it is immense.

---

* This ayat, and in fact the whole sura up to ayat 27, was occasioned by a slanderous rumour
concerning one of the wives of the Prophet.

16   Why, when you heard it, did you not say,
         'We have no business speaking about this.
             Glory be to You! This is a terrible slander!'?

17   Allah warns you never to repeat the like of it again
         if you are believers.

18   Allah makes the Signs clear to you
         and Allah is All-Knowing, All-Wise.

19   People who love to see filth being spread about
         concerning those who believe
      will have a painful punishment
         both in this world and the Next World.
      Allah knows and you do not know.

20   Were it not for Allah's favour to you and His mercy . . .
         and that Allah is All-Gentle, Most Merciful.

21   You who believe! do not follow in the footsteps of Shaytan.
         Anyone who follows in Shaytan's footsteps should know
             that he commands indecency and wrongdoing.
      Were it not for Allah's favour upon you and His mercy,
         not one of you would ever have been purified.
      But Allah purifies whomever He wills.
         Allah is All-Hearing, All-Knowing.

22   Those of you possessing affluence and ample wealth
         should not make oaths that they will not give
             to their relatives and the very poor
      and those who have made hijra in the way of Allah.*
         They should rather pardon and overlook.
      Would you not love Allah to forgive you?
         Allah is Ever-Forgiving, Most Merciful.

23   Those who accuse women who are chaste,
         but who are careless and yet believe,
      are cursed in both this world and the Next World,
         and they will have a terrible punishment
24   on the Day when their tongues and hands and feet
         will testify against them about what they were doing.

---

* This refers to some believers who vowed to stop supporting certain dependants because of their involvement in spreading the rumour.

25   On that Day Allah will pay them in full what is due to them,
        and they will know that Allah is the Clear Truth.

26   Corrupt women are for corrupt men
        and corrupt men are for corrupt women,
    Good women are for good men
        and good men are for good women.
    The latter are innocent of what they say.
        They will have forgiveness and generous provision.

27   You who believe! do not enter houses
        other than your own
    until you have asked permission
        and greeted their inhabitants.
    That is better for you,
        so that hopefully you will pay heed.
28   And if you find no one at home do not go in
        until permission has been granted you.
    And if you are told to go away then go away.
        That is purer for you.
    Allah knows what you do.

29   There is nothing wrong in your entering houses
        where no one lives
        and where there is some service for you.
    Allah knows what you divulge
        and what you conceal.

30   Say to the believers that they should lower their eyes
        and guard their private parts.
        That is purer for them.
    Allah is aware of what they do.

31   Say to the believing women that they should lower their eyes
        and guard their private parts
        and not display their adornments –
            except for what normally shows –
        and draw their head-coverings across their breasts.
    They should only display their adornments to their husbands
        or their fathers or their husbands' fathers,
        or their sons or their husbands' sons
        or their brothers or their brothers' sons
        or their sisters' sons
        or other women

or those they own as slaves
or their male attendants who have no sexual desire
or children who still have no awareness
of women's private parts.
Nor should they stamp their feet
so that their hidden ornaments are known.
Turn to Allah every one of you, believers,
so that hopefully you will be successful.

32   Marry off those among you who are unmarried
and those of your slaves and slavegirls who are righteous.
If they are poor, Allah will enrich them from His bounty.
Allah is All-Encompassing, All-Knowing.

33   Those who cannot find the means to marry should be abstinent
until Allah enriches them from His bounty.
If any slaves you own want to make a contract to free themselves,
write it for them if you know of good in them
and give them some of the wealth Allah has given you.
Do not force your slavegirls to prostitute themselves
if they desire to be virtuous women
out of your desire for the goods of this world.
If anyone forces them,
then after they have been forced,
Allah is Ever-Forgiving, Most Merciful.

34   We have sent down Clear Signs to you
and the example of those who passed away before you
and an admonition for the godfearing.

35   Allah is the Light of the heavens and the earth.
The metaphor of His Light
is that of a niche
in which is a lamp,
the lamp inside a glass,
the glass like a brilliant star,
lit from a blessed tree, an olive,
neither of the east nor of the west,
its oil all but giving off light
even if no fire touches it.
Light upon Light.
Allah guides to His Light whomever He wills
and Allah makes metaphors for mankind
and Allah has knowledge of all things.

36 In houses which Allah has permitted to be built
   and in which His name is remembered,
 there are men who proclaim His glory
   morning and evening,

37 not distracted by trade or commerce
   from the remembrance of Allah
    and the establishment of the prayer
     and the payment of zakat;
   fearing a day when all hearts and eyes will be in turmoil –

38 so that Allah may reward them for the best of what they did
   and give them more from His unbounded favour.
 Allah provides for anyone He wills without reckoning.

39 But the actions of those who disbelieve
   are like a mirage in the desert.
 A thirsty man thinks it is water
   but when he reaches it,
    he finds it to be nothing at all,
   but he finds Allah there.
 He will pay him his account in full.
   Allah is swift at reckoning.

40 Or they are like the darkness of a fathomless sea
   which is covered by waves
    above which are waves
     above which are clouds,
   layers of darkness,
    one upon the other.
 If he puts out his hand,
   he can scarcely see it.
 Those Allah gives no light to,
   they have no light.

41 Do you not see that everyone in the heavens and earth
   glorifies Allah,
 as do the birds with their outspread wings?
   Each one knows its prayer and glorification.
 Allah knows what they do.

42 The kingdom of the heavens and earth belongs to Allah
   and Allah is the final destination.

43 Do you not see that Allah propels the clouds
   then makes them coalesce

then heaps them up,
and then you see the rain come pouring
out of the middle of them?
And He sends down mountains from the sky
with hail inside them,
striking with it anyone He wills
and averting it from anyone He wills.
The brightness of His lightning almost blinds the sight.

44   Allah revolves night and day.
There is surely a lesson in that for people with inner sight.

45   Allah created every animal from water.
Some of them go on their bellies,
some of them on two legs,
and some on four.
Allah creates whatever He wills.
Allah has power over all things.

46   We have sent down Signs making things clear.
Allah guides whomever He wills to a straight path.

47   They say, 'We believe in Allah
and in the Messenger
and we obey.'
Then after that a group of them turn away.
Such people are not believers.

48   When they are summoned to Allah and His Messenger,
so that he may judge between them,
a group of them immediately turn away.

49   But if right is on their side,
they come to him most submissively!

50   Is there a sickness in their hearts
or do they have misgivings
or do they fear that Allah and His Messenger
will be unjust to them?
No, it is simply that they are wrongdoers.

51   The reply of the believers
when they are summoned to Allah and His Messenger
so that he can judge between them,

is to say, 'We hear and we obey.'
They are ones who are successful.

52   All who obey Allah and His Messenger
and have awe of Allah and taqwa of Him,
they are the ones who are victorious.

53   They have sworn by Allah with their most earnest oaths
that if you give them the command, they will go out.
Say: 'Do not swear.
Honourable obedience is enough.
Allah is aware of what you do.'

54   Say: 'Obey Allah and obey the Messenger.
Then if they turn away
he is only responsible for what he is charged with
and you are responsible for what you are charged with.
If you obey him, you will be guided.'
The Messenger is only responsible for clear transmission.

55   Allah has promised those of you
who believe and do right actions
that He will make them successors in the land
as He made those before them successors,
and will firmly establish for them their deen
with which He is pleased
and give them, in place of their fear, security.
'They worship Me, not associating anything with Me.'
Any who disbelieve after that, such people are deviators.

56   Establish the prayer and pay zakat and obey the Messenger
so that hopefully mercy will be shown to you.

57   Do not imagine that those who disbelieve
are able to escape Allah on earth.
Their shelter will be the Fire.
What an evil destination!

58   You who believe! those you own as slaves
and those of you who have not yet reached puberty
should ask your permission to enter at three times:
before the Dawn Prayer,
when you have undressed at noon,

and after the 'Isha' Prayer –
three times of nakedness for you.
There is nothing wrong for you or them at other times
in moving around among yourselves from one to another.
In this way Allah makes the Signs clear to you.
Allah is All-Knowing, All-Wise.

59   Once your children have reached puberty,
they should ask your permission to enter
as those before them also asked permission.
In this way Allah makes His Signs clear to you.
Allah is All-Knowing, All-Wise.

60   As for women who are past child-bearing age
and no longer have any hope of getting married,
there is nothing wrong in their removing their outer clothes,
provided they do not flaunt their adornments;
but to refrain from doing so is better for them.
Allah is All-Hearing, All-Knowing.

61   There is no objection to the blind, no objection to the lame,
no objection to the sick nor to yourselves
if you eat in your own houses
or your fathers' houses or your mothers' houses
or your brothers' houses or your sisters' houses
or the houses of your paternal uncles or paternal aunts
or the houses of your maternal uncles or maternal aunts
or places to which you own the keys
or those of your friends.
There is nothing wrong in your eating together
or eating separately.
And when you enter houses greet one another
with a greeting from Allah, blessed and good.
In this way Allah makes the Signs clear to you
so that hopefully you will use your intellect.

62   The believers are those
who believe in Allah and His Messenger
and who, when they are with him
on a matter of common concern,
do not leave until they have asked him for permission.
Those people who ask you for permission
are the ones who truly believe in Allah and His Messenger.

If they ask your permission to attend to their own affairs,
    give permission to any of them you please;
        and ask Allah's forgiveness for them.
    Allah is Ever-Forgiving, Most Merciful.

63   Do not make the Messenger's summoning of you
        the same as your summoning of one another.
    Allah knows those of you who sneak away.
        Those who oppose his command should
            beware of a testing trial coming to them
        or a painful punishment striking them.

64   Everything in the heavens and the earth belongs to Allah.
        He knows what you are engaged upon.
    On the Day when they are returned to Him,
        He will inform them of what they did.
    Allah has knowledge of all things.

Sura 25

Al-Furqan
Discrimination

In the name of Allah, All-Merciful, Most Merciful

1   Blessed be He who has sent down the Discrimination to His slave
      so that he can be a warner to all beings;

2   He to whom the kingdom of the heavens and the earth belongs.
      He does not have a son
        and He has no partner in the Kingdom.
      He created everything and determined it most exactly.

3   But they have adopted gods apart from Him
      which do not create anything
        but are themselves created.
      They have no power to harm or help themselves.
      They have no power over death or life or resurrection.

4   Those who disbelieve say,
      'This is nothing but a lie he has invented
        and other people have helped him to do it.
      They have brought injustice and falsehood.'

5   They say, 'It is myths of previous peoples
      which he has had transcribed
    and which are read out to him
      in the morning and the evening.'

6   Say: 'The One Who sent it down
      is He Who knows all hidden secrets
        in the heavens and earth.
      He is Ever-Forgiving, Most Merciful.'

7 They say, 'What is the matter with this Messenger,
   that he eats food and walks in the market-place?
  Why has an angel not been sent down to him
   so that it can be a warner along with him?

8 Why has treasure not been showered down on him?
   Why does he not have a garden to give him food?'
  The wrongdoers say, 'You are merely following
   a man who is bewitched.'

9 See how they make comparative judgements about you.
   They are misguided
    and cannot find the way.

10 Blessed be He who, if He wishes,
   will grant you better than that:
  Gardens with rivers flowing under them;
   and He will grant you Palaces.

11 But instead, they deny the Hour;
   and We have prepared a Searing Blaze
    for those who deny the Hour.

12 When it sees them coming from a long way off,
   they will hear it seething and rasping.

13 When they are flung into a narrow place in it,
   shackled together in chains,
  they will cry out there for destruction.

14 'Do not cry out today for just one destruction,
   cry out for many destructions!'

15 Say: 'Is that better, or the Garden of Eternal Life
   which has been promised to the godfearing?
    That is their recompense and destination.'

16   They will have in it whatever they want
    timelessly, for ever.
   It is a binding promise of your Lord.

17 On the Day We gather them together,
   and those they worship besides Allah,
  and say, 'Did you misguide these slaves of Mine
   or did they stray from the way of their own accord?'

18 they will say, 'Glory be to You!

It would not have been fitting for us
to have taken any protectors apart from You.
But You let them and their fathers enjoy themselves
so that they forgot the Reminder.
They were people devoid of good.'

19 So now they have disowned you for what you said,
and they cannot avert it or give you any help.
As for anyone among you who has done wrong,
We will make him suffer great punishment.

20 We never sent any Messengers before you
who did not eat food and walk in the market-place.
But We have made some of you a trial for others
to see if you will be steadfast?
Your Lord sees everything.

21 Those who do not expect to meet Us say,
'Why have angels not been sent down to us?
Why do we not see our Lord?'
They have become arrogant about themselves
and are excessively insolent.

22 On the Day they see the angels,
there will be no good news that Day for the evildoers.
They will say, 'There is an absolute ban.'

23 We will advance on the actions they have done
and make them scattered specks of dust.

24 The Companions of the Garden on that Day
will have better lodging and a better resting-place,

25 on the Day when Heaven is split apart in clouds,
and the angels are sent down rank upon rank.

26 The Kingdom that Day will belong in truth to the All-Merciful.
It will be a hard Day for the unbelievers,

27 the Day when a wrongdoer will bite his hands and say,
'Alas for me! If only I had gone the way of the Messenger!

28 Alas for me! If only I had not taken so-and-so for a friend!

29 He led me astray from the Reminder after it came to me.'
Shaytan always leaves man in the lurch.

30 The Messenger says, 'My Lord, my people
treat this Qur'an as something to be ignored.'

31   In this way We have assigned to every Prophet
        an enemy from among the evildoers.
    But your Lord is a sufficient guide and helper.

32   Those who disbelieve say, 'Why was the Qur'an
        not sent down to him all in one go?'
    It is so that We may fortify your heart by it.
        We have recited it distinctly, little by little.

33   Every time they come to you with a difficult point,
        We bring you the truth and the best of explanations.

34   Those who are herded headlong into Hell,
        such people are in the worst position.
    They are the most misguided from the way.

35   We gave Musa the Book and appointed
        his brother Harun with him as a helper.

36   We said, 'Go to the people who have denied Our Signs,'
        and We annihilated them completely.

37   And when the people of Nuh denied the Messengers,
        We drowned them and made them a Sign for all mankind.
    We have prepared a painful punishment for the wrongdoers.

38   The same goes for 'Ad and Thamud
        and the Companions of the Well
            and many generations in between.

39   We gave examples to each one of them
        and each one of them We utterly wiped out.

40   They themselves have come across the city
        which was rained on by an evil rain.*
    Did they not then see it?
        But they do not expect to rise again.

41   When they see you they only make a mockery of you:
        'Is this the one Allah has sent as a Messenger?

42   He might almost have misled us from our gods
        had we not stuck to them steadfastly!'
    They will soon know,

---

* Referring to the ruins of Sodom, the city of the Prophet Lut, which was on the trade route from Makka to Syria, a journey regualarly made by the Makkan caravans.

when they see the punishment,
    whose way is the most misguided.

43   Have you seen him who has taken his whims
      and desires to be his god?
    Will you then be his guardian?

44   Do you suppose that most of them hear or understand?
      They are just like cattle.
    Indeed they are even more astray!

45   Do you not see how your Lord stretches out shadows?
      If He had wished He could have made them stationary.
    Then We appoint the sun to be the pointer to them.
46   Then We draw them back to Ourselves in gradual steps.

47   It is He who made the night a cloak for you
      and sleep a rest,
    and He made the day a time for rising.

48   It is He who sends out the winds,
      bringing advance news of His mercy.
    And We send down from heaven pure water
49   so that by it We may bring a dead land to life
    and give drink to many of the animals and people We created.

50   We have variegated it for them so that they might pay heed
      but most people spurn anything else but unbelief.

51   If We had wished We could have sent a warner to every town.

52   So do not obey the unbelievers but use this
      to battle against them with all your might.

53   It is He who has unloosed both seas –
      one sweet and refreshing,
        the other salty and bitter –
    and put a dividing line between them,
      an impassable barrier.

54   And it is He who created human beings from water
      and then gave them relations by blood and marriage.
        Your Lord is All-Powerful.

55   Yet they worship instead of Allah
       what can neither help nor harm them.
   The unbelievers are always biased against their Lord.

56   We only sent you to bring good news
       and to give warning.

57   Say: 'I do not ask you for any wage for it –
       only that anyone who wants to
   should make his way towards his Lord.'

58   Put your trust in the Living who does not die
       and glorify Him with praise.
   He is well aware of the wrong actions of His slaves:
59   He who created the heavens and the earth
          and everything in between them
             in six days,
       and then established Himself firmly on the Throne;
         the All-Merciful –
       ask anyone who is informed about Him.

60   When they are told to prostrate to the All-Merciful,
       they say, 'And what is the All-Merciful?
   Are we to prostrate to something you command us to?'
       And it merely makes them run away all the more.

61   Blessed be He who placed constellations in the sky
       and put a blazing lamp and shining moon among them.

62   It is He who made night and day succeed each other
       for those who want to pay heed or to give thanks.

63   The slaves of the All-Merciful
       are those who walk lightly on the earth
   and, who, when the ignorant speak to them, say, 'Peace';
64   those who pass the night
       prostrating and standing before their Lord;
65   those who say, 'Our Lord, avert from us the punishment of Hell.
       Its punishment is inescapable pain.
66   It is indeed an evil lodging and abode';
67   those who, when they spend, are neither extravagant nor mean,
       but take a stance midway between the two;
68   those who do not call on any other god together with Allah
       and do not kill anyone Allah has made inviolate,

except with the right to do so,
and do not fornicate;
anyone who does that will receive an evil punishment

69 and on the Day of Rising his punishment will be doubled
and he will be humiliated in it timelessly, for ever,

70 except for those who repent
and believe and act rightly:
Allah will transform the wrong actions
of such people into good –
Allah is Ever-Forgiving, Most Merciful –

71 for certainly all who repent and act rightly
have turned sincerely towards Allah;

72 those who do not bear false witness
and who, when they pass by worthless talk,
pass by with dignity;

73 those who, when they are reminded of the Signs of their Lord,
do not turn their backs, deaf and blind to them;

74 those who say, 'Our Lord, give us joy in our wives and children
and make us a good example for the godfearing';

75 such people will be repaid for their steadfastness
with the Highest Paradise,
where they will meet with welcome and with 'Peace'.

76 They will remain in it timelessly, for ever.
What an excellent lodging and abode!

77 Say: 'What has My Lord to do with you if you do not call on Him?
But you have denied the truth,
so punishment is bound to come.'

Sura 26

Ash-Shu'ara'
The Poets

1   Ta Sin Mim
2   Those are the Signs of the Clear Book.

3   Perhaps you will destroy yourself with grief
        because they will not become believers.

4   If We wished We could send down a Sign to them from heaven,
        before which their heads would be bowed low in subjection.

5   But no fresh reminder from the All-Merciful reaches them
        without their turning away from it.

6   They have denied the truth,
        but the news of what they mocked
          will certainly come to them.

7   Have they not looked at the earth and seen how We have made
        every sort of beneficial species grow in it?

8   There is certainly a Sign in that,
        yet most of them are not believers.
9   Truly your Lord is the Almighty, the Most Merciful.

10   When your Lord called out to Musa:
        'Go to the wrongdoing people,
11   the people of Pharaoh.
        Will they not be godfearing?'

12	He said, 'My Lord, I fear they will deny me
13	and that my breast will be constricted
	and that my tongue will not be free,
	so send Harun as a Messenger as well.
14	They hold a wrong action against me
	and I fear that they may kill me.'
15	He said, 'By no means! Go, both of you, with Our Signs.
	We will certainly be together with you, listening.
16	Go to Pharaoh and say,
	"We are the Messenger of the Lord of all the worlds
17	to tell you to send the tribe of Israel away with us."'
18	He said, 'Did we not bring you up among us as a child
	and did you not spend many years of your life among us?
19	Yet you did the deed you did and were ungrateful.'
20	He said, 'At the time I did it I was one of the misguided
21	and so I fled from you when I was in fear of you
	but my Lord gave me right judgement
	and made me one of the Messengers.
22	And anyway you can only reproach me with this favour
	because you made the tribe of Israel into slaves!'
23	Pharaoh said, 'What is the Lord of all the worlds?'
24	He said, 'The Lord of the heavens and the earth
	and everything between them
	if you knew for sure.'
25	He said to those around him, 'Are you listening?'
26	He said, 'Your Lord and the Lord of your forefathers,
	the previous peoples.'
27	He said, 'This Messenger, who has been sent to you, is mad.'
28	He said, 'The Lord of the East and the West
	and everything between them
	if you used your intellect.'
29	He said, 'If you take any god other than me,
	I will certainly throw you into prison.'
30	He said, 'Even if I were to bring you something undeniable?'

31   He said, 'Produce it then if you are someone telling the truth.'

32   So he threw down his staff and there it was,
         unmistakably a snake.
33   And he drew out his hand and there it was,
         pure white to those who looked.

34   He said to the High Council round about him,
         'This certainly is a skilled magician
35   who desires by his magic
         to expel you from your land,
         so what do you recommend?'
36   They said, 'Detain him and his brother
         and send out marshals to the cities,
37   to bring you all the skilled magicians.'

38   So the magicians were assembled
         for a meeting on a specified day.

39   The people were asked, 'Are you all assembled
40   so we can follow the magicians
         if they are the winners?'

41   When the magicians came, they said to Pharaoh,
         'Will we be rewarded if we are the winners?'
42   He said, 'Yes, and in that case
         you will be among those brought near.'

43   Musa said to them, 'Throw whatever it is you are going to throw!'

44   They threw down their ropes and staffs and said,
         'By the might of Pharaoh we are the winners.'
45   But Musa threw down his staff and at once
         it swallowed up what they had fabricated.

46   The magicians threw themselves down, prostrating.

47   They said, 'We believe in the Lord of all the worlds,
48   the Lord of Musa and Harun.'

49   He said, 'Have you believed in him
         before I authorised you?
         He is your chief who taught you magic.
         But you will soon know!

I will cut off your alternate hands and feet
and I will crucify every one of you.'

50   They said, 'We do not care!
We are returning to our Lord.
51   We remain hopeful that our Lord
will forgive us our mistakes
for being the first of the believers.'

52   We revealed to Musa:
'Travel with Our slaves by night.
You will certainly be pursued.'

53   Pharaoh sent marshals into the cities:
54   'These people are a small group
55   and we find them irritating
56   and we constitute a vigilant majority.'

57   We expelled them from gardens and springs,
58   from treasures and a splendid situation.
59   So it was! And We bequeathed them to the tribe of Israel.

60   So they pursued them towards the east.
61   And when the two hosts came into sight of one another
Musa's companions said, 'We will surely be overtaken!'
62   He said, 'Never! My Lord is with me and He will guide me.'

63   So We revealed to Musa, 'Strike the sea with your staff.'
And it split in two, each part like a towering cliff.
64   And We brought the others right up to it.
65   We rescued Musa and all those who were with him.
66   Then We drowned the rest.

67   There is certainly a Sign in that
yet most of them are not believers.
68   Truly your Lord is the Almighty, the Most Merciful.

69   Recite to them the story of Ibrahim
70   when he said to his father and his people,
'What do you worship?'
71   They said, 'We worship idols
and will continue to cling to them.'
72   He said, 'Do they hear you when you call
73   or do they help you or do you harm?'

74   They said, 'No, but this is what
         we found our fathers doing.'

75   He said, 'Have you really thought about what you worship,
76   you and your fathers who came before?
77   They are all my enemies –
         except for the Lord of all the worlds:
78   He who created me and guides me;
79   He who gives me food and gives me drink;
80   and when I am ill, it is He who heals me;
81   He who will cause my death, then give me life;
82   He who I sincerely hope will forgive my mistakes
         on the Day of Reckoning.
83   My Lord, give me right judgement
         and unite me with the righteous;
84   and make me highly esteemed among the later peoples;
85   and make me one of the inheritors
                of the Garden of Delight;
86   and forgive my father – he was one of the misguided;
87   and do not disgrace me on the Day they are raised up,
88   the Day when neither wealth nor sons will be of any use –
89   except to those who come to Allah
                with sound and flawless hearts.'

90   The Garden will be brought near to the godfearing.
91   The Blazing Fire will be displayed to the misled.

92   They will be asked, 'Where are those
         you used to worship besides Allah?
93   Can they help you or even help themselves?'

94   They will be bundled into it head first,
         they and the misled,
95   and every one of Iblis's regiments.

96   Arguing in it with one another, they will say,
97   'By Allah, we were plainly misguided
98   when We equated you with the Lord of all the worlds.
99   It was only the evildoers who misguided us
100   and now we have no one to intercede for us;
101   we do not have a single loyal friend.
102   If only we could have another chance
         then we would be among the believers!'

103	There is certainly a Sign in that, yet most of them are not believers.
104	Truly your Lord is the Almighty, the Most Merciful.
105	The people of Nuh denied the Messengers.
106	When their brother Nuh said to them, 'Will you not be godfearing?
107	I am a faithful Messenger to you
108	so have taqwa of Allah and obey me.

109	I do not ask you for any wage for it.
	        My wage is the responsibility of no one
	                but the Lord of all the worlds.

110	so have taqwa of Allah and obey me.'
111	they said, 'Why should we believe you when the vilest people follow you?'
112	He said, 'What do I know about what they have been doing?
113	Their reckoning is the concern of my Lord alone if you were but aware.
114	I am not going to chase away the believers.
115	I am only a clear warner.'
116	They said, 'Nuh, if you do not desist you will be stoned.'
117	He said, 'My Lord, my people have denied me
118	so make a clear judgement between me and them and rescue me and the believers who are with me.'
119	So We rescued him and those with him in the loaded ship.
120	Then afterwards We drowned the rest.
121	There is certainly a Sign in that, yet most of them are not believers.
122	Truly your Lord is the Almighty, the Most Merciful.
123	'Ad denied the Messengers
124	when their brother Hud said to them, 'Will you not be godfearing?
125	I am a faithful Messenger to you
126	so have taqwa of Allah and obey me.

127	I do not ask you for any wage for it.
	        My wage is the responsibility of no one
	                but the Lord of all the worlds.

128	Do you build a tower on every hilltop, just to amuse yourselves,

129	and construct great fortresses,
	hoping to live for ever,
130	and when you attack,
	attack as tyrants do?
131	So have taqwa of Allah and obey me.
132	Have taqwa of Him
	who has supplied you with what you know,
133	supplied you with livestock and children
134	and gardens and clear springs.
135	I fear for you the punishment of a terrible Day.'

136	They said, 'It makes no difference to us
	whether you preach or do not preach.
137	This is only what the previous peoples did.
138	We are not going to be punished.'

139	So they denied him and We destroyed them.
	There is certainly a Sign in that,
	yet most of them are not believers.
140	Truly your Lord is the Almighty, the Most Merciful.

141	Thamud denied the Messengers,
142	when their brother Salih said to them,
	'Will you not be godfearing?
143	I am a faithful Messenger to you
144	so have taqwa of Allah and obey me.
145	I do not ask you for any wage for it.
	My wage is the responsibility of no one
	but the Lord of all the worlds.
146	Are you going to be left secure amid what is here,
147	amid gardens and clear springs,
148	and cultivated fields
	and palms with supple spathes?
149	Will you continue hewing houses from the mountains
	with exultant skill?
150	So have taqwa of Allah and obey me.
151	Do not obey the orders of the profligate,
152	those who corrupt the earth and do not put things right.'

153	They said, 'You are merely someone bewitched.
154	You are nothing but a human being like ourselves,
	so produce a Sign if you are telling the truth.'

155	He said, 'Here is a she-camel. She has a time for drinking and you have a time for drinking – on specified days.
156	Do not do anything to harm her or the punishment of a terrible day will come down on you.'
157	But they hamstrung her and woke up full of remorse,
158	for the punishment did come down them.
	There is certainly a Sign in that, yet most of them are not believers.
159	Truly your Lord is the Almighty, the Most Merciful.
160	The people of Lut denied the Messengers,
161	when their brother Lut said to them, 'Will you not be godfearing?
162	I am a faithful Messenger to you.
163	so have taqwa of Allah and obey me.
164	I do not ask you for any wage for it. My wage is the responsibility of no one but the Lord of all the worlds.
165	Of all beings, do you lie with males,
166	leaving the wives Allah has created for you? You are a people who have overstepped the limits.'
167	They said, 'Lut, if you do not desist you will be expelled.'
168	He said, 'I am someone who detests the deed you perpetrate.
169	My Lord, rescue me and my family from what they are doing.'
170	Therefore We rescued him and all his family –
171	except for an old woman who remained behind.
172	Then We utterly destroyed the rest
173	and made a Rain come pouring down upon them. How evil is the rain of those who are warned!
174	There is certainly a Sign in that, yet most of them are not believers.
175	Truly your Lord is the Almighty, the Most Merciful.
176	The Companions of the Thicket denied the Messengers,
177	when Shu'ayb said to them, 'Will you not be godfearing?

178	I am a faithful Messenger to you.
179	so have taqwa of Allah and obey me.
180	I do not ask you for any wage for it.
	My wage is the responsibility of no one
	but the Lord of all the worlds.
181	Give full measure.
	Do not skimp.
182	Weigh with a level balance.
183	Do not diminish people's goods
	and do not go about the earth, corrupting it.
184	Have taqwa of Him
	who created you and the earlier creatures.'
185	They said, 'You are merely someone bewitched.
186	You are nothing but a human being like ourselves.
	We think you are a liar.
187	So make lumps from heaven fall down on us
	if you are telling the truth.'
188	He said, 'My Lord knows best what you are doing.'
189	They denied him and the punishment
	of the Day of Shadow came down on them.
	It was indeed the punishment of a terrible Day.
190	There is certainly a Sign in that,
	yet most of them are not believers.
191	Truly your Lord is the Almighty, the Most Merciful.
192	Truly it is revelation
	sent down by the Lord of all the worlds.
193	The Faithful Ruh brought it down
194	to your heart
	so you might be one of the Warners
195	in a clear Arabic tongue.
196	It is certainly in the scriptures of the previous peoples.
197	Is it not indeed a Sign for them that
	the scholars of the tribe of Israel have knowledge of it?
198	If We had sent it down to a non-Arab
199	who had then recited it to them,
	they still would not believe in it.

200   That is how We thread it
            into the hearts of the evildoers.
201   They will not believe in it
            until they see the painful punishment.
202   It will come upon them suddenly
            when they are not expecting it.

203   They will say, 'Can we be granted a reprieve?'
204   Do they want to hasten Our punishment?

205   Do you think, if We let them enjoy themselves for years
206   and then what they were promised comes to them,
207   that what they enjoyed will be of any use to them?

208   We have never destroyed a city
            without giving it prior warning
209   as a reminder.
            We were never unjust.

210   The shaytans did not bring it down.
211   It does not befit them
            and they are not capable of it.
212   They are debarred from hearing it.

213   So do not call on any other god along with Allah
            or you will be among those who will be punished.

214   Warn your near relatives.
215   and take the believers who follow you under your wing.

216   If they disobey you, say, 'I am free of what you do.'

217   Put your trust in the Almighty, the Most Merciful,
218   He who sees you when you stand up to pray
219   and your movements with those who prostrate.
220   He is the All-Hearing, the All-Knowing.

221   Shall I tell you whom the shaytans descend upon?
222   They descend on every evil liar.
223   They give them a hearing
            and most of them are liars.

224   And as for poets,
            it is the misled who follow them.

225	Do you not see how they ramble on in every style
226	and say things which they do not do,
227	except those who believe and do right actions

and remember Allah repeatedly
and defend themselves after they have been wronged?
Those who do wrong will soon know
the kind of reversal they will receive!

Sura 27

An-Naml
The Ant

In the name of Allah, All-Merciful, Most Merciful

1   Ta Sin
   Those are the Signs of the Qur'an and a Clear Book.

2   It is guidance and good news for the believers,

3   those who establish the prayer and pay zakat
    and are certain about the Next World.

4   As for those who do not believe in the Next World,
    We have made their actions appear good to them
     and they wander about blindly.

5   Such people will receive an evil punishment
    and will be the greatest losers in the Next World.

6   You receive the Qur'an directly
    from One who is All-Wise, All-Knowing.

7   When Musa said to his people, 'I can make out a fire.
    I will bring you news from it or at least a burning brand
     so that hopefully you will be able to warm yourselves.'

8   But when he reached it, a voice called out to him,
    'Blessed be him who is by the Fire,
     and all who are around it.
    Glory be to Allah,
     the Lord of all the worlds!

9   Musa, I am Allah,
     the Almighty, the All-Wise.

10   Throw down your staff.'
        Then when he saw it slithering like a snake
            he turned and fled and did not turn back again.
                'Have no fear, Musa.
        In My Presence the Messengers have no fear –

11   except for one who did wrong
        and then changed evil into good –
            for I am Ever-Forgiving, Most Merciful.

12   Put your hand inside your shirt front.
            It will emerge pure white,
                yet quite unharmed –
        one of nine Signs to Pharaoh and his people.
            They are a people of deviators.'

13   When Our Signs came to them in all their clarity,
            they said, 'This is downright magic,'
14   and they repudiated them wrongly and haughtily,
            in spite of their own certainty about them.
        See the final fate of the corrupters.

15   We gave knowledge to Dawud and Sulayman who said,
            'Praise be to Allah who has favoured us
                over many of His slaves who are believers.'

16   Sulayman was Dawud's heir.
            He said, 'Mankind!
          we have been taught the speech of birds
            and we have been given everything.
         This is indeed a manifest blessing.'

17   Sulayman's troops,
            made up of jinn and men and birds,
        were assembled for him,
            paraded in tight ranks.

18   Then, when they reached the Valley of the Ants,
            an ant said, 'Ants! enter your dwellings
        so that Sulayman and his troops
            do not crush you unwittingly.'
19   He smiled, laughing at its words, and said,
            'My Lord, keep me thankful for the blessing
        You have bestowed on me and on my parents,
            and keep me acting rightly, pleasing You,

and admit me, by Your mercy,
among Your slaves who are righteous.'

20   He inspected the birds and said,
'How is it that I do not see the hoopoe?
Or is it absent without leave?
21   I will certainly punish it most severely
or slaughter it
if it does not bring me clear authority.'

22   However, it was not long delayed, and then it said,
'I have comprehended something which you have not
and bring you accurate intelligence from Sheba.
23   I found a woman ruling over them
who has been given everything.
She possesses a mighty throne.
24   I found both her and her people
prostrating to the sun instead of Allah.
Shaytan has made their actions seem good to them
and debarred them from the Way
so they are not guided
25   and do not prostrate to Allah,
Who brings out what is hidden
in the heavens and the earth,
and knows what you conceal
and what you divulge.
26   Allah – there is no god but Him –
the Lord of the Mighty Throne.'

27   He said, 'We shall soon see
if you have told the truth
or are a liar.
28   Take this letter of mine
and deliver it to them
and then withdraw from them a little
and see how they respond.'

29   She said, 'Council! a noble letter
has been delivered to me.
30   It is from Sulayman and says:
"In the name of Allah,
All-Merciful, Most Merciful.
31   Do not rise up against me,
but come to me in submission."'

32 She said, 'Council! give me your opinion about this matter.
        It is not my habit to make a final decision
            until I have heard what you have to say.'
33 They said, 'We possess strength and we possess great force.
        But the matter is in your hands
            so consider what you command.'
34 She said, 'When kings enter a city, they lay waste to it
        and make its mightiest inhabitants the most abased.
            That is what they too will do.
35   I will send them a gift and then wait and see
            what the messengers bring back.'

36 When it reached Sulayman he said,
        'Would you give me wealth
            when what Allah has given me
        is better than what He has given you?
    No, rather it is you who delight in your gift.
37   Return to them.
    We will come to them
        with troops they cannot face
    and we will expel them from it
        abased and humiliated.'

38 He said, 'Council! who among you will bring me her throne
        before they come to me in submission?'
39 An ifreet of the jinn said,
        'I will bring it to you
            before you get up from your seat.
        I am strong and trustworthy enough to do it.'
40 He who possessed knowledge of the Book said,
        'I will bring it to you
            before your glance returns to you.'
    And when he saw it standing firmly in his presence,
        he said, 'This is part of my Lord's favour to test me
            to see if I will give thanks or show ingratitude.
        Whoever gives thanks only does so to his own gain.
        Whoever is ungrateful, my Lord is Rich Beyond Need, Generous.'

41 He said, 'Disguise her throne.
        We shall see whether she is guided
            or someone who is not guided.'
42 Then when she came, she was asked,
        'Is your throne like this?'
    She said, 'It is exactly like it.'

'We were given knowledge before her
and were already Muslims,

43   but what she worshipped besides Allah impeded her.
She was from an unbelieving people.'

44   She was told: 'Enter the courtyard,' but when she saw it
she supposed it to be a pool and bared her legs.
He said, 'It is a courtyard paved with glass.'
She said, 'My Lord, I have wronged myself
but I have submitted with Sulayman
to the Lord of all the worlds.'

45   To Thamud We sent their brother Salih
telling them to worship Allah,
but straightaway they divided in two,
arguing with one another.

46   He said, 'My people, why are you so anxious
to hasten the bad before the good?
If only you would ask for forgiveness from Allah,
so that mercy might perhaps be shown to you.'

47   They said, 'We see you, and those with you, as an evil omen.'
He said, 'No, your evil omen is with Allah;
you are merely a people undergoing a trial.'

48   There was a group of nine men in the city
causing corruption in the land
and not putting things right.

49   They said, 'Let us make an oath to one another by Allah
that we will fall on him and his family in the night
and then say to his protector, "We did not witness
the destruction of his family and we are telling the truth."'

50   They hatched a plot and We hatched a plot
while they were not aware.

51   So look at the end result of all their plotting;
We utterly destroyed them and their whole people!

52   These are the ruins of their houses because of the wrong they did.
There is certainly a Sign in that for people with knowledge.

53   We rescued those who believed and were godfearing.

54   And when Lut said to his people:
'Do you approach depravity with open eyes?

55   Do you come with lust to men instead of women?
You are a people who are deeply ignorant.'

56   the only response of his people was to say:
        'Drive the family of Lut out of your city!
    They are people who keep themselves pure!'

57   So We rescued him and his family – except for his wife.
        We ordained her to be one of those who stayed behind.
58   We rained down a rain upon them.
        How evil is the rain of those who are warned!

59   Say: 'Praise be to Allah
        and peace be upon His slaves whom He has chosen.'
    Is Allah better, or what you associate with Him?

60   He Who created the heavens and the earth
        and sends down water for you from the sky
    by which We make luxuriant gardens grow –
        you could never make their trees grow.
    Is there another god besides Allah?
        No indeed, but they are people
            who equate others with Him!

61   He Who made the earth a stable dwelling place
        and appointed rivers flowing through its midst
            and placed firmly embedded mountains on it
        and set a barrier between the two seas.
    Is there another god besides Allah?
        No indeed, but most of them do not know it!

62   He Who responds to the oppressed when they call on Him
            and removes their distress,
        and has appointed you as khalifs on the earth.
    Is there another god besides Allah?
        How little you pay heed!

63   He Who guides you in the darkness of land and sea
        and sends out the winds bringing advance news of His mercy.
    Is there another god besides Allah?
        Exalted is Allah above what they associate with Him!

64   He Who originates creation and then regenerates it
        and provides for you from out of heaven and earth.
    Is there another god besides Allah?
        Say: 'Bring your proof if you are being truthful.'

65   Say: 'No one in the heavens and the earth knows the Unseen
        except Allah.'
    They are not aware of when they will be raised.

66   No, their knowledge stops short of the Next World.
        In fact they have doubts about it.
            In fact they are blind to it.

67   Those who disbelieve say,
        'When we and our fathers are turned to dust
            will we then be brought forth again?
68   We have been promised this before,
        we and our fathers.
    This is nothing but myths and legends
        of previous peoples.'

69   Say: 'Travel about the earth
        and see the final fate of the evildoers.'

70   Do not grieve over them
        and do not let the plots they make distress you.

71   They say, 'When will this promise be fulfilled
        if you are telling the truth?'

72   Say: 'It may well be that some of
        what you are anxious to hasten on
            is right behind you.'

73   Allah shows favour to mankind
        but most of them are not thankful.

74   Certainly your Lord knows what their hearts keep hidden
        and what they divulge.

75   Certainly there is no hidden thing in either heaven or earth
        which is not in a Clear Book.

76   Certainly this Qur'an narrates to the tribe of Israel
        most of the things about which they differ.

77   Certainly it is guidance and a mercy for the believers.

78   Certainly your Lord will decide between them
                with His just judgement.
        He is the Almighty, the All-Knowing.

79   So put your trust in Allah.
                You are clearly on a path of truth.

80   You will not make dead men hear
                and you will not make deaf men hear the call
                        when they turn their backs in flight.

81   You will not guide blind men out of their error.
                You will not make anyone hear except for those
        who believe in Our Signs and so are Muslims.

82   When the Word is justly carried out against them,
                We will produce a Beast from the earth
                        which will speak to them.
        Truly mankind had no certainty about Our Signs.

83   On that Day We will collect from every community
                a crowd of those who denied Our Signs,
                        paraded in tight ranks.

84   Then when they arrive He will say,
                'Did you deny My Signs even though
        you did not have proper knowledge of them.
                What were you doing?'

85   The Word will be carried out against them
                for the wrong they did
                        and they will not speak.

86   Do they not see that We have made the night for them to rest in
                and the day for seeing?
        There are certainly Signs in that for people who believe.

87   On the Day the Trumpet is blown
                and everyone in the heavens
                        and everyone on the earth
                                is terrified –
                        except those Allah wills,
                everyone will come to Him abject.

88   You will see the mountains you reckoned to be solid
        going past like clouds –
    the handiwork of Allah
        who gives to everything its solidity.
    He is aware of what you do.

89   Those who perform good actions
        will receive better than them
    and will be safe that Day from terror.

90   Those who perform bad actions
        will be flung head first into the Fire:
    'Are you being repaid for anything other than what you did?'

91   'I have simply been ordered to worship the Lord of this land
        which He has declared sacred –
            everything belongs to Him –
    and I have been ordered to be one of the Muslims
92   and to recite the Qur'an.'
    Whoever is guided is only guided to his own good;
        if anyone is misguided just say,
           'I am only a warner.'

93   Say: 'Praise be to Allah.
        He will show you His Signs
           and you will recognise them.
    Your Lord is not unaware of what you do.'

Sura 28

Al-Qasas
The Story

In the name of Allah, All-Merciful, Most Merciful

1   Ta Sin Mim

2   Those are the Signs of the Clear Book.

3   We recite to you with truth some news of Musa and Pharaoh
        for people who believe.

4   Pharaoh exalted himself arrogantly in the land
        and divided its people into camps,
    oppressing one group of them
        by slaughtering their sons
           and letting their women live.
    He was one of the corrupters.

5   We desired to show kindness to those
        who were oppressed in the land
          and to make them leaders
        and make them inheritors

6   and establish them firmly in the land
        and to show Pharaoh and Haman and their troops
    the very thing that they were fearing from them.

7   We revealed to Musa's mother, 'Suckle him and then
        when you fear for him cast him into the sea.
    Do not fear or grieve; We will return him to you
        and make him one of the Messengers.'

8   The family of Pharaoh picked him up
        so that he might be an enemy

and a source of grief to them.
Certainly Pharaoh and Haman
and their troops were in the wrong.

9   The wife of Pharaoh said,
           'A source of delight for me and for you;
              do not kill him.
      It may well be that he will be of use to us
           or perhaps we could adopt him as a son.'
             They were not aware.

10   Musa's mother felt a great emptiness in her heart
           and she almost gave him away;
      only We fortified her heart so that
           she would be one of the believers.

11   She said to his sister, 'Go after him.'
           And she kept an eye on him from afar
             but they were not aware.

12   We first made him refuse all wet-nurses,
           so she said, 'Shall I show you to a household
      who will feed him for you and be good to him?'

13   That is how We returned him to his mother
           so that she might delight her eyes and feel no grief
      and so that she would know that Allah's promise is true.
           But most of them do not know this.

14   And when he reached his full strength and maturity,
           We gave him judgement and knowledge.
      That is how We recompense good-doers.

15   He entered the city at a time when its inhabitants were unaware
           and found two men fighting there –
      one from his party and the other from his enemy.
           The one from his party asked for his support
             against the other from his enemy.
           So Musa hit him, dealing him a fatal blow.
      He said, 'This is part of Shaytan's handiwork.
           He truly is an outright and misleading enemy.'

16   He said, 'My Lord, I have wronged myself. Forgive me.'
           So He forgave him.

He is the Ever-Forgiving, the Most Merciful.

17   He said, 'My Lord, because of Your blessing upon me,
         I will never be a supporter of evildoers.'

18   Morning found him in the city, fearful and on his guard.
         Then suddenly the man
             who had sought his help the day before,
         shouted for help from him again.
      Musa said to him, 'You are clearly a misguided man.'

19   But when he was about to grab the man
         who was their common enemy,
      he said, 'Musa! do you want to kill me
         just as you killed a person yesterday?
      You only want to be a tyrant in the land;
         you do not want to be a reformer.'

20   A man came running from the furthest part of the city,
         saying, 'Musa, the Council are conspiring to kill you,
             so leave!
         I am someone who brings you good advice.'

21   So he left there fearful and on his guard, saying,
         'My Lord, rescue me from the people of the wrongdoers!'
22   When he turned his face in the direction of Madyan, he said,
         'Hopefully my Lord will guide me to the right way.'

23   When he arrived at the water of Madyan,
         he found a crowd of people drawing water there.
      Standing apart from them, he found two women,
         holding back their sheep.
      He said, 'What are you two doing here?'
         They said, 'We cannot draw water
      until the shepherds have driven off their sheep.
         You see our father is a very old man.'
24   So he drew water for them and then
         withdrew into the shade and said,
      'My Lord, I am truly in need of any good
         You have in store for me.'

25   One of them came walking shyly up to him
         and said, 'My father invites you
      so that he may pay you your wage

for drawing water for us.'
When he came to him and told him the whole story
    he said, 'Have no fear,
you have escaped from wrongdoing people.'

26   One of them said, 'Hire him, father.
        The best person to hire
is someone strong and trustworthy.'

27   He said, 'I would like to marry you to one
        of these two daughters of mine on condition
            that you work for me for eight full years.
        If you complete ten, that is up to you.
            I do not want to be hard on you.
        You will find me, Allah willing,
            to be one of the righteous.'
28   He said, 'That is agreed between me and you.
        Whichever of the two terms I fulfil,
      there should be no bad feeling towards me.
        Allah is Guardian over what we say.'

29   When Musa had fulfilled the appointed term
        and had set off with his family,
      he noticed a fire from one side of the Mount.
    He said to his family, 'Stay here, I can see a fire.
        Hopefully I will bring you back some news from it
            or a burning branch from the fire
      so that you will be able to warm yourselves.'

30   But when he reached it a voice called out to him
        from the right hand side of the valley
            in the part which was full of blessing,
                from out of the bush:
    'Musa, I am Allah, the Lord of all the worlds.
31   Throw down your staff!'
Then when he he saw it slithering like a snake
      he turned and fled and did not turn back again.
    'Musa, approach and have no fear!
      You are one of those who are secure.
32   Put your hand inside your shirt front.
      It will emerge pure white yet quite unharmed.
And hug your arms to your sides to still your fear.
      These are two proofs from your Lord

for Pharaoh and his ruling circle.
They are a deviant people.'

33   He said, 'My Lord, I killed one of them
and I am afraid they will kill me;

34   and my brother Harun is more eloquent than me
so send him with me to support me and back me up.
I am afraid they will call me a liar.'

35   He said, 'We will reinforce you with your brother
and by Our Signs will give you both authority,
so that they will not be able to lay a hand on you.
You and those who follow you will be the victors.'

36   But when Musa brought them Our Clear Signs
they said, 'This is nothing but trumped-up magic.
We never heard anything like this
among our earlier forefathers.'

37   Musa said, 'My Lord knows best
who has come with guidance from Him
and who will have the best Home in the end.
The wrongdoers will certainly not be successful.'

38   Pharaoh said, 'Council, I do not know
of any other god for you apart from Me.
Haman, kindle a fire for me over the clay
and build me a lofty tower so that perhaps
I may be able to climb up to Musa's god!
I consider him a blatant liar.'

39   He and his troops were arrogant in the land
without any right.
They thought that they would not return to Us.

40   So We seized him and his troops
and flung them into the sea.
See the final fate of the wrongdoers!

41   We made them leaders, summoning to the Fire,
and on the Day of Rising they will not be helped.

42   We pursued them with a curse in this world
and on the Day of Rising they will be hideous and spurned.

43   We gave Musa the Book after destroying the earlier nations,
to awaken people's hearts and as a guidance and a mercy
so that hopefully they might pay heed.

44   You were not on the western side
             when We gave Musa the command.
        You were not a witness.

45   Yet We produced further generations
             and ages passed.
        Nor did you live among the people of Madyan
             and recite Our Signs to them,
        yet We have sent you news of them.

46   Nor were you on the side of the Mount
                  when We called,
              yet it is a mercy from your Lord
        so that you can warn a people
             to whom no warner came before,
        so that hopefully they will pay heed.

47   If a disaster had struck them
             because of what they had already done,
        they would have said, 'Our Lord,
              why did You not send us a Messenger
        so that we could have followed Your Signs
             and been believers?'

48   But when the truth did come to them from Us they said,
             'Why has he not been given the same as Musa was given?'
        But did they not previously reject what Musa was given?
             They say, 'Two magicians who back each other up.'
                  And they say, 'We reject both of them.'

49   Say: 'Bring a Book, then, from Allah
             which guides better than both of them
        and follow it if you are telling the truth.'

50   If they do not respond to you then know that
             they are merely following their whims and desires.
        And who could be further astray
             than someone who follows his whims and desires
                  without any guidance from Allah?
        Allah does not guide the people of the wrongdoers.

51   We have conveyed the Word to them
             so that hopefully they will pay heed.

52 Those We gave the Book before this believe in it.

53 When it is recited to them they say,
   'We believe in it; it is the truth from our Lord.
 We were already Muslims before it came.'

54 They will be given their reward twice over
   because they have been steadfast
 and because they ward off the bad with the good
   and give from what We have provided for them.

55 When they hear worthless talk they turn away from it
   and say, 'We have our actions and you have your actions.
 Peace be upon you.
   We do not desire the company of the ignorant.'

56 You cannot guide those you would like to
   but Allah guides those He wills.
 He has best knowledge of the guided.

57 They say, 'If we follow the guidance with you,
   we shall be forcibly uprooted from our land.'
 Have We not established a safe haven for them
   to which produce of every kind is brought,
    provision direct from Us?
 But most of them do not know it.

58 How many cities We have destroyed
   which lived in insolent ingratitude!
 There are their houses,
   never again inhabited after them,
    except a little.
 It was We who were their Heir.

59 Your Lord would never destroy any cities
   without first sending to the chief of them
    a Messenger to recite Our Signs to them.
 We would never destroy any cities
   unless their inhabitants were wrongdoers.

60 Anything you have been given is only the enjoyment
   of the life of this world and its finery.
 What is with Allah is better and longer lasting.
   So will you not use your intellect?

61   Is someone whom We have promised good
         and who then obtains it,
     the same as someone whom We have given
         enjoyment in the life of this world
            and who then, on the Day of Rising,
         is one of those brought to punishment?

62   On the Day when He summons them He will say,
         'Where are they, those you claimed were My associates?'

63   Those against whom the Word has been justly carried out
         will say, 'Our Lord, those people we misled,
            we only misled them as we too were misled.
     We disown responsibility to You.
         It was not us they were worshipping!'

64   They will be told, 'Call on your partner-gods!'
         They will call on them but
            they will not respond to them.
     They will see the punishment.
         Oh, if only they had been guided!

65   On the Day when He summons them He will say,
         'How did you respond to the Messengers?'

66   That Day the facts will be unclear to them
         and they will not be able to question one another.

67   But as for those who repent, believe and act rightly,
         they will hopefully be successful.

68   Your Lord creates and chooses whatever He wills.
         The choice is not theirs.
            Glory be to Allah!
     He is exalted above anything they associate with Him!

69   Your Lord knows what their hearts conceal
         and what they divulge.

70   He is Allah.
     There is no god but Him.
     Praise be to Him in this world
         and the Next World.

Judgement belongs to Him.
> You will be returned to Him.

71   Say: 'What do you think?
> If Allah made it permanently night for you
>> till the Day of Rising,
> what god is there other than Allah
>> to bring you light?
> Do you not then hear?'

72   Say: 'What do you think?
> If Allah made it permanently day for you
>> till the Day of Rising,
> what god is there other than Allah
>> to bring you night to rest in?
> Do you not then see?'

73   But part of His mercy is that He has made
> both night and day for you
so that you can have your rest and seek His bounty,
> and so that hopefully you will be thankful.

74   On the Day when He summons them He will say,
> 'Where are they, those you claimed to be My associates?'

75   We will drag out a witness from each nation
> and will say, 'Produce your evidence!'
They will know then that the truth is with Allah
> and that what they invented has forsaken them.

76   Qarun was one of the people of Musa
> but he lorded it over them.
We gave him treasures, the keys to which alone
> were a heavy weight for a party of strong men.
When his people said to him, 'Do not gloat.
> Allah does not love people who gloat.

77   Seek the abode of the Next World
> with what Allah has given you,
without forgetting your portion of this world.
> And do good as Allah has been good to you.
And do not seek to cause corruption in the earth.
> Allah does not love corrupters.'

78   he said, 'I have only been given it
> because of knowledge I have.'

Did he not know that before him
    Allah had destroyed generations
with far greater strength than his
    and far more possessions?
The evildoers will not be questioned about their sins.

79   He went out among his people in his finery.
    Those who desired the life of this world said,
'Oh! If only we had the same as Qarun has been given!
    What immense good fortune he possesses.'

80   But those who had been given knowledge said,
    'Woe to you! Allah's reward is better
      for those who believe and act rightly.
    But only the steadfast will obtain it.'

81   We caused the earth to swallow up both him and his house.
    There was no group to come to his aid, besides Allah,
      and he was not someone who is helped.

82   Those who had longed to take his place the day before
    woke up saying, 'Allah expands the provision
      of any of His slaves He wills
        or restricts it.
If Allah had not shown great kindness to us,
    we would have been swallowed up as well.
Ah! Truly the unbelievers are not successful.'

83   That abode of the Next World –
    We grant it to those who do not seek
      to exalt themselves in the earth
    or to cause corruption in it.
The successful outcome is for the godfearing.

84   Anyone who does a good action
    will get something better.
As for anyone who does a bad action,
    those who have done bad actions
will only be repaid for what they did.

85   He who has imposed the Qur'an upon you
    will most certainly bring you back home again.
Say: 'My Lord knows best who has brought true guidance
    and who is plainly misguided.'

86   You did not expect to be given the Book.
     It is nothing but a mercy from your Lord.
So do not lend support to the unbelievers.

87   Do not let them debar you from Allah's Signs
     after they have been sent down to you.
Call people to your Lord
     and on no account be one of the idolators.

88   Do not call on any other god along with Allah.
     There is no god but Him.
All things are passing except His Face.
     Judgement belongs to Him.
You will be returned to Him.

Sura 29

Al-'Ankabut
The Spider

In the name of Allah, All-Merciful, Most Merciful

1   Alif Lam Mim

2   Do people imagine that they will be left to say,
           'We believe,' and will not be tested?

3   We tested those before them so that Allah
           would know the truthful
               and would know the liars.

4   Or do those who do bad actions
           imagine they can outstrip Us?
       How bad their judgement is!

5   As for those who look forward to meeting Allah,
           Allah's appointed time is certainly coming.
       He is the All-Hearing, the All-Knowing.

6   Whoever does jihad does it entirely for himself.
           Allah is Rich Beyond Need of any being.

7   As for those who believe and do right actions,
           We will erase their bad actions from them,
       and recompense them for the best of what they did.

8   We have instructed man to honour his parents,
           but if they endeavour to make you associate with Me
       something about which you have no knowledge,
           do not obey them.

It is to Me that you will return
 and I will inform you about the things you did.

9   As for those who believe and do right actions,
 We will admit them among the righteous.

10 There are some people who say, 'We believe in Allah,'
 and then, when they suffer harm in Allah's cause,
  they take people's persecution for Allah's punishment;
 but if help comes from your Lord they say, 'We were with you.'
 Does Allah not know best what is in every person's heart?

11 Allah knows those who believe
 and He knows the hypocrites.

12 Those who disbelieve say to those who believe,
 'Follow our way and we will bear the weight of your mistakes.'
 They will not bear the weight of a single one of their mistakes.
  Truly they are liars.

13 They will bear their own burdens
 and other burdens together with their own.
 On the Day of Rising they will be questioned
 about what they invented.

14 We sent Nuh to his people and he remained among them
  for fifty short of a thousand years;
 yet the Flood engulfed them while they were wrongdoers.

15 We rescued him and the occupants of the Ark
 and made that into a Sign for all the worlds.

16 And Ibrahim, when he said to his people,
 'Worship Allah and have taqwa of Him.
  That is better for you if you only knew.

17 Instead of Allah you worship only idols.
  You are inventing a lie.
 Those you worship besides Allah
  have no power to provide for you.
 So seek your provision from Allah
  and worship Him and give thanks to Him.
 It is to Him you will be returned.'

18 And if you deny it, nations before you also denied the truth.
 The Messenger is only responsible for clear transmission.

19   Have they not seen how Allah brings creation out of nothing,
        then reproduces it?
           That is easy for Allah.

20   Say: 'Travel about the earth
        and see how He brought creation out of nothing.
    Then later Allah will bring about the next existence.
        Allah has power over all things.
21   He punishes anyone He wills
        and has mercy on anyone He wills.
           You will be returned to Him.
22   There is no way out for you in earth or heaven.
        You have no protector or helper besides Allah.'

23   Those who reject Allah's Signs and the meeting with Him,
        such people can despair of My mercy,
    such people will have a painful punishment.

24   The only answer of his people was to say:
        'Kill him or burn him!'
           But Allah rescued him from the fire.
        There are certainly Signs in that
           for people who are believers.

25   He said, 'You have adopted idols apart from Allah
        as tokens of mutual affection in this world.
    But then on the Day of Rising
        you will reject one another
           and curse one another.
    The Fire will be your shelter.
        You will have no helpers.'

26   And Lut believed in him.
        He said, 'I am leaving this place
           to follow the pleasure of my Lord.
        He is the Almighty, the All Wise.'

27   We gave him Ishaq and Ya'qub and placed
        Prophethood and the Book among his progeny.
           We gave him his reward in this world
        and in the Next World he will be among the righteous.

28   When Lut said to his people, 'You are committing an obscenity
        not perpetrated before you by anyone in all the worlds.

29 Do you lie with men and waylay them on the road
  and commit depravities within your gatherings?'
the only answer of his people was to say,
  'Bring us Allah's punishment if you are telling the truth.'
30 He said, 'My Lord, help me against the people of corruption!'

31 When Our messengers came with the good news to Ibrahim,
  they said, 'We are going to destroy the people of this city.
   Truly its inhabitants are wrongdoers.'
32 He said, 'Lut is in it.'
They said, 'We know very well who is in it.
  We are going to rescue him and his family –
   except for his wife.
  She will be one of those who stay behind.'

33 When Our Messengers came to Lut,
  he was distressed on their account,
   feeling incapable of protecting them.
They said, 'Do not fear and do not grieve.
  We are going to rescue you and your family –
   except for your wife;
  she will be one of those who stay behind.
34 We will bring down on the inhabitants of this city
  a devastating punishment from heaven
   because of their deviance.'

35 We have left a Clear Sign of them behind
  for people who use their intellect.

36 And to Madyan We sent their brother Shu'ayb.
  He said, 'My people, worship Allah
   and look to the Last Day
  and do not act unjustly on earth, corrupting it.'
37 But they denied him so the earthquake seized them
  and morning found them lying flattened in their homes.

38 And 'Ad and Thamud –
  it must be clear to you from their dwelling places!
Shaytan made their actions seem good to them
  and so debarred them from the Way,
even though they were intelligent people.

39   And Qarun and Pharaoh and Haman –
Musa came with the Clear Signs to them,

but they were arrogant on the earth.
They could not outstrip Us.

40   We seized each one of them for their wrong actions.
Against some We sent a sudden squall of stones;
some of them were seized by the Great Blast;
some We caused the earth to swallow up;
and some We drowned.
Allah did not wrong them;
rather they wronged themselves.

41   The metaphor of those who take protectors besides Allah
is that of a spider which builds itself a house;
but no house is flimsier than a spider's house,
if they only knew.

42   Allah knows what you call upon besides Himself.
He is the Almighty, the All-Wise.

43   Such metaphors – We devise them for mankind;
but only those with knowledge understand them.

44   Allah created the heavens and the earth with truth.
There is certainly a Sign in that for the believers.

45   Recite what has been revealed to you of the Book
and establish the prayer.
The prayer precludes indecency and wrongdoing.
And remembrance of Allah is greater still.
Allah knows what you do.

46   Only argue with the People of the Book in the kindest way –
except in the case of those of them who do wrong –
saying, 'We believe in what has been sent down to us
and what was sent down to you.
Our God and your God are one and we submit to Him.'

47   Accordingly We have sent down the Book to you,
and those to whom We gave the Book believe in it,
and some of these people believe in it as well.
Only the unbelievers deny Our Signs.

48   You never recited any Book before it
nor did you write one down with your right hand.

If you had, the purveyors of falsehood
would have voiced their doubts.

49   No, it is Clear Signs reposited in the hearts
of those who have been given knowledge.
Only wrongdoers deny Our Signs.

50   They say, 'Why have no Signs
been sent down to him from his Lord?'
Say: 'The Signs are with Allah.
I am only a clear warner.'

51   Is it not enough for them that We have
sent down to you the Book
which is recited to them?
There is certainly a mercy and reminder in that
for people who believe.

52   Say: 'Allah is a sufficient witness between me and you.'
He knows everything in the heavens and the earth.
Those who believe in falsehood and reject Allah,
they are the losers.

53   They ask you to hasten the punishment.
If it were not for a stipulated term,
the punishment would have come to them already.
It will come upon them suddenly
when they are not expecting it.

54   They ask you to hasten the punishment
but Hell already encircles the unbelievers.

55   On the Day the punishment envelops them
from above them and from underneath their feet,
He will say, 'Taste what you were doing!'

56   My slaves, you who believe,
My earth is wide, so worship Me alone!

57   Every self will taste death.
Then you will be returned to Us.

58   As for those who believe and do right actions,
We will lodge them in lofty chambers in the Garden,

with rivers flowing under them,
remaining in them timelessly, for ever.
How excellent is the reward of those who act:

59   those who are steadfast and put their trust in their Lord.

60   How many creatures do not carry their provision with them!
Allah provides for them and He will for you.
He is the All-Hearing, the All-Knowing.

61   If you ask them, 'Who created the heavens and the earth
and made the sun and moon subservient?'
they will say, 'Allah.'
So how have they been perverted?

62   Allah expands the provision of any of His slaves He wills
and restricts it.
Allah has knowledge of all things.

63   If you ask them, 'Who sends down water from the sky,
bringing the earth back to life again after it was dead?'
they will say, 'Allah.'
Say: 'Praise be to Allah.'
But most of them do not use their intellect.

64   The life of this world is nothing but a game and a diversion.
The abode of the Next World –
that is truly Life if they only knew.

65   When they embark in ships, they call on Allah,
making their deen sincerely His,
but then when He delivers them safely to land,
they associate others with Him.

66   Let them be ungrateful for what We have given them!
Let them enjoy themselves – they will soon know!

67   Do they not see that We have established a safe haven
while people all round them are violently dispossessed?
So why do they believe in falsehood
and reject the blessing of Allah?

68   Who could do greater wrong than someone
who invents lies against Allah

or denies the truth when it comes to him?
Is there not shelter in Hell for the unbelievers?

69   As for those who do jihad in Our Way,
           We will guide them to Our Paths.
       Truly Allah is with the good-doers.

Sura 30

Ar-Rum
The Romans

In the name of Allah, All-Merciful, Most Merciful

1   Alif Lam Mim
2 The Romans have been defeated
3   in the land nearby,
    but after their defeat
  they will themselves be victorious
4   in a few years' time.
  The affair is Allah's from beginning to end.
    On that day, the believers will rejoice
5   in Allah's help.
  He grants victory to whomever He wills.
    He is the Almighty, the Most Merciful.

6   That is Allah's promise.
  Allah does not break His promise.
    But most people do not know it.

7   They know an outward aspect of the life of this world
    but are heedless of the Next World.

8   Have they not reflected within themselves?
     Allah did not create the heavens and the earth
      and everything between them
     except with truth and for a fixed term.
  Yet many people reject the meeting with their Lord.

9   Have they not travelled in the earth
     and seen the final fate of those before them?
  They had greater strength than them and cultivated the land

and inhabited it in far greater numbers than they do.
Their Messengers also came to them with the Clear Signs.
  Allah would never have wronged them;
    but they wronged themselves.

10   Then the final fate of those who did evil will be the Worst
    because they denied Allah's Signs and mocked at them.

11   Allah originates creation,
    then will regenerate it,
  then you will be returned to Him.

12   On the Day the Hour arrives
    the evildoers will be in despair.
13   None of their partner-gods will intercede for them.
    They will reject their partner-gods.

14   On the Day the Hour arrives,
    that Day they will be split up.
15   As for those who believed and did right actions,
    they will be made joyful in a verdant meadow.
16   But as for those who disbelieved and denied Our Signs
    and the meeting of the Next World,
  they will be summoned to the punishment.

17   So glory be to Allah when you start the night
    and when you greet the day.
18   Praise be to Him in the heavens and the earth,
    in the afternoon and when you reach midday.
19   He brings forth the living from the dead
    and brings forth the dead from the living
  and brings the earth to life after it was dead.
    In the same way you too will be brought forth.

20   Among His Signs is that He created you from dust
    and here you are now, widespread human beings!

21   Among His Signs is that
    He created spouses for you of your own kind
      so that you might find tranquillity in them.
    And He has placed affection and compassion between you.
There are certainly Signs in that for people who reflect.

22   Among His Signs is the creation of the heavens and earth
            and the variety of your languages and colours.
      There are certainly Signs in that for every being.

23   Among His Signs are your sleep by night and day
            and your seeking after His bounty.
      There are certainly Signs in that for people who hear.

24   Among His Signs is that He shows you lightning,
            a source of fear and eager hope,
      and sends down water from the sky,
            bringing the dead earth back to life by it.
      There are certainly Signs in that
            for people who use their intellect.

25   Among His Signs is that heaven and earth
            hold firm by His command.
      Then, when He calls you forth from the earth,
            you will emerge at once.

26   Everyone in the heavens and earth belongs to Him.
            All are submissive to Him.

27   It is He who originated the creation and then regenerates it.
            That is very easy for Him.
      His is the most exalted designation in the heavens and the earth.
            He is the Almighty, the All-Wise.

28   He has made an example for you from among yourselves.
            Are any of the slaves you own partners with you
                  in what We have provided for you
            so that you are equal in respect of it,
                  you fearing them the same as one another?
            In that way We make Our Signs clear
                  for people who use their intellect.

29   Yet those who do wrong pursue their whims and desires
            without any knowledge.
      Who can guide those whom Allah has led astray?
            They will have no helpers.

30   So set your face firmly towards the Deen,
            as a pure natural believer,
      Allah's natural pattern on which He made mankind.

There is no changing Allah's creation.
That is the true Deen –
    but most people do not know it –
31   turning towards Him.
Have taqwa of Him and establish the prayer.
    Do not be among the idolators:
32 those who split up their deen, and form into sects,
    each faction exulting in what they have.

33 When harm touches people they call on their Lord,
    turning in repentance to Him.
But then, when He gives them a taste of mercy from Him,
a group of them immediately associate others with their Lord
34   showing ingratitude for what We have given them.
    'Enjoy yourselves – you will soon know.'

35 Or have We sent down some authority to them,
    which advocates associating others with Him?

36 When We give people a taste of mercy, they rejoice in it,
    but when something bad happens to them
because of what they themselves have done,
    they immediately lose all hope.

37 Do they not see that Allah expands provision for whoever He wills
    and also restricts it?
There are certainly Signs in that for people who believe.

38 Give relatives their due, and the poor and travellers.
    That is best for those who seek the pleasure of Allah.
    They are the ones who are successful.

39 What you give with usurious intent,
    aiming to get back a greater amount from people's wealth,
    does not become greater with Allah.
But anything you give as zakat, seeking the Face of Allah –
    all who do that will get back twice as much.

40 Allah is He who created you,
    then provides for you,
then will cause you to die
    and then bring you back to life.
Can any of your partner-gods do any of that?

Glory be to Him and He is exalted
above anything they associate with Him!

41   Corruption has appeared in both land and sea
        because of what people's own hands have brought about
so that they may taste something of what they have done
        so that hopefully they will turn back.

42   Say: 'Travel about the earth and see the final fate of those before.
        Most of them were idolators.'

43   So set your face firmly towards the True Deen,
        before a Day comes from Allah
           which cannot be turned back.
        On that Day they will be split up.

44   Those who disbelieved
        will find that their unbelief was against themselves.
Those who did right
        were making the way easy for themselves;
45   so that He may repay with His bounty
        those who believed and did right actions.
           He certainly does not love the unbelievers.

46   Among His Signs is that He sends the winds
           bearing good news,
        to give you a taste of His mercy,
and to make the ships run by His command,
        and to enable you to seek His bounty
so that hopefully you will be thankful.

47   Before you We sent other Messengers to their people,
        and they too brought them the Clear Signs.
We took revenge on those who did evil;
        and it is Our duty to help the believers.

48   It is Allah who sends the winds which stir up clouds
        which He spreads about the sky however He wills.
He forms them into dark clumps and you see the rain
        come pouring out from the middle of them.
When He makes it fall on those of His slaves He wills,
        they rejoice,
49   even though before He sent it down on them
           they were in despair.

50 So look at the effect of the mercy of Allah,
   how He brings the dead earth back to life.
  Truly He is the One Who brings the dead to life.
   He has power over all things.
51 But if We send a wind, and they see it turning yellow,
   still they persist after that in disbelieving.

52 You will not make dead men hear;
   you will not make deaf men hear the call,
  when they turn their backs in flight.

53 You will not guide blind men away from their misguidance.
   You will not make anyone hear except for those
  who believe in Our Signs and so are Muslims.

54 It is Allah who created you from a weak beginning
   then after weakness gave you strength
  then after strength ordained weakness and grey hair.
   He creates whatever He wills.
  He is All-Knowing, All-Powerful.

55 On the Day the Last Hour arrives, the evildoers
   will swear they have not even tarried for an hour.
  That is the extent to which they are deceived.

56 Those who have been given knowledge and faith will say,
   'You tarried in accordance with Allah's Decree
    until the Day of Rising.
   And this is the Day of Rising, but you did not know it.'

57 On that Day the excuses of those who did wrong
   will not help them
  nor will they be able to appease Allah.

58 We have made all kinds of examples for people in this Qur'an.
   If you bring them a Sign those who disbelieve will say,
    'You are just purveyors of falsehood!'
59 In that way Allah seals up the hearts of those who do not know.

60 So be steadfast. Allah's promise is true.
  Do not let those who have no certainty belittle you.

Sura 31

Luqman

1	Alif Lam Mim
2	Those are the Signs of the Wise Book –
3	guidance and mercy for the good-doers:
4	those who establish the prayer and pay zakat
	and are certain of the Next World.

5　Such people are following guidance from their Lord.
　　They are the ones who are successful.

6　But there are some people who trade in distracting tales
　　to misguide people from Allah's Way
　　　knowing nothing about it
　　and to make a mockery of it.
　Such people will have a humiliating punishment.

7　When Our Signs are recited to such a person,
　　he turns away arrogantly as if he had not heard,
　　　as if there were a great weight in his ears.
　So give him news of a painful punishment.

8　For those who believe and do right actions
　　there are Gardens of Delight,
9　to remain in them timelessly, for ever.
　　Allah's promise is true.
　He is the Almighty, the All-Wise.

10　It is Allah Who created the heavens
　　with no support – you can see them –

and cast firmly embedded mountains on the earth
    so that it would not move under you,
and scattered about in it creatures of every kind.
    And We send down water from the sky
and make every generous species grow in it.

11   This is Allah's creation.
    Show me then what those besides Him have created!
      The wrongdoers are clearly misguided.

12   We gave Luqman wisdom:
    'Give thanks to Allah.
Whoever gives thanks
    only does so for his own good.
Whoever is ungrateful,
    Allah is Rich Beyond Need, Praiseworthy.'

13   When Luqman said to his son, counselling him,
    'My son, do not associate anything with Allah.
Associating others with Him is a terrible wrong.'

14   We have instructed man concerning his parents.
    Bearing him caused his mother great debility
      and the period of his weaning was two years:
'Give thanks to Me and to your parents.
    I am your final destination.
15   But if they try to make you associate something with Me
    about which you have no knowledge,
      do not obey them.
Keep company with them correctly and courteously in this world
    but follow the Way of him who turns to Me.
Then you will return to Me and I will inform you
    about the things you did.'

16   'My son, even if something weighs as little as a mustard-seed
      and is inside a rock
    or anywhere else in the heavens or earth,
      Allah will bring it out.
    Allah is All-Pervading, All-Aware.
17   My son, establish the prayer
    and command what is right and forbid what is wrong
and be steadfast in the face of all that happens to you.
    That is certainly the most resolute course to follow.

18   Do not avert your face from people out of haughtiness
         and do not strut about arrogantly on the earth.
      Allah does not love anyone who is vain or boastful.
19   Be moderate in your tread and lower your voice.
      The most hateful of voices is the donkey's bray.'

20   Do you not see that Allah has subjected to you
         everything in the heavens and earth
    and has showered His blessings upon you,
         both outwardly and inwardly?
    Yet there are people who argue about Allah
         without knowledge or guidance
           or any illuminating Book.

21   When they are told: 'Follow what Allah has sent down,'
         they say, 'No, we will follow what we found our fathers doing.'
    What! Even if Shaytan is calling them
         to the punishment of the Blazing Fire?

22   Those who submit themselves completely to Allah
           and do good
        have grasped the Firmest Handhold.
    The end result of all affairs is with Allah.

23   And do not let the unbelief of those who disbelieve sadden you.
         They will return to Us
    and We will inform them about the things they did.
         Allah knows what the heart contains.

24   We will let them enjoy themselves a little,
         then drive them to a harsh punishment.

25   If you asked them, 'Who created the heavens and earth?'
         they would say, 'Allah!'
    Say: 'Praise be to Allah!'
         But most of them do not know.
26   Everything in the heavens and earth belongs to Allah.
         Allah is the Rich Beyond Need, the Praiseworthy.

27   If all the trees on earth were pens and all the sea,
         with seven more seas besides, were ink
    Allah's words still would not run dry.
         Allah is Almighty, All-Wise.

28　　Your creation and rising is only like that of a single self.
　　　　Allah is All-Hearing, All-Seeing.

29　　Do you not see that Allah makes night merge into day
　　　　and day merge into night,
　　　and that He has made the sun and moon subservient,
　　　　each one running for a specified time,
　　　and that Allah is aware of what you do?

30　　That is because Allah – He is the Truth,
　　　　and what you call upon besides Him is falsehood.
　　　　　Allah is the All-High, the Most Great.

31　　Do you not see that ships sail on the sea by Allah's blessing
　　　　so that He can show you something of His Signs?
　　　There are certainly Signs in that
　　　　for everyone who is steadfast and thankful.
32　　When the waves hang over them like canopies,
　　　　they call on Allah, making their deen sincerely His.
　　　But then when He delivers them safely to the land,
　　　　some of them are ambivalent.
　　　None but a treacherous, thankless man denies Our Signs.

33　　Mankind! have taqwa of your Lord and fear a day
　　　　when no father will be able to atone for his son,
　　　　　or son for his father, in any way.
　　　Allah's promise is true.
　　　　So do not let the life of this world delude you
　　　and do not let the Deluder delude you concerning Allah.

34　　Truly Allah has knowledge of the Hour
　　　　and sends down abundant rain
　　　　　and knows what is in the womb.
　　　And no self knows what it will earn tomorrow
　　　　and no self knows in what land it will die.
　　　　　Allah is All-Knowing, All-Aware.

Sura 32

As-Sajda
Prostration

1 Alif Lam Mim
2 The revelation of the Book,
       without any doubt of it,
   is from the Lord of the worlds.

3 Or do they say, 'He has invented it'?
       No indeed! It is the truth from your Lord
   to warn a people to whom, before you, no warner came,
       so that hopefully they will be guided.

4 Allah is He who created the heavens and the earth
       and everything between them in six days
   and then established Himself firmly upon the Throne.
       You have no protector or intercessor apart from Him.
           So will you not pay heed?

5 He directs the whole affair from heaven to earth.
       Then it will again ascend to Him
   on a Day whose length is a thousand years
       by the way you measure.

6 That is the Knower of the Unseen and the Visible,
       the Almighty, the Most Merciful:
7 He who has created all things in the best possible way.
       He commenced the creation of man from clay;
8 then produced his seed from an extract of base fluid;
9   then formed him and breathed His Ruh into him

and gave you hearing, sight and hearts.
What little thanks you show!

10   They say, 'When we have been absorbed into the earth,
          are we then to be in a new creation?'
      In fact they reject the meeting with their Lord.

11   Say: 'The Angel of Death,
          who has been given charge of you,
              will take you back
      and then you will be sent back to your Lord.'

12   If only you could see the evildoers
          hanging their heads in shame before their Lord:
      'Our Lord, we have seen and we have heard,
          so send us back again and we will act rightly.
              Truly we now have certainty.'

13   'Had We so willed We could have given guidance to everyone,
          but now My Words are shown to be true:
      that I shall fill up Hell entirely with jinn and human beings.
14   So taste it.
      Because you forgot the meeting on this Day,
          We have forgotten you.
      Taste the punishment of eternal timelessness
          for what you did.'

15   The people who truly do believe in Our Signs
          are those who fall to the ground prostrating
              when they are reminded of them,
          and glorify their Lord with praise,
              and are not arrogant.
16   Their sides eschew their beds
              as they call on their Lord
                  in fear and ardent hope.
          And they give of what
              We have provided for them.

17   No self knows the delight that is hidden away for it
          in recompense for what it used to do.

18   Is someone who believe like someone who is a deviator?
          They are not the same!

19   As for those who believe and do right actions,
         they will have the Gardens of Safe Refuge
            as hospitality for what they used to do.

20   But as for those who are deviators,
         their refuge is the Fire.
     Every time that they want to get out,
         they are put straight back into it again
     and they are told, 'Taste the punishment of the Fire,
         which you denied.'

21   We will give them a taste of lesser punishment
         before the greater punishment,
     so that hopefully they will turn back.

22   Who could do greater wrong than someone
         who is reminded of the Signs of his Lord
            and then turns away from them?
     We will take revenge on the evildoers.

23   We gave Musa the Book – be in no doubt
         about the meeting with him –
     and made it a guidance for the tribe of Israel.

24   We appointed leaders from among them,
         guiding by Our command when they were steadfast
            and when they had certainty about Our Signs.

25   On the Day of Rising your Lord will decide between them
         regarding everything about which they differed.

26   Are they not guided by the many generations
         We destroyed before them,
     among whose ruined homes they walk around?
         There are certainly Signs in that.
            So will they not listen?

27   Do they not see how We drive water to barren land
         and bring forth crops by it
     which their livestock and they themselves both eat?
         So will they not see?

28   They say, 'When will this victory come
         if you are telling the truth?'

29   Say: 'On the Day of Victory
                the faith of those who disbelieved
                    will be of no use to them.
                They will be granted no reprieve.'

30   So turn from them and wait.
                They too are waiting.

Sura 33

Al-Ahzab
The Confederates

In the name of Allah, All-Merciful, Most Merciful

1 O Prophet! have taqwa of Allah and do not obey
  the unbelievers and hypocrites.
 Allah is All-Knowing, All-Wise.

2 Follow what has been revealed to you from your Lord.
  Allah is aware of what you do.

3 And put your trust in Allah.
  Allah suffices as a Guardian.

4 Allah has not allotted to any man
  two hearts within his breast,
   nor has He made
 those of your wives you equate with your mothers
  your actual mothers,*
   nor has He made
 your adopted sons your actual sons.
 These are just words coming out of your mouths.
  But Allah speaks the truth
   and He guides to the Way.

5 Call them after their fathers.
  That is closer to justice in Allah's sight.
 And if you do not know who their fathers were
  then they are your brothers in the deen

---

* This refers to a type of divorce in which men would equate their wives with their mothers, thus preventing any further relations with them.

and people under your patronage.
You are not to blame for any honest mistake you make
but only for what your hearts premeditate.
Allah is Ever-Forgiving, Most Merciful.

6   The Prophet has more right to the believers
than their own selves,
and his wives are their mothers.
But blood-relations have more rights to one another
in the Book of Allah
than the believers and Muhajirun.
All the same, you should act correctly by your friends;
that is inscribed in the Book.

7   When We made a covenant with all the Prophets –
with you and with Nuh and Ibrahim
and Musa and 'Isa son of Maryam –
We made a binding covenant with them,
8   so that He might question the truly sincere
about their sincerity;
and He has prepared a painful punishment for the unbelievers.

9   You who believe! remember Allah's blessing upon you
when forces came against you
and We sent a wind against them
and other forces you could not see.*
Allah sees what you do.

10   When they came at you from above you and below you,
when your eyes rolled and your hearts rose to your throats,
and you thought unworthy thoughts about Allah,
11   at that point the believers were tested and severely shaken.

12   When the hypocrites and people
with sickness in their hearts said,
'What Allah and His Messenger promised us
was mere delusion.'
13   and a group of them said, 'People of Yathrib,
Your position is untenable so return!'
some of them asked the Prophet to excuse them, saying,

---

* Ayats 9-25 refer to the 'Battle of the Trench' when Madina was invaded by a force made up of an alliance of the Makkan tribe of Quraysh and several other Arab tribes but they became discouraged and left after a few days without offering battle.

'Our houses are exposed,' when they were not exposed;
it was merely that they wanted to run away.

14   If they had been overrun from every side,
and had then been asked to revert to unbelief,
they would have done so and hesitated very little about it.

15   Yet they had previously made a contract with Allah
that they would never turn their backs.
Contracts made with Allah will be asked about.

16   Say: 'Flight will not benefit you if you try to run away
from death or being killed.
Then you will only enjoy a short respite.'

17   Say: 'Who is going to shield you from Allah
if He desires evil for you or desires mercy for you?'
They will find no one to protect or help them besides Allah.

18   Allah knows the obstructers among you
and those who say to their brothers, 'Come to us,'
and who only come to fight a very little,

19   and are begrudging towards you.
Then when fear comes, you see them looking at you,
their eyes rolling like people scared to death.
But when fear departs they flay you with sharp tongues,
grasping for wealth.
Such people do not believe
and Allah will make their actions come to nothing.
That is easy for Allah.

20   They think that the Confederates have not departed
and if the Confederates did appear
then they would wish they were out in the desert
with the desertArabs,
asking for news of you.
If they were with you they would only fight a very little.

21   You have an excellent model in the Messenger of Allah,
for all who put their hope in Allah and the Last Day
and remember Allah much.

22   When the believers saw the Confederates they said:
'This is what Allah and His Messenger promised us.

Allah and His Messenger told us the truth.'
It only increased them in faith and in submission.

23   Among the believers there are men who have been true
          to the contract they made with Allah.
      Some of them have fulfilled their pact by death
          and some are still waiting to do so,
                not having changed in any way at all.

24   So that Allah might recompense the truly sincere
                for their sincerity
      and punish the hypocrites, if He wills,
                or turn towards them.
      Allah is Ever-Forgiving, Most Merciful.

25   Allah sent back those who disbelieved in their rage
          without their achieving any good at all.
      Allah saved the believers from having to fight.
          Allah is Most Strong, Almighty.

26   He brought down from their fortresses
          those of the People of the Book who supported them
                and cast terror into their hearts.
      You killed some of them and some you took prisoner.*

27   He bequeathed their land, their houses and their wealth to you,
          and another land you had not yet trodden on.
                Allah has power over all things.

28   O Prophet, tell your wives:
          'If you desire the life of this world and its finery,
                come and I will give you all you need
                      and release you with kindness.
29   But if you desire Allah and His Messenger
                and the abode of the Next World,
          Allah has prepared an immense reward
                for those among you who are good-doers.'

30   Wives of the Prophet! if any of you
                commits an obvious act of indecency
      she will receive double the punishment.
          That is an easy matter for Allah.

---

* This refers to Banu Qurayza, a Jewish tribe of Madina who betrayed the Muslims during the Battle of the Ditch.

31   But those of you who are obedient to Allah and His Messenger
                and act rightly
            will be given their reward twice over;
        and We have prepared generous provision for them.

32   Wives of the Prophet! you are not like other women
                provided you are godfearing.
        Do not be too soft-spoken in your speech
                lest someone with sickness in his heart
                        become desirous.
            Speak correct and courteous words.
33   Remain in your houses and do not display your beauty
                as it was previously displayed in the Time of Ignorance*
        Establish the prayer and pay zakat
                and obey Allah and His Messenger.
        Allah desires to remove all impurity from you,
                People of the House,
            and to purify you completely.
34   And remember the Signs of Allah
                and the wise words
        which are recited in your rooms.
            Allah is All-Pervading, All-Aware.

35   Men and women who are Muslims,
                men and women who are believers,
                men and women who are obedient,
                men and women who are truthful,
                men and women who are steadfast,
                men and women who are humble,
                men and women who give sadaqa,
                men and women who fast,
                men and women who guard their private parts,
                men and women who remember Allah much:
        Allah has prepared forgiveness for them and an immense reward.

36   When Allah and His Messenger have decided something
                it is not for any man or woman of the believers
                        to have a choice about it.
        Anyone who disobeys Allah and His Messenger
                is clearly misguided.

37   When you said to him whom Allah has blessed
                and you yourself have greatly favoured,

---

* The time before the coming of the Prophet and the revelation of the Qur'an.

'Keep your wife to yourself and have taqwa of Allah,'
while concealing something in yourself
which Allah wished to bring to light,
you were fearing people when Allah has more right to your fear.
Then when Zayd divorced her We married her to you
so that there should be no restriction for the believers
regarding the wives of their adopted sons
when they have divorced them.
Allah's command is always carried out.

38   There is no restriction on the Prophet
regarding anything Allah allots to him.
This was Allah's pattern with those who passed away before –
and Allah's command is a pre-ordained decree –
39   those who conveyed Allah's Message and had taqwa of Him,
fearing no one except Allah.
Allah suffices as a Reckoner.

40   Muhammad is not the father of any of your men,
but the Messenger of Allah and the Final Seal of the Prophets.
Allah has knowledge of all things.

41   You who believe! remember Allah much,
42   and glorify Him in the morning and the evening.
43   It is He Who calls down blessing on you,
as do His angels,
to bring you out of the darkness into the light.
He is Most Merciful to the believers.
44   Their greeting on the Day they meet Him will be 'Peace!'
and He has prepared a generous reward for them.

45   O Prophet! We have sent you as a witness,
and a bringer of good news and a warner,
46   and a caller to Allah by His permission
and a light-giving lamp.
47   Give good news to the believers that they will receive
immense favour from Allah.
48   Do not obey the unbelievers and hypocrites
and disregard their abuse of you.
Put your trust in Allah.
Allah suffices as Protector.

49   You who believe! when you marry believing women
and then divorce them before you have touched them,

there is no 'idda for you to calculate for them,
    so give them a gift and let them go with kindness.

50   O Prophet! We have made halal for you:
    your wives to whom you have given dowries
    and any slavegirls you own
        from the booty Allah has allotted you
    and the daughters of your paternal uncles
    and the daughters of your paternal aunts
    and the daughters of your maternal uncles
    and the daughters of your maternal aunts
        who have made hijra with you
    and any believing woman who gives herself to the Prophet
        if the Prophet desires to marry her:
    exclusively for you as opposed to the rest of the believers –
        We know very well what We have prescribed for them
            regarding their wives and any slavegirls they possess –
    in order that there be no restriction on you.
        Allah is Ever-Forgiving, Most Merciful.

51   You may refrain from any of them you will
        and keep close to you any of them you will.
    And if you desire any you have left alone,
        there is nothing wrong in that.
    This makes it more likely they will be comforted
        and not be grieved,
    and all of them will be content with what you give them.
        Allah knows what is in your hearts.
    Allah is All-Knowing, All-Forbearing.

52   After that no other women are halal for you
        nor may you exchange them for other wives,
    even though their beauty might be pleasing to you,
        except for any you own as slaves.
    Allah is watchful over all things.

53   You who believe! do not go into the Prophet's rooms
        except when you are invited to come and eat.
    Do not wait there while the food is being cooked.
        However, when you are called, go in,
            and when you have eaten, disperse,
        not remaining there to chat with one another.
    Doing that causes annoyance to the Prophet
        though he is too reticent to tell you so.

But Allah is not reticent with the truth.
> When you ask his wives for something,
>> ask them from behind a screen.
> That is purer for your hearts and their hearts.
It is not right for you to cause annoyance
>> to the Messenger of Allah
> or ever to marry his wives after him.
To do that would be a dreadful thing in Allah's sight.

54   Whether you divulge a thing or conceal it,
>> Allah has knowledge of all things.

55   They incur no blame in respect of their fathers
>> or their sons or their brothers
>> or their brothers' or sisters' sons,
>> or their women or any slaves they own.
> Have taqwa of Allah.
>> Allah is witness of all things.

56   Allah and His angels call down blessings on the Prophet.
>> You who believe! call down blessings on him
> and ask for complete peace and safety for him.

57   As for those who abuse Allah and His Messenger,
>> Allah's curse is on them in this world and the Next World.
> He has prepared a humiliating punishment for them.

58   And those who abuse men and women who are believers,
>> when they have not merited it,
> bear the weight of slander and clear wrongdoing.

59   O Prophet! Tell your wives and daughters
>> and the women of the believers
>> to draw their outer garments closely round themselves.
> This makes it more likely that they will be recognised
>> and not be harmed.
> Allah is Ever-Forgiving, Most Merciful.

60   If the hypocrites and those with sickness in their hearts
>> and the rumour-mongers in Madina do not desist,
>>> We will set you onto them.
> Then they will only be your neighbours there a very short time.

61   They are an accursed people.

Wherever they are found they should be seized
and mercilessly put to death.

62   This is Allah's pattern with those who passed away before.
You will not find any alteration in Allah's pattern.

63   People will ask you about the Last Hour.
Say: 'Only Allah has knowledge of it.
What will make you understand?
It may be that the Last Hour is very near.'

64   Allah has cursed the unbelievers
and prepared a Searing Blaze for them
65   where they will remain timelessly, for ever and ever,
not finding any protector or any helper.

66   They will say on the Day their faces are rolled over in the Fire,
'If only we had obeyed Allah and obeyed the Messenger!'
67   And they will say, 'Our Lord,
we obeyed our masters and great men
and they misguided us from the Way.
68   Our Lord, give them double the punishment
and curse them many times over!'

69   You who believe! do not be like those who abused Musa.
Allah absolved him of what they said
and he was highly honoured in Allah's sight.

70   You who believe! have taqwa of Allah
and speak words which hit the mark.
71   He will put your actions right for you
and forgive you your wrong deeds.
All who obey Allah and His Messenger
have won a mighty victory.

72   We offered the Trust* to the heavens,
the earth and the mountains
but they refused to take it on and shrank from it.
But man took it on.
He is indeed wrongdoing and ignorant.

---

* The Trust is moral responsibility or honesty, and all the duties which Allah has ordained.

73   This was so that Allah might punish
            the men and women of the hypocrites,
                and the men and women of the idolators,
        and turn towards the men and women of the believers.
            Allah is Ever-Forgiving, Most Merciful.

Sura 34

Saba'
Sheba

In the name of Allah, All-Merciful, Most Merciful

1 Praise be to Allah,
    to Whom everything in the heavens
        and everything in the earth belongs,
and praise be to Him in the Next World.
    He is the All-Wise, the All-Aware.

2 He knows what goes into the earth
    and what comes out of it,
and what comes down from heaven
    and what goes up into it.
And He is the Most Merciful, the Ever-Forgiving.

3 Those who disbelieve say, 'The Hour will never come.'
    Say: 'Yes, by my Lord, it certainly will come!'
He is the Knower of the Unseen, Whom not even
    the weight of the smallest particle eludes,
        either in the heavens or in the earth;
nor is there anything smaller or larger than that
    which is not in a Clear Book.
4 This is so that He may recompense
    those who believe and do right actions.
They will have forgiveness and generous provision.

5 But those who strive against Our Signs,
    trying to nullify them,
will have a punishment of agonising pain.

6　　Those who have been given knowledge see
　　　　that what has been sent down to you
　　　　　　from your Lord is the truth
　　　and that it guides to the Path of the Almighty, the Praiseworthy.

7　　Those who disbelieve say,
　　　　'Shall we lead you to a man who will tell you
　　　that when you have completely disintegrated,
　　　　you will then be recreated all anew?
8　　Has he invented a lie against Allah or is he possessed?'
　　　　No indeed! Those who do not believe in the Next World
　　　　　　are in punishment and deeply misguided.

9　　Have they not looked at the sky and the earth
　　　　in front of them and behind them?
　　　If We willed We would cause the earth to swallow them up
　　　　or make great lumps fall down on them from the sky.
　　　There is certainly a Sign in that for every remorseful slave.

10　　We gave Dawud great favour from Us:
　　　　'O mountains and birds! echo with him in his praise!'
　　　　　And We made iron malleable for him:
11　　'Make full-length coats of mail, measuring the links with care.
　　　　And act rightly, all of you, for I see what you do.'

12　　And We gave Sulayman power over the wind –
　　　　a month's journey in the morning
　　　　　and a month's in the afternoon.
　　　And We made a fount of molten brass flow out for him.
　　　　And some of the jinn worked in front of him
　　　　　by his Lord's permission.
　　　And if a single one of them deviates at all from Our command,
　　　　We make him taste the punishment of the Searing Blaze.

13　　They made for him anything he wished:
　　　　high arches and statues,
　　　　　huge dishes like cisterns,
　　　　great built-in cooking vats.
　　　'Work, family of Dawud, in thankfulness!'
　　　　But very few of My slaves are thankful.
14　　Then when We decreed that he should die,
　　　　nothing divulged his death to them
　　　　　except the worm which ate his staff;
　　　so that when he fell down it was made clear to the jinn

that if they had truly had knowledge of the Unseen
they need not have stayed there
suffering humiliating punishment.

15   There was also a sign for Saba in their dwelling place:
    two gardens – one to the right and one to the left.
'Eat of your Lord's provision
    and give thanks to Him:
a bountiful land and a most forgiving Lord.'

16   But they turned away so We unleashed against them
    the flood from the great dam
and exchanged their two gardens for two others
    containing bitter-tasting plants
    and tamarisk and a few lote trees.

17   That is how We repaid them for their ingratitude.
    Are any but the ungrateful repaid like this?

18   We placed between them and the cities We had blessed
    other clearly conspicuous cities,
making them measured stages on the way:
    'Travel between them in safety by night and day.'

19   They said, 'Our Lord, put more distance
    between our staging posts.'
They wronged themselves
    so We made legends of them
    and scattered them without a trace.
There are certainly Signs in that
    for everyone who is steadfast and thankful.

20   Iblis was correct in his assessment of them
    and they followed him,
except for a group of believers.

21   He had no authority over them
    except to enable Us to know
those who believe in the Next World
    from those who are in doubt about it.
Your Lord is the Preserver of all things.

22   Say: 'Call on those you make claims for besides Allah.
    They have no power over even the smallest particle,
    either in the heavens or in the earth.
    They have no share in them.
    He has no need of their support.'

23 Intercession with Him will be of no benefit
       except from someone who has His permission.
So that when the terror has left their hearts
       they will say, 'What did your Lord say?'
They will say, 'The truth.
       He is the All-High, the Most Great.'

24 Say: 'Who provides for you from the heavens and earth?'
       Say: 'Allah.
It is certain that one or the other of us, either we or you,
       is following guidance or else clearly astray.'

25 Say: 'You will not be asked about any evil we committed
       and we will not be asked about what you did.'

26 Say: 'Our Lord will bring us all together
       and then will judge between us with the truth.
He is the Just Decider, the All-Knowing.'

27 Say: 'Show me those you have joined to Him as associates.
       No indeed! He is Allah, the Almighty, the All-Wise.'

28 We only sent you for the whole of mankind,
       to bring good news and to give warning.
             But most of mankind do not know it.

29 They say, 'When will this promise come about
       if you are telling the truth?'

30 Say: 'You have a promised appointment on a Day
       which you cannot delay or advance a single hour.'

31 Those who disbelieve say,
       'We will never believe in this Qur'an,
             nor in what came before it.'
If only you could see when the wrongdoers,
       standing in the presence of their Lord,
cast accusations back and forth at one another!
       Those deemed weak will say to those deemed great,
'Were it not for you, we would have been believers!'

32   Those deemed great will say to those deemed weak,
'Did we debar you from the guidance when it came to you?
       No, it is you who were evildoers.'

33   Those deemed weak will say to those deemed great,
        'No, it was your scheming night and day
            when you commanded us to reject Allah
               and assign equals to Him.'
      But they will show their remorse when they see the punishment.
        We will put iron collars
            round the necks of those who disbelieve.
        Will they be repaid for anything but what they did?

34   We never sent a warner into any city
            without the affluent people in it saying,
               'We reject what you have been sent with.'
35   They also said, 'We have more wealth and children.
            We are not going to be punished.'

36   Say: 'My Lord expands the provision of anyone He wills
            or restricts it.
            But the majority of mankind do not know it.'

37   It is not your wealth or your children
               that will bring you near to Us –
            only in the case of people who believe and act rightly;
      such people will have a double recompense for what they did.
        They will be safe from all harm in the High Halls of Paradise.

38   But people who strive against Our Signs,
            trying to nullify them,
            such people will be summoned to the punishment.

39   Say: 'My Lord expands the provision
            of any of His slaves He wills
               or restricts it.
            But anything you expend will be replaced by Him.
            He is the Best of Providers.'

40   On the Day We gather them all together
             and then say to the angels,
            'Was it you whom these people were worshipping?'
41   they will say, 'Glory be to You! You are our Protector, not them.
            No, they were worshipping the jinn.
               They mostly had faith in them.'

42   'Today you possess no power to help or harm one another.'
      And We will say to those who did wrong,
    'Taste the punishment of the Fire which you denied.'

43   When Our Clear Signs are recited to them, they say,
      'This is nothing but a man who wants to debar you
        from what your fathers used to worship.'
    They say, 'This is nothing but an invented lie.'
    Those who disbelieve say to the truth when it comes to them,
    'This is nothing but downright magic.'

44   We have not given them any books which they are studying
      nor did We send, before you, any warner to them.

45   Those before them also denied the truth
      but these people do not have even a tenth
        of what We gave to them.
    They denied My Messengers.
      And how complete was My denial!

46   Say: 'I exhort you to do one thing alone:
      to stand before Allah
        in pairs and on your own
      and then reflect.
    Your companion is not possessed.
      He is only a warner come to you
        ahead of a terrible punishment.'

47   Say: 'I have not asked you for any wage –
      it is all for you.
    My wage is the responsibility of Allah alone.
      He is witness of everything.'

48   Say: 'My Lord hurls forth the Truth –
      the Knower of all unseen things.'

49   Say: 'The Truth has come.
      Falsehood cannot originate
        or regenerate.'

50   Say: 'If I am misguided, it is only to my detriment.
      But if I am guided, it is by what my Lord reveals to me.
        He is All-Hearing, Close-at-hand.'

51   If you could only see when they are terrified,
           and there is no way out,
      and they are seized from a nearby place.

52   They will say, 'We believe in it,'
           but how can they reach out for it
              from a distant place
53   when before they had rejected it,
           shooting forth about the Unseen
              from a distant place?

54   A barrier will be set up between them
           and the thing that they desire,
        just as was done with their kind before.
      They too were in a state of crippling doubt.

Sura 35

Fatir
The Bringer into Being

In the name of Allah, All-Merciful, Most Merciful

1 Praise be to Allah,
the Bringer into Being of the heavens and earth,
He who made the angels messengers,
with wings – two, three or four.
He adds to creation in any way He wills.
Allah has power over all things.

2 Any mercy Allah opens up to people, no one can withhold,
and any He withholds, no one can afterwards release.
He is the Almighty, the All-Wise.

3 Mankind! remember Allah's blessing upon you.
Is there any creator other than Allah
providing for you from heaven and earth?
There is no god but Him.
So how have you been perverted?

4 If they deny you, Messengers before you were also denied.
All matters return to Allah.

5 Mankind! Allah's promise is true.
Do not let the life of this world delude you
and do not let the Deluder delude you about Allah.

6 Shaytan is your enemy
so treat him as an enemy.
He summons his party
to be among the people of the Searing Blaze.

7   Those who disbelieve will suffer a harsh punishment.
            But those who believe and do right actions
                will receive forgiveness and an immense reward.

8   And what of him the evil of whose actions
            appears fine to him
                so that he sees them as good?
        Allah misguides whomever He wills
            and guides whomever He wills.
        So do not let yourself waste away
            out of regret for them.
        Allah knows what they do.

9   It is Allah who sends the winds which raise the clouds
            which We then drive to a dead land
        and by them bring the earth to life after it was dead.
            That is how the Resurrection will occur.

10   If anyone wants power, all power belongs to Allah.
            All good words rise to Him
                and He elevates all virtuous deeds.
        But people who plot evil deeds
            will suffer a harsh punishment.
        The plotting of such people is profitless.

11   Allah created you from dust
            and then from a drop of sperm
                and then made you into pairs.
        No female becomes pregnant or gives birth
            except with His knowledge.
        And no living thing lives long
            or has its life cut short
        without that being in a Book.
            That is easy for Allah.

12   The two seas are not the same:
            the one is sweet, refreshing, delicious to drink,
                the other salty, bitter to the taste.
        Yet from both of them you eat fresh flesh
            and extract ornaments for yourselves to wear;
        and you see ships on them, cleaving through the waves
            so that you can seek His bounty
        and so that hopefully you will be thankful.

13 He makes night merge into day and day merge into night,
>   and He has made the sun and moon subservient,
>   each one running until a specified time.
>   That is Allah, your Lord.
>   All Sovereignty is His.
>   Those you call on besides Him
>   have no power over even the smallest speck.

14 If you call on them they will not hear your call,
>   and were they to hear, they would not respond to you.
>   On the Day of Rising they will reject
>   your making associates of them.
>   No one can inform you like One who is All-aware.

15 Mankind! you are the poor in need of Allah
>   whereas Allah is the Rich Beyond Need, the Praiseworthy.
16 If He wills He can dispense with you
>   and bring about a new creation.
17 That is not difficult for Allah.

18 No burden-bearer can bear another's burden.
>   If someone weighed down
>   calls for help to bear his load,
>   none of it will be borne for him,
>   even by his next of kin.
>   You can only warn those
>   who fear their Lord in the Unseen
>   and establish the prayer.
>   Whoever is purified, is purified for himself alone.
>   Allah is your final destination.

19 The blind and seeing are not the same
20 >   nor are darkness and light
21 >   nor are cool shade and fierce heat.

22 The living and dead are not the same.
>   Allah makes anyone He wills hear
>   but you cannot make those in the grave hear.

23 You are only a warner.

24 We have sent you with the truth
>   bringing good news and giving warning.
>   There is no community to which a warner has not come.

25   If they deny you, those before them also denied the truth.
         Their Messengers came to them with Clear Signs,
              and psalms and the Illuminating Book.

26   Then I seized hold of those who disbelieved
         and how absolute was My rejection!

27   Do you not see that Allah sends down water from the sky
         and by it We bring forth fruits of varying colours?
     And in the mountains there are streaks of white and red,
         of varying shades, and rocks of deep jet black.
28   And mankind and beasts and livestock
         are likewise of varying colours.
     Only those of His slaves with knowledge
         have fear of Allah.
     Allah is Almighty, Ever-Forgiving.

29   Those who recite the Book of Allah and establish the prayer
         and give of what We have provided for them,
              secretly and openly,
     hope for a transaction which will not prove profitless:
30   that He may pay them their wages in full
     and give them more from His unbounded favour.
         He is Ever-Forgiving, Ever-Thankful.

31   What We have revealed to you of the Book is the truth,
         confirming what came before it.
     Allah is aware of and sees His slaves.

32   Then We made Our chosen slaves inherit the Book.
         But some of them wrong themselves;
              some are ambivalent;
     and some outdo each other in good by Allah's permission.
         That is the great favour.

33   They will enter Gardens of Eden
         where they will be adorned with gold bracelets and pearls,
         and where their clothing will be of silk.
34   They will say, 'Praise be to Allah
     Who has removed all sadness from us.
     Truly our Lord is Ever-Forgiving, Ever-Thankful:
35   He who has lodged us,
              out of His munificence,

in the Abode of Permanence
where no weariness or fatigue affects us.'

36   But for those who disbelieve there will be the Fire of Hell.
They will not be killed off so that they die
and its punishment will not be lightened for them.
That is how We repay every thankless man.

37   They will shout out in it, 'Our Lord!
take us out! We will act rightly,
differently from the way we used to act!'
Did We not let you live long enough
for anyone who was going to pay heed
to pay heed?
And did not the warner come to you?
Taste it then!
There is no helper for the wrongdoers.

38   Allah knows the Unseen of the heavens and earth.
Allah knows what the heart contains.

39   It is He who made you khalifs on the earth.
So whoever disbelieves, his unbelief is against himself.
In Allah's sight, the unbelief of the unbelievers
only increases their loathsomeness;
the unbelief of the unbelievers only increases their loss.

40   Say: 'Have you thought about your partner gods,
those you call upon besides Allah?
Show me what they have created of the earth;
or do they have a partnership in the heavens?'
Have We given them a Book whose Clear Signs they follow?
No indeed! The wrongdoers promise each other
nothing but delusion.

41   Allah keeps a firm hold on the heavens and earth,
preventing them from vanishing away.
And if they vanished no one could then keep hold of them.
Certainly He is Most Forbearing, Ever-Forgiving.

42   They swore by Allah with their most earnest oaths
that if a warner came to them
they would be better guided
than any other community.

But then when a warner did come to them,
> it only increased their aversion,

43   shown by their arrogance in the land and evil plotting.
> But evil plotting envelops only those who do it.

Do they expect anything
> but the pattern of previous peoples?

You will not find any changing in the pattern of Allah.
> You will not find any alteration in the pattern of Allah.

44   Have they not travelled in the land
> and seen the final fate of those before them?

They were far greater than them in strength.
> Allah cannot be withstood in any way,
> > either in the heavens or on earth.
> He is All-Knowing, All-Powerful.

45   If Allah were to take mankind to task for what they have earned,
> He would not leave a single creature crawling on it,
> > but He is deferring them until a specified time.
> Then, when their time comes, Allah sees His slaves!

Sura 36

Ya Sin

In the name of Allah, All-Merciful, Most Merciful

1   Ya Sin
2   By the Wise Qur'an.
3   Truly you are one of the Messengers
4   on a Straight Path.

5   The revelation of the Almighty, the Most Merciful
6   so that you may warn a people
          whose fathers were not warned
      and who are therefore unaware.

7   The Sentence has been justly carried out against most of them
       so they do not believe.

8   We have put iron collars round their necks
       reaching up to the chin,
   so that their heads are forced back.

9   We have placed a barrier in front of them
       and a barrier behind them,
   blindfolding them so that they cannot see.

10 It makes no difference to them
       whether you warn them
         or do not warn them:
       they will not believe.

11   You can only warn those who act on the Reminder
                and fear the All-Merciful in the Unseen.
        Give them the good news of forgiveness and a generous reward.

12   We bring the dead to life
                and We record what they send ahead
                        and what they leave behind.
        We have listed everything in a clear register.

13   Make an example for them of the inhabitants of the city
                when the Messengers came to it.

14   When We sent them two and they denied them both,
                so We reinforced them with a third.
        They said, 'Truly We have been sent to you as Messengers.'

15   They said, 'You are nothing but human beings like ourselves.
                The All-Merciful has not sent down anything.
                        You are simply lying.'

16   They said, 'Our Lord knows
                        we have been sent as Messengers to you.
17   We are only responsible for clear transmission.'

18   They said, 'We see an evil omen in you.
                If you do not stop we will stone you
        and you will suffer a painful punishment at our hands.'

19   They said, 'Your evil omen is in yourselves.
                Is it not just that you have been reminded?
                        No, you are an unbridled people!'

20   A man came running from the far side of the city,
                saying, 'My people! follow the Messengers!
21   Follow those who do not ask you for any wage
                and who have received guidance.
22   Why indeed should I not worship Him
                        Who brought me into being,
                Him to Whom you will be returned?
23   Am I to take as gods instead of Him those whose intercession,
                if the All-Merciful desires harm for me,
        will not help me at all and cannot save me?
24   In that case I would clearly be misguided.
25   I believe in your Lord so listen to me!'

26   He was told, 'Enter the Garden!'
        He said, 'If my people only knew
27   how my Lord has forgiven me
     and placed me among the honoured ones!'

28   We did not send down to his people
        any host from heaven after him
           nor would We send one down.
29   It was but one Great Blast
        and they were extinct.

30   Alas for My slaves!
        No Messenger comes to them
           without their mocking him.

31   Do they not see how many generations before them
        We have destroyed
     and that they will not return to them?

32   Each and every one will be summoned to Our presence.

33   A Sign for them is the dead land which We bring to life
        and from which We bring forth grain of which they eat.
34   We place in it gardens of dates and grapes,
        and cause springs to gush out in it,
35   so they may eat its fruits –
     they did not do it themselves.
     So will they not be thankful?

36   Glory be to Him who created all the pairs:
        from what the earth produces
           and from themselves
     and from things unknown to them.

37   A Sign for them is the night –
        We peel the day away from it
           and there they are in darkness.
38   And the sun runs to its resting place.
        That is the decree of the Almighty, the All-Knowing.
39   And We have decreed set phases for the moon,
        until it ends up looking like an old palm spathe.
40   It is not for the sun to overtake the moon
        nor for the night to outstrip the day;
           each one is swimming in a sphere.

41   A Sign for them is that We carried their families
         in the laden ship.

42   And We have created for them the like of it
         in which they sail.

43   If We wished, We could drown them
         with no one to hear their cry,
    and then they would not be saved –

44   except as an act of mercy from Us,
    to give them enjoyment for a time.

45   They are told, 'Have taqwa of what is before you and behind you
         so that hopefully you will have mercy shown to you.'

46   Not one of your Lord's Signs comes to them
         without their turning away from it.

47   And when they are told, 'Spend from the provision
         Allah has given you,'
    those who disbelieve say to those who believe,
         'Why should we feed someone whom,
    if He wished, Allah would feed Himself?
         You are clearly in error.'

48   And they say, 'When will this promise come about
         if you are telling the truth?'

49   What are they waiting for but one Great Blast
         to seize them while they are quibbling?

50   They will not be able to make a will
         or return to their families.

51   The Trumpet will be blown and at once they will
         be sliding from their graves towards their Lord.

52   They will say, 'Alas for us!
         Who has raised us from our resting-place?
    This is what the All-Merciful promised us.
         The Messengers were telling the truth.'

53   It will be but one Great Blast,
         and they will all be summoned to Our presence.

54   Today no self will be wronged in any way.
         You will only be repaid for what you did.

55   The Companions of the Garden
         are busy enjoying themselves today,
56   they and their wives reclining on couches in the shade.
57   They will have fruits there and whatever they request.

58   'Peace!'
     A word from a Merciful Lord.

59   'Keep yourselves apart today, you evildoers!
60   Did I not make a contract with you,
             tribe of Adam,
           not to worship Shaytan,
         who truly is an outright enemy to you,
61   but to worship Me?
     That is a straight path.
62   He has led huge numbers of you into error.
         Why did you not use your intellect?
63   This is the Hell that you were promised.
64   Roast in it today because you were unbelievers.'

65   Today We seal up their mouths
         and their hands speak to us,
     and their feet bear witness
         to what they have earned.

66   If We wished, We could put out their eyes.
         Then, though they might race for the path,
             how would they see?

67   If We wished, We could transform them where they stand
         so they would neither be able to go out nor return.

68   When We grant long life to people,
         We return them to their primal state.
     So will you not use your intellect?

69   We did not teach him poetry nor would it be right for him.
         It is simply a reminder and a clear Qur'an
70   so that you may warn those who are truly alive
         and so that the Word may be carried out
             against the unbelievers.

71   Have they not seen how We created for them,
         by Our own handiwork,

livestock which are under their control?

72   We have made them tame for them
      and some they ride and some they eat.

73   And they have other uses for them,
      and milk to drink.
    So will they not be thankful?

74   They have taken gods besides Allah
      so that perhaps they may be helped.

75   They cannot help them even though
      they are an army mobilised in their support.

76   So do not let their words distress you.
      We know what they keep secret
        and what they divulge.

77   Does not man see that We created him from a drop
      yet there he is, an open antagonist!

78   He makes likenesses of Us and forgets his own creation,
      saying, 'Who will give life to bones when they are decayed?'

79   Say 'He who made them in the first place
      will bring them back to life.
    He has total knowledge of each created thing;

80   He Who produces fire for you from green trees
      so that you use them to light your fires.'

81   Does He who created the heavens and earth
      not have the power to create the same again?
    Yes indeed! He is the Creator, the All-Knowing.

82   His command when He desires a thing
      is just to say to it, 'Be!' and it is.

83   Glory be to Him Who has the Dominion
      of all things in His Hand.
    You will be returned to Him .

Sura 37

As-Saffat
Those in Ranks

In the name of Allah, All-Merciful, Most Merciful

1	By those drawn up in ranks,
2	and by the warners crying warning,
3	and by the reciters of the Reminder:
4	your God is One:
5	Lord of the heavens and the earth
	and everything between them;
	Lord of the Easts.
6	We have adorned the lowest heaven
	with the beauty of the stars
7	and guarded it against every defiant shaytan.
8	They cannot eavesdrop on the Highest Assembly
	and they are stoned from every side,
9	repelled with harshness –
	they will suffer eternal punishment –
10	except for him who snatches a snippet
	and then is pursued by a piercing flame.
11	Ask them for a fatwa:
	is it they who are stronger in structure
	or other things We have created?
	We created them from sticky clay.
12	No wonder you are surprised as they laugh with scorn!
13	When they are reminded they do not pay heed.
14	When they see a Sign they only laugh with scorn.
15	They say, 'This is just downright magic.

16   When we are dead and turned to dust and bones
                 will we then be raised up again alive?
17   And our early forefathers as well?'
18   Say: 'Yes, and you will be in a despicable state.'

19   There will be but one Great Blast and then their eyes will open.
20   They will say, 'Alas for us! This is the Day of Reckoning!'
21   This is the Day of Decision you used to deny.

22   Assemble those who did wrong
                 together with their associates
       and what they worshipped
23   besides Allah,
       and guide them to the Path of the Blazing Fire!
24   And call them to a halt.
                 They will be asked:
25   'Why are you not helping one another?'
26   No, today they come in absolute submission.

27   They will confront each other, questioning one another.
28   One group will say,
       'You used to come at us from a position of power.'
29   The others will say, 'The truth is that you were not believers.
30   We had no authority over you.
                 Rather you were unbridled people.
31   Our Lord's Word has been carried out against us,
                 that we would taste it.
32   We misled you and we were ourselves misled.'

33   On that Day they will be partners in the punishment.
34   That is how We deal with evildoers.

35   When they were told, 'There is no god but Allah,'
                 they were arrogant.
36   They said, 'Are we to forsake our gods for a mad poet?'

37   Rather he has brought the truth
                 and confirmed the Messengers.

38   You will definitely taste the painful punishment
39   and you will only be repaid for what you did –
40   except for Allah's chosen slaves.

41	They will have preordained provision:
42	sweet fruits and high honour
43	in Gardens of Delight
44	on couches face to face;
45	a cup from a flowing spring
	will pass round among them,
46	as white as driven snow,
	delicious to those who drink,
47	which has no headache in it
	and does not leave them stupefied.
48	There will be dark-eyed maidens with them,
	with eyes reserved for them alone,
49	just like closely guarded pearls.
50	They will confront each other, questioning one another.
51	One of them will say,
	'I used to have a friend
52	who would say to me,
	"Are you one of those
	who say that it is true:
53	that when we have died
	and are turned to dust and bones,
	we will face a Reckoning?"'
54	He will say, 'Are you looking down?'
55	So he will look down and see him
	in the midst of the Blazing Fire
56	and say, 'By Allah, you almost ruined me!
57	If it were not for the blessing of my Lord,
	I would have been among those arraigned.
58	Are we not going to die,
59	except for our first death?
	Are we not going to be punished?
60	Truly this is the Great Victory!
61	It is for the like of this that all workers should work!'
62	Is that better by way of hospitality or the tree of Zaqqum
63	which We have made to be an ordeal for the wrongdoers?
64	It is a tree that emerges in the depths of the Blazing Fire.
65	Its fruits are just like the heads of shaytans.
66	They will eat from it and fill their bellies with it.
67	Then they will have a boiling brew to drink on top of it.
68	Then their destination will be the Blazing Fire.

| 69 | They found their fathers misguided |
| 70 | and they are following hard upon their heels. |

71	Most of the earlier peoples went astray before them
72	though We sent warners to them.
73	See the final fate of those who were warned –
74	except for Allah's chosen slaves.

75	Nuh called out to Us and what an excellent Responder We are!
76	We rescued him and his family from the terrible plight
77	and made his descendants the survivors;
78	and We left the later people to say of him:
79	'Peace be upon Nuh among all beings!'

| 80 | That is how we recompense the good-doers. |
| 81 | He truly was one of Our slaves who are believers. |

| 82 | Then We drowned the rest. |

83	One of his followers in faith was Ibrahim
84	when he came to his Lord with an unblemished heart,
85	and said to his father and his people,
	'What are you worshipping?
86	Is it falsehood – gods besides Allah – that you desire?
87	So what are your thoughts about the Lord of all the worlds?'

88	He took a look at the stars
89	and said, 'I am sick.'
90	So they turned their backs on him.

91	He turned surreptitiously to their gods and said, 'Do you not eat?
92	What is the matter with you that you do not speak?'
93	He turned on them, striking out with his right hand.

94	They came rushing back to him.
95	He said, 'Do you worship something you have carved
96	when Allah created both you and what you do?'
97	They said, 'Build a pyre for him and fling him into the blaze!'
98	They tried to outwit him but We made them the lowest.

99	He said, 'I am going towards my Lord; He will be my guide.
100	My Lord, bestow on me a right-acting child!'
101	And We gave him the good news of a forbearing boy.

102	When he was of an age to work with him, he said,
	'My son, I have seen in a dream that I must sacrifice you.
	What do you think about this?'
	He said, 'Do as you are ordered, father.
	Allah willing, you will find me resolute.'
103	Then when they had both submitted
	and he had laid him face down on the ground,
104	We called out to him, 'Ibrahim!
105	you have fulfilled your vision.'
	That is how We recompense good-doers.
106	This was indeed a most manifest trial.
107	We ransomed him with a mighty sacrifice
108	and left the later people saying of him:
109	'Peace be upon Ibrahim.'
110	That is how We recompense good-doers.
111	He truly was one of Our believing slaves.
112	We gave him the good news of Ishaq,
	a Prophet, one of the righteous.
113	We showered blessings upon him and upon Ishaq.
	Among their descendants are good-doers
	and also people who clearly wrong themselves.
114	We showed great kindness to Musa and Harun.
115	We rescued them and their people
	from their terrible plight.
116	We supported them and so they were the victors.
117	We gave them the clarifying Book
118	and guided them on the Straight Path,
119	and left the later people saying of them,
120	'Peace be upon Musa and Harun!'
121	That is how We recompense good-doers.
122	They truly were among Our slaves who are believers.
123	Ilyas was one of the Messengers.
124	When he said to his people,
	'Will you not be godfearing?
125	Do you call on Baal
	and abandon the Best of Creators?
126	Allah is your Lord and Lord of your forefathers,
	the previous peoples,'

127	they denied him
	and so they will be among those arraigned –
128	except for Allah's chosen slaves.
129	We left the later people saying of him,
130	'Peace be upon the family of Yasin!'
131	That is how We recompense good-doers.
132	He truly was one of Our slaves who are believers.
133	And Lut was one of the Messengers.
134	When We rescued him and all his family –
135	except an old woman among those who stayed behind.
136	Then We utterly destroyed the rest.
137	And you pass by them in the daytime
	and at night.
138	So will you not use your intellect?
139	Yunus too was one of the Messengers.
140	When he ran away to the fully laden ship
141	and cast lots and lost.
142	Then the fish devoured him and he was to blame.
143	Had it not been that he was a man who glorified Allah,
144	he would have remained inside its belly
	until the Day they are raised again.
145	So We cast him up onto the beach and he was sick;
146	and We caused a gourd tree to grow over him.
147	We sent him to a hundred thousand or even more.
148	They believed
	and so We gave them enjoyment for a time.
149	Ask them for a fatwa:
	does your Lord have daughters
	while they themselves have sons?
150	Or did We create the angels female,
	with them as witnesses?
151	No indeed! It is one of their blatant lies to say,
152	'Allah has given birth'.
	They are truly liars.
153	Has He chosen daughters over sons?
154	What is the matter with you?
	How do you reach your judgement?
155	Will you not pay heed?

156   Or do you have some clear authority?
157   Bring your Book, then,
          if you are telling the truth!

158   They claim there is a blood-tie between Him and the jinn
       but the jinn know very well that they will be arraigned.

159   Glory be to Allah above what they describe –
160   except for Allah's chosen slaves.

161   You and those you worship:
162   you will entice no one to them
163   except for him who is to roast in the Blazing Fire.

164   'There is not one of us who does not have a known station.
165   We are those drawn up in ranks.
166   We are those who glorify.'

167   They used to say,
168   'If we had only had a Reminder
          from the previous peoples,
169   we would certainly have been
          sincere slaves of Allah!'
170   But they have rejected it
       and they will soon know!

171   Our Word was given before to Our slaves, the Messengers,
172   that they would certainly be helped.
173   It is Our army which will be victorious.

174   Therefore turn from them for a time.
175   And watch them, for they will soon see!

176   Are they trying to hasten Our punishment?
177   When it descends in their courtyard –
          how evil will be the morning
            of those who were warned!

178   So turn from them for a time.
179   And watch, for they will soon see!

180   Glory be to your Lord, the Lord of Might,
       beyond anything they describe.

181   And peace be upon the Messengers.
182   And praise be to Allah,
                    the Lord of all the worlds!

Sura 38

Sâd

In the name of Allah, All-Merciful, Most Merciful

1   Sâd
By the Qur'an holding the Remembrance.

2   But those who disbelieve are full of vainglory
        and entrenched in hostility.

3   How many generations We have destroyed before them!
        And they cried out when it was too late to escape.

4   They are surprised that a warner should come
        to them from among themselves.
The unbelievers say, 'This is a lying magician.

5   Has he turned all the gods into One God?
        That is truly astonishing!'

6   Their leaders went off saying,
        'Carry on as you are! Hold fast to your gods.
        This is clearly something planned.

7   We have not heard of this in the old religion.
        This is merely something contrived.

8   Has the Reminder been sent down to him out of all of us?'
        They are in doubt about My Reminder.
They have yet to taste My punishment.

9   Or do they possess the treasuries of your Lord's mercy,
        the Almighty, the Ever-Giving?

10   Or does the kingdom of the heavens and earth
        and everything between them belong to them?
Let them, in that case, climb the ropes to heaven!

11   Even a whole army of Confederates will be routed there!

12   Before them the people of Nuh denied the truth,
          as did 'Ad and Pharaoh of the Stakes,
13   and Thamud and the people of Lut
          and the Companions of the Thicket.*
          Those too were Confederates.
14   Each one of them denied the Messengers
          and so My punishment was justly carried out.

15   These people too are only awaiting a single Blast
          and it will not be repeated.
16   They say, 'Our Lord, advance our share to us
          before the Day of Reckoning.'

17   Be steadfast in the face of what they say
          and remember Our slave Dawud,
             who possessed true strength.
          He truly turned to his Lord.
18   We subjected the mountains to glorify with him
          in the evening and at sunrise.
19   And also the birds, flocking together,
          all of them turned to Him.
20   We made his kingdom strong
          and gave him wisdom and decisive speech.

21   Has the story of the litigants reached you?
          How they climbed up to the Upper Room
22   and came in on Dawud
          who was alarmed by them.
     They said, 'Do not be afraid. We are two litigants,
          one of whom has acted unjustly towards the other,
     so judge between us with truth and do not be unjust
          and guide us to the Right Path.
23   This brother of mine has ninety-nine ewes
          and I have only one.
     He said, "Let me have charge of it,"
          and got the better of me with his words.'

24   He said, 'He has wronged you by asking for your ewe
          to add to his ewes.
     Truly many partners are unjust to one another –

---

* The 'Thicket' may be a description or the name of an actual place. It may be another name for the people of Madyan.

except those who believe and do right actions,
>and how few they are!'
Dawud realised that We had put him to the test.
He begged forgiveness from his Lord
>and fell down prone, prostrating, and repented.
25 So We forgave him for that
>and he has nearness to Us
>>and a good Homecoming.

26 'Dawud! We have made you a khalif on the earth,
>so judge between people with truth
and do not follow your own desires,
>letting them misguide you from the Way of Allah.
Those who are misguided from the Way of Allah
>will receive a harsh punishment
because they forgot the Day of Reckoning.'

27 We did not create heaven and earth
>and everything between them
>>to no purpose.
That is the opinion of those who disbelieve.
Woe to those who disbelieve, because of the Fire!

28 Would We make those who believe and do right actions
>the same as those who cause corruption on the earth?
Would We make those who are godfearing
>the same as the dissolute?

29 It is a Book We have sent down to you, full of blessing,
>so let people of intelligence ponder its Signs
>>and take heed.

30 We gave Dawud Sulayman.
>What an excellent slave!
>>He truly turned to his Lord.
31 When swift horses, champing at the bit,
>were displayed before him in the afternoon,
32 he said, 'I have put the love of good things
>above the remembrance of my Lord
until the sun disappeared behind its veil.
33 >Return them to me!'
And he set about slashing
>through their shanks and necks.

34   We tested Sulayman and placed
         a lifeless body on his throne.
            Then he repented.

35   He said, 'My Lord, forgive me and give me a kingdom
         the like of which will never be granted to anyone after me.
            Truly You are the Ever-Giving.'

36   So We subjected the wind to him
         to blow at his command,
            softly, wherever he directed.

37   And the shaytans, every builder and diver,

38   and others of them, yoked together in chains.

39   'This is Our gift: so bestow it or withhold it
         without reckoning.'

40   He will have nearness to Us
         and a good Homecoming.

41   Remember Our slave Ayyub when he called on his Lord:
         'Shaytan has afflicted me with exhaustion and suffering.'

42   'Stamp your foot! Here is a cool bath
         and water to drink.'

43   We gave him back his family
         and the same again with them
            as a mercy from Us
         and a reminder for people of intellect.

44   'Take a bundle of rushes in your hand and strike with that
         but do not break your oath.'
     We found him steadfast.
         What an excellent slave!
     He truly turned to his Lord.

45   And remember Our slaves Ibrahim, Ishaq and Ya'qub,
         men of true strength and inner sight.

46   We purified their sincerity
         through sincere remembrance of the Abode.

47   In Our eyes they are among the best of chosen men.

48   Remember Our slaves Isma'il, Al-Yasa' and Dhu'l-Kifl;
         each of them was among the best of men.

49   This is a Reminder.
     The godfearing will have a good Homecoming:

50   Gardens of Eden, whose gates will be open to them,

51   where they will recline,
            calling for plentiful fruit and drink;

52 and there will be dark-eyed maidens with them
with eyes reserved for them alone.

53 This is what you are promised on the Day of Reckoning.

54 This is Our provision which will never run out.

55 This! Whereas for the profligate
there is an evil Homecoming:

56 Hell, where they will roast.
What an evil resting-place!

57 This! So let them taste it –
boiling water and scalding pus,

58 and other such torments.

59 This! A crowd hurtling in with you.
There is no welcome for them.
They will certainly roast in the Fire.

60 They will say, 'No, it is you who have no welcome.
It is you who brought it upon us.
What an evil place to settle!'

61 They will say, 'Our Lord, give him who brought this on us
double the punishment in the Fire!'

62 They will say, 'How is it that we do not see some men
whom we used to count among the worst of people?

63 Did we turn them into figures of fun?
Did our eyes disdain to look at them?'

64 All this is certainly true –
the bickering of the people of the Fire.

65 Say: 'I am only a warner.
There is no god except Allah,
the One, the All-Conquering,

66 Lord of the heavens and the earth
and everything between them,
the Almighty, the Endlessly Forgiving.'

67 Say: 'This is momentous news

68 yet you ignore it!

69 I knew nothing of the Highest Assembly
when they debated.

70 It is only revealed to me
that I am a clear warner.'

71 Your Lord said to the angels,
'I am going to create a human being out of clay.

72   When I have formed him
           and breathed My Ruh into him,
             fall down in prostration to him!'

73   So the angels prostrated,
        all of them together,

74   except for Iblis who was arrogant
     and was one of the unbelievers.

75   He said, 'Iblis, what prevented you prostrating
       to what I created with My own Hands?
     Were you overcome by arrogance
       or are you one of the exalted?'

76   He said, 'I am better than him.
       You created me from fire
         but You created him from clay.'

77   He said, 'Get out!
       you are accursed!

78   My curse is upon you
     until the Day of Reckoning.'

79   He said, 'My Lord, grant me a reprieve
     until the Day they are raised again.'

80   He said, 'You are among the reprieved
81   until the Day whose time is known.'

82   He said, 'By Your might, I will mislead all of them
83   except for Your chosen slaves among them.'

84   He said, 'By the truth – and I speak the truth –
85   I will fill up Hell with you
     and every one of them who follows you.'

86   Say: 'I do not ask you for any wage for it,
       nor am I a man of false pretentions.

87   It is simply a reminder to all the worlds.

88   You will come to know
         what it is talking about
           after a while.'

Sura 39

Az-Zumar
The Companies

1   The revelation of the Book
      is from Allah, the Almighty, the All-Wise.

2   We have sent down the Book to you with truth.
      So worship Allah, making your deen sincerely His.

3   Indeed is the sincere deen not Allah's alone?
      If people take protectors besides Him –
    'We only worship them so that they
      may bring us nearer to Allah' –
    Allah will judge between them regarding
      the things about which they differed.
    Allah does not guide anyone who is an ungrateful liar.

4   If Allah had desired to have a son
      He would have chosen
        whatever He wished
    from what He has created.
        Glory be to Him!
    He is Allah, the One, the All-Conquering.

5   He created the heavens and the earth with truth.
      He wraps the night around the day
        and wraps the day around the night,
    and has made the sun and moon subservient,
        each one running for a specified term.
    Is He not indeed the Almighty, the Endlessly Forgiving?

6   He created you from a single self,
            then produced its mate from it,
       and sent down livestock to you –
            eight kinds in pairs.
       He creates you stage by stage
            in your mothers' wombs
                in a threefold darkness.
       That is Allah, your Lord.
            Sovereignty is His.
       There is no god but Him.
            So what has made you deviate?

7   If you are ungrateful, Allah is rich beyond need of any of you
            and He is not pleased with ingratitude in His slaves.
       But if you are grateful, He is pleased with you for that.
            No burden-bearer can bear another's burden.
       Then you will return to your Lord
            and He will inform you of what you did.
       He knows what the heart contains.

8   When harm touches man he calls upon his Lord,
            turning in repentance to Him.
       Then when He grants him a blessing from Him,
            he forgets what he was calling for before
                and ascribes rivals to Allah,
            so as to misguide others from His Way.
       Say: 'Enjoy your unbelief for a little while.
            You are among the Companions of the Fire.'

9   What of him who spends the night hours in prayer,
            prostrating and standing up,
                mindful of the Next World,
            hoping for the mercy of his Lord?
       Say: 'Are they the same – those who know
            and those who do not know?'
       It is only people of intelligence who pay heed.

10   Say: 'Slaves of Mine who believe! have taqwa of your Lord.
       For those who do good in this world there is good
            and Allah's earth is spacious.
       The steadfast will be paid their wages in full
            without any reckoning.'

11   Say: 'I am commanded to worship Allah,
            making my deen sincerely His.
12   And I am commanded to be the first of the Muslims.'

13   Say: 'I fear, were I to disobey my Lord,
            the punishment of a Terrible Day.'

14   Say: 'It is Allah I worship, making my deen sincerely His,
15   so worship anything you will apart from Him!'
        Say: 'The real losers are those who lose themselves
            and their families on the Day of Rising.'
                Is not that a clear loss?
16   They will have awnings of Fire above them
            and awnings below them.
        By that Allah strikes fear into His slaves:
            'So have taqwa, My slaves, of Me!'

17   Those who shun the worship of false gods
            and turn towards Allah
                will have good news.
        So give good news to My slaves.
18   Those who listen well to what is said
            and follow the best of it,
        they are the ones whom Allah has guided,
            they are the people of intelligence.

19   But as for those against whom the decree of Punishment
            is justly carried out,
        can you rescue those who are in the Fire?

20   But those who have taqwa of their Lord
            will have high-ceilinged Halls,
        and more such Halls built one above the other,
            and rivers flowing under them.
        That is Allah's promise.
            Allah does not break His promise.

21   Do you not see that Allah sends down water from the sky
            and threads it through the earth to emerge as springs
        and then by it brings forth crops of varying colours,
            which then wither and you see them turning yellow
                and then He makes them into broken stubble?
        There is a reminder in that for people of intelligence.

22   Is he whose breast is opened to Islam,
            and who is therefore illuminated by his Lord . . . ?
        Woe to those whose hearts are hardened
            against the remembrance of Allah!
        Such people are clearly misguided.

23   Allah has sent down the Supreme Discourse,
            a Book consistent in its frequent repetitions.
        The skins of those who fear their Lord tremble at it
            and then their skins and hearts yield softly
                to the remembrance of Allah.
        That is Allah's guidance by which He guides whoever He wills.
            And no one can guide those whom Allah misguides.

24   Is someone who tries to shield himself with his face
            from the worst of the torment on the Day of Rising . . . ?
        The wrongdoers will be told, 'Taste what you have earned.'

25   Those before them also denied the truth
            and the punishment came upon them
                from where they did not expect.
26   So Allah made them taste disgrace in the life of this world
            and the punishment of the Next World is far worse
                if they only knew.

27   We have given people all kinds of examples in this Qur'an,
            so that hopefully they will pay heed –
28   an Arabic Qur'an with no distortion in it,
            so that hopefully they will be godfearing.

29   Allah has made a comparison for them of a man
            owned by several partners in dispute with one another
                and another man wholly owned by a single man.
            Are they the same?
                Praise be to Allah!
        The fact is that most of them do not know.

30   You will die and they too will die.
31   Then on the Day of Rising you will argue
                in the presence of your Lord.

32   Who could do greater wrong than those who lie about Allah
            and deny the truth when it comes to them?
        Do the unbelievers not have a dwelling place in Hell?

33 He who brings the truth
        and those who confirm it –
    those are the godfearing.

34 They will have anything they wish for from their Lord.
        That is the recompense of good-doers.
35 So that Allah may erase from them the worst of what they did
        and pay them their wages for the best of what they did.

36 Is Allah not enough for His slave?
        Yet they try to scare you with others apart from Him.
    If Allah misguides anyone, he has no guide
37   and if Allah guides anyone, he cannot be misguided.
    Is Allah not Almighty, Exactor of Revenge?

38 If you ask them, 'Who created the heavens and the earth?'
        they will say, 'Allah.'
    Say: 'So what do you think?
        If Allah desires harm for me,
    can those you call upon besides Allah remove His harm?
        Or if He desires mercy for me,
    can they withhold His mercy?'
        Say: 'Allah is enough for me.
    All those who truly trust put their trust in Him.'

39 Say: 'My people, do as you think best;
        that is what I am doing.
    You will soon know
40   who will receive a punishment which disgraces him
    and will unleash against himself
        an everlasting punishment.'

41 We have sent down to you the Book for mankind with truth.
        So whoever is guided is guided to his own good
            and whoever is misguided, it is to his detriment.
        You are not set over them as a guardian.

42 Allah takes back people's souls when their death arrives
        and those who have not yet died, while they are asleep.
    He keeps hold of those whose death has been decreed
        and sends the others back for a specified term.
    There are certainly Signs in that for people who reflect.

43   Or have they adopted intercessors besides Allah?
         Say: 'Even though they do not control a thing
            and have no awareness?'
44   Say: 'Intercession is entirely Allah's affair.
         The kingdom of the heavens and earth is His.
            Then you will be returned to Him.'

45   When Allah is mentioned on His own,
         the hearts of those who do not believe in the Next World
            shrink back shuddering,
         but when others apart from Him are mentioned,
            they jump for joy.

46   Say: 'O Allah, Originator of the heavens and the earth,
         Knower of the Unseen and the Visible,
      You will judge between Your slaves
         regarding what they differed about.'

47   If those who did wrong owned everything on earth,
         and the same again with it,
      they would offer it as a ransom to save themselves
         from the evil of the punishment on the Day of Rising.
      What confronts them from Allah
         will be something they did not reckon with.
48   What confronts them will be the evil actions which they earned
         and what they used to mock at will engulf them.

49   When harm touches man he calls on Us.
         Then when We grant him a blessing from Us he says,
      'I have only been given this because of my knowledge.'
         In fact it is a trial but most of them do not know it.
50   Those who came before them also said that,
         but what they earned did not avail them.
51   The evil deeds they earned caught up with them.
         And the evil deeds which the wrongdoers
            among these people earn
         will also catch up with them
      and they can do nothing to prevent it.

52   Do they not know that Allah
         expands the provision of anyone He wills
            and restricts it?
      There are certainly Signs in that for people who believe.

53 Say: 'My slaves, you who have transgressed against yourselves,
     do not despair of the mercy of Allah.
   Truly Allah forgives all wrong actions.
     He is the Ever-Forgiving, the Most Merciful.'

54 Turn in repentance to your Lord and submit to Him
     before punishment comes upon you,
       for then you cannot be helped.

55 Follow the best that has been sent down to you from your Lord
     before the punishment comes upon you suddenly
       when you are not expecting it;
56 lest anyone should say, 'Alas for me
     for neglecting what Allah was due,
       and being one of the scoffers!'
57 or lest they should say,
     'If only Allah had guided me,
       I would have been godfearing,'
58 or lest he should say, when he sees the punishment,
     'If only I could have another chance
       so that I could be a good-doer!'

59 'No, the fact is that My Signs came to you
     but you denied them and were arrogant
       and were one of the unbelievers.'

60 On the Day of Rising you will see those who lied against Allah
     with their faces blackened.
   Do the arrogant not have a dwelling place in Hell?

61 Allah will give security those who were godfearing
     in their victorious Safe Haven.
   No evil will touch them and they will know no sorrow.

62 Allah is the Creator of everything
     and He is Guardian over everything.
63 The keys of the heavens and earth belong to Him.
     It is those who reject Allah's Signs who are the losers.

64 Say: 'Do you order me to worship something other than Allah,
     you ignorant people?'

65 It has been revealed to you and those before you:
     'If you associate others with Allah,

your actions will come to nothing
and you will be among the losers.'

66   No! Worship Allah and be among the thankful.

67   They do not measure Allah with His true measure.
The whole earth will be a mere handful
for Him on the Day of Rising,
the heavens folded up in His right hand.
Glory be to Him!
He is exalted above the partners they ascribe!

68   The Trumpet will be blown
and those in the heavens
and those in the earth
will all lose consciousness,
except those Allah wills.
Then it will be blown a second time
and at once they will be standing upright,
looking on.

69   And the earth will shine with the Pure Light of its Lord;
the Book will be put in place;
the Prophets and witnesses will be brought;
it will be decided between them with the truth;
and they will not be wronged.

70   Every self will be repaid in full for what it did.
He knows best what they are doing.

71   Those who disbelieve will be driven to Hell in companies
and when they arrive there and its gates are opened
its custodians will say to them,
'Did Messengers from yourselves not come to you,
reciting your Lord's Signs to you and warning you
of the meeting on this Day of yours?'
They will say, 'Indeed they did, but the decree of punishment
is justly carried out against the unbelievers.'

72   They will be told, 'Enter the gates of Hell
and stay there timelessly, for ever.
How evil is the abode of the arrogant!'

73   And those who have taqwa of their Lord
will be driven to the Garden in companies
and when they arrive there, finding its gates open,

its custodians will say to them, 'Peace be upon you!
You have done well so enter it timelessly, for ever.'

74 They will say, 'Praise be to Allah
Who has fulfilled His promise to us
and made us the inheritors of this land,
letting us settle in the Garden wherever we want.
How excellent is the wage of those who work!'

75 You will see the angels circling round the Throne,
glorifying their Lord with praise.
It will be decided between them with truth.
And it will be said:
'Praise be to Allah,
the Lord of all the worlds.'

Sura 40

Ghafir
Forgiving

In the name of Allah, All-Merciful, Most Merciful

1   Ha Mim
2   The revelation of the Book is from Allah,
      the Almighty, the All-Knowing.

3   The Forgiver of wrong action, the Accepter of repentance,
      the Severe in retribution, the Possessor of abundance.
   There is no god but Him. He is the final destination.

4   No one disputes Allah's Signs except those who disbelieve.
      Do not let their free movement about the earth deceive you.

5   The people of Nuh denied the truth before them,
      and the Confederates after them.
   Every nation planned to seize its Messenger
      and used false arguments to rebut the truth.
   So I seized them, and how was My retribution!

6   So your Lord's Words about those who disbelieve proved true,
      that they are indeed the Companions of the Fire.

7   Those who bear the Throne, and all those around it,
      glorify their Lord with praise and believe in Him
         and ask forgiveness for those who believe:
   'Our Lord, You encompass everything in mercy and knowledge!
      Forgive those who turn to You and who follow Your Way
         and safeguard them from the punishment
            of the Blazing Fire.

8   Our Lord, admit them to the Gardens of Eden
        You have promised them,
          and all of their parents, wives and children who acted rightly.
          Truly You are the Almighty, the All-Wise.

9   And safeguard them from evil acts.
    Those You safeguard from evil acts
        are truly the recipients of Your mercy on that Day.
          That is the Mighty Victory.'

10   Those who disbelieved will be addressed:
        'Allah's hatred of you,
    when you were called to faith but then chose unbelief,
        is even greater than your hatred of yourselves.'

11   They will say, 'Our Lord,
        twice You caused us to die
          and twice You gave us life.
        We admit our wrong actions.
          Is there no way out?'

12   That is because when Allah alone is called upon you disbelieve,
        but if others are associated with Him, you believe.
    Judgement belongs to Allah, the All-High, the All-Great.

13   It is He who shows you His Signs
        and sends down provision to you out of heaven.
    But none pay heed save those who repent.

14   So call upon Allah, making your deen sincerely His,
        even though the unbelievers detest it.

15   He is the Raiser of ranks, the Possessor of the Throne,
        He sends the Ruh by His command
          to whichever of His slaves He wills
    so that he may warn mankind about the Day of Meeting:

16   the Day when they will issue forth
    and when not one thing about them
        will be hidden from Allah.
    'To whom does the kingdom belong today?
        To Allah, the One, the Conqueror!

17   Every self will be repaid today for what it earned.
        Today there will be no injustice.
          Allah is swift at reckoning.'

18   And warn them of the Day of Immediacy
            when hearts rise choking to the throat.
        The wrongdoers will have no close friend
            nor any intercessor who might be heard.

19   He knows the eyes' deceit
            and what people's breasts conceal.

20   Allah will judge with truth;
            and those you call upon apart from Him
                will not judge with anything at all.
        It is Allah who is the All-Hearing, the All-Seeing.

21   Have they not travelled in the earth
            and seen the final fate of those before them?
        They were greater than them in strength
            and left far deeper traces on the earth,
        yet Allah seized them for their wrong actions
            and they had no one to protect them from Allah.
22   That was because their Messengers brought them the Clear Signs
            but they remained unbelievers.
                So Allah seized them.
        He is Most Strong, Severe in Retribution.

23   We sent Musa with Our Signs and clear authority
24   to Pharaoh, Haman and Qarun.
                But they said, 'A lying magician.'
25   When he brought them the truth from Us they said,
            'Slaughter the sons of those who believed with him
                but let their women live.'
        The stratagems of the unbelievers are nothing but errors.

26   Pharaoh said, 'Let me kill Musa and let him call upon his Lord!
            I am afraid that he may change your deen
                and bring about corruption in the land.'
27   Musa said, 'I seek refuge in my Lord and your Lord
            from every proud man who does not believe
                in the Day of Reckoning.'

28   A man among Pharaoh's people who had faith,
            but kept his faith concealed, said,
        'Are you going to kill a man for saying "My Lord is Allah"
            when he has brought you Clear Signs from your Lord?
        If he is telling a lie, be it on his own head.

But if he is telling the truth,
then some of what he is promising you
will certainly happen to you.
Allah does not guide any unbridled inveterate liar.

29 My people! the kingdom is yours today,
as masters in the land,
but who will help us against Allah's violent force,
if it comes upon us?'
Pharoah said, 'I only show you what I see myself
and I only guide you to the path of rectitude.'

30 The man who had faith said, 'My people!
I fear for you a day like that of the Confederates,
31 the same as happened to the people of Nuh and 'Ad
and Thamud and those who followed after them.
Allah does not want any injustice for His slaves.
32 My people! I fear for you the Day of Calling Out,
33 the Day when you will turn your backs in flight,
having no one to protect you from Allah.
Whoever Allah misguides will have no guide.
34 Yusuf brought you the Clear Signs before,
but you never stopped doubting what he brought to you
to the extent that when he died, you said,
"Allah will never send another Messenger after him."
That is how Allah misguides
those who are unbridled and full of doubt.'

35 Those who argue about the Signs of Allah
without any authority coming to them
do something hateful in the sight of Allah
and in the sight of the people who believe.
That is how Allah seals up
the heart of every arrogant oppressor.

36 Pharaoh said, 'Haman, build me a tower
so that perhaps I may gain means of access,
37 access to the heavens,
so that I can look on Musa's God.
Truly I think he is a liar.'
That is how Pharaoh's evil actions
were made attractive to him
and he debarred others from the Path.
Pharaoh's scheming led to nothing but ruin.

38   The man who believed said, 'My people! follow me
          and I will guide you to the path of rectitude.
39   My people! the life of this world is only fleeting enjoyment.
          It is the Next World which is the abode of permanence.
40   Whoever does an evil act will only be repaid with its equivalent.
          But whoever acts rightly,
                male or female,
                    being a believer,
                such a person will enter the Garden,
          provided for in it without any reckoning.
41   My people! how is it that I call you to salvation
          while you call me to the Fire?
42   You call me to reject Allah
          and to associate something with Him
                about which I have no knowledge,
          while I call you to the Almighty, the Endlessly Forgiving.
43   There is no question that what you call me to
          has no foundation either in this world or the Next World,
                that our return is to Allah,
          and that the profligate will be Companions of the Fire.
44   You will remember what I am telling you.
          I consign my destiny completely to Allah.
                Truly Allah sees His slaves.'

45   So Allah safeguarded him from the evil things they plotted
          and a most evil torment engulfed Pharaoh's people –
46   the Fire, morning and night, to which they are exposed;
          and on the Day the Hour takes place:
      'Admit Pharaoh's people to the harshest punishment!'

47   When they are squabbling with one another in the Fire,
          the weak will say to those deemed great,
      'We were your followers, so why do you not
          relieve us of a portion of the Fire?'
48   Those deemed great will say, 'All of us are in it.
          Allah has clearly judged between His slaves.'

49   Those in the Fire will say to the custodians of Hell,
          'Call on your Lord to make the punishment less for us
                for just one day.'
50   They will ask, 'Did your Messengers
                not bring you the Clear Signs?'
          They will answer, 'Yes.'

They will say, 'Then you call!'
But the calling of the unbelievers only goes astray.

51   We will certainly help Our Messengers
          and those who believe
      both in the life of this world
          and on the Day the witnesses appear,

52   the Day when the excuses of the wrongdoers
          will not help them.
      The curse will be on them
          and they will have the most evil Home.

53   We gave Musa the guidance
          and bequeathed the Book to the tribe of Israel,

54   as guidance and a reminder for people of intelligence.

55   So remain steadfast. Allah's promise is true.
          Ask forgiveness for your wrong action
              and glorify your Lord with praise
          in the evening and the early morning.

56   Certainly those who argue about the Signs of Allah
          without any authority having come to them
      have nothing in their breasts except for pride
          which they will never be able to vindicate.
      Therefore seek refuge with Allah.
          He is the All-Hearing, the All-Seeing.

57   The creation of the heavens and earth
          is far greater than the creation of mankind.
      But most of mankind do not know it.

58   The blind and the seeing are not the same.
      Nor are those who believe and do right actions
          the same as evildoers.
      What little heed they pay!

59   The Hour is coming – there is no doubt about it.
          But most of mankind do not believe.

60   Your Lord says, 'Call on Me and I will answer you.
          Those who who are too proud to worship Me
              will enter Hell abject.'

61   Allah is He who appointed the night for you
            so that you might rest in it,
                and the day for seeing.
      Allah pours out His favour on mankind
            but most people do not show thanks.

62   That is Allah, your Lord,
            the Creator of all things.
      There is no god but Him –
            so how have you been perverted?

63   That is how those who deny Allah's Signs have been perverted.

64   It is Allah who made the earth a stable home for you
                and the sky a dome,
            and formed you, giving you the best of forms,
      and provided you with good and wholesome things.
            That is Allah, your Lord.
      Blessed be Allah, the Lord of all the worlds!

65   He is the Living –
            there is no god but Him –
      so call on Him, making your deen sincerely His.
            Praise be to Allah, the Lord of all the worlds.

66   Say: 'I have been forbidden to worship
                those you call upon besides Allah
            when the Clear Signs came to me from my Lord
      and I have been commanded to submit
            to the Lord of all the worlds.'

67   It is He who created you from earth,
            then from a drop of sperm,
                then from a clot of blood,
      then He brings you out as infants,
            then so you may achieve full strength,
      then so you may become old men –
            though some of you may die before that time –
      so that you may reach a predetermined age
            and so that hopefully you will use your intellect.

68   It is He who gives life and causes to die.
            When He decides on something,
      He just says to it, 'Be!' and it is.

69   Do you not see those who argue about Allah's Signs?
       How have they been turned around?

70   Those who deny the Book
       and that with which We sent Our Messengers
          will certainly come to know
71   when they have shackles and chains around their necks
       and are dragged along the ground
72   into the boiling water
       and then are thrown into the Fire!

73   Then they will be asked,
       'Where are those besides Allah you associated with Him?'
74   and they will reply, 'They have forsaken us.
       Or rather we were not calling to anything at all before.'
          That is how Allah misguides the unbelievers.

75   'That is because you exulted on the earth,
       without any right to do so;
          and strutted about.
76   Enter the gates of Hell,
       remaining in it timelessly, for ever.
    How evil is the abode of the arrogant!'

77   So be steadfast, Allah's promise is true.
       Whether We show you some
    of what We have promised them,
       or take you back to Us,
    they will in any case be returned to Us.

78   We sent Messengers before you.
       Some of them We have told you about
          and others We have not told you about.
    No Messenger can bring a Sign
       except with Allah's permission.
    But when Allah's command comes
       the matter will be decided with truth
    and then and there the liars will be lost.

79   It is Allah who has given you livestock,
       some for you to ride and some to eat.

80   You gain various benefits from them,
                and on them you can obtain what your hearts desire,
        and on them and on ships you are transported.

81   He shows you His Signs,
                so which of Allah's Signs do you deny?

82   Have they not travelled in the land
                and seen the final fate of those before them?
        They were more numerous than them and greater in strength
                and left more and deeper traces on earth,
        but what they earned was of no use to them.

83   When their Messengers brought them the Clear Signs,
                they exulted in the knowledge they had
        and then were engulfed by the very things they mocked.

84   When they saw Our violent force,
                they said, 'We believe in Allah alone
                        and reject what we associated with Him.'
85   But when they saw Our violent force
                their faith was of no use to them.
        That is the pattern Allah has always followed with His slaves.
                Then and there the unbelievers were lost.

Sura 41

Fussilat
Made Plain

In the name of Allah, All-Merciful, Most Merciful

1   Ha Mim
2   A revelation from the All-Merciful, the Most Merciful.

3   A Book whose verses have been demarcated
         for people who know
             as an Arabic Qur'an,
4   bringing good news and giving warning;
         but most of them have turned away
             and do not hear.

5   They say, 'Our hearts are covered up
         against what you call us to
     and there is a heaviness in our ears.
         There is a screen between us and you.
     So act – we are certainly acting.'

6   Say: 'I am only a human being like yourselves.
         It is revealed to me that your god is One God.
     So be straight with Him and ask for His forgiveness.'
         Woe to those who associate others with Him:
7   those who do not pay zakat and deny the Next World.

8   Those who believe and do right actions
         will have a wage which never fails.

9   Say: 'Do you reject Him who created the earth in two days,
         and make others equal to Him?
         That is the Lord of all the worlds.'

10   He placed firmly embedded mountains on it, towering over it,
               and blessed it and measured out its nourishment in it,
                    laid out for those who seek it – all in four days.

11   Then He turned to heaven when it was smoke
               and said to it and to the earth,
                    'Come willingly or unwillingly.'
               They both said, 'We come willingly.'

12   In two days He determined them as seven heavens
               and revealed, in every heaven, its own mandate.
        We adorned the lowest heaven with lamps
               and guarded it.
        That is the decree of the Almighty, the All-Knowing.

13   If they turn away, then say, 'I warn you of a lightning-bolt
               like the lightning-bolt of 'Ad and of Thamud.'

14   When the Messengers came to them
                    from in front and from behind,
               saying, 'Do not worship anyone but Allah.'
        they said, 'If our Lord had willed,
                    He could have sent angels down,
               so we reject the Message you have been sent with.'

15   'Ad were arrogant in the land, without any right,
               saying, 'Who has greater strength than us?'
        Did they not see that Allah, who created them,
               had greater strength than them?
                    But they renounced Our Signs.

16   So We sent a howling wind against them
               on disastrous ill-fated days
        to make them taste the punishment
               of degradation in this world.
        But the punishment of the Next World
               is even more degrading.
        And they will not be helped.

17   As for Thamud, We guided them,
               but they preferred blindness to guidance.
        So the lightning-bolt of the humiliating punishment
               seized them on account of what they earned.

18   And We rescued those who believed and were godfearing.

19   On the Day We crowd the enemies of Allah into the Fire
               and they are driven in close-packed ranks,

20   when they reach it, their hearing, sight and skin
          will testify against them concerning what they did.
21   They will ask their skins, 'Why did you testify against us?'
          and they will reply, 'Allah gave us speech
              as He has given speech to everything.
          He created you in the first place
              and you will be returned to Him.
22   You did not think to shield yourselves from
          your hearing, sight and skin testifying against you
      and you thought that Allah would never know
          much of what you did.
23   It is that thought you had about your Lord that has destroyed you
          so now you find yourselves among the lost.'

24   Even if they are steadfast, the Fire will still be their residence!
          If they ask for favour, no favour will be given.
25   We have assigned to them close comrades
          who have made
      what is before them and behind them
          seem good to them.
      And the statement about the nations,
          both of jinn and men,
      who passed away before them
          has proved true of them as well.
      Certainly they were lost.

26   Those who disbelieve say, 'Do not listen to this Qur'an.
          Drown it out so that hopefully you will gain the upper hand.'
27   We will make those who disbelieve suffer a severe punishment
          and repay them for the worst of what they did.
28   That is the repayment of the enemies of Allah – the Fire.
          They will have it for their Eternal Home
      as repayment for their renunciation of Our Signs.

29   Those who disbelieve say, 'Our Lord,
          show us those jinn and men who misguided us
              and we will place them beneath our feet
          so that they will be among the lowest of the low.'

30   The angels descend on those who say,
          'Our Lord is Allah,' and then go straight:
      'Do not fear and do not grieve
          but rejoice in the Garden you have been promised.

31   We are your protectors
        in the life of this world and the Next World.
      You will have there all that your selves could wish for.
        You will have there everything you demand.

32   Hospitality from One who is Ever-Forgiving, Most Merciful.'

33   Who could say anything better
      than someone who summons to Allah
        and acts rightly
      and says, 'I am one of the Muslims'?

34   A good action and a bad action are not the same.
      Repel the bad with something better
    and, if there is enmity between you and someone else,
      he will be like a bosom friend.

35   None will obtain it but those who are truly steadfast.
      None will obtain it but those who have great good fortune.

36   If an evil urge from Shaytan eggs you on,
      seek refuge in Allah.
    He is the All-Hearing, the All-Knowing.

37   Among His Signs are the night and day and the sun and moon.
      Do not prostrate to the sun nor to the moon.
    Prostrate to Allah who created them, if you worship Him.

38   If they grow arrogant, those who are with your Lord
      glorify Him night and day and never grow tired.

39   Among His Signs is that you see the earth laid bare
      and then when We send down water on it
        it quivers and swells.
    He who gives it life is He who gives life to the dead.
      Certainly He has power over all things.

40   Those who adulterate Our Signs are not concealed from Us.
      Who is better – someone who will be thrown into the fire
        or someone who will arrive in safety on the Day of Rising?
    Do what you like.
      He sees whatever you do.

41   Those who reject the Remembrance when it comes to them –
      truly it is a Mighty Book;

42   falsehood cannot reach it from before it or behind it –
         it is a revelation from One who is All-Wise, Praiseworthy.

43   Nothing has been said to you
         that was not said to the Messengers before you.
      Your Lord is the Possessor of forgiveness
         but also of painful retribution.

44   If We had made it a Qur'an in a foreign tongue
         they would have said,
      'Why have its Signs not been made plain?
         What! A foreign language for an Arab?'
      Say: 'It is guidance and healing for people who believe.
         Those who do not believe have heaviness in their ears
            and for them it is blindness.
      Such people are being called from a very distant place.'

45   We gave Musa the Book but there was disagreement about it.
         And had it not been for a prior Word from your Lord,
      the judgement between them would already have been made.
         They are indeed in grave doubt about it.

46   Whoever acts rightly, it is for his own good.
         Whoever does evil, it is to his detriment.
      Your Lord does not wrong His slaves.

47   Knowledge of the Hour is referred to Him.
         And no fruit emerges from its husk,
      nor does any female get pregnant or give birth,
         without His knowledge.
      On the Day He calls out to them: 'Where are My associates?'
         they will say, 'We declare to you that none of us is a witness.'
48   What they called upon before will have forsaken them
         and they will realise they have no way of escape.

49   Man never tires of praying for what is good
         and if evil touches him,
            he despairs and loses hope.
50   But if We let him taste mercy from Us
         after he has suffered hardship,
            then he says, 'This is my due.
      I do not think that the Hour is going to come.
         And if am returned to my Lord,
      I will definitely find the best reward with Him.'

But We will inform those who disbelieve
> of what they did
and make them suffer a ruthless punishment.

51   When We grant blessing to a man,
> he turns away and draws aside
but when any evil touches him,
> he is full of endless prayers!

52   Say: 'What do you think? If it is from Allah
and you reject it, who could be more misguided
> than someone entrenched in hostility towards it?'

53   We will show them Our Signs on the horizon
> and within themselves
until it is clear to them that it is the truth.
> Is it not enough for your Lord
that He is Witness of everything?

54   What! Are they in doubt about the meeting with their Lord?
> What! Does He not encompass all things?

Sura 42

Ash-Shura
Counsel

1   Ha Mim

2   'Ayn Sin Qaf

3   That is how He sends revelation to you and those before you.
Allah is the Almighty, the All-Wise.

4   Everything in the heavens
and everything in the earth
belongs to Him.
He is the Most High, the Magnificent.

5   The heavens are all but rent asunder from above
when the angels glorify their Lord with praise
and ask forgiveness for those who are on the earth.
Allah is the Ever-Forgiving, the Most Merciful.

6   As for those who take others besides Him as protectors,
Allah will take care of them.
You are not set over them as a guardian.

7   Accordingly We have revealed to you an Arabic Qur'an
so that you may warn the Mother of Cities*
and those around it,
and give warning of the Day of Gathering
about which there is no doubt:
one group in the Garden,
the other in the Blazing Fire.

---

* Makka.

8   If Allah had willed, He would have made them a single nation.
           But He admits whomever He wills into His mercy
       and the wrongdoers have no protector and no helper.

9   Have they then taken others besides Him as protectors?
           But Allah is the Protector.
               He gives life to the dead.
           He has power over all things.

10   The judgement concerning anything
           you differ about is Allah's concern.
               That is Allah, my Lord –
           I have put my trust in Him and to Him I turn –
11   the Bringer into Being of the heavens and the earth:
           He has given you mates from among yourselves,
               and given mates to the livestock,
                   in that way multiplying you.
               Nothing is like Him.
           He is the All-Hearing, the All-Seeing.

12   The Keys of the heavens and earth belong to Him.
           He expands the provision of anyone He wills
               or restricts it.
           He has knowledge of all things.

13   He has laid down the same deen for you as He enjoined on Nuh:
           that which We have revealed to you
       and which We enjoined on Ibrahim, Musa and 'Isa:
           'Establish the deen and do not make divisions in it.'
       What you call the idolators to follow is very hard for them.
           Allah chooses for Himself anyone He wills
               and guides to Himself those who turn to Him.

14   They only split up after knowledge came to them,
           tyrannising one another.
       And were it not for a prior decree from your Lord
           for a specified term,
           the judgement between them
               would already have been made.
       Those who inherited the Book after them
           are indeed in grave doubt about it.

15   So call and go straight as you have been ordered to.
           Do not follow their whims and desires but say,

'I believe in a Book sent down by Allah
and I am ordered to be just between you.
Allah is our Lord and your Lord.
We have our actions and you have your actions.
There is no debate between us and you.
Allah will gather us all together.
He is our final destination.'

16 The argument of those who argue about Allah,
once He has been acknowledged,
has no basis whatsoever with their Lord.
There is anger upon them
and they will have a harsh punishment.

17 It is Allah who has sent down the Book with truth
and with the Just Balance.
What will make you realise?
Perhaps the Hour is close.

18 Those who do not believe in it try to hasten it.
But those who believe in it are afraid of it.
They know it is the truth.
Those who doubt the Hour are greatly misguided.

19 Allah is very gentle with His slaves.
He provides for anyone He wills.
He is the Most Strong, the Almighty.

20 If anyone desires to cultivate the Next World,
We will increase him in his cultivation.
If anyone desires to cultivate this world,
We will give him some of it
but he will have no share in the Next World.

21 Or do they have partners who have laid down a deen for them
for which Allah has not given any authority?
Were it not for the prior Word of Decision,
the judgement between them
would already have been made.
The wrongdoers will have a painful punishment.

22 You will see the wrongdoers afraid of what they have earned,
when it is about to land right on top of them,

whereas those who believe and do right actions
    will be in the lush Meadows of the Gardens.
They will have whatever they wish for with their Lord.
    That is the great favour.

23   That is the good news which Allah gives to His slaves
    who believe and do right actions.
Say: 'I do not ask you for any wage for this –
    except for you to love your near of kin.
If anyone does a good action,
    We will increase the good of it for him.
Allah is Ever-Forgiving, Ever-Thankful.'

24   Or do they ask, 'Has he invented a lie about Allah?'
    If Allah willed, He could seal up your heart.
By His Words Allah wipes out the false
    and confirms the truth.
He knows what the heart contains.

25   It is He who accepts repentance from His slaves
    and pardons evil acts and He knows what they do.

26   He responds to those who believe and do right actions
    and gives them increase from His favour.
But the unbelievers will have a harsh punishment.

27   Were Allah to expand the provision of His slaves,
    they would act as tyrants on the earth.
But He sends down whatever He wills
    in a measured way.
He is aware of and He sees His slaves.

28   It is He who sends down abundant rain,
    after they have lost all hope,
        and unfolds His mercy.
He is the Protector, the Praiseworthy.

29   Among His Signs is the creation of the heavens and earth
    and all the creatures He has spread about in them.
And He has the power to gather them together
    whenever He wills.

30   Any disaster that strikes you
    is through what your own hands have earned
        and He pardons much.

31   You will not be able to thwart Him on the earth
      and you have no protector or helper besides Allah.

32   Among His Signs are the tall ships
      sailing like mountains through the sea.
33   If He wills He makes the wind stop blowing
      and then they lie motionless on its back.
      There are certainly Signs in that
      for everyone who is steadfast and thankful.
34   Or He wrecks them for what they have earned
      though He pardons much.

35   Those who argue about Our Signs should know
      that they have no way of escape.

36   Whatever you have been given is only
      the enjoyment of the life of this world.
      What is with Allah is better and longer lasting
      for those who believe and trust in their Lord:
37   those who avoid major wrong actions and indecencies
      and who, when they are angered, then forgive;
38   those who respond to their Lord and establish the prayer,
      and manage their affairs by mutual consultation
      and spend from what We have provided for them;
39   those who, when they are wronged, defend themselves.

40   The repayment of a bad action is one equivalent to it.
      But if someone pardons and puts things right,
        his reward is with Allah.
      Certainly He does not love wrongdoers.

41   But if people do defend themselves when they are wronged,
      nothing can be held against them for doing that.
42   There are only grounds against those who wrong people
      and act as tyrants in the earth without any right to do so.
      Such people will have a painful punishment.
43   But if someone is steadfast and forgives,
      that is the most resolute course to follow.

44   Whoever Allah misguides
      has no one to protect them after that.
      You will see the wrongdoers saying,
        when they see the punishment,
          'Is there no way back?'

45 You will see them as they are exposed to it,
    abject in their abasement,
      glancing around them furtively.
Those who believe will say, 'Truly the losers
    are those who lose themselves and their families
      on the Day of Rising.'
The wrongdoers are in an everlasting punishment.
46 They have no one to protect or help them apart from Allah.
    There is no way out for anyone Allah misguides.

47 Respond to your Lord before a Day comes from Allah
    which cannot be turned back.
On that Day you will have no hiding-place
    and no means of denial.
48 But if they turn away, We have not sent you to be their guardian.
    You are only responsible for transmission.
When We let a man taste mercy from Us
    he exults in it.
But if something bad strikes him for what he has done
    he is ungrateful.

49 The kingdom of the heavens and earth belongs to Allah.
    He creates whatever He wills.
He gives daughters to whoever He wishes;
    and He gives sons to whoever He wishes;
50 or He gives them both sons and daughters;
    and He makes whoever He wishes barren.
Truly He is All-Knowing, All-Powerful.

51 It does not befit Allah to address any human being
    except by inspiration, or from behind a veil,
or He sends a messenger who then reveals
    by His permission whatever He wills.
      He is indeed Most High, All-Wise.
52 Accordingly We have revealed to you a Ruh
    by Our command.
You had no idea of what the Book was, nor faith.
    Nonetheless We have made it a Light by which
      We guide those of Our slaves We will.
Truly you are guiding to a Straight Path:
53   the Path of Allah
to Whom everything in the heavens
    and everything on the earth belongs.
Indeed all matters return eventually to Allah.

Sura 43

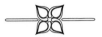

Az-Zukhruf
The Gold Ornaments

In the name of Allah, All-Merciful, Most Merciful

1	Ha Mim
2	By the Book which makes things clear.

3 We have made it an Arabic Qur'an
   so that hopefully you will use your intellect.

4 It is in the Source Book with Us,
   high-exalted, full of wisdom.

5 Shall We then deprive you of the Reminder
   for being a profligate people?

6 How many Prophets We sent to the previous peoples!
7   But no Prophet came to them without their mocking him;
8 and so We destroyed people with greater power than they have
      and the pattern of the previous peoples has gone before.

9 If you were to ask them, 'Who created the heavens and the earth?'
      they would reply,
   'The Almighty, the All-Knowing created them.'

10 It is He who made the earth a cradle for you
      and made pathways for you in it
   so that hopefully you would be guided.

11 It is He who sends down water in due measure from the sky
      by which We bring a dead land back to life.
   That is how you too will be brought forth.

12   It is He who created all species
            and gave you ships and livestock for you to ride,
13   so that you might sit firmly on their backs
            and remember your Lord's blessing
                while you are seated on them, saying,
      'Glory be to Him who has subjected this to us.
            We could never have accomplished it by ourselves.
14   Indeed we are returning to our Lord!'

15   They have assigned to Him a portion of His creatures!
            Truly man is openly ungrateful.

16   Has He then taken daughters from what He has created
            and chosen sons for you?

17   When any of them is given the good news of the very thing
            which he himself has ascribed to the All-Merciful
                his face darkens and he is furious.
18   'What! Someone brought up among pretty trinkets
            who cannot produce a cogent argument!'

19   They have designated the angels as female,
            those who are in the presence of the All-Merciful!
      Were they present to witness their creation?
            Their testimony will be recorded
                and they will be asked about it!

20   They say, 'If the All-Merciful had so willed,
            we would not have worshipped them.'
      They have no knowledge of that.
            They are only conjecturing.
21   Or did We give them a Book before,
            which they are holding to?

22   No, in fact they say, 'We found our fathers following a religion
            and we are simply guided in their footsteps.'

23   Similarly We never sent any warner before you to any city
            without the affluent among them saying,
      'We found our fathers following a religion
            and we are simply following in their footsteps.'

24   Say: 'What if I have come with better guidance
         than what you found your fathers following?'
      They say, 'We reject what you have been sent with.'

25   So We took revenge on them.
         And see the final fate of the deniers!

26   When Ibrahim said to his father and his people,
         'I am free of everything you worship,
27   except for Him who brought me into being,
         Who will certainly guide me,'
28   he made it an ongoing word among his descendants
         so that perhaps they might turn back.

29   I let those people and their forefathers enjoy themselves
            until the truth came to them
         and a Messenger to make it clear.
30   But when the truth came to them they said,
         'This is magic and we reject it.'

31   They say, 'Why was this Qur'an not sent down
         to one of the great men of the two cities?'*

32   Is it they, then, who allocate the mercy of your Lord?
         We have allocated their livelihood among them
            in the life of this world
         and raised some of them above others in rank
            so that some of them are subservient to others.
      But the mercy of your Lord is better than anything they amass.

33   Were it not that mankind might all become one community,
         We would have given those who reject the All-Merciful
            silver roofs to their houses
         and silver stairways to ascend
34   and silver doors to their houses
         and silver couches on which to recline,
35   and gold ornaments.
      All that is merely the trappings of the life of this world.
         But the Next World with your Lord
            is for those the godfearing.

36   If someone shuts his eyes to the remembrance of the All-Merciful,
         We assign him a shaytan who becomes his bosom friend –

* Makka and At-Ta'if.

37   they debar them from the path,
                yet they still think they are guided –
38   until, when he reaches Us, he says,
             'If only there were the distance of the two Easts
             between you and me!'
             What an evil companion!
39   It will not benefit you today, since you did wrong,
             that you share equally in the punishment.

40   Can you make the dead hear or guide the blind
             and those who are patently misguided?

41   Either We will extricate you and take revenge on them
42   or let you see what We have promised them.
         They are completely in Our power.

43   So hold fast to what has been revealed to you.
             You are on a straight path.

44   It is certainly a reminder to you and to your people
             and you will be questioned.

45   Ask those We sent before you as Our Messengers:
             Have We ever designated any gods to be worshipped
                besides the All-Merciful?

46   We sent Musa with Our Signs to Pharaoh and his nobles.
             He said, 'I am the Messenger of the Lord of the worlds.'
47   But when he came to them with Our Signs,
             they merely laughed at them.
48   We showed them no Sign
             that was not greater than the one before it.
         We seized them with punishment
             so that hopefully they would turn back.
49   They said, 'Magician, invoke your Lord for us
               by the contract He has made with you
             and we shall certainly follow the guidance.'
50   But when We removed the punishment from them,
             they immediately broke their word.

51   Pharaoh called to his people, saying, 'My people,
               does the kingdom of Egypt not belong to me?
         Do not all these rivers flow under my control?
               Do you not then see?

52   Am I not better than this man who is contemptible
       and can scarcely make anything clear?
53   Why have gold bracelets not been put upon his arms
       and why is there not a train of angels accompanying him?'
54   In that way he swayed his people and they succumbed to him.
       They were a people of deviators.
55   Then when they had provoked Our wrath,
       We took revenge on them
         and drowned every one of them.
56   We made them a thing of the past,
       an example for later peoples.

57   When an example is made of the son of Maryam
       your people laugh uproariously.
58   They retort, 'Who is better then, our gods or him?'
       They only say this to you for argument's sake.
         They are indeed a disputatious people.
59   He is only a slave on whom We bestowed Our blessing
       and whom We made an example for the tribe of Israel.

60   If We wished We could appoint angels in exchange for you
       to succeed you on the earth.

61   He is a Sign of the Hour.
       Have no doubt about it.
     But follow me.
       This is a straight path.
62   Do not let Shaytan bar your way.
       He truly is an outright enemy to you.

63   And when 'Isa came with the Clear Signs,
       he said, 'I have come to you with Wisdom
     and to clarify for you some of the things
       about which you have differed.
     Therefore have taqwa of Allah and obey me.
64   Allah is my Lord and your Lord
           so worship Him.
       This is a straight path.'

65   The various factions among them differed.
       Woe then to those who did wrong
     on account of the punishment of a painful Day!

66   What are they waiting for,
            but the Hour to come upon them suddenly
               when they are not expecting it?

67   On that Day the closest friends
            will be enemies to one another –
            except for the godfearing.

68   'My slaves, you will feel no fear today;
            you will know no sorrow.'

69   As for those who believed in Our Signs
            and became Muslims:

70   'Enter the Garden,
            you and your wives,
               delighting in your joy.'

71   Platters and cups of gold will passed around among them
            and they will have there all that their hearts desire
               and their eyes find delight in.
            'You will remain in it timelessly, for ever.

72   That is the Garden you will inherit for what you did.

73   There will be many fruits in it for you to eat.'

74   The evildoers will remain timelessly, for ever,
            in the punishment of Hell.

75   It will not be eased for them.
            They will be crushed there by despair.

76   We have not wronged them;
            it was they who were wrongdoers.

77   They will call out, 'Malik,*
            let your Lord put an end to us!'
            He will say, 'You will stay the way you are.'

78   We brought you the truth
            but most of you hated the truth.

79   Or have they hatched a plot?
            It is We who are the Plotter!

80   Or do they imagine that We do not hear
            their secrets and their private talk?

---

* The angel in charge of the custodians of Hell.

On the contrary Our messengers
　　are right there with them
　　　　writing it down!

81　Say: 'If the All-Merciful had a son,
　　　I would be the first to worship him.'
82　Glory be to the Lord of the heavens and the earth,
　　　the Lord of the Throne,
　　　　　beyond what they describe.

83　So leave them to plunge and play around
　　　until they meet their Day which they are promised.

84　It is He who is God in heaven and God on earth.
　　　He is the All-Wise, the All-Knowing.
85　Blessed be Him to whom belongs
　　　the sovereignty of the heavens and the earth
　　　　　and everything in between them.
　　The knowledge of the Hour is with Him.
　　　You will be returned to Him.

86　Those you call upon apart from Him
　　　possess no power of intercession –
　　only those who bore witness to the truth
　　　and have full knowledge.
87　If you asked them who created them,
　　　they would say, 'Allah!'
　　So how have they been perverted?

88　And as for his words, 'My Lord,
　　　these are people who do not believe!'
89　turn from them and say, 'Peace!
　　　You will soon come to know.'

Sura 44

Ad-Dukhan
Smoke

In the name of Allah, All-Merciful, Most Merciful

1	Ha Mim
2	By the Book which makes things clear.
3	We sent it down on a blessed night;
	We are constantly giving warning.
4	During it every wise decree is specified
5	by a command from Our presence.
	We are constantly sending out
6	as a mercy from your Lord.
	He is the All-Hearing, the All-Knowing:
7	the Lord of the heavens and the earth
	and everything in between them,
	if you are people with certainty.
8	There is no god but Him –
	He gives life and causes to die –
	your Lord and the Lord of your forefathers,
	the previous peoples.
9	Yet they play around in doubt.
10	So be on the watch for a day when heaven
	brings forth a distinctive smoke,
11	which enshrouds mankind.
	'This is a painful punishment!
12	Our Lord, remove the punishment from us.
	We are really believers.'

13 How can they expect a Reminder when
    a clear Messenger has already come to them?
14 But then they turned away from him and said,
    'He is an instructed madman!'

15 We remove the punishment a little,
    and you revert!
16 On the day We launch the Great Assault
    We will certainly take Our revenge.

17 Before them We put Pharaoh's people to the test
    when a noble Messenger came to them, saying
18 'Hand over to me the slaves of Allah.
    I am a trustworthy Messenger to you.'
19 And: 'Do not exalt yourselves above Allah.
    I come to you with clear authority.
20   I have sought refuge
    with my Lord and your Lord
      against your stoning me.
21   If you do not believe in me,
      then at least leave me alone.'

22 He called out to his Lord,
    'These are evildoing people.'

23 'Set out with My slaves by night.
    You will certainly be pursued.
24   Leave the sea divided as it is.
    They are an army who will be drowned.'

25 How many gardens and fountains they left behind,
26   and ripe crops and noble residences.
27 What comfort and ease they had delighted in!
28   So it was.
    Yet We bequeathed these things to another people.
29   Neither heaven nor earth shed any tears for them
      and they were granted no reprieve.
30   We rescued the tribe of Israel
      from the humiliating punishment,
31   from Pharaoh – he was haughty,
      one of the profligate.
32   We chose them knowingly
      above all other people

33   and We gave them Signs
         containing a clear trial.

34   These people say,
35   'There is nothing more than our first death.
         We will not be raised up a second time.
36   Bring us our fathers if you are telling the truth.'

37   Are they better or the people of Tubba'
         and those before them whom We destroyed?
     They were certainly evildoers.

38   We did not create the heavens and the earth
         and everything between them as a game.
39   We did not create them except with truth
         but most of them do not know it.

40   The Day of Decision will be their appointment all together:
41   the Day when friends will be of no avail at all to one another,
           and they will not be helped –
42   except for those Allah has mercy on.
     He is the Almighty, the Most Merciful.

43   The Tree of az-Zaqqum
44   is the food of the wicked,
45   seething in the belly like molten brass,
46   as boiling water bubbles and seethes.
47   'Seize him and drag him bodily
         into the middle of the Blazing Fire.
48   Then pour the punishment
         of boiling water on his head.'
49   'Taste that! You are the mighty one, the noble one!
50   This is the very thing you used to doubt.'

51   The godfearing will be in a safe place
52   amid gardens and fountains,
53   wearing fine silk and rich brocade,
         face to face with one another.
54   So it will be.
     We will marry them to dark-eyed maidens.
55   They will call there for fruit of every kind,
         in complete security.
56   They will not taste any death there –
         other than the first one.

He will safeguard them from
the punishment of the Blazing Fire.

57   A favour from your Lord.
That is the Great Victory.

58   We have made it easy in your own tongue
so that hopefully they will pay heed.

59   So watch and wait.
They too are waiting.

Sura 45

Al-Jathiyya
Kneeling

In the name of Allah, All-Merciful, Most Merciful

1   Ha Mim
2   The revelation of the Book
         is from Allah, the Almighty, the All-Wise.

3   In the heavens and earth
         there are certainly Signs for the believers.
4   And in your creation and all the creatures
             He has spread about
         there are Signs for people with certainty.
5   And in the alternation of night and day
             and the provision Allah sends down from the sky,
         bringing the earth to life by it after it has died,
             and the varying direction of the winds,
         there are Signs for people who use their intellect.

6   Those are Allah's Signs
         which We recite to you with truth.
     In what discourse, then,
             after Allah and His Signs,
                 will they believe?

7   Woe to every wicked liar
8   who hears the Signs of Allah recited to him
     and then persists in his arrogance
             as if he had never heard them.
     Give him the news of a painful punishment.

9　　　When he does learn something of Our Signs,
　　　　　he makes a mockery of them.
　　　Such people will have a humiliating punishment.
10　　　　Hell is right at their heels.
　　　Nothing they have earned will be of any use to them,
　　　　　nor will those they took as protectors besides Allah.
　　　They will have a terrible punishment.

11　　　　This is guidance.
　　　And those who reject the Signs of their Lord
　　　　　will have a punishment of agonising pain.

12　　　It is Allah who has made the sea subservient to you
　　　　　so that the ships sail on it at His command,
　　　　　　enabling you to seek His bounty,
　　　　　so that hopefully you will be thankful.
13　　　And He has made everything in the heavens
　　　　　and everything on the earth subservient to you.
　　　　　　It is all from Him.
　　　There are certainly Signs in that for people who reflect.

14　　　Tell those who believe that they should forgive those
　　　　　who feel no fear about the Days of Allah,
　　　when He will repay people according to what they earned.

15　　　Whoever acts rightly, it is for his own good.
　　　　　Whoever does evil, it is to his detriment.
　　　Then you will be returned to your Lord.

16　　　We gave the Book and Judgement
　　　　　and Prophethood to the tribe of Israel
　　　and provided them with good things
　　　　　and favoured them over all other people.
17　　　We made the Commandments very clear to them
　　　　　and they only differed after knowledge came to them,
　　　　　　tyrannising one other.
　　　Your Lord will decide between them on the Day of Rising
　　　　　regarding the things they differed about.

18　　　Then We placed you on the right road of Our Command,
　　　　　so follow it.
　　　Do not follow the whims and desires of those who do not know.

19   They will not help you in any way against Allah.
       The wrongdoers are protectors of one another
but Allah is the Protector of the godfearing.

20   This is clear insight for mankind
       and guidance and mercy
          for people with certainty.

21   Or do those who perpetrate evil deeds
       suppose that We will make them
like those who believe and do right actions,
       so that their lives and deaths will be the same?
         How bad their judgement is!

22   Allah created the heavens and earth with truth
       so that every self might be repaid for what it earned
         and they will not be wronged.

23   Have you seen him who takes
       his whims and desires to be his god,
and whom Allah has misguided knowingly,
       sealing up his hearing and his heart
         and placing a blindfold over his eyes?
Who then will guide him after Allah?
       So will you not pay heed?

24   They say, 'There is nothing but our existence in this world.
       We die and we live and nothing destroys us except time.'
They have no knowledge of that.
       They are only conjecturing.

25   When Our Clear Signs are recited to them
       their only argument is to say,
'Bring us our fathers if you are telling the truth.'

26   Say: 'Allah gives you life, then causes you to die,
       and then will gather you together for the Day of Rising
         about which there is no doubt.
But most people do not know it.'

27   The kingdom of the heavens and earth belongs to Allah
       and, on the Day that the Hour arrives,
         that Day the liars will be lost.

28 You will see every nation on its knees,
  every nation summoned to its Book:
  'Today you will be repaid for what you did.
29 This is Our Book speaking against you with the truth.
  We have been recording everything you did.'

30 As for those who believed and did right actions,
  their Lord will admit them into His mercy.
   That is the Clear Victory.
31 But as for those who disbelieved:
  'Were My Signs not recited to you?
And yet you proved arrogant;
  you were a people of evildoers?
32 When you were told, "Allah's promise is true
  and so is the Hour, of which there is no doubt,"
you said, "We have no idea what the Hour is.
  We have only been conjecturing.
   We are by no means certain."'

33 The evil deeds they did will appear before them
  and the things they mocked at will engulf them.
34 They will be told, 'Today We have forgotten you
  as you forgot the meeting of this your Day.
Your refuge is the Fire and you have no helpers.
35   That is because you made a mockery of Allah's Signs
   and the life of this world deluded you.'
Therefore, today they will not get out of it.
  They will not be able to appease Allah.

36 All praise belongs to Allah,
  the Lord of the heavens
   and the Lord of the earth,
  Lord of all the worlds.
37 All greatness belongs to Him
  in the heavens and earth
He is the Almighty, the All-Wise.

Sura 46

Al-Ahqaf
The Sand-Dunes

In the name of Allah, All-Merciful, Most Merciful

1   Ha Mim

2   The revelation of the Book
        is from Allah, the Almighty, the All-Wise.

3   We have not created the heavens and earth
        and everything between them
    except with truth and for a set term.
        But those who disbelieve turn away from
    what they have been warned about.

4   Say: 'Have you thought about those
        you call upon apart from Allah?
    Show me what they have created on the earth.
        Or do they have a partnership in the heavens?
    Produce a Book for me before this one
        or a shred of knowledge
            if you are telling the truth.'

5   Who could be further astray than those
        who call on other things besides Allah,
    which will not respond to them until the Day of Rising
        and which are unaware of their prayers?

6   When mankind is gathered together,
        they will be their enemies
    and will reject their worship.

7   When Our Clear Signs are recited to them,
        those who reject say to the truth

when it comes to them,
'This is downright magic.'

8 Or do they say, 'He has invented it'?
    Say: 'If I have invented it,
        then you possess no power
    to help me against Allah in any way.
        He knows best what you hold forth about.
        He is witness enough between me and you.
        He is the Ever-Forgiving, the Most Merciful.'

9 Say: 'I am nothing new among the Messengers.
        I have no idea what will be done with me or you.
    I only follow what has been revealed to me.
        I am only a clear warner.'

10 Say: 'What do you think?
        If it is from Allah and you reject it,
    when a witness from the tribe of Israel
        testifies to its similarity and believes
            while you are arrogant . . . !
    Allah certainly does not guide wrongdoing people.'

11 Those who disbelieve say of those who believe,
        'If there was any good in it,
            they would not have beaten us to it.'
    And since they have not been guided by it,
        they are bound to say,
    'This is an antiquated falsehood.'

12 But before it there was the Book of Musa
        as a model and a mercy.
    And this is a corroborating Book
        in the Arabic tongue
    so that you may warn those who do wrong,
        and as good news for the good-doers.

13 Those who say, 'Our Lord is Allah,' and then go straight
        will feel no fear and will know no sorrow.
14 Such people are the Companions of the Garden,
        remaining in it timelessly, for ever,
            as repayment for what they did.

15   We have instructed man to be good to his parents.
         His mother bore him with difficulty
     and with difficulty gave birth to him;
         and his bearing and weaning take thirty months.
     Then when he achieves his full strength
         and reaches forty, he says, 'My Lord,
     keep me thankful for the blessing
         You bestowed on me and on my parents,
     and keep me acting rightly, pleasing You.
         And make my descendants righteous.
     I have turn in repentance to You
         and I am truly one of the Muslims.'

16   Those are people whose best deeds will be accepted
         and whose wrong deeds will be overlooked.
     They are among the Companions of the Garden,
         in fulfilment of the true promise made to them.

17   But what of him who says to his parents, 'Fie on you!
         Do you promise me that I will be resurrected
             when generations before me have passed away?'
     They both call on Allah for help: 'Woe to you!
         Believe! Allah's promise is true.'
     But he says, 'This is nothing but the myths of previous peoples.'

18   Those are people of whom the statement about the nations,
         both of jinn and men, who passed away before them,
         has also proved true; truly they were the lost.

19   Everyone will be ranked according to what they did.
         We will pay them in full for their actions
         and they will not be wronged.

20   On the Day when those who disbelieved are exposed to the Fire:
         'You dissipated the good things you had in your worldly life
         and enjoyed yourself in it.
         So today you are being repaid
             with the punishment of humiliation
             for being arrogant in the earth without any right
             and for being deviators.'

21   Remember the brother of 'Ad
         when he warned his people by the sand-dunes –
     and warners passed away before and after him –

'Worship no one but Allah.
I fear for you the punishment of a terrible Day.'

22 They said, 'Have you come to us to divert us from our gods?
Bring us what you have promised us
if you are telling the truth.'

23 He said, 'All knowledge is with Allah.
I only transmit to you what I have been sent with.
But I see that you are a people who are ignorant.'

24 When they saw it as a storm cloud advancing on their valleys
they said, 'This is a storm cloud which will give us rain.'
No, rather it is what you desired to hasten –
a wind containing painful punishment,

25 destroying everything at its Lord's command!
When morning came you could see nothing
but their dwellings.
That is how We repay the people of the evildoers.

26 We established them far more firmly
than We have established you
and gave them hearing, sight and hearts.
But their hearing, sight and hearts
were of no use to them at all
when they renounced Allah's Signs
and what they mocked at engulfed them.

27 We destroyed the cities round about you
and have variegated the Signs
so that hopefully they will turn back.

28 Why have those they took as gods besides Allah,
to bring them near to Him,
not come to their aid?
No, in fact they have forsaken them!
That was a fiction, something they invented.

29 And We diverted a group of jinn towards you
to listen to the Qur'an.
When they were in earshot of it they said, 'Be quiet and listen.'
When it was over they went back to their people, warning them.

30 They said, 'Our people, we have heard a Book
which was sent down after Musa,
confirming what came before it,
guiding to the truth and to a straight path.

31   Our people, respond to Allah's caller and believe in Him.
        He will forgive you some of your wrong actions
           and save you from a painful punishment.
32   Those who do not respond to Allah's caller
        cannot thwart Allah on earth
     and have no protectors apart from Him.
        Such people are clearly misguided.'

33   Do they not see that Allah –
        He who created the heavens and the earth
           and was not wearied by creating them –
     has the power to bring the dead to life?
        Yes indeed! He has power over all things.

34   On the Day when those who disbelieved are exposed to the Fire,
        they will be asked, 'Is this not the truth?'
           They will say, 'Yes, by our Lord.'
     He will say, 'Then taste the punishment for having believed.'

35   So be steadfast
        as the Messengers with firm resolve
           were also steadfast.
        And do not seek to hasten it for them.
     On the Day they see what they were promised,
        it will be as if they had only tarried
           for just one hour of a single day.
        It has been transmitted!
     Will any be destroyed except for deviant people?

Sura 47

Muhammad

In the name of Allah, All-Merciful, Most Merciful

1   As for those who disbelieve and bar others from the Way of Allah,
         Allah will make their actions go astray.
2   But as for those who believe and do right actions
             and believe in what has been sent down to Muhammad –
             and it is the truth from their Lord –
     He will erase their bad actions from them
             and better their condition.
3   That is because those who disbelieve follow falsehood
             whereas those who believe
                 follow the truth from their Lord.
     In that way Allah makes comparisons for mankind.

4   Therefore when you meet those who disbelieve
             strike their necks.
     Then when you have decimated them,
             tie their bonds tightly
     and set them free or ransom them,
             until the war is finally over.
     That is how it is to be.
             If Allah willed, He could avenge Himself on them.
     But it is so that He can test some of you by means of others.
             As for those who fight in the Way of Allah,
                 He will not let their actions go astray.
5   He will guide them and better their condition
6   and He will admit them into the Garden
             which He has made known to them.

7   You who believe!
         if you help Allah, He will help you
            and make your feet firm.

8   But those who disbelieve will have utter ruin
         and He will make their actions go astray.

9   That is because they hate what Allah has sent down,
         so He has made their actions come to nothing.

10   Have they not travelled about the earth
         and seen the final fate of those before them?
            Allah destroyed them utterly.
         And those who disbelieved will suffer the same fate.

11   That is because Allah is the Protector of those who believe
         and because those who disbelieve have no protector.

12   Allah will admit those who believe to Gardens
         with rivers flowing under them.
    Those who disbelieve have their enjoyment,
            eating as cattle eat,
         but the Fire will be their final residence.

13   How many cities We have destroyed,
         greater in strength than your city
            which has driven you out,
         and there was no one to help them.

14   Is someone on a clear path from his Lord
         like those whose bad actions
    have been made to seem good to them
         and who follow their own desires?

15   An image of the Garden which is promised
         to those who are godfearing:
    in it there are rivers of water which will never spoil
   and rivers of milk whose taste will never change
         and rivers of wine, delightful to all who drink it,
            and rivers of honey of undiluted purity;
         in it they will have fruit of every kind
            and forgiveness from their Lord.
   Is that like those who will be in the Fire timelessly, for ever,
         with boiling water to drink which lacerates their bowels?

16   Among them are those who listen to you and then,
         when they leave your presence,
    say to those who have been given knowledge,

'What was that he just said?'
They are those whose hearts Allah has sealed up
and who follow their own desires.

17   He increases in guidance those who are already guided
and gives them their taqwa.

18   What are they awaiting but for the Hour
to come upon them suddenly?
Its Signs have already come.
What good will their Reminder be to them
when it does arrive?

19   Know then that there is no god except Allah
and ask forgiveness for your wrongdoing,
and for the men and women who believe.

20   Those who believe say, 'If only a sura could be sent down.'
But when a straightforward sura is sent down
and fighting is mentioned in it,
you see those with sickness in their hearts looking at you
with the look of someone about to faint from fear of death.
More fitting for them
21   would be obedience and honourable words.
Once the matter is resolved upon,
being true to Allah would be better for them.

22   Is it not likely that, if you did turn away,
you would cause corruption in the earth
and sever your ties of kinship?
23   Such are the people Allah has cursed,
making them deaf and blinding their eyes.

24   Will they not then ponder the Qur'an
or are there locks upon their hearts?

25   Those who have turned back in their tracks
after the guidance became clear to them,
it was Shaytan who talked them into it
and filled them with false hopes.
26   That is because they said to those
who hate what Allah has sent down,
'We will obey you in part of the affair.'
But Allah knows their secrets.

27   How will it be when the angels take them in death,
           beating their faces and their backs?
28   That is because they followed what angers Allah
           and hated what is pleasing to Him.
      So He made their actions come to nothing.

29   Or did those with sickness in their hearts imagine
           that Allah would not expose their malevolence?
30   If We wished, We would show them to you
           and you would know them by their mark
      and know them by their ambivalent speech.
           Allah knows your actions.

31   We will test you until We know
           the true fighters among you
               and those who are steadfast
           and test what is reported of you.

32   Those who disbelieve and obstruct the Way of Allah,
           and are entrenched in hostility towards the Messenger
      after the guidance has become clear to them,
           do not harm Allah in any way
      and He makes their actions come to nothing.

33   You who believe! obey Allah and obey the Messenger.
           Do not make your actions of no worth.

34   Those who disbelieve and obstruct the Way of Allah,
           and then disbelieve,
      Allah will not forgive them.

35   Do not become faint-hearted and call for peace
           when you are uppermost and Allah is with you –
      He would never cheat you of your deeds.

36   The life of this world is merely a game and a diversion.
           If you believe and are godfearing,
               He will pay you your wages
           and not ask you for all your wealth.

37   If He did ask you for it and put you under pressure,
           you would be tight-fisted
      and it would bring out your malevolence.

38   Here you are then: people who are called upon
              to spend in the Way of Allah
                  and then some of you are tight-fisted!
      But whoever is tight-fisted
          is only tight-fisted to himself.
      Allah is Rich and you are poor.
          If you turn away, He will replace you
      with a people other than yourselves
          and they will not be like you.

Sura 48

Al-Fath
Victory

In the name of Allah, All-Merciful, Most Merciful

1	Truly We have granted you a clear victory,
2	so that Allah may forgive you your earlier errors and any later ones and complete His blessing upon you, and guide you on a Straight Path.
3	and so that Allah may help you with a mighty help.*
4	It is He who sent down serenity into the hearts of the believers thereby increasing their faith with more faith – the legions of the heavens and the earth belong to Allah. Allah is All-Knowing, All-Wise –
5	so that He may admit the men and women of the believers into Gardens with rivers flowing under them, remaining in them timelessly, for ever, and erase their bad actions from them; and in Allah's sight that is a mighty victory.
6	And so that He might punish the men and women of the hypocrites and the men and women of the idolators – those who think bad thoughts about Allah. They will suffer an evil turn of fate.

---

* This sura was occasioned by the expedition of al-Hudaybiyya in which the Prophet, accompanied by a large number of Companions, went to Makka to perform 'umra but was prevented from entering the city and forced to stop at a place named al-Hudaybiyya. Eventually a treaty was signed which, though apparently disadvantageous to the Muslims, paved the way for the victory of Islam within a very short time.

Allah is angry with them,
and has cursed them
and prepared Hell for them.
What an evil destination!

7   The legions of the heavens and the earth belong to Allah.
Allah is Almighty, All-Wise.

8   We have sent you bearing witness,
bringing good news and giving warning
9   so that you might all believe in Allah and His Messenger
and honour Him and respect Him
and glorify Him in the morning and the evening.

10 Those who pledge you their allegiance
pledge allegiance to Allah.*
Allah's hand is over their hands.
He who breaks his pledge
only breaks it against himself.
But as for him who fulfils the contract
he has made with Allah,
We will pay him an immense reward.

11 Those Arabs who remained behind will say to you,
'Our wealth and families kept us occupied,
so ask forgiveness for us.'
They say with their tongues what is not in their hearts.
Say: 'Who can control Allah for you in any way
whether He wants harm for you
or wants benefit for you?'
Allah is aware of what you do.

12 No, you thought that the Messenger and the believers
were not going to return to their families,
and that seemed pleasing to your hearts
and you thought evil thoughts
and you were a blighted people.

13 Whoever does not believe in Allah and His Messenger –
We have prepared a Blazing Fire for the unbelievers.

---

* This refers to an incident at al-Hudaybiyya when, owing to the danger of their situation, the Muslims renewed their pledge of allegiance to the Prophet under a tree there.

14   The kingdom of the heavens and the earth belongs to Allah.
            He forgives those He wills and punishes those He wills.
                Allah is Ever-Forgiving, Most Merciful.

15   When you go out to get the booty,
            those who remained behind will say,
        'Allow us to follow you,'
            desiring to alter Allah's words.
        Say: 'You may not follow us.
            That is what Allah said before.'
        They will say, 'It is only because you envy us.'
            No indeed! How little they have understood!

16   Say to the Arabs who remained behind:
            'You will be called up against a people
                who possess great force
            whom you must fight unless they submit.
        If you obey, Allah will give you an excellent reward.
            But if you turn your backs as you did before,
        He will punish you with a painful punishment.'

17   There is no constraint on the blind,
            nor on the lame, nor on the sick.
        We will admit all who obey Allah and His Messenger
            into Gardens with rivers flowing under them.
        But We will punish with a painful punishment
            anyone who turns his back.

18   Allah was pleased with the believers
            when they pledged allegiance to you under the tree.
        He knew what was in their hearts,
            and sent down serenity to them
        and has rewarded them with an imminent victory,
19   and with much booty which they will take.
                Allah is Almighty, All-Wise.
20   Allah has promised you much booty
            which you will take,
        and has hastened this for you
            and held people's hands back from you,
        so that it might be a Sign to the believers,
            and so that He might guide you to a straight path.
21   And other booty you do not yet have the power to take –
            Allah has already encompassed it.
                Allah has power over all things.

22   If those who disbelieve should fight you,
            they would turn their backs
            and then find no one to protect or help them.
23   That is Allah's pattern which has passed away before.
            You will not find any changing in the pattern of Allah.

24   It is He who held their hands back from you,
            and your hands from them
                in the valley of Makka,
            after giving you the upper hand over them.
            Allah sees what you do.

25   They are those who disbelieve
            and debarred you from the Masjid al-Haram
        and prevented the sacrifice
            from reaching its proper place,
        and had it not been for some men and women
            who are believers,
        whom you did not know
            and might trample underfoot,
        and so unknowingly incur blame
            on their account –
        so that Allah might admit into His mercy
                those He wills –
        and had those among them who disbelieve
            been clearly distinguishable,
        We would have punished them
            with a painful punishment.

26   Those who disbelieve filled their hearts with fanatical rage –
            the fanatical rage of the Time of Ignorance* –
        and Allah sent down serenity to His Messenger
            and to the believers,
        and bound them to the expression of taqwa
            which they had most right to
                and were most entitled to.
            Allah has knowledge of all things.

27   Allah has confirmed His Messenger's vision with truth:
            'You will enter the Masjid al-Haram in safety,
                Allah willing,
            shaving your heads and cutting your hair
                without any fear.'

---

* The time before the coming of the Prophet and the revelation of the Qur'an.

He knew what you did not know and ordained,
    in place of this,
    an imminent victory.

28   It is He who sent His Messenger
      with the Guidance and the Deen of Truth
        to exalt it over every other deen
      and Allah suffices as a witness.

29   Muhammad is the Messenger of Allah,
      and those who are with him
        are fierce to the unbelievers,
      merciful to one another.
You see them bowing and prostrating,
    seeking Allah's good favour
      and His pleasure.
Their mark is on their faces,
    the traces of prostration.
That is their likeness in the Torah.
    And their likeness in the Injil
is that of a seed which puts up a shoot
    and makes it strong so that it thickens
      and grows up straight upon its stalk,
    filling the sowers with delight –
so that by them He may infuriate the unbelievers.
    Allah has promised those of them
      who believe and do right actions
    forgiveness and an immense reward.

Sura 49

Al-Hujurat
The Private Quarters

In the name of Allah, All-Merciful, Most Merciful

1   You who believe! do not put yourselves forward
       in front of Allah and of His Messenger;
         and have taqwa of Allah.
       Allah is All-Hearing, All-Knowing.

2   You who believe! do not raise your voices
       above the voice of the Prophet
    and do not be as loud when speaking to him
       as you are when speaking to one another,
    lest your actions should come to nothing
       without your realising it.

3   Those who lower their voices
       when they are with the Messenger of Allah
    are people whose hearts Allah has tested for taqwa.
       They will have forgiveness and an immense reward.

4   As for those who call out to you
        from outside your private quarters,
       most of them do not use their intellect.
5   If they had only been patient until you came out to them,
       it would have been better for them.
    But Allah is Ever-Forgiving, Most Merciful.

6   You who believe! if a deviator brings you a report,
       scrutinize it carefully in case you attack people in ignorance
        and so come to greatly regret what you have done.

7   Know that the Messenger of Allah is among you.
           If he were to obey you in many things,
               you would suffer for it.
       However, Allah has given you love of faith
           and made it pleasing to your hearts,
       and has made unbelief, deviance and disobedience
           hateful to you.
       People such as these are rightly guided.

8   It is a great favour from Allah and a blessing.
           Allah is All-Knowing, All-Wise.

9   If two parties of the believers fight, make peace between them.
           But if one of them attacks the other unjustly,
       fight the attackers until they revert to Allah's command.
           If they revert, make peace between them with justice,
               and be even-handed.
           Allah loves those who are even-handed.

10   The believers are brothers,
           so make peace between your brothers
               and have taqwa of Allah
           so that hopefully you will gain mercy.

11   You who believe! people should not ridicule others
           who may be better than themselves;
       nor should any women ridicule other women
           who may be better than themselves.
       And do not find fault with one another
           or insult each other with derogatory nicknames.
       How evil it is to have a name for evil conduct
           after coming to faith!
       Those people who do not turn from it are wrongdoers.

12   You who believe! avoid most suspicion.
               Indeed some suspicion is a crime.
           And do not spy and do not backbite one another.
       Would any of you like to eat his brother's dead flesh?
           No, you would hate it.
       And have taqwa of Allah.
           Allah is Ever-Returning, Most Merciful.

13   Mankind! We created you from a male and female,
           and made you into peoples and tribes

so that you might come to know each other.
The noblest among you in Allah's sight
is the one with the most taqwa.
Allah is All-Knowing, All-Aware.

14   The desert Arabs say, 'We believe.'
Say: 'You do not believe.
Say rather, "We have become Muslim,"
for faith has not yet entered into your hearts.
If you obey Allah and His Messenger,
He will not undervalue your actions in any way.
Allah is Ever-Forgiving, Most Merciful.'

15   The believers are only those
who have believed in Allah and His Messenger
and then have had no doubt
and have done jihad with their wealth
and themselves in the Way of Allah.
They are the ones who are true to their word.

16   Say: 'Do you presume to teach Allah your deen
when Allah knows everything in the heavens
and everything in the earth?
Allah has knowledge of all things.'

17   They think they have done you a favour by becoming Muslims!
Say: 'Do not consider your Islam a favour to me.
No indeed! It is Allah who has favoured you
by guiding you to faith if you are telling the truth.'

18   Allah knows the unseen things of the heavens and the earth.
Allah sees what you do.

Sura 50

Qaf

In the name of Allah, All-Merciful, Most Merciful

1   Qaf
By the Glorious Qur'an!

2   Nonetheless they are amazed that a warner
should have come to them
from among themselves
and those who disbelieve say,
'What an extraordinary thing!
3   When we are dead and turned to dust . . . ?
That would be a most unlikely return!'

4   We know exactly how the earth eats them away.
We possess an all-preserving Book.

5   But they denied the truth when it came to them.
They are, therefore, in a very muddled state.

6   Have they not looked at the sky above them:
how We structured it and made it beautiful
and how there are no fissures in it?
7   And the earth: how We stretched it out
and cast firmly embedded mountains onto it
and caused luxuriant plants of every kind to grow in it,
8   an instruction and a reminder for every penitent human being.

9   And We sent down blessed water from the sky
and made gardens grow by it
and grain for harvesting

10   and soaring date-palms with layered spathes,
11   as provision for Our slaves;
      by it We brought a dead land back to life.
      That is how the Emergence will take place.

12   Before them the people of Nuh also denied the truth
        and the Companions of Rass and Thamud,
13   and 'Ad and Pharaoh and the brothers of Lut
14   and the Companions of the Thicket and the people of Tubba'.
      Each one denied the Messengers and My promise proved true.

15   Were We exhausted by the first creation?
      Yet they are dubious about the new creation.

16   We created man and We know what his own self whispers to him.
      We are nearer to him than his jugular vein.

17   And the two recording angels are recording,
      sitting on the right and on the left.

18   He does not utter a single word,
      without a watcher by him, pen in hand!

19   The throes of death come revealing the truth.
      That is what you were trying to evade!

20   The Trumpet will be blown.
      That is the Day of the Threat.

21   Every self will come together with a driver and a witness:
22   'You were heedless of this
      so We have stripped you of your covering
      and today your sight is sharp.'

23   His inseparable comrade will say,
      'This is what I have ready for you.'

24   'Hurl into Hell every obdurate unbeliever,
25   impeder of good, doubt-causing aggressor,
26   who set up another god together with Allah.
      Hurl him into the terrible punishment.'

27   His inseparable comrade will say,
         'Our Lord, I did not make him overstep the limits.
            He was, in any case, far astray.'

28   He will say, 'Do not argue in My presence
         when I gave you advance warning of the Threat.
29   My Word, once given, is not subject to change
         and I do not wrong My slaves.'

30   On the Day He says to Hell, 'Are you full?'
         it will ask, 'Are there no more to come?'

31   And the Garden will be brought up close to the godfearing,
         not far away:
32   'This is what you were promised.
         It is for every careful penitent:
33   those who fear the All-Merciful in the Unseen
         and come with a contrite heart.
34   Enter it in peace.
     This is the Day of Timeless Eternity.'

35   They will have there everything they want
         and with Us there is still more.

36   How many generations before them We destroyed
         who had greater force than them
            and scoured many lands!
         Did they find any way of escape?

37   There is a reminder in that for anyone who has a heart,
         or who listens well, having seen the evidence.

38   We created the heavens and the earth,
         and everything between them,
            in six days
         and We were not affected by fatigue.

39   So be patient in the face of what they say
         and glorify your Lord with praise
     before the rising of the sun and before it sets.
40   And glorify Him during the night
            and after you have prostrated.

41   Listen out for the Day when the Summoner
                shall call out from a nearby place.

42   The Day they hear the Blast in truth,
                that is the Day of Emergence.

43   It is We who give life and cause to die
                and We are their final destination.

44   The Day the earth splits open all around them
                as they come rushing forth,
        that is a gathering, easy for Us to accomplish.

45   We know best what they say.
                You are not a dictator over them.
        So remind, with the Qur'an,
                whomever fears My Threat.

Sura 51

Adh-Dhariyat
The Scatterers

In the name of Allah, All-Merciful, Most Merciful

1	By the scatterers scattering,
2	and those bearing weighty loads,
3	and those speeding along with ease,
4	and those apportioning the command:
5	what you are promised is certainly true –
6	the Judgement will certainly take place!
7	By Heaven with its oscillating orbits,
8	you certainly have differing beliefs.
9	Averted from it is he who is averted.
10	Death to the conjecturers:
11	those who flounder
	in a glut of ignorance,
12	asking, 'When is the Day of Judgement?'
13	On the Day they are tormented by the Fire:
14	'Taste your torment! This is what
	you were trying to hasten!'
15	The godfearing will be among Gardens and Fountains,
16	receiving what their Lord has given them.
	Certainly before that they were good-doers.
17	The part of the night they spent asleep was small
18	and they would seek forgiveness before the dawn.

19 And beggars and the destitute
received a due share of their wealth.

20 There are certainly Signs in the earth for people with certainty;
21 and in yourselves as well. Do you not then see?

22 Your provision is in heaven – and what you are promised.

23 By the Lord of heaven and earth, it is certainly the truth,
just as you have speech.

24 Has the story reached you of the honoured guests of Ibrahim?
25 When they entered his dwelling and said, 'Peace!'
he said, 'Peace, to people we do not know.'
26 So he slipped off to his household and brought a fattened calf.
27 He offered it to them and then exclaimed,
'Do you not then eat?'
28 He felt afraid of them but they said, 'Do not be afraid!'
and gave him the good news of a son imbued with knowledge.
29 His wife came up with a shriek and struck her face
and said, 'What, and me a barren old woman!'
30 They said, 'That is what your Lord says.
He is the All-Wise, the All-Knowing.'
31 He inquired, 'What, then, is your business, messengers?'
32 They said, 'We have been sent to a people of evildoers
33 to unleash upon them lumps of clay
34 earmarked by your Lord for the profligate.'

35 We brought out all the believers who were there
36 but found in it only one house of Muslims.
37 And We left a Sign in it
for those who fear the painful punishment.

38 And also in Musa when We sent him to Pharaoh
with clear authority.
39 But he turned away with his forces,
saying, 'A magician or a madman!'
40 So We seized him and his armies
and hurled them into the sea,
and he was to blame.

41 And also in 'Ad when We unleashed against them
the barren wind,
42 which left nothing it touched without turning it to dust.

43   And also in Thamud, when they were told:
        'Enjoy yourselves a while!'

44   But they spurned their Lord's command,
        so the Blast seized them as they looked.

45   They could not stand upright and they were not helped.

46   And the people of Nuh before,
        they were a people of deviators.

47   As for heaven – We built it with great power
        and gave it its vast expanse.

48   And the earth – We spread it like a carpet
        and how well We smoothed it out!

49   And We created all things in pairs
        so that hopefully you would pay heed.

50   So flee to Allah.
        Truly I bring you a clear warning from Him.

51   Do not set up another god together with Allah.
        Truly I bring you a clear warning from Him.

52   Equally, no Messenger came to those before them
        without their saying, 'A magician or a madman!'

53   Did they bequeathe this to one another?
        Indeed they are an unbridled people.

54   So turn away from them,
        for you are not to blame.

55   And remind them,
        for truly the believers benefit from being reminded.

56   I only created jinn and man to worship Me.

57   I do not require any provision from them
        and I do not require them to nourish Me.

58   Truly Allah, He is the Provider,
        the Possessor of Strength, the Sure.

59   Those who do wrong will have their due,
        the same as that of their friends.
            So they should not hurry Me!

60   Woe then to those who disbelieved on account of
        the Day they have been promised!

Sura 52

At-Tur
The Mount

In the name of Allah, All-Merciful, Most Merciful

1	By the Mount
2	and an Inscribed Book
3	on an Unfurled Scroll,
4	by the Visited House,
5	by the Raised Canopy,
6	by the Overflowing Ocean:
7	your Lord's punishment will certainly take place.
8	No one can ward it off.

9	On the Day when heaven sways to and fro
10	and the mountains shift about,
11	woe that Day to the deniers,
12	who play at frivolous games –
13	the Day they are shoved roughly
	into the Fire of Hell:
14	'This is the Fire which you denied!
15	So is this magic?
	Or is it that you do not see?
16	Roast in it! And bear it patiently
	or do not bear it patiently.
	It makes no difference either way.
	You are simply being repaid for what you did.'

17	The godfearing will be in Gardens of Delight,
18	savouring what their Lord has given them.
	Their Lord will safeguard them from
	the punishment of the Blazing Fire:

19	'Eat and drink with relish for what you did.'
20	They will recline on couches ranged in rows and We will marry them to dark-eyed maidens.
21	And We will unite those who believed with their offspring, who followed them in faith, and We will not undervalue their own actions in any way. Every man is in pledge for what he earned.
22	We will supply them with any kind of fruit and meat that they desire.
23	They will pass round there a drinking cup to one another with no foolish talk and no wrong action in it.
24	Circulating among them there will be youths like hidden pearls.
25	Some of them will come up to others and they will question one another.
26	They will say, 'Beforehand we used to live in fear among our families.
27	But Allah was gracious to us and safeguarded us from the punishment of the searing wind.
28	Beforehand we certainly used to call on Him because He is the All-Good, the Most Merciful.'
29	Remind them then! For, by the blessing of your Lord, you are neither a soothsayer nor a madman.
30	Or do they say, 'He is a poet and We are waiting for something bad to happen to him'?
31	Say: 'Wait then! I am waiting with you.'
32	Is it their intellects that direct them to say this or is it that they are an unbridled people?
33	Or do they say, 'He has simply made it up'? No, the truth is they do not believe.
34	Let them produce a discourse like it if they are telling the truth.
35	Or were they created out of nothing, or are they the creators?
36	Or did they create the heavens and the earth? No, in truth they have no certainty.

37   Or do they possess the treasuries of your Lord
         or do they have control of them?

38   Or do they have a ladder on which they listen?
         Then let their listener bring clear evidence.

39   Or does He have daughters
         whereas you have sons?

40   Or do you ask them for a wage
         so they are weighed down with debt?

41   Or is the Unseen in their hands
         so they can write out what is to happen?

42   Or do they desire to dupe you?
         But the duped ones are those who disbelieve.

43   Or do they have some god other than Allah?
         Glory be to Allah above any idol they propose!

44   If they saw a lump of heaven falling down,
         they would just say, 'Banked-up clouds!'

45   Leave them then until they meet their Day
         when they will be struck down by the Blast:

46   the Day their ploys will not profit them at all
         and they will not be helped.

47   And those who do wrong will have
         a punishment besides that
but most of them do not know it.

48   So wait steadfastly for the judgement of your Lord –
         you are certainly before Our eyes.
And glorify and praise your Lord when you get up.

49   And glorify Him in the night and when the stars fade out.

Sura 53

An-Najm
The Star

In the name of Allah, All-Merciful, Most Merciful

1	By the star when it descends,
2	your companion is not misguided or misled;
3	nor does he speak from whim.

4	It is nothing but Revelation revealed,
5	taught him by one immensely strong,
6	possessing power and splendour.
	He stood there stationary –
7	there on the highest horizon.
8	Then he drew near and hung suspended.
9	He was two bow-lengths away
	or even closer.
10	Then He revealed to His slave what He revealed.

11	His heart did not lie about what he saw.
12	What! Do you dispute with him about what he saw?

13	He saw him again another time
14	by the Lote-tree of the Final Limit,
15	beside which is the Garden of Refuge,
16	when that which covered the Lote-tree
	covered it.
17	His eye did not waver nor did he look away.
18	He saw some of the Greatest Signs of his Lord.

19	Have you really considered al-Lat and al-'Uzza
20	and Manat, the third, the other one?*

* These are the names of some of the idols worshipped by the Arabs.

21   Do you have males and He females?
22   That is a most unfair division!

23   They are nothing but names which you yourselves have given,
                  you and your forefathers.
            Allah has sent down no authority for them.
            They are following nothing but conjecture
                  and what their own selves desire.
            And that when guidance has reached them from their Lord!

24   Shall man then have whatever he covets?
25   The last and the first belong to Allah.

26   And how many angels there are in the heavens
                  whose intercession is of no avail at all
           until Allah has authorised those He wills
                  and is pleased with them!

27   Those who do not believe in the Next World
                  give the angels female names.
28   They have no knowledge of this.
                  They are only following conjecture.
           Conjecture is of no avail whatever against the truth.
29   So turn away from him who turns away
                  from Our remembrance
           and desires nothing but the life of this world.

30   That is as far as their knowledge extends.
                Your Lord knows best those who are misguided from His Way
                  and He knows best those who are guided.

31   Everything in the heavens and everything in the earth
                belongs to Allah
           so that He can repay those who do evil for what they did
                and repay those who do good with the Very Best.

32   To whomever avoids the major wrong actions and indecencies –
                except for minor lapses –
           truly your Lord is vast in forgiveness.
           He has most knowledge of you
                when He first produced you from the earth,
           and when you were embryos in your mothers' wombs.
                So do not claim purity for yourselves.
           He knows best those who are godfearing.

33 Have you seen him who turns away
34   and gives little, and that grudgingly?

35 Does he have knowledge of the Unseen,
        enabling him to see?

36 Or has he not been informed what is in the texts of Musa
37   and of Ibrahim, who paid his dues in full:

38 that no burden-bearer can bear another's burden;

39 that man will have nothing but what he strives for;

40 that his striving will most certainly be seen;

41 that he will then receive repayment of the fullest kind;

42 that the ultimate end is with your Lord;

43 that it is He Who brings about both laughter and tears;

44 that it is He Who brings about both death and life;

45 that He created the two sexes – male and female –
46   out of a sperm-drop when it spurted forth;

47 that He is responsible for the second existence;

48 that it is He Who enriches and Who satisfies;

49 that it is He Who is the Lord of Sirius;

50 that He destroyed 'Ad, the earlier people,
51   and Thamud as well, sparing none of them,
52 and the people of Nuh before –
        they were most unjust and exorbitant –
53 and the Upturned City which He turned upside down
54   so that what enveloped it enveloped it.

55 Which one of your Lord's blessings do you then dispute?

56 This is a warning like the warnings of old.

57   The Imminent is imminent!

58   No one besides Allah can unveil it.

59   Are you then amazed at this discourse
60   and laugh and do not cry,
61   treating life as a game?

62   Prostrate before Allah and worship Him!

Sura 54

Al-Qamar
The Moon

In the name of Allah, All-Merciful, Most Merciful

1   The Hour has drawn near and the moon has split.

2   If they see a Sign they turn away, saying
        'There is no end to this witchcraft!'

3   They have denied the truth
        and followed their whims and desires,
            but everything has its time.

4   News has come to them which contains a threa –
5   consummate wisdom – but warnings are profitless.

6   Turn away from them then.
        On the Day the Summoner summons them
            to something unspeakably terrible,
7   they will emerge from their graves
            with downcast eyes,
                like swarming locusts,
8   necks outstretched, eyes transfixed,
            rushing headlong to the Summoner.
    The unbelievers will say, 'This is a pitiless day!'

9   Before them the people of Nuh denied the truth.
        They denied Our slave,
            saying, 'He is madman,'
        and he was driven away with jeers.

10   He called upon his Lord:
                  'I am overwhelmed, so help me!'

11   So We opened the gates of heaven
                  with torrential water
12   and made the earth burst forth
                  with gushing springs.
        And the waters met together
                  in a way which was decreed.

13   We bore him on a planked and well-caulked ship,
14   which ran before Our eyes –
        a reward for him who had been rejected.

15   We left it as a Sign.
                But is there any rememberer there?
16   How terrible were My punishment and warnings!

17   We have made the Qur'an easy to remember.
                But is there any rememberer there?

18   'Ad denied the truth.
                How terrible were My punishment and warnings!
19   We unleashed a howling wind against them
                on a day of unremitting horror.
20   It plucked up men like uprooted stumps.
21   How terrible were My punishment and warnings!

22   We have made the Qur'an easy to remember.
                But is there any rememberer there?

23   Thamud denied the warnings.
24   They said, 'Are we to follow a human being, one of us?
                Then we would truly be misguided, quite insane!
25   Has the Reminder been given to him of all of us?
                No indeed! He is an impudent liar.'
26   'They will know tomorrow who the impudent liar is.
27   We will send the she-camel as a trial for them.
       Just keep a watchful eye on them and be steadfast.
28   Inform them that the water
                is to be shared out between them,
                   each drinking by turn.'
29   They called on their companion
                and he set to it and hamstrung her.

30   How terrible were My punishment and warnings!
31   We sent a single Blast against them
                  and they were just like a thatcher's reeds.

32   We have made the Qur'an easy to remember.
          But is there any rememberer there?

33   The people of Lut denied the warnings.
34   We unleashed a sudden squall of stones
                  against all of them,
              except the family of Lut,
                  who We rescued before dawn.
35   It was a blessing direct from Our presence.
          That is how We recompense the grateful.
36   He warned them of Our onslaught
          but they dismissed the warnings.
37   They even wanted to seduce his guests!
              So We put out their eyes:
          'Taste My punishment and warnings!'
38   Early morning brought them enduring punishment:
39   'Taste My punishment and warnings!'

40   We have made the Qur'an easy to remember
          But is there any rememberer there?

41   Warnings came to Pharaoh's people.
42   They dismissed every one of Our Signs
                  and so We seized them
          with the seizing of One who is Almighty, All-Powerful.

43   Are your unbelievers better than those peoples'?
          Or have you been given exemption in the Books?
44   Or do they say, 'We are an assembly who will win'?
45   The assembly will be routed
                  and will turn their backs in flight.

46   In fact the Hour is their promised appointment
          and the Hour is more disastrous and bitter!

47   The evildoers are indeed misguided and insane
48   on the Day that they are dragged
                  face-first into the Fire:
              'Taste the scorching touch of Saqar!'

49   We have created all things in due measure.

50   Our command is only one word,
        like the blinking of an eye.

51   We destroyed those of your kind in the past.
        But is there any rememberer there?

52   Everything they did is in the Books.
53   Everything is recorded, big or small.

54   The godfearing
        will be amid Gardens and Rivers,
55   on seats of honour
    in the presence of an All-Powerful King.

Sura 55

Ar-Rahman
The All-Merciful

In the name of Allah, All-Merciful, Most Merciful

1	The All-Merciful
2	taught the Qur'an.
3	He created man
4	and taught him clear expression.
5	The sun and the moon both run with precision.
6	The shrubs and the trees all bow down in prostration.
7	He erected heaven and established the balance,
8	so that you would not transgress the balance.
9	Give just weight – do not skimp in the balance.
10	He laid out the earth for all living creatures.
11	In it are fruits and date-palms with covered spathes,
12	and grains on leafy stems and fragrant herbs.
13	*So which of your Lord's blessings do you both then deny?**
14	He created man from dry earth like baked clay;
15	and He created the jinn from a fusion of fire.
16	*So which of your Lord's blessings do you both then deny?*

---

* The sura is addressed to the jinn and mankind, the two species who are accountable for their actions in this world. See ayat 33.

17   The Lord of the two Easts and the Lord of the two Wests.

18   *So which of your Lord's blessings do you both then deny?*

19   He has let loose the two seas, converging together,
20   with a barrier between them they do not break through.

21   *So which of your Lord's blessings do you both then deny?*

22   From out of them come glistening pearls and coral.

23   *So which of your Lord's blessings do you both then deny?*

24   His, too, are the ships sailing like mountain peaks on the sea.

25   *So which of your Lord's blessings do you both then deny?*

26   Everyone on it will pass away;
27   but the Face of your Lord will remain,
                     Master of Majesty and Generosity.

28   *So which of your Lord's blessings do you both then deny?*

29   Everyone in the heavens and earth requests His aid.
               Every day He is engaged in some affair.

30   *So which of your Lord's blessings do you both then deny?*

31   Soon We will settle your affairs, you two weighty throngs.

32   *So which of your Lord's blessings do you both then deny?*

33   Company of jinn and men, if you are able to pierce through
               the confines of the heavens and earth, pierce through them.
       You will not pierce through except with a clear authority.

34   *So which of your Lord's blessings do you both then deny?*

       He will pursue you with a piercing flame
35   and fiery smoke,
       and you will not be helped.

36   *So which of your Lord's blessings do you both then deny?*

37 When heaven is split apart and goes red like dregs of oil.

38 *So which of your Lord's blessings do you both then deny?*

39 That Day no man or jinn will be asked about his sin.

40 *So which of your Lord's blessings do you both then deny?*

41 The evildoers will be recognised by their mark
and seized by their forelocks and their feet.

42 *So which of your Lord's blessings do you both then deny?*

43 This is Hell which the evildoers deny.
44 They will go back and forth between fire and scalding water.

45 *So which of your Lord's blessings do you both then deny?*

46 For those who fear the Station of their Lord
there are two Gardens.

47 *So which of your Lord's blessings do you both then deny?*

48 Shaded by spreading branches.

49 *So which of your Lord's blessings do you both then deny?*

50 In them are two clear flowing springs.

51 *So which of your Lord's blessings do you both then deny?*

52 In them are two kinds of every fruit.

53 *So which of your Lord's blessings do you both then deny?*

54 They will be reclining on couches lined with rich brocade,
the fruits of the Gardens hanging close to hand.

55 *So which of your Lord's blessings do you both then deny?*

56 In them are maidens with eyes for them alone,
untouched before them by either man or jinn.

57 *So which of your Lord's blessings do you both then deny?*

58   Like precious gems of ruby and pearl.

59   *So which of your Lord's blessings do you both then deny?*

60   Will the reward for doing good be anything other than good?

61   *So which of your Lord's blessings do you both then deny?*

62   As well as those two there will be two other Gardens.

63   *So which of your Lord's blessings do you both then deny?*

64   Of deep viridian green.

65   *So which of your Lord's blessings do you both then deny?*

66   In them are two gushing springs.

67   *So which of your Lord's blessings do you both then deny?*

68   In them are fruits and date-palms and pomegranates.

69   *So which of your Lord's blessings do you both then deny?*

70   In them are sweet, lovely maidens.

71   *So which of your Lord's blessings do you both then deny?*

72   Dark-eyed, secluded in cool pavilions.

73   *So which of your Lord's blessings do you both then deny?*

74   Untouched before them by either man or jinn.

75   *So which of your Lord's blessings do you both then deny?*

76   Reclining on green quilts and exquisite rugs.

77   *So which of your Lord's blessings do you both then deny?*

78   Blessed be the name of your Lord,
       Master of Majesty and Generosity.

Sura 56

Al-Waqi'a
The Occurrence

1   When the Great Event occurs,
2   none will deny its occurrence;
3   bringing low, raising high.

4   When the earth is convulsed
5   and the mountains are crushed
6   and become scattered dust in the air.

7   And you will be classed into three:
8   the Companions of the Right:
   what of the Companions of the Right?
9   the Companions of the Left:
   what of the Companions of the Left?
10   and the Forerunners,
       the Forerunners.

11   Those are the Ones Brought Near
12   in Gardens of Delight.
13   A large group of the earlier people
14   but few of the later ones.
15   On sumptuous woven couches,
16   reclining on them face to face.
17   There will circulate among them, ageless youths,
18   carrying goblets and decanters
       and a cup from a flowing spring –
19   it does not give them any headache
       nor does it leave them stupefied.

20	And any fruit they specify
21	and any bird-meat they desire.
22	And dark-eyed maidens
23	like hidden pearls.
24	As recompense for what they did.
25	They will hear no prattling in it
	nor any word of wrong.
26	All that is said is, 'Peace! Peace!'

27	And the Companions of the Right:
	what of the Companions of the Right?
28	Amid thornless lote-trees
29	and fruit-laden acacias
30	and wide-spreading shade
31	and outpouring water
32	and fruits in abundance
33	never failing, unrestricted.
34	And on elevated couches
35	We have brought maidens into being
36	and made them purest virgins,
37	devoted, passionate, of like age,
38	for the Companions of the Right.
39	A large group of the earlier people
40	and a large group of the later ones.

41	And the Companions of the Left:
	what of the Companions of the Left?
42	Amid searing blasts and scalding water
43	and the murk of thick black smoke,
44	providing no coolness and no pleasure.
45	Before that they were living in luxury,
46	persisting in immense wrongdoing
47	and saying, 'When we are dead
	and turned to dust and bones,
	shall we then be raised again
48	or our forefathers, the earlier peoples?'

49	Say: 'The earlier and the later peoples
	will certainly all be gathered
50	to the appointment of a specified Day.
51	Then you, you misguided, you deniers
52	will eat from the tree of Zaqqum,
53	filling your stomachs with it

54   and drink scalding water on top of it,
55   slurping like thirst-crazed camels.
56   This will be their hospitality on the Day of Judgment!'

57   We created you so why do you not confirm the truth?

58   Have you thought about the sperm that you ejaculate?
59   Is it you who create it
            or are We the Creator?
60   We have decreed death for you
            and We will not be forestalled
61   in replacing you
            with others the same as you
                and re-forming you
            in a way you know nothing about.
62   You have known the first formation,
            so will you not pay heed?

63   Have you thought about what you cultivate?
64   Is it you who make it germinate
            or are We the Germinator?
65   If We wished We could have made it broken stubble.
            You would then be left devoid of crops, distraught:
66   'We are ruined,
67   in fact we are destitute!'

68   Have you thought about the water that you drink?
69   Is it you who sent it down from the clouds
            or are We the Sender?
70   If We wished We could have made it bitter,
            so will you not give thanks?

71   Have you thought about the fire that you light?
72   Is it you who make the trees that fuel it grow
            or are We the Grower?
73   We have made it to be a reminder
            and a comfort for travellers in the wild.

74   So glorify the name of your Lord, the Magnificent!

75   And I swear by the falling of the stars –
76   and that is a mighty oath if you only knew –
77   it truly is a Noble Qur'an
78   in a well protected Book.

79   No one may touch it except the purified.

80   Revelation sent down from the Lord of all the worlds.

81   Do you nonetheless regard this discourse with scorn

82   and do you show thanks for your provision
            by your denial of the truth?

83   Why then, when death reaches his throat

84   and you are at that moment looking on –

85   and We are nearer him than you but you cannot see –

86   why then, if you are not subject to Our command,

87   do you not send it back if you are telling the truth?

88   But the truth is that if he is one of Those Brought Near,

89   there is solace and sweetness and a Garden of Delight.

90   And if he is one of the Companions of the Right,

91   'Peace be upon you!' from the Companions of the Right.

92   And if he is one of the misguided deniers,

93   there is hospitality of scalding water

94   and roasting in the Blazing Fire.

95   This is indeed the Truth of Certainty.

96   So glorify the Name of your Lord, the Magnificent!

Sura 57

Al-Hadid

Iron

In the name of Allah, All-Merciful, Most Merciful

1   Everything in the heavens and the earth glorifies Allah.
        He is the Almighty, the All-Wise.

2   The kingdom of the heavens and the earth belongs to Him.
        He gives life and causes to die.
            He has power over all things.

3   He is the First and the Last, the Outward and the Inward.
        He has knowledge of all things.

4   It is He Who created the heavens and the earth in six days,
        then established Himself firmly on the Throne.
    He knows what goes into the earth and what comes out of it,
        what comes down from heaven and what goes up into it.
    He is with you wherever you are – Allah sees what you do.

5   The kingdom of the heavens and the earth belongs to Him.
        All things return to Allah.

6   He makes night merge into day and day merge into night.
        He knows what the heart contains.

7   Believe in Allah and His Messenger
        and give of that to which He has made you successors.
    Those of you who believe and give
        will have an immense reward.

8   And what is the matter with you with you
        that you do not believe in Allah,
    when the Messenger calls you
        to believe in your Lord,

and He has made a covenant with you
if you are believers?

9   It is He who sends down Clear Signs to His slave
to bring you out of the darkness to the light.
Allah is All-Gentle with you, Most Merciful.

10   And how is it with you that you do not give in the Way of Allah,
when the inheritance of the heavens and the earth
belongs to Allah?
Those of you who gave and fought before the Victory*
are not the same as those who gave and fought afterwards.
They are higher in rank.
But to each of them Allah has promised the Best.
Allah is aware of what you do.

11   Who will make a good loan to Allah
so that He may multiply it for him?
He will have a generous reward.

12   On the Day you see the men and women of the believers,
with their light streaming out in front of them,
and to their right:
'Good news for you today of Gardens
with rivers flowing under them,
remaining in them timelessly, for ever.
That is the Great Victory.'

13   That Day the men and women of the hypocrites
will say to those who believe,
'Wait for us so that we can borrow some of your light.'
They will be told, 'Go back and look for light!'
And a wall will be erected between them with a gate in it,
on the inside of which there will be mercy
but before whose exterior lies the punishment.

14   They will call out to them, 'Were we not with you?'
They will reply, 'Indeed you were.
But you made trouble for yourselves
and hung back and and doubted
and false hopes deluded you until Allah's command arrived.
The Deluder deluded you about Allah.

---

* Generally taken to refer to the Conquest of Makka, although some commentators say that it
refers to the Treaty of al-Hudaybiyya.

15   So today no ransom will be accepted from you
        or from those who disbelieved.
           Your refuge is the Fire.
           It is your master.
        What an evil destination!'

16   Has the time not arrived for the hearts of those who believe
        to yield to the remembrance of Allah
           and to the truth He has sent down,
    so they are not like those who were given the Book before
        for whom the time seemed over long
           so that their hearts became hard?
    Many of them are deviators.

17   Know that Allah brings the earth to life after it was dead.
        We have made the Signs clear to you
    so that hopefully you will use your intellect.

18   The men and women who give sadaqa
        and make a good loan to Allah
    will have it increased for them
        and they will have a generous reward.

19   Those who believe in Allah and His Messengers –
        such people are the truly sincere –
    and the martyrs who are with their Lord
        will receive their wages and their light.
    But those who disbelieve and deny Our Signs,
        will be Companions of the Blazing Fire.

20   Know that the life of this world is merely a game and a diversion
        and ostentation and a cause of boasting among yourselves
           and trying to outdo one another in wealth and children:
    like the plant-growth after rain which delights the cultivators,
        but then it withers and you see it turning yellow,
           and then it becomes broken stubble.
    In the Next World there is terrible punishment
        but also forgiveness from Allah and His good pleasure.
    The life of this world is nothing but the enjoyment of delusion.

21   Race each other to forgiveness from your Lord and to a Garden,
        whose breadth is like that of heaven and earth combined,
    made ready for those who believe
        in Allah and His Messengers.

That is Allah's favour which He gives to those He wills.
Allah's favour is indeed immense.

22 Nothing occurs, either in the earth or in yourselves,
without its being in a Book before We make it happen.
That is something easy for Allah.

23 That is so that you will not be grieved
about the things that pass you by
or exult about the things that come to you.
Allah does not love any vain or boastful man:

24 those who are tight-fisted
and tell others to be tight-fisted.
If anyone turns away,
Allah is the Rich Beyond Need, the Praiseworthy.

25 We sent Our Messengers with the Clear Signs
and sent down the Book and the Balance with them
so that mankind might establish justice.
And We sent down iron in which there lies great force
and which has many uses for mankind,
so that Allah might know those who help Him
and His Messengers in the Unseen.
Allah is All-Strong, Almighty.

26 We sent Nuh and Ibrahim
and placed Prophethood and the Book
among their descendants.
Some of them are guided but many of them are deviators.

27 Then We sent Our Messengers following in their footsteps
and sent 'Isa son of Maryam after them, giving him the Injil.
We put compassion and mercy
in the hearts of those who followed him.
They invented monasticism –
We did not prescribe it for them –
purely out of desire to gain the pleasure of Allah,
but even so they did not observe it
as it should have been observed.
To those of them who believed We gave their reward
but many of them are deviators.

28 You who believe! have taqwa of Allah
and believe in His Messenger.

He will give you a double portion of His mercy
and grant you a Light by which to walk
and forgive you.
Allah is Ever-Forgiving, Most Merciful.

29   So that the People of the Book may know
that they have no power at all
over any of Allah's favour
and that all favour is in the Hand of Allah.
He gives it to anyone He wills.
Allah's favour is indeed immense.

Sura 58

Al-Mujadala
The Disputer

In the name of Allah, All-Merciful, Most Merciful

1   Allah has heard the words of the woman*
        who disputes with you about her husband
            and lays her complaint before Allah.
        Allah hears the two of you talking together.
            Allah is All-Hearing, All-Seeing.

2   Those of you who divorce your wives
        by equating them with your mothers,
            they are not your mothers.**
    Your mothers are only those who gave birth to you.
        What you are saying is wrong and a slanderous lie.
    But Allah is Ever-Pardoning, Ever-Forgiving.

3   Those who divorce their wives
        by equating them with their mothers,
    and then wish to go back on what they said,
            must set free a slave
        before the two of them may touch one another.
    This is what you are enjoined to do.
        Allah is aware of what you do.

4   Anyone who cannot find the means
        must fast for two consecutive months
            before the two of them may touch one another again.

---

* This refers to Khawla bint Tha'laba who went to the Prophet, peace be upon him, to complain when her husband divorced her by the form of divorce mentioned in this sura when he was suffering from dementia.
** This refers to a type of divorce in which men would equate their wives with their mothers, thus preventing any further relations with them.

And anyone who is unable to do that must feed sixty poor people.
That is to affirm your faith in Allah and His Messenger.
These are Allah's limits.
The unbelievers will have a painful punishment.

5   Those who oppose Allah and His Messenger
will be subdued and overcome
as those before them were also subdued and overcome.
We have sent down Clear Signs.
The unbelievers will have a humiliating punishment.

6   On the Day Allah raises up all of them together,
He will inform them of what they did.
Allah has recorded it while they have forgotten it.
Allah is a Witness of all things.

7   Do you not see that Allah knows
what is in the heavens and on the earth?
Three men cannot confer together secretly
without Him being the fourth of them,
or five without Him being the sixth of them,
or fewer than that or more
without Him being with them wherever they are.
Then He will inform them on the Day of Rising of what they did.
Allah has knowledge of all things.

8   Do you not see those who were forbidden
to confer together secretly
returning to the very thing they were forbidden to do,
and conferring together secretly in wrongdoing and enmity
and disobedience to the Messenger?
And when they come to you they greet you
with words Allah has never used in greeting you,
and say to themselves
'Why does Allah not punish us for what we say?'
Hell will be enough for them!
They will roast in it.
What an evil destination!

9   You who believe! when you confer together secretly,
do not do so in wrongdoing and enmity
and disobedience to the Messenger;
rather confer together in goodness and taqwa of Allah.
Have taqwa of Allah – Him to Whom you will be gathered.

10   Conferring in secret is from Shaytan,
         to cause grief to those who believe;
     but it cannot harm them at all,
         unless by Allah's permission.
     So let the believers put their trust in Allah.

11   You who believe! when you are told:
         'Make room in the gathering,'
     then make room and Allah will make room for you!
         And when it is said, 'Get up', get up.
     Allah will raise in rank those of you who believe
         and those who have been given knowledge.
     Allah is aware of what you do.

12   You who believe! when you consult the Messenger privately
         precede your private consultation by giving sadaqa –
            that is better for you and purer.
         But if you cannot find the means,
     Allah is Ever-Forgiving, Most Merciful.

13   Are you afraid to give gifts of sadaqa
         before your private consultation?
     If you do not and Allah turns to you,
         at least establish the prayer and pay zakat,
            and obey Allah and His Messenger.
         Allah is aware of what you do.

14   Do you not see those who have turned to people
            with whom Allah is angry?
         They belong neither to you nor to them.
            And they swear to falsehood
            and do so knowingly.
15   Allah has prepared a terrible punishment for them.
         How evil is what they have been doing!
16   They made their oaths into a cloak
         and barred the Way of Allah,
         so they will have a humiliating punishment.
17   Neither their wealth nor their children
         will help them at all against Allah.
     Such people are the Companions of the Fire,
         remaining in it timelessly, for ever.

18   On the Day Allah raises up all of them them together
         they will swear to Him just as they have sworn to you

and imagine they have something to stand upon.
No indeed! It is they who are the liars.

19   Shaytan has gained mastery over them
        and made them forget the remembrance of Allah.
            Such people are the party of Shaytan.
No indeed! It is the party of Shaytan who are the losers.

20   Those who oppose Allah and His Messenger,
        such people will be among the most abased.
21   Allah has written, 'I will be victorious,
        I and and My Messengers.'
Allah is Most Strong, Almighty.

22   You will not find people who believe in Allah and the Last Day
        having love for anyone who opposes Allah and His Messenger,
    though they be their fathers, their sons,
            their brothers or their clan.
        Allah has inscribed faith upon such people's hearts
            and will reinforce them with a Ruh from Him
    and admit them into Gardens with rivers flowing under them,
        remaining in them timelessly, for ever.
    Allah is pleased with them and they are pleased with Him.
        Such people are the party of Allah.
    Truly it is the party of Allah who are successful.

Sura 59

Al-Hashr
The Gathering

In the name of Allah, All-Merciful, Most Merciful

1   Everything in the heavens
   and everything in the earth glorifies Allah.
  He is the Almighty, the All-Wise.

2   It is He who expelled those who disbelieved
   among the People of the Book
  from their homes to the first gathering-place.*
 You did not think that they would leave
  and they thought that their fortresses
   would protect them from Allah.
 Then Allah came upon them
  from where they least expected it
   and cast terror into their hearts.
 Their houses were pulled down by their own hands
  and by the hands of the believers.
 People of insight, take note!

3   If Allah had not prescribed banishment for them,
  He would have punished them in his world.
 But in the Next World they will have the punishment of the Fire.

4   That is because they were entrenched in hostility
  towards Allah and His Messenger.
 If anyone is hostile towards Allah,
  Allah is Severe in Retribution.

---

* This refers to the Bani Nadir, a Jewish tribe of Madina, who were banished from Madina in 4
AH on account of their persistent treachery towards the Muslims.

5   Whatever palm-trees you cut down,
            or left standing upright on their roots,
        it was done by Allah's permission
            in order to disgrace the deviators.

6   Whatever booty from them Allah has given to His Messenger –
            and you spurred on neither horse nor camel in its acquisition,
                but Allah gives power to His Messengers
                    over anyone He wills,
                    Allah has power over all things –
7   whatever booty Allah gives to His Messenger from city dwellers
            belongs to Allah and to the Messenger
                and to near relatives and orphans
                    and the very poor and travellers,
                so that it does not become something
            which merely revolves between the rich among you.
        Whatever the Messenger gives you you should accept
            and whatever he forbids you you should forgo.
        Have taqwa of Allah – Allah is severe in retribution.
8   It is for the poor of the Muhajirun
        who were driven from their homes and wealth
                desiring the favour and the pleasure of Allah
                    and supporting Allah and His Messenger.
            Such people are the truly sincere.

9   Those who were already settled in the abode,
            and in faith, before they came,
        love those who have made hijra to them
            and do not find in their hearts
        any need for what they have been given
            and prefer them to themselves
                even if they themselves are needy.
        It is the people who are safe-guarded
            from the avarice of their own selves
                who are successful.

10   Those who have come after them say,
            'Our Lord, forgive us and our brothers
                who preceded us in faith
            and do not put any rancour in our hearts
                towards those who believe.
        Our Lord, You are All-Gentle, Most Merciful.'

11   Did you not see the hypocrites saying to their brothers,
       those among the People of the Book who disbelieve,
    'If you are driven out we will leave with you,
       we will never obey anyone to your detriment.
    And if you are fought against we will help you'?
       Allah bears witness that they are truly liars.

12   If they are driven out they will not leave with them.
       If they are fought against they will not help them.
    And if they did help them they would turn their backs,
       and then they would not be helped.

13   You are a greater cause of terror in their breasts than Allah!
       That is because they are people who do not understand.

14   They will not fight against you all together as a group
       except in fortified towns or behind high walls.
    Their hostility towards each other is intense.
       They are full of bravado in each other's company.
    You consider them united but their hearts are scattered.
       That is because they are people who do not use their intellect.

15   They are the same as those a short time before them who tasted
       the evil consequences of what they did.*
       They will have a painful punishment.

16   They are like Shaytan
       when he says to a human being, 'Disbelieve,'
          and then when he disbelieves, says,
            'I wash my hands of you.
          Truly I fear Allah, the Lord of all the worlds.'

17   The final fate of both of them
is that they will be timelessly, for ever in the Fire.
    That is the repayment of the wrongdoers.

18   You who believe! have taqwa of Allah
       and let each self look to what
          it has sent forward for Tomorrow.
       Have taqwa of Allah.
          Allah is aware of what you do.

19   Do not be like those who forgot Allah
       so He made them forget themselves.
    Such people are the deviators.

20   The Companions of the Fire
       and the Companions of the Garden

---

* A reference to another Madinan Jewish tribe, the Bani Qaynuqa, who had also been banished from Madina in 2 AH for treachery.

are not the same.
It is the Companions of the Garden who are the victors.

21 If We had sent down this Qur'an onto a mountain,
        you would have seen it humbled,
            crushed to pieces out of fear of Allah.
    We make such examples for people
        so that hopefully they will reflect.

22 He is Allah – there is no god but Him.
        He is the Knower of the Unseen and the Visible.
            He is the All-Merciful, the Most Merciful.
23 He is Allah – there is no god but Him.
        He is the King, the Most Pure, the Perfect Peace,
    the Trustworthy, the Safeguarder, the Almighty,
            the Compeller, the Supremely Great.
        Glory be to Allah above all they associate with Him.
24 He is Allah – the Creator, the Maker, the Giver of Form.
        To Him belong the Most Beautiful Names.
    Everything in the heavens and earth glorifies Him.
        He is the Almighty, the All-Wise.

Sura 60

Al-Mumtahana
The Woman Tested

In the name of Allah, All-Merciful, Most Merciful

1   You who believe!
         do not take My enemy and your enemy as friends,
              showing love for them when they have rejected
                   the truth that has come to you,
              driving out the Messenger and yourselves
                   simply because you believe in Allah your Lord.
     If you go out to do jihad in My Way and seeking My pleasure,
         keeping secret the love you have for them,
     I know best what you conceal and what you make known.
         Any of you who do that have strayed from the right way.
2   If they come upon you, they will be your enemies and stretch out
         their hands and tongues against you with evil intent,
              and they would dearly love you to disbelieve.

3   Neither your blood relations nor your children
         will be of any use to you.
     On the Day of Rising He will differentiate between you.
         Allah sees what you do.

4   You have an excellent example in Ibrahim and those with him,
         when they said to their people, 'We wash our hands of you
              and all that you worship apart from Allah,
                   and we reject you.
     Between us and you there will be enmity and hatred for ever
         unless and until you believe in Allah alone.'
     Except for Ibrahim's words to his father:
         'I will ask forgiveness for you but I have no power
              to help you in any way against Allah.'

'Our Lord, we have put our trust in You.
    and have turned in repentance to You.
        You are our final destination.

5   Our Lord, do not make us a target for those who disbelieve
    and forgive us.
Our Lord, You are the Almighty, the All-Wise.'

6   There is an excellent example in them for you to follow,
    that is for those whose hope is in Allah and the Last Day.
        But if anyone turns away,
Allah is the Rich Beyond Need, the Praiseworthy.

7   It may well be that Allah will restore the love
    between you and those of them who are now your enemies.
        Allah is All-Powerful.
    Allah is Ever-Forgiving, Most Merciful.

8   Allah does not forbid you from being good to those
    who have not fought you in the deen
        or driven you from your homes,
    or from being just towards them.
        Allah loves those who are just.

9   Allah merely forbids you from taking as friends
    those who have fought you in the deen
        and driven you from your homes
            and who supported your expulsion.
    Any who take them as friends are wrongdoers.

10   You who believe! when women who believe
    come to you as muhajirun,
        submit them to a test.
    Allah has best knowledge of their faith.
If you know they are believers,
    do not return them to the unbelievers.
They are not halal for the unbelievers
    nor are the unbelievers halal for them.
Give the unbelievers whatever dowry they paid.
    And there is nothing wrong in your marrying them
    provided you pay them their due.
Do not hold to any marriage ties with women who disbelieve.
    Ask for what you paid
        and let them ask for what they paid.

That is Allah's judgement.
Allah will judge between them.
Allah is All-Knowing, All-Wise.

11   If any of your wives rejoin the unbelievers,
you should have compensation.
So repay to those whose wives have gone
the dowry they paid out.
Have taqwa of Allah – Him in Whom you believe.

12   O Prophet! When women who believe come to you
pledging allegiance to you on the grounds
that they will not associate anything with Allah
or steal or fornicate or kill their children
or give a false ascription of paternity –
making up lies about their bodies –
or disobey you in respect of anything right,
then accept their pledge and ask forgiveness for them.
Allah is Ever-Forgiving, Most Merciful.

13   You who believe! do not make friends of people
with whom Allah is angry,
who have despaired of the Next World
as the unbelievers have despaired
of the inhabitants of the graves.

Sura 61

As-Saff
The Ranks

In the name of Allah, All-Merciful, Most Merciful

1 Everything in the heavens
     and everything in the earth glorifies Allah.
  He is the Almighty, the All-Wise.

2 You who believe! why do you say what you do not do?

3 It is deeply abhorrent to Allah
  that you should say what you do not do.

4 Allah loves those who fight in His Way in ranks
  like well-built walls.

5 Remember when Musa said to his people,
    'My people, why do you mistreat me
when you know that I am the Messenger of Allah to you?'
    So when they deviated,
  Allah made their hearts deviate.
Allah does not guide people who are deviators.

6 And when 'Isa son of Maryam said,
    'Tribe of Israel, I am the Messenger of Allah to you,
      confirming the Torah which came before me
   and giving you the good news of a Messenger after me
     whose name is Ahmad.'
When he brought them the Clear Signs,
  they said, 'This is downright magic.'

7   Who could do greater wrong than someone
            who invents a lie against Allah
                when he has been called to Islam?
            Allah does not guide wrongdoing people.

8   They desire to extinguish Allah's Light
            with their mouths
        but Allah will perfect His Light,
            though the unbelievers hate it.

9   It is He who sent His Messenger with guidance
            and the Deen of Truth
        to exalt it over every other deen,
            though the idolators hate it.

10   You who believe! shall I direct you to a transaction
            which will save you from a painful punishment?
11   It is to believe in Allah and His Messenger
            and do jihad in the Way of Allah
                with your wealth and your selves.
            That is better for you if you only knew.

12   He will forgive you your wrong actions
            and admit you into Gardens
                with rivers flowing under them,
        and fine dwellings in the Gardens of Eden.
                That is the Great Victory.
13   And other things you love:
        support from Allah and imminent victory.
            Give good news to the believers!

14   You who believe! be helpers of Allah as 'Isa son of Maryam
            said to the Disciples, 'Who will be my helpers to Allah?'
        The Disciples said, 'We will be the helpers of Allah.'
                One faction of the tribe of Israel believed
                    and the other disbelieved.
                So We supported those who believed against their enemy
                    and they became victorious.

Sura 62

Al-Jumu'a
The Jumu'a Prayer

In the name of Allah, All-Merciful, Most Merciful

1 Everything in the heavens
    and everything in the earth glorifies Allah,
    the King, the All-Pure, the Almighty, the All-Wise.

2 It is He who raised up among the unlettered people
    a Messenger from them to recite His Signs to them
        and purify them
    and teach them the Book and Wisdom,
    even though before that they were clearly misguided.
3   And others of them who have not yet joined them.
        He is the Almighty, the All-Wise.
4   That is Allah's favour which He gives to whomever He wills.
        Allah's favour is indeed immense.

5 The metaphor of those who were charged with the Torah
        but then have not upheld it,
    is that of a donkey loaded with weighty tomes.
    How evil is the metaphor of those who deny Allah's Signs!
        Allah does not guide wrongdoing people.

6 Say: 'You Jews, if you claim to be the friends of Allah
        to the exclusion of all other people,
    then wish for death if you are telling the truth.'
7   But they will never ever wish for it
            because of what they have done.
        Allah knows the wrongdoers.

8   Say: 'Death, from which you are fleeing,
            will certainly catch up with you.
        Then you will be returned
            to the Knower of the Unseen and the Visible
        and He will inform you about what you did.'

9   You who believe! when you are called to the prayer
            on the Day of Jumu'a,
        hasten to the remembrance of Allah
            and abandon trade.
        That is better for you if you only knew.
10   Then when the prayer is finished
            spread through the earth
        and seek Allah's bounty and remember Allah much
            so that hopefully you will be successful.
11   But when they see a chance of trade or entertainment
            they scatter off to it and leave you standing there.
        Say: 'What is with Allah is better than trade or entertainment.
            Allah is the Best of Providers.'

Sura 63

Al-Munafiqun
The Hypocrites

In the name of Allah, All-Merciful, Most Merciful

1   When the hypocrites come to you they say,
        'We bear witness that you are the Messenger of Allah.'
            Allah knows that you are indeed His Messenger
        and Allah bears witness that the hypocrites are certainly liars.

2   They have made their oaths into a cloak
        and barred the Way of Allah.
    What they have done is truly evil.

3   That is because they have believed and then returned to unbelief.
        So their hearts have been sealed up
            and they cannot understand.

4   When you see them, their outward form appeals to you,
        and if they speak you listen to what they say.
    But they are like propped-up planks of wood.
        They imagine every cry to be against them.
    They are the enemy, so beware of them.
        Allah fight them! How they are perverted!

5   When they are told, 'Come, and the Messenger of Allah
        will ask forgiveness for you,' they turn their heads
            and you see them turn away in haughty arrogance.

6   In their case it makes no difference
        whether you ask forgiveness for them
            or do not ask forgiveness for them.
        Allah will never forgive them.
            Allah does not guide deviant people.

7   They are the people who say, 'Do not spend
            on those who are with the Messenger of Allah,
                so that they may go away.'
     The treasuries of the heavens and earth belong to Allah.
            But the hypocrites do not understand this.

8   They say, 'If we return to Madina,
            the mightier will drive out the inferior.'
     But all might belongs to Allah
            and to His Messenger and the believers.
     But the hypocrites do not know this.

9   You who believe! do not let your wealth or children
            divert you from the remembrance of Allah.
                Whoever does that is lost.
10   Give from what We have provided for you
            before death comes to one of you and he says,
     'My Lord, if only you would give me a little more time
            so that I can give sadaqa and be one of the righteous!'

11   Allah will not give anyone more time,
            once their time has come.
     Allah is aware of what you do.

Sura 64

At-Taghabun
Profit and Loss

In the name of Allah, All-Merciful, Most Merciful

1   Everything in the heavens and everything on earth glorifies Allah.
      Sovereignty and praise belong to Him.
        He has power over all things.

2   It is He who created you.
      Yet among you are those who disbelieve
        and those who believe.
      Allah sees what you do.

3   He created the heavens and the earth with truth
      and formed you, giving you the best of forms.
        And He is your final destination.

4   He knows everything in the heavens and earth.
      He knows what you keep secret and what you divulge.
        Allah knows what the heart contains.

5   Has the news not reached you of those who disbelieved before
      and tasted the evil consequences of what they did?
        They will have a painful punishment.

6   That is because their Messengers brought them the Clear Signs
      but they said, 'Are human beings going to guide us?'
        So they disbelieved and turned away.
      But Allah is completely independent of them.
        Allah is Rich Beyond Need, Praiseworthy.

7   Those who disbelieve claim that they will never be raised again.
      Say: 'Oh yes, by my Lord, you certainly will be raised again!

And then you will be informed about what you did.
That is easy for Allah.'

8   So believe in Allah and His Messenger
       and in the Light We have sent down.
       Allah is aware of what you do.

9   On the Day He gathers you for the Day of Gathering –
       that is the Day of Profit and Loss.
       As for those who believe in Allah and act rightly,
          We will erase their bad actions from them
             and admit them into Gardens
          with rivers flowing under them,
       remaining in them timelessly, for ever and ever.
          That is the Great Victory!
10   But as for those who disbelieve and deny Our Signs
          they are the Companions of the Fire,
             remaining in it timelessly, for ever.
          What an evil destination!

11   No misfortune occurs except by Allah's permission.
          Whoever believes in Allah –
             He will guide his heart.
          Allah has knowledge of all things.

12   Obey Allah and obey the Messenger.
          But if you turn your backs,
       the Messenger is only responsible
          for clear transmission.

13   Allah – there is no god but Him.
          So let the believers put their trust in Allah.

14   You who believe! some of your wives and children
          are an enemy to you, so be wary of them.
       But if you pardon and exonerate and forgive,
          Allah is Ever-Forgiving, Most Merciful.
15   Your wealth and children are a trial.
          But with Allah there is an immense reward.
16   So have taqwa of Allah, as much as you are able to,
          and listen and obey and spend for your own benefit.
       It is the people who are safe-guarded
          from the avarice of their own selves
             who are successful.

17   If you make a generous loan to Allah
          He will multiply it for you
              and forgive you.
      Allah is All-Thankful, Most Forbearing.

18   The Knower of the Unseen and the Visible,
          the Almighty, the All-Wise.

Sura 65

At-Talaq
Divorce

In the name of Allah, All-Merciful, Most Merciful

1   O Prophet! When any of you divorce women,
        divorce them during their period of purity
            and calculate their 'idda carefully.
        And have taqwa of Allah, your Lord.
    Do not evict them from their homes,
        nor should they leave,
    unless they commit an outright indecency.
        Those are Allah's limits,
    and anyone who oversteps Allah's limits
        has wronged himself.
    You never know, it may well be that after that
        Allah will cause a new situation to develop.

2   Then when they have reached the end of their 'idda
        either retain them with correctness and courtesy
            or part from them with correctness and courtesy.
    Call two upright men from among yourselves as witnesses
        and they should carry out the witnessing for Allah.
    This is admonishment for all who believe
            in Allah and the Last Day.
        Whoever has taqwa of Allah – He will give him a way out
3   and provide for him from where he does not expect.
        Whoever puts his trust in Allah – He will be enough for him.
            Allah always achieves His aim.
        Allah has appointed a measure for all things.

4   In the case of those of your wives
            who are past the age of menstruation,
                if you have any doubt, their 'idda should be three months,
                    and that also applies to those
                        who have not yet menstruated.
      The time for women who are pregnant is when they give birth.
            Whoever has taqwa of Allah –
                He will make matters easy for him.
5   That is Allah's command which He has sent down to you.
            Whoever has taqwa of Allah –
                He will erase his bad actions from him
                    and greatly increase his reward.

6   Let them live where you live, according to your means.
            Do not put pressure on them, so as to harass them.
      If they are pregnant, maintain them until they give birth.
            If they are suckling for you, give them their wages
                and consult together with correctness and courtesy.
      But if you make things difficult for one another,
            another woman should do the suckling for you.
7   He who has plenty should spend out from his plenty,
            but he whose provision is restricted should spend
                from what Allah has given him.
      Allah does not demand from any self more than He has given it.
            Allah will appoint after difficulty, ease.

8   How many cities spurned
            their Lord's command and His Messengers!
      And so We called them harshly to account
            and punished them with a terrible punishment.
9   They tasted the evil consequences of what they did
            and the end of their affair was total loss.
10   Allah has prepared a terrible punishment for them.
            So have taqwa of Allah, people of intelligence –
                those who believe –
            Allah has sent down a reminder to you,
11   a Messenger reciting Allah's Clear Signs to you
            to bring those who believe and do right actions
                out of the darkness into the Light.
      Whoever believes in Allah and acts rightly,
            We will admit him into Gardens
                with rivers flowing under them
            remaining in them timelessly, for ever and ever.
                Allah has provided for him excellently!

12   It is Allah who created the seven heavens
                    and of the earth the same number,
                the Command descending down through all of them,
            so that you might know that Allah has power over all things
                    and that Allah encompasses all things in His knowledge.

Sura 66

At-Tahrim
The Prohibition

In the name of Allah, All-Merciful, Most Merciful

1   O Prophet! Why do you make haram
        what Allah has made halal for you,
            seeking to please your wives?
        Allah is Ever-Forgiving, Most Merciful.

2   Allah has made the expiation of your oaths obligatory for you.
        Allah is your Master – He is the All-Knowing, the All-Wise.

3   The Prophet confided a certain matter to one of his wives,
        then when she divulged it Allah disclosed that to him,
            and he communicated part of it and withheld part of it.
        When he told her of it, she said, 'Who told you of this?'
    He said, 'The All-Knowing and All-Aware informed me of it.'

4   If the two of you would only turn to Allah,
        for your hearts clearly deviated . . .*
    But if you support one another against him,
        Allah is his Protector and so are Jibril
            and every right-acting man of the believers
    and, furthermore, the angels too will come to his support.

5   It may be that if he does divorce you,
        his Lord will give him in exchange
            better wives than you:
    Muslim women, believing women,
        obedient women, penitent women,

---

* This sura was occasioned by an incident when one wife of the Prophet betrayed a confidential
matter to another of his wives and the 'two' mentioned here are the two wives concerned.

women who worship, women who fast much –
    previously married women as well as virgins.

6   You who believe! safeguard yourselves and your families
        from a Fire whose fuel is people and stones.
Harsh, terrible angels are in charge of it
    who do not disobey Allah
in respect of any order He gives them
    and carry out what they are ordered to do.

7   'You who disbelieve! do not try to excuse yourselves today.
    You are merely being repaid for what you did.'

8   You who believe! repent sincerely to Allah.
    It may be that your Lord will erase your bad actions from you
        and admit you into Gardens
           with rivers flowing under them
    on the Day when Allah will not disgrace the Prophet
        and those who believed along with him.
    Their light will stream out ahead of them and on their right.
They will say, 'Our Lord, perfect our light for us and forgive us!
    You have power over all things.'

9   O Prophet! do jihad against the unbelievers and hypocrites
    and be harsh with them.
Their refuge is Hell.
    What an evil destination!

10   Allah has made an example for those who disbelieve:
    the wife of Nuh and the wife of Lut.
They were married to two of Our righteous slaves
    but they betrayed them
        and were not helped at all against Allah.
They were told, 'Enter the Fire along with all who enter it.'

11   Allah has made an example for those who believe:
    the wife of Pharaoh when she said,
'My Lord, build a house in the Garden for me in Your presence
    and rescue me from Pharaoh and his deeds
        and rescue me from this wrongdoing people.'
12   And Maryam, the daughter of 'Imran,
    who guarded her chastity – We breathed Our Ruh into her
        and she confirmed the Words of her Lord and His Books
        and was one of the obedient.

Sura 67

Al-Mulk
The Kingdom

In the name of Allah, All-Merciful, Most Merciful

1   Blessed be He who has the Kingdom in His Hand!
       He has power over all things.

2   He who created death and life
       to test which of you is best in action.
    He is the Almighty, the Ever-Forgiving.

3   He who created the seven heavens in layers.
          You will not find any flaw
             in the creation of the All-Merciful.
    Look again – do you see any gaps?
4   Then look again and again.
    Your sight will return to you
          dazzled and exhausted!

5   We have adorned the lowest heaven with lamps
       and made some of them stones for the shaytans
    for whom We have prepared the punishment of the Blaze.

6   Those who reject their Lord will have
          the punishment of Hell.
             What an evil destination!
7   When they are flung into it
       they will hear it gasping harshly as it seethes.
8   It all but bursts with rage.
          Each time a group is flung into it
             its custodians will question them:
          'Did no warner come to you?'

9   They will say, 'Yes indeed,
            a warner did come to us
                but we denied him and said,
            "Allah has sent nothing down.
                You are just greatly misguided."'

10   They will say, 'If only we had really listened and used our intellect,
            we would not have been Companions of the Blaze.'

11   Then they will acknowledge their wrong actions.
            Away with the Companions of the Blaze!

12   Those who fear their Lord in the Unseen
            will have forgiveness and an immense reward.

13   Whether you keep your words secret
            or say them out loud
        He knows what the heart contains.

14   Does He who created not then know?
            He is the All-Pervading, the All-Aware.

15   It is He who made the earth submissive to you,
            so walk its broad trails and eat what it provides.
                The Resurrection is to Him.

16   Do you feel secure against Him Who is in heaven
            causing the earth to swallow you up
        when suddenly it rocks from side to side?

17   Or do you feel secure against Him Who is in heaven
            releasing against you a sudden squall of stones,
        so that you will know how true My warning was?

18   Those before them also denied
            but then how great was My denial!

19   Have they not looked at the birds above them,
            with wings outspread and folded back?
        Nothing holds them up but the All-Merciful.
            He sees all things.

20   Who is there who could be a force for you,
            to come to your support,
                apart from the All-Merciful?
        The unbelievers are only living in delusion.

21   Who is there who could provide for you
         if He withholds His provision?
     Yet still they obstinately persist in insolence and evasion.

22   Who is better guided:
         he who goes grovelling on his face
     or he who walks upright on a straight path?

23   Say: 'It is He who brought you into being
         and gave you hearing, sight and hearts.
             What little thanks you show!'

24   Say: 'It is He who scattered you about the earth
         and you will be gathered to Him.'

25   They say, 'When will this promise come about
         if you are telling the truth?'

26   Say: 'The knowledge is with Allah alone
         and I am only a clear warner.'

27   When they see it right up close,
         the faces of those who disbelieve
             will be appalled
         and they will be told,
     'This is what you were calling for.'

28   Say: 'What do you think?
         If Allah destroys me and those with me,
             or if He has mercy on us,
         who can shelter the unbelievers
             from a painful punishment?'

29   Say: 'He is the All-Merciful.
     We believe in Him
         and trust in Him.
     You will soon know
         who is clearly misguided.'

30   Say: 'What do you think?
         If, one morning, your water disappears into the earth
             who will bring you running water?'

Sura 68

Al-Qalam
The Pen

In the name of Allah, All-Merciful, Most Merciful

1   Nun
By the Pen and what they write down!

2   By the blessing of your Lord, you are not mad.

3   You will have a wage which never fails.

4   Indeed you are truly vast in character.

5   So you will see and they will see
6   which of you is mad.

7   Your Lord knows best who is misguided from His Way
and He knows best those who are guided.

8   So do not obey those who deny the truth.

9   They wish that you would conciliate them,
then they too would be conciliating.

10   But do not obey any vile swearer of oaths,
11   any backbiter, slandermonger,
12   impeder of good, evil aggressor,
13   gross, coarse and furthermore, despicable,
14   simply because he possesses wealth and sons.

15   When Our Signs are recited to him, he says,
'Just myths of previous peoples!'

16   We will brand him on the snout!

17   We have tried them as We tried the owners of the garden
            when they swore that they would harvest in the morning
18   but did not say the redeeming words, 'If Allah wills'.

19   So a visitation from your Lord came upon it while they slept
20   and in the morning it was like burnt land stripped bare.

21   In the morning they called out to one another,
22   'Leave early for your land if you want to pick the fruit.'
23   So they set off, quietly saying to one another,
24   'Do not let any poor man into it today while you are there.'
25   They left early, intent on carrying out their scheme.

26   But when they saw it, they said, 'We must have lost our way.
27   No, the truth is we are destitute!'
28   The best of them said, 'Did I not say to you,
            "Why do you not glorify Allah?"'
29   They said, 'Glory be to our Lord!
            Truly we have been wrongdoers.'
30   They turned to face each other in mutual accusation.
31   They said, 'Woe to us! We were indeed inordinate.
32   Maybe our Lord will give us
            something better than it in exchange.
                We entreat our Lord.'

33   Such is the punishment.
            And the punishment of the Next World is much greater
            if they only knew.

34   The godfearing
            will have Gardens of Delight with their Lord.

35   Would We make the Muslims the same as the evildoers?

36   What is the matter with you?
            On what basis do you judge?

37   Or do you have a Book which you study,
38   so that you may have anything in it you choose?
39   Or do you have oaths which bind Us,
                extending to the Day of Rising,
            that you will have whatever you decide?

40   Ask them which of them stands as guarantor for that!

41   Or do they have Divine partners?
         Then let them produce their partners
            if they are telling the truth!

42   On the Day when legs are bared
         and they are called on to prostrate,
            they will not be able to do so.
43   Their eyes will be downcast, darkened by debasement;
         for they were called on to prostrate
when they were in full possession of their faculties.

44   So leave anyone who denies this discourse to Me!
         We will lead them, step by step, into destruction
            from where they do not know.
45   I will allow them more time.
         My subterfuge is sure.

46   Or do you ask them for a wage
         so they are weighed down with debt?
47   Or is the Unseen in their hands,
         so they can write out what is to happen?

48   So wait steadfastly for the judgement of your Lord.
         Do not be like the Companion of the Fish*
            when he called out in absolute despair.
49   Had a blessing from his Lord not overtaken him,
         he would have been thrown up on the naked shore,
            for he was at fault.
50   But his Lord chose him and made him one of the righteous.

51   Those who disbelieve all but strike you down
         with their evil looks
            when they hear the Reminder
         and say, 'He is quite mad.'

52   But it is nothing less than a Reminder to all the worlds.

---

*The Prophet Yunus.

Sura 69

Al-Haqqa
The Undeniable

In the name of Allah, All-Merciful, Most Merciful

1	The Undeniable! What is the Undeniable?
2	What will convey to you what the Undeniable is?
3	Thamud and 'Ad denied the Crushing Blow.
4	Thamud were destroyed by the Deafening Blast.
5	'Ad were destroyed by a savage howling wind.

6	Allah subjected them to it for seven whole nights
	    and eight whole days without a break.
	You could see the people flattened in their homes
	    just like the hollow stumps of uprooted palms.

7	Do you see any remnant of them left?
8	Pharaoh and those before him and the Upturned Cities made a great mistake.
9	They disobeyed the Messenger of their Lord so He seized them in an ever-tightening grip.
10	When the waters rose We carried you in the ship
11	to make it a reminder for you and something to be retained by retentive ears.
12	So when the Trumpet is blown with a single blast,

13	and the earth and the mountains
	    are lifted and crushed
	        with a single blow,

14	On that Day, the Occurrence will occur
15	and Heaven will be split apart,
	for that Day it will be very frail.
16	The angels will be gathered round its edge.
	On that Day, eight will bear the Throne of their Lord
	above their heads.
17	On that Day you will be exposed –
	no concealed act you did
	will stay concealed.

18	As for him who is given his Book in his right hand,
	he will say, 'Here, come and read my Book!
19	I counted on meeting my Reckoning.'
20	He will have a very pleasant life
21	in an elevated Garden,
22	its ripe fruit hanging close to hand.
23	'Eat and drink with relish
	for what you did before in days gone by!'

24	But as for him who is given his Book in his left hand,
25	he will say, 'If only I had not been given my Book
26	and had not known about my Reckoning!
27	If only death had really been the end!
28	My wealth has been of no avail to me.
29	My power has vanished.'
30	'Seize him and truss him up.
31	Then roast him in the Blazing Fire.
32	Then bind him in a chain
	which is seventy cubits long.
33	He used not to believe in Allah the Magnificent,
34	nor did he urge the feeding of the poor.
35	Therefore here today he has no friend
36	nor any food except exuding pus
37	which no one will eat except those
	who were in error.'

38	I swear both by what you see
39	and what you do not see,
40	that this is the word of a noble Messenger.

41	It is not the word of a poet –
	how little faith you have!
42	Nor the word of a fortune-teller –
	how little heed you pay!

43 It is a revelation from the Lord of all the worlds.

44 If he had made up any sayings and ascribed them to Us,
45   We would have seized him by force,
46 and then We would have cut off his life-blood
47   and not one of you could have protected him.

48 It is a reminder to the godfearing.

49 We know that some of you will deny it.

50 It is a cause of great distress to those who disbelieve.

51 And it is undeniably the Truth of Certainty.

52 Glorify then the name of your Lord, the Magnificent.

Sura 70

Al-Ma'arij
The Ascending Steps

In the name of Allah, All-Merciful, Most Merciful

1   An inquirer asked about an impending punishment.

2   It is for the unbelievers and cannot be averted,
3   from Allah – the Lord of the Ascending Steps.
4   The angels and the Spirit ascend to Him in a day
        whose length is fifty thousand years.

5   Therefore be patient with a patience which is beautiful.

6   They see it as something distant,
7   but We see it as very close.

8   On the Day the sky is like molten brass
9   and the mountains like tufts of coloured wool.
10 no good friend will ask about his friend
11   even though they can see each other.
    An evildoer will wish he could ransom himself
        from the punishment of that Day,
            by means of his sons,
12   or his wife or his brother
13   or his family who sheltered him
14   or everyone else on earth,
        if that only meant that he could save himself.

15 But no! It is a Raging Blaze
16   stripping away the limbs and scalp,

17   which calls for all who drew back
               and turned away,
18   and amassed and hoarded up.

19   Truly man was created headstrong –
20   desperate when bad things happen,
21   begrudging when good things come –
22   except for those who do the prayer
23   and are constant in it;
24   those in whose wealth there is a known share
25   for beggars and the destitute;
26   those who affirm the Day of Judgement,
27   those who are fearful of the punishment of their Lord
28   (no one is safe from the punishment of his Lord);
29   those who guard their private parts
30   except from their wives and any slaves they own,
                    in which case they incur no blame,
31   but if anyone desires any more than that,
                    they have overstepped the limits;
32   those who honour their trusts and contracts;
33   those who stand by their testimony;
34   those who safeguard their prayer;
35   such people will be in Gardens, highly honoured.

36   What is the matter with those who disbelieve?
               They run about in front of you,
                    with outstretched necks
                    and staring eyes,
37   on the right and on the left
                    in scattered groups!

38   Does each one of them aspire to be admitted
               into a Garden of Delight?

39   Certainly not! We created them
               from what they know full well.

40   No! I swear by the Lord of the Easts and Wests
               that We have the power
41   to replace them with something better than them.
               We will not be outstripped.

42   So leave them to plunge and play around
               until they meet their Day which they are promised.

43   The Day they will emerge swiftly from their graves
               as if rushing to rally to the flag,
44   eyes downcast, darkened by debasement,
      that will be the Day which they were promised.

Sura 71

Nuh
Noah

In the name of Allah, All-Merciful, Most Merciful

1 We sent Nuh to his people: 'Warn your people
  before a painful punishment comes to them.'

2 He said, 'My people, I am a clear warner to you.
3 Worship Allah, have taqwa of Him and obey me.
4 He will forgive you your wrong actions
  and defer you until a specified time.
 When Allah's time comes it cannot be deferred,
  if you only knew.'

5 He said, 'My Lord, I have called my people night and day
6 but my calling has only made them more evasive.
7 Indeed, every time I called them to Your forgiveness,
  they put their fingers in their ears,
   wrapped themselves up in their clothes
    and were overweeningly arrogant.
8 Then I called them openly.
9 Then I addressed them publicly
  and addressed them privately.
10 I said, "Ask forgiveness of your Lord.
  Truly He is Endlessly Forgiving.
11 He will send heaven down on you in abundant rain
12 and reinforce you with more wealth and sons,
   and grant you gardens and grant you waterways.
13 What is the matter with you that you do not hope
  for honour from Allah,
14 when He created you by successive stages?

15   Do you not see how He created seven heavens in layers,
16   and placed the moon as a light in them
            and made the sun a blazing lamp?
17   Allah caused you to grow from the earth
18   then will return you to it
            and bring you out again.
19   Allah has spread the earth out as a carpet for you
20   so that you could use its wide valleys as roadways."'

21   Nuh said, 'My Lord, they have disobeyed me
            and followed those whose wealth and children
            have only increased them in loss.
22   They have hatched a mighty plot
23   saying, "Do not abandon your gods.
    Do not abandon Wadd or Suwa'
        or Yaghuth or Ya'uq or Nasr."*
24   They have misguided many people.
    Do not increase the wrongdoers
        in anything but misguidance!'

25   Because of their errors they were drowned
        and put into the Fire.
    They found no one to help them besides Allah.

26   Nuh said, 'My Lord!
        do not leave a single one of the unbelievers on earth!
27   If You leave any they will misguide Your slaves
        and spawn nothing but more dissolute unbelievers.
28   My Lord! forgive me and my parents
        and all who enter my house as believers,
            and all the men and women of the believers.
    But do not increase the wrongdoers except in ruin!'

---

* These are the names of various pagan gods worshipped by the people of Nuh.

Sura 72

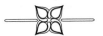

Al-Jinn
The Jinn

1   Say: 'It has been revealed to me that a band of the jinn listened
       and said, "We have heard a most amazing Recitation.

2   It leads to right guidance so we believe in it
       and will not associate anyone with our Lord.

3   He – exalted be the Majesty of our Lord! –
       has neither wife nor son.

4   The fools among us have uttered a vile slander against Allah.

5   We did not think it possible for either man or jinn
         to tell a lie against Allah.

6   Certain men from among mankind used to seek refuge
       with certain men from among the jinn
         but they increased them in wickedness.

7   They thought – as you also think –
       that Allah would never raise up anyone.

8   We tried, as usual, to travel to heaven in search of news
       but found it filled with fierce guards and meteors.

9   We used to sit there on special seats to listen in.
       But anyone listening now
         finds a fiery meteor in wait for him.

10   We have no idea whether evil is intended for those on earth,
       or whether their Lord intends them to be rightly guided.

11   Among us there are some who are righteous
       and some who are other than that.
         We follow many different paths.

12   We realised we would never thwart Allah on earth
       and would never thwart Him by flight,

13   and when we heard the guidance, we believed in it.

Anyone who believes in his Lord need fear
neither belittlement nor tyranny.

14   Some of us are Muslims
and some are deviators.
Those who have become Muslim
are those who sought right guidance;

15   the deviators will be firewood for Hellfire."'

16   If only they were to go straight on the Path,
We would give them abundant water to drink

17   so that We could test them by it.
Whoever turns aside from the remembrance of his Lord,
He will introduce him to an arduous punishment.

18   All mosques belong to Allah
so do not call on anyone else besides Allah.

19   When the slave of Allah stands calling on Him,
they almost swarm all over him.

20   Say: 'I call only upon my Lord
and do not associate anyone else with Him.'

21   Say: 'I possess no power to do you harm
or to guide you right.'

22   Say: 'No one can protect me from Allah
and I will never find any refuge apart from Him –

23   only in transmitting from Allah, conveying His Messages.
As for him who disobeys Allah and His Messenger,
he will have the Fire of Hell,
remaining in it timelessly, for ever and ever.'

24   So that when they see what they were promised,
they will know who has less support and smaller numbers.

25   Say: 'I do not know whether what you are promised is close
or whether my Lord will appoint a longer time before it.'

26   He is the Knower of the Unseen,
and does not divulge His Unseen to anyone –

27   except a Messenger with whom He is well pleased,
and then He posts sentinels before him and behind him,

28   so that He may know that they have indeed
transmitted the Messages of their Lord.
He encompasses what is in their hands
and has counted the exact number of everything.

Sura 73

Al-Muzzammil
The Enwrapped

In the name of Allah, All-Merciful, Most Merciful

1 You who are enwrapped in your clothing!
2   stay up at night, except a little,
3   half of it, or a little less,
4   or a little more,
    and recite the Qur'an distinctly.

5 We will impose a weighty Word upon you.

6 Certainly rising at night has a stronger effect
    and is more conducive to concentration.

7 In the daytime much of your time
    is taken up by business matters.

8 Remember the Name of your Lord,
    and devote yourself to Him completely.
9 Lord of the East and West –
    there is no god but Him –
    so take Him as your Guardian.

10 Be steadfast in the face of what they say
    and cut yourself off from them –
      but courteously.

11 Leave the deniers, who live a life of ease, to Me,
    and tolerate them a little longer.

12	With Us there are shackles and a Blazing Fire
13	and food that chokes and a painful punishment,
14	on the Day the earth and mountains shake
	and the mountains become like shifting dunes.

15	We have sent you a Messenger to bear witness against you
	just as We sent Pharaoh a Messenger.
16	But Pharaoh disobeyed the Messenger,
	so We seized him with terrible severity.

17	How will you safeguard yourselves, if you disbelieve,
	against a Day which will turn children grey,
18	by which heaven will be split apart?
	His promise will be fulfilled.

19	This truly is a reminder, so let anyone who wills
	take the Way towards his Lord.

20	Your Lord knows that you stay up
	nearly two-thirds of the night –
	or half of it, or a third of it –
	and a group of those with you.
	Allah determines the night and day.
	He knows you will not keep count of it,
	so He has turned towards you.
	Recite as much of the Qur'an as is easy for you.
	He knows that some of you are ill
	and that others are travelling in the land
	seeking Allah's bounty,
	and that others are fighting in the Way of Allah.
	So recite as much of it as is easy for you.
	And establish the prayer and pay zakat
	and lend a generous loan to Allah.
	Whatever good you send ahead for yourselves
	you will find it with Allah as something better
	and as a greater reward.
	And seek forgiveness from Allah.
	Allah is Ever-Forgiving, Most Merciful.

Sura 74

Al-Muddaththir
The Enveloped

In the name of Allah, All-Merciful, Most Merciful

1	You who are enveloped in your cloak!
2	Arise and warn.
3	Magnify your Lord.
4	Purify your clothes.
5	Shun all filth.
6	Do not give out of a desire for gain.
7	Be steadfast for your Lord.
8	For when the Trumpet is blown,
9	that Day will be a difficult day,
10	not easy for the unbelievers.
11	Leave the person I created on his own to Me, alone,
12	him to whom I have given great wealth
13	and sons who stay with him,
14	and whose way I have smoothed.
15	Then he wants Me to add yet more!
16	No indeed! He is obdurate about Our Signs.
17	I will force him to climb a fiery slope.

18	He reflected and considered.
19	Curse him, how he considered!
20	Again curse him, how he considered!
21	Then he looked.
22	Then he frowned and glowered.
23	Then he drew back and was proud.
24	He said, 'This is nothing but magic from the past.
25	This is nothing but the words of a human being.'
26	I will roast him in Saqar.
27	What will convey to you what Saqar is?
28	It does not spare and does not ease up,
29	ceaselessly scorching the flesh.
30	There are nineteen in charge of it.
31	We have only appointed angels as masters of the Fire
	and We have only specified their number
	as a trial for those who disbelieve;
	so that those who were given the Book
	might gain in certainty,
	and those who believe
	might increase in their faith,
	and both those who were given the Book
	and the believers
	might have no doubt;
	and so that those with sickness in their hearts
	and the unbelievers
	might say, 'What did Allah intend by this example?'
	In this way Allah misguides those He wills
	and guides those He wills.
	No one knows the legions of your Lord but Him.
	This is nothing but a reminder to all human beings.
32	No indeed! By the moon
33	and the night when it withdraws
34	and the dawn when it grows bright,
35	it truly is one of the greatest of all things,
36	a warning to human beings:
37	for any of you who want to go forward
	or hang back.
38	Every self is held in pledge against what it earned,
39	except for the companions of the Right.

40	In Gardens they will ask
41	the evildoers:
42	'What caused you to enter Saqar?'
43	They will say, 'We were not among those who prayed
44	and we did not feed the poor.
45	We plunged with those who plunged
46	and denied the Day of Judgment
47	until the Certain came to us.'
48	The intercession of the interceders will not help them.
49	What is the matter with them
	that they run from the Reminder
50	like panicked donkeys
51	fleeing from a lion?
52	In fact each one of them wants to be given an unfurled scroll.
53	No indeed! The truth is they do not fear the Next World.
54	No indeed! It is truly a reminder
55	to which anyone who wills may pay heed.
56	But they will only pay heed if Allah wills.
	He is entitled to be feared and entitled to forgive.

Sura 75

Al-Qiyama
The Rising

1   No! I swear by the Day of Rising!

2   No! I swear by the self-reproaching self.

3   Does man imagine We will not reassemble his bones?
4   On the contrary! We are well able to reshape his fingers.

5   Yet man still wants to deny what is ahead of him,
6   asking, 'So when is the Day of Rising?'

7   But when the eyesight is dazzled,
8   and the moon is eclipsed,
9   and the sun and moon are fused together,
10   on that Day man will say, 'Where can I run?'
11   No indeed! There will be no safe place.

12   That Day the only resting place will be your Lord.

13   That Day man will be told what he did and failed to do.

14   In fact, man will be clear proof against himself
15   in spite of any excuses he might offer.

16   Do not move your tongue trying to hasten it.
17   Its collection and recitation are Our affair.
18   So when We recite it, follow its recitation.
19   Then its explanation is Our concern.

20   No indeed! But you love this fleeting world
21   and you disregard the Next World.

22   Faces that Day will be radiant,
23   gazing at their Lord.
24   And faces that Day will be glowering,
25   realising that a back-breaking blow has fallen.

26   No indeed! When it reaches the gullet
27   and he hears the words, 'Who can heal him now?'
28   and he knows it is indeed the final parting,
29   and one leg is entwined with the other:
30   that Day he will be driven to your Lord.

31   He neither affirmed the truth nor did he pray,
32   but rather denied the truth and turned away.
33   and then went off to his family, swaggering.

34   It is coming closer to you and closer.
35   Then closer to you and closer still.

36   Does man reckon he will be left to go on unchecked?

37   Was he not a drop of ejaculated sperm,
38   then a blood-clot which He created and shaped,
39   making from it both sexes, male and female?

40   Is He who does this not able to bring the dead to life?

Sura 76

Al-Insan
Man

In the name of Allah, All-Merciful, Most Merciful

1   Has man ever known a point of time
        when he was not something remembered?

2   We created man from a mingled drop to test him,
        and We made him hearing and seeing.
3   We guided him on the Way,
        whether he is thankful or unthankful.

4   We have made ready for the unbelievers
        shackles and chains and a Searing Blaze.

5   The truly good will drink from a cup
        mixed with the coolness of camphor,
6   a spring from which Allah's slaves will drink,
        making it gush forth at will abundantly.

7   They fulfil their vows and fear a Day
        whose evil will spread far and wide.
8   They give food, despite their love for it,
        to the poor and orphans and captives:
9   'We feed you only out of desire for the Face of Allah.
        We do not want any repayment from you or any thanks.
10   Truly We fear from our Lord a glowering, calamitous Day.'

11   So Allah has safeguarded them from the evil of that Day
        and has made them meet with radiance and pure joy,
12   and will reward them for their steadfastness
        with a Garden and with silk.

13   Reclining in it on couches, they will experience there
        neither burning sun nor bitter cold.

14   Its shading branches will droop down over them,
        its ripe fruit hanging ready to be picked.

15   Vessels of silver and goblets of pure crystal
        will be passed round among them,

16   crystalline silver –
        they have measured them very exactly.

17   They will be given there a cup to drink
        mixed with the warmth of ginger.

18   In it there is a flowing spring called Salsabil.

19   Ageless youths will circulate among them,
           serving them.
    Seeing them, you would think them scattered pearls.

20   Seeing them, you see delight and a great kingdom.

21   They will wear green garments of fine silk and rich brocade.
        They will be adorned with silver bracelets.
    And their Lord will give them a pure draught to drink.

22   'This is your reward.
        Your striving is fully acknowledged.'

23   It is We who have sent the Qur'an down to you little by little.

24   Therefore wait patiently for the judgement of your Lord.
        Do not obey any evildoer or thankless man among them.

25   Remember the Name of your Lord
        in the morning and the evening.

26   Prostrate to Him during the night
        and glorify Him throughout the long night.

27   These people love this fleeting world
        and have put the thought of a Momentous Day
           behind their backs.

28   We created them and made their joints strong,
        and if We wish We can replace them
           with others like them.

29   This truly is a Reminder,
        so whoever wills
    should take the Way towards his Lord.

30 But you will not will unless Allah wills.
    Allah is All-Knowing, All-Wise.

31 He admits whomever He wills into His mercy.
    But He has prepared a painful punishment
        for the wrongdoers

Sura 77

Al-Mursalat
Those Sent Forth

In the name of Allah, All-Merciful, Most Merciful

1	By those sent forth in succession,
2	by the violently gusting blasts,
3	by the scatterers scattering,
4	by the winnowers winnowing,
5	by those hurling a reminder,
6	excusing or warning,
7	what you are promised will certainly happen.
8	When the stars are extinguished,
9	when heaven is split open,
10	when the mountains are pulverised,
11	when the Messengers' time is appointed –
12	until what day is that deferred?
13	Until the Day of Decision.
14	And what will teach you what the Day of Decision is?
15	*On that Day, woe to the deniers!*
16	Did We not destroy the earlier peoples,
17	then succeed them with later ones?
18	That is how We deal with evildoers.
19	*On that Day, woe to the deniers!*
20	Did We not create you from a base fluid,
21	then place it in a secure repository
22	for a recognised term?

23   It is We who determine.
          What an excellent Determiner!

24   *On that Day, woe to the deniers!*

25   Did We not make the earth a receptacle
26   for the living and the dead?
27   Did We not place firmly embedded mountains on it,
          soaring high into the air,
      and give you sweet fresh water to drink?

28   *On that Day, woe to the deniers!*

29   Proceed to that which you denied!
30   Proceed to a shadow which forks into three
31   but gives no shade or protection from the flames,
32   shooting up great sparks the size of castles,
33   like a herd of yellow camels.

34   *On that Day, woe to the deniers!*

35   This is the Day they will not say a single word,
36   nor will they be allowed to offer any excuses.

37   *On that Day, woe to the deniers!*

38   'This is the Day of Decision.
          We have gathered you and the earlier peoples.
39   So if you have a ploy, use it against Me now!'

40   *On that Day, woe to the deniers!*

41   The people with taqwa will be amid shade and fountains
42   and have any fruits that they desire:
43   'Eat and drink with relish for what you did.
44   This is the way We reward good-doers.'

45   *On that Day, woe to the deniers!*

46   'Eat and enjoy yourselves for a little while.
          You are evildoers.'

47   *On that Day, woe to the deniers!*

48   When they are told to bow, they do not bow.

49   *On that Day, woe to the deniers!*

50   In what discourse after this, then, will they believe?

Sura 78

An-Naba'
The News

In the name of Allah, All-Merciful, Most Merciful

1	About what are they asking one another?
2	About the momentous news:
3	the thing about which they differ.
4	No indeed! They will soon know!
5	Again, no indeed! They will soon know!
6	Have We not made the earth a flat carpet
7	and the mountains its pegs?
8	We have created you in pairs.
9	We made your sleep a break.
10	We made the night a cloak.
11	We made the day for earning a living.
12	We built seven firm layers above you.
13	We installed a blazing lamp.
14	We sent down cascading water from the clouds
15	so that by it We might bring forth grains and plants
16	and luxuriant gardens.

17   The Day of Decision is a fixed appointment:
18   the Day the Trumpet is blown
                  and you come in droves,
19   and heaven is opened
                  and becomes doorways,
20   and the mountains are shifted
                  and become a mirage.

21   Hell lies in wait –
22   a homecoming for the profligate
23   remaining in it for countless aeons,
24   not tasting any coolness there or any drink,
25   except for boiling water and scalding pus –
26   a fitting recompense.

27   They did not expect to have a reckoning
28   and utterly denied Our Signs.
29   We have recorded all things in writing.
30   So taste!
      We will increase you only in punishment.

31   For the godfearing there is triumph:
32   Gardens and grape vines,
33   and nubile maidens of similar age,
34   and an overflowing cup,
35   where they will hear no prattle
                  and no denial,
36   a recompense from your Lord,
                  a commensurate gift.

37   Lord of the heavens and earth
            and everything between them,
                  the All-Merciful.
      They will not have the power to speak to Him.

38   On the Day when the Spirit and the angels stand in ranks,
            no one will speak,
      except for him who is authorised by the All-Merciful
            and says what is right.

39   That will be the True Day.
            So whoever wills should
      take the way back to his Lord.

40   We have warned you of an imminent punishment
          on the Day when a man will see what he has done,
      and the unbeliever will say, 'Oh, if only I were dust!'

Sura 79

An-Nazi'at
The Pluckers

In the name of Allah, All-Merciful, Most Merciful

1	By those who pluck out harshly,
2	and those who draw out gently,
3	and those who glide serenely,
4	and those who outrun easily,
5	and those who direct affairs.
6	On the Day the first blast shudders,
7	and the second blast follows it,
8	hearts that Day will be pounding
9	and eyes cast down.
10	They will say, 'Are we to be restored to how we were?
11	when we have become perished, worm-eaten bones?'
12	They say, 'That will clearly be a losing restoration!'
13	There will be but one Great Blast,
14	and at once they will be on the surface, wide awake!
15	Has the story of Musa reached you:
16	when his Lord called out to him
	in the holy valley of Tuwa?
17	'Go to Pharaoh – he has overstepped the limits –
18	and say: "Do you resolve to purify yourself.
19	I will guide you to your Lord
	so that you may fear Him?"'

20	Then he showed him the Great Sign.
21	But he denied it and disobeyed,
22	and then he hastily backed away.
23	But then he rallied and called out,
24	saying, 'I am your Lord Most High!'
25	So Allah made an example of him seizing him with punishment in the Next World and in this world.
26	There is certainly instruction in that for those who fear.
27	Are you stronger in structure or is heaven? He built it.
28	He raised its vault high and made it level.
29	He darkened its night and brought forth its morning light.
30	After that He smoothed out the earth
31	and brought forth from it its water and its pastureland
32	and made the mountains firm,
33	for you and for your livestock to enjoy.
34	When the Great Calamity comes:
35	that Day man will remember what he has striven for
36	and the Blazing Fire will be displayed for all who can see.
37	As for him who overstepped the bounds
38	and preferred the life of this world,
39	the Blazing Fire will be his refuge.
40	But as for him who feared the Station of his Lord and forbade the lower self its appetites,
41	the Garden will be his refuge.
42	They ask you about the Hour: 'When will it come?'
43	What are you doing mentioning it?
44	Its coming is your Lord's affair.
45	You are only the warner of those who fear it.

46   On the Day they see it,
                it will be as if they had only lingered
              for the evening or the morning of a single day.

Sura 80

'Abasa
He Frowned

In the name of Allah, All-Merciful, Most Merciful

1   He frowned and turned away
2   because the blind man came to him.*
3   But how do you know?
        Perhaps he would be purified
4   or reminded,
        and the reminder benefit him.

5   As for him who thinks himself self-sufficient,
6   you give him your complete attention,
7   but it is not up to you whether or not he is purified.

8   But as for him who comes to you eagerly
9   showing fearfulness,
10 from him you are distracted.

11 No indeed! Truly it is a reminder,
12   and whoever wills pays heed to it.
13 Inscribed on Honoured Pages,
14   exalted, purified
15 by the hands of scribes,
16   noble, virtuous.

17 Curse man for his ingratitude!

18 From what thing did He create him?

---

* The blind man was 'Abdullah ibn Umm Maktum. The Prophet stopped him doing what he was doing because he was hoping that some of the nobles of Quraysh would become Muslim and he was eager for that to happen.

19   From a drop of sperm He created him
            and proportioned him.

20   Then He eases the way for him.

21   Then He causes him to die and buries him.

22   Then, when He wills, He raises him from the dead.

23   No indeed!
         He has not done what He ordered him.

24   Man has only to look at his food.

25   We pour down plentiful water,

26   then split the earth into furrows.

27   Then We make grain grow in it,

28   and grapes and herbs

29   and olives and dates

30   and luxuriant gardens

31   and orchards and meadows,

32   for you and your livestock to enjoy.

33   When the Deafening Blast comes,

34   the Day a man will flee from his brother

35   and his mother and his father,

36   and his wife and his children:

37   on that Day every man among them will have
            concerns enough of his own.

38   That Day some faces will be radiant,

39   laughing, rejoicing.

40   That Day some faces will be dust-covered,

41   overcast with gloom.

42   Those are the dissolute unbelievers.

Sura 81

At-Takwir
The Compacting

In the name of Allah, All-Merciful, Most Merciful

1	When the sun is compacted in blackness,
2	when the stars fall in rapid succession,
3	when the mountains are set in motion,
4	when the camels in foal are neglected,
5	when the wild beasts are all herded together,
6	when the oceans surge into each other,
7	when the selves are arranged into classes,
8	when the baby girl buried alive is asked
9	for what crime she was killed,
10	when the Pages are opened up,
11	when the Heaven is peeled away,
12	when the Fire is set ablaze,
13	when the Garden is brought up close:
14	then each self will know what it has done.
15	No! I swear by the planets with their retrograde motion,
16	swiftly moving, self-concealing,
17	and by the night when it draws in,
18	and by the dawn when it exhales,
19	truly it is the speech of a noble Messenger,
20	possessing great strength,
	securely placed with the Lord of the Throne,
21	obeyed there, trustworthy.
22	Your companion is not mad.
23	He saw him on the clear horizon.

24   Nor is he miserly with the Unseen.

25   Nor is it the word of an accursed Shaytan.

26   So where, then, are you going?

27   It is nothing but a Reminder to all the worlds,
28   to whomever among you wishes to go straight.

29   But you will not will unless Allah wills,
         the Lord of all the Worlds.

Sura 82

Al-Infitar
The Splitting

In the name of Allah, All-Merciful, Most Merciful

1	When the sky is split apart,
2	when the stars are strewn about,
3	when the seas flood and overflow,
4	when the graves are emptied out,
5	each self will know
	what it has sent ahead and left behind.
6	O man! what has deluded you in respect of your Noble Lord?
7	He Who created you and formed you and proportioned you
8	and assembled you in whatever way He willed.
9	Yes indeed! But still you deny the Judgement.
10	Standing over you are guardians,
11	noble, recording,
12	who know what you do.
13	The truly good will be in perfect Bliss.
14	The dissolute will be in a Blazing Fire.
15	They will roast in it on the Day of Judgment
16	and will never escape from it.
17	What will convey to you what the Day of Judgement is?
18	Again! What will convey to you what the Day of Judgement is?

19   It is the Day when a self will have no power
                to help any other self in any way.
      The command that Day will be Allah's alone.

Sura 83

Al-Mutaffifin
The Stinters

In the name of Allah, All-Merciful, Most Merciful

1	Woe to the stinters!
2	Those who, when they take a measure from people, exact full measure,
3	but when they give them a measure or weight, hand over less than is due.
4	Do such people not realise that they will be raised up
5	on a Terrible Day,
6	the Day mankind will stand before the Lord of all the worlds?
7	No indeed! The book of the dissolute is in Sijjin.
8	And what will convey to you what Sijjin is?
9	A clearly written Book.
10	Woe that Day to the deniers:
11	those who deny the Day of Reckoning.
12	No one denies it except for every evil aggressor.
13	When Our Signs are recited to him, he says, 'Just myths and legends of the previous peoples!'
14	No indeed! Rather what they have earned has rusted up their hearts.
15	No indeed! Rather that Day they will be veiled from their Lord.
16	Then they will roast in the Blazing Fire.
17	Then they will be told, 'This is what you denied.'

18   No indeed! The book of the truly good is in 'Illiyun.

19   And what will convey to you what 'Illiyun is?

20   A clearly written book.

21   Those brought near will witness it.

22   The truly good will be in perfect Bliss

23   on couches gazing in wonder.

24   You will recognise in their faces the radiance of delight.

25   They are given the choicest sealed wine to drink,

26   whose seal is musk –

         let people with aspiration aspire to that! –

27   mixed with Tasnim:

28   a fountain at which Those Brought Near will drink.

29   Those who did evil used to laugh at those who believed.

30   When they passed by them,

         they would wink at one another.

31   When they returned to their families,

         they would make a joke of them.

32   When they saw them,

         they would say, 'Those people are misguided.'

33   But they were not sent as guardians over them.

34   So today those who believe are laughing at the unbelievers,

35   on couches, gazing in wonder.

36   Have not the unbelievers been rewarded for what they did?

Sura 84

Al-Inshiqaq
The Bursting

In the name of Allah, All-Merciful, Most Merciful

1   When the sky bursts open,
2   hearkening to its Lord as it is bound to do!

3   When the earth is flattened out
4   and disgorges what is inside it
       and empties out,
5   hearkening to its Lord as it is bound to do!

6   O Man! You are toiling laboriously towards your Lord
     but meet Him you will!

7   As for him who is given his Book in his right hand,
8   he will be given an easy reckoning
9   and return to his family joyfully.

10   But as for him who is given his Book behind his back,
11   he will cry out for destruction
12   but will be roasted in a Searing Blaze.

13   He used to be joyful in his family.
14   He thought that he was never going to return.
15   But in fact his Lord was always watching him!

16   No, I swear by the evening glow,
17   and the night and all it shrouds,
18   and the moon when it is full,
19   you will mount up stage by stage!

20   What is the matter with them that they do not believe
21   and, when the Qur'an is recited to them, do not prostrate?

22   In fact those who disbelieve say that it is lies.
23   But Allah knows best what they are storing in their hearts.

24   Give them the news of a painful punishment –
25   except those who believe and do right actions:
             they will have a wage which never fails.

Sura 85

Al-Buruj
The Houses of the Zodiac

In the name of Allah, All-Merciful, Most Merciful

1 By Heaven with its Houses of the Zodiac,
2   and the Promised Day,
3   and the witness and the witnessed,
4 cursed be the Companions of the Pit –
5   the fire well stocked with fuel –
6 when they were seated right beside it
7   witnessing what they did to the believers.

8 The only reason they punished them
      was because they believed in Allah,
         the Almighty, the All-Praiseworthy –
9   Him to whom the Kingdom of the heavens
         and the earth belongs.
      Allah is Witness of all things.

10 Those who persecute men and women of the believers,
      and then do not repent,
         will have the punishment of Hell,
      will have the punishment of the Burning.
11 But those who believe and do right actions
      will have Gardens with rivers flowing under them.
         That is the Great Victory.

12 Your Lord's Assault is very fierce indeed.

13 He originates and regenerates.

14   He is the Ever-Forgiving, the All-Loving,
15   the Possessor of the Throne, the All-Glorious,
16   the Doer of whatever He desires.

17   Has the story reached you of the legions
18   of Pharaoh and Thamud?

19   Yet those who disbelieve insist on their denial
20   while Allah is encircling them from behind.

21   It is indeed a Glorious Qur'an
22   preserved on a Tablet.

Sura 86

At-Tariq
The Night-Comer

In the name of Allah, All-Merciful, Most Merciful

1	By Heaven and the Night-Comer!
2	And what will convey to you what the Night-Comer is?
3	The Piercing Star!
4	There is no self which has no guardian over it.
5	Man has only to look at what he was created from.
6	He was created from a spurting fluid,
7	emerging from between the back-bone and the breast-bone.
8	He certainly has the power to return him to life.
9	on the Day when the secrets are sought out
10	and man will have no strength or helper.
11	By Heaven with its cyclical systems
12	and the earth with its splitting seeds,
13	it is truly a Decisive Word.
14	It is no joke.
15	They are hatching a plot.
16	I too am hatching a plot.
17	So bear with the unbelievers –
	bear with them for a while.

Sura 87

Al-A'la
The Most High

In the name of Allah, All-Merciful, Most Merciful

1	Glorify the Name of your Lord, the Most High:
2	He who created and moulded;
3	He who determined and guided;
4	He who brings forth green pasture,
5	then makes it blackened stubble.
6	We will cause you to recite
	so that you do not forget –
7	except what Allah wills.
	He knows what is voiced out loud
	and what is hidden.
8	We will ease you to the Easy Way.
9	Remind, then, if the reminder benefits.
10	He who has fear will be reminded;
11	but the most miserable will shun it,
12	those who will roast in the Greatest Fire
13	and then neither die nor live in it.
14	He who has purified himself will have success,
15	he who invokes the Name of his Lord and prays.
16	Yet still you prefer the life of this world
17	when the Next World is better and longer lasting.
18	This is certainly in the earlier texts,
19	the texts of Ibrahim and Musa.

Sura 88

Al-Ghashiyya
The Overwhelmer

1   Has news of the Overwhelmer reached you?

2   Some faces on that Day will be downcast,
3   labouring, toiling endlessly,
4   roasting in a red-hot Fire,
5   drinking from a boiling spring.
6   They have no food but a bitter thorny bush
7   which neither nourishes nor satisfies.

8   Some faces on that Day will be radiant,
9   well-pleased with their efforts
10   in an elevated Garden
11   where no prattle is ever heard.
12   In it is a gushing spring
13   and raised-up couches,
14   and set-out goblets,
15   and lined-up cushions,
16   and spread-out rugs.

17   Have they not looked at the camel –
       how it was created?
18   and at the sky –
       how it was raised up?
19   and at the mountains –
       how they were embedded?
20   and at the earth –
       how it was smoothed out?

21 So remind them!
    You are only a reminder.
22 You are not in control of them.

23 But as for anyone who turns away and disbelieves,
24   Allah will punish him with the Greatest Punishment.

25 Certainly it is to Us they will return.
26   Then their Reckoning is Our concern.

Sura 89

Al-Fajr
The Dawn

In the name of Allah, All-Merciful, Most Merciful

1	By the dawn
2	and ten nights,
3	and the even and odd,
4	and the night when it travels on,
5	is there not in that an oath for the intelligent?

6	Do you not see what your Lord did with 'Ad –
7	Iram of the Columns
8	whose like was not created in any land –
9	and Thamud who carved out rocks in the valley-side,
10	and Pharaoh of the Stakes,
11	all of whom were tyrants in their lands
12	and caused much corruption in them?
13	So your Lord unleashed on them a scourging punishment;
14	your Lord is always lying in wait.

15	As for man, when his Lord tests him
	by honouring him and favouring him,
	he says, 'My Lord has honoured me!'

16	But then when He tests him
	by restricting his provision,
	he says, 'My Lord has humiliated me!'

17	No indeed! You do not honour orphans
18	nor do you urge the feeding of the poor;
19	you devour inheritance with voracious appetites
20	and you have an insatiable love of wealth.

21	No indeed! When the earth is crushed and ground to dust
22	and your Lord arrives with the angels rank upon rank
23	and that Day Hell is produced,
24	that Day man will remember;
	but how will the remembrance help him?
25	He will say, 'Oh! If only I had prepared in advance
	for this life of mine!'
26	That Day no one will punish as He punishes
27	and no one will shackle as He shackles.
28	'O self at rest and at peace,
29	return to your Lord,
	well-pleasing and well-pleased!
30	Enter among My slaves! Enter My Garden.'

Sura 90

Al-Balad
The City

In the name of Allah, All-Merciful, Most Merciful

1	I swear by this city –
2	and you are resident in this city –
3	and by a father and what he fathered,
4	We created man in trouble.
5	Does he imagine that no one has power over him?
6	He says, 'I have consumed vast quantities of wealth.'
7	Does he imagine that no one has seen him?
8	Have We not given him two eyes,
9	and a tongue and two lips
10	and shown him the two highways?
11	But he has not braved the steep ascent.
12	What will convey to you what the steep ascent is?
13	It is freeing a slave
14	or feeding on a day of hunger
15	an orphaned relative
16	or a poor man in the dust;
17	then to be one of those who believe
	and urge each other to steadfastness
	and urge each other to compassion.
18	Those are the Companions of the Right.
19	Those who reject Our signs,
	they are the Companions of the Left.
20	Above them is a sealed vault of Fire.

Sura 91

Ash-Shams
The Sun

In the name of Allah, All-Merciful, Most Merciful

1	By the sun and its morning brightness,
2	and the moon when it follows it,
3	and the day when it displays it,
4	and the night when it conceals it
5	and the sky and what erected it
6	and the earth and what extended it.
7	and the self and what proportioned it
8	and inspired it with depravity or taqwa,
9	he who purifies it has succeeded,
10	he who covers it up has failed.
11	Thamud denied in their excessive tyranny –
12	when the worst of them rushed ahead,
13	and the Messenger of Allah had said to them, 'This is the she-camel of Allah, so let her drink!'
14	But they denied him and they hamstrung her, so their Lord crushed them for their sin and flattened them.
15	And He does not fear the consequences.

Sura 92

Al-Layl
The Night

1	By the night when it conceals
2	and the day when it reveals
3	and the creation of male and female,
4	there is a vast difference in your striving.
5	As for him who gives out and is godfearing
6	and confirms the Good,
7	We will pave his way to Ease.
8	But as for him who is stingy and self-satisfied,
9	and denies the Good,
10	We will pave his way to Difficulty.
11	His wealth will not help him
	when he plummets to the depths.
12	Assuredly guidance is up to Us
13	and both the Last and First belong to Us.
14	I have warned you of a Fire which rages,
15	in which only the most wretched will roast –
16	those who denied and turned away.
17	Those with most taqwa will be far removed from it:
18	those who give their wealth to purify themselves –
19	not to repay someone else for a favour done –
20	desiring only the Face of their Lord Most High.
21	They will certainly be satisfied.

Sura 93

Ad-Duha
The Morning Brightness

In the name of Allah, All-Merciful, Most Merciful

1	By the morning brightness
2	and the night when it is still,
3	your Lord has not abandoned you
	nor does He hate you.
4	The Last will be better for you than the First.
5	Your Lord will soon give to you and you will be satisfied.
6	Did He not find you orphaned and shelter you?
7	Did He not find you wandering and guide you?
8	Did He not find you impoverished and enrich you?
9	So as for orphans, do not oppress them,
10	and as for beggars, do not berate them.
11	And as for the blessing of your Lord, speak out!

Sura 94

Al-Inshirah
The Expanding

In the name of Allah, All-Merciful, Most Merciful

1	Did We not expand your breast for you
2	and remove your load from you
3	which weighed down your back?
4	Did We not raise high your renown?
5	For truly with hardship comes ease;
6	truly with hardship comes ease.
7	So when you have finished, work on,
8	and make your Lord your goal!

Sura 95

At-Tin
The Fig

In the name of Allah, All-Merciful, Most Merciful

1   By the fig and the olive
2   and Mount Sinai
3   and this safe land,
4   We created man in the finest mould.

5   Then We reduced him to the lowest of the low,
6   except for those who believe and do right actions:
           they will have a wage which never fails.

7   What could make you deny the Reckoning after this?
8   Is Allah not the Justest of Judges?

Sura 96

Al-'Alaq
The Blood-clot

1   Recite: In the Name of your Lord who created,
2   created man from clots of blood.

3   Recite: And your Lord is the Most Generous,
4   He who taught by the pen,
5   taught man what he did not know.

6   No indeed! Truly man is unbridled
7   seeing himself as self-sufficient.

8   Truly it is to your Lord that you will return.

9   Have you seen him who prevents
10   a slave when he goes to pray?
11   Do you think he is rightly guided
12   or commands taqwa?
13   Or do you see how he has denied
            and turned away?
14   Does he not know that Allah sees?

15   No indeed! If he does not desist,
        We will grab him by the forelock,
16   a lying, sinful forelock.
17   Let him call his attendants;
18   We will call the Guards of Hell!

19   No indeed! Do not obey him,
        but prostrate and draw near.

Sura 97

Al-Qadr
Power

In the name of Allah, All-Merciful, Most Merciful

1   Truly We sent it down on the Night of Power.
2   And what will convey to you what the Night of Power is?
3   The Night of Power is better than a thousand months.

4   In it the angels and the Ruh descend
         by their Lord's authority
            with every ordinance.

5   It is Peace –
         until the coming of the dawn.

Sura 98

Al-Bayyina
The Clear Sign

In the name of Allah, All-Merciful, Most Merciful

1   The People of the Book who disbelieved and the idolators
     would not be cut off until the Clear Sign came to them:
2   a Messenger from Allah reciting purified texts
3   containing upright precepts.

4   Those who were given the Book did not divide into sects
     until after the Clear Sign came to them.
5   They were only ordered to worship Allah,
     making their deen sincerely His
       as people of pure natural faith,
   and to establish the prayer and pay zakat –
     that is the correct deen.

6   The People of the Book who disbelieve and the idolators
     will be in the Fire of Hell,
       remaining in it timelessly, for ever.
     They are the worst of creatures.
7   But those who believe and do right actions –
     they are the best of creatures.
8   Their reward is with their Lord:
     Gardens of Eden with rivers flowing under them,
       remaining in them timelessly, for ever and ever.
     Allah is pleased with them
       and they are pleased with Him.
   That is for those who fear their Lord.

Sura 99

Az-Zilzal
The Earthquake

In the name of Allah, All-Merciful, Most Merciful

1	When the earth is convulsed with its quaking
2	and the earth then disgorges its charges
3	and man asks, 'What is wrong with it?',
4	on that Day it will impart all its news
5	because your Lord has inspired it.
6	That Day people will emerge segregated
	to see the results of their actions.
7	Whoever does an atom's weight of good will see it.
8	Whoever does an atom's weight of evil will see it.

Sura 100

Al-'Adiyat
The Chargers

In the name of Allah, All-Merciful, Most Merciful

1	By the charging horses panting hard,
2	striking sparks from their flashing hooves,
3	raiding at full gallop in the early dawn,
4	leaving a trailing dust-cloud in their wake,
5	cleaving through the middle of the foe,
6	truly man is ungrateful to his Lord
7	and indeed he bears witness to that.
8	Truly he is fierce in his love of wealth.
9	Does he not know that when the graves are emptied out,
10	and the heart's contents are brought into the open,
11	that Day their Lord will certainly be aware of them.

Sura 101

Al-Qari'a
The Crashing Blow

In the name of Allah, All-Merciful, Most Merciful

1	The Crashing Blow!
2	What is the Crashing Blow?
3	What will convey to you what the Crashing Blow is?
4	It is the Day when mankind will be like scattered moths
5	and the mountains like tufts of coloured wool.
6	As for him whose balance is heavy,
7	he will have a most pleasant life.
8	But as for him whose balance is light,
9	his motherland is Hawiya.
10	And what will convey to you what that is?
11	A raging Fire!

Sura 102

At-Takathur
Competition

In the name of Allah, All-Merciful, Most Merciful

1   Fierce competition for this world distracted you
2   until you visited the graves.

3   No indeed, you will soon know!
4   Again no indeed, you will soon know!

5   No indeed, if you only knew with the Knowledge of Certainty,
6   you will certainly see the Blazing Fire!
7   Then you will certainly see it with the Eye of Certainty.

8   Then you will be asked that Day about the pleasures you enjoyed.

Sura 103

Al-'Asr
The Late Afternoon

In the name of Allah, All-Merciful, Most Merciful

1   By the Late Afternoon,
2   truly man is in loss –
3   except for those who believe and do right actions
        and urge each other to the truth
    and urge each other to steadfastness.

Sura 104

Al-Humaza
The Backbiter

In the name of Allah, All-Merciful, Most Merciful

1   Woe to every faultfinding backbiter
2   who has amassed wealth and hoarded it!
3   He thinks his wealth will make him live for ever.

4   No indeed!
        He will be flung into the Shatterer.
5   And what will convey to you what the Shatterer is?

6   The kindled Fire of Allah
7   reaching right into the heart.
8   It is sealed in above them
9   in towering columns.

Sura 105

Al-Fil
The Elephant

In the name of Allah, All-Merciful, Most Merciful

1   Do you not see what your Lord did
        with the Companions of the Elephant?*
2   Did He not bring all their schemes to nothing,
3   unleashing upon them flock after flock of birds,
4   bombarding them with stones of hard-baked clay,
5   making them like stripped wheat-stalks eaten bare?

---

* An army from Yemen containing an elephant which attacked Makka in the year of the
Prophet's birth, may Allah bless him and grant him peace.

Sura 106

Quraysh

In the name of Allah, All-Merciful, Most Merciful

1   In acknowledgment of the established tradition of Quraysh,
2   their tradition of the winter and summer caravans:
3   so let them worship the Lord of this House
4   who has preserved them from hunger
     and secured them from fear.

Sura 107

Al-Ma'un
Helping Others

In the name of Allah, All-Merciful, Most Merciful

1	Have you seen him who denies the deen?
2	He is the one who harshly rebuffs the orphan
3	and does not urge the feeding of the poor.
4	So woe to those who pray,
5	and are forgetful of their prayer,
6	those who show off
7	and deny help to others.

Sura 108

Al-Kawthar
The Great Abundance

In the name of Allah, All-Merciful, Most Merciful

1   Truly We have given you the Great Abundance.
2   So pray to your Lord and sacrifice.
3   It is the one who hates you who is cut off without an heir.

Sura 109

Al-Kafirun
The Rejectors

In the name of Allah, All-Merciful, Most Merciful

1	Say: 'Unbelievers!
2	I do not worship what you worship
3	and you do not worship what I worship.
4	Nor will I worship what you worship
5	nor will you worship what I worship.
6	You have your deen and I have my deen.'

Sura 110

An-Nasr
Victory

In the name of Allah, All-Merciful, Most Merciful

1 When Allah's help and victory have arrived
2   and you have seen people entering Allah's deen in droves,
3 then glorify your Lord's praise and ask His forgiveness.
        He is the Ever-Relenting.

Sura 111

Al-Masad
Palm Fibre

In the name of Allah, All-Merciful, Most Merciful

1   Ruin to the hands of Abu Lahab and ruin to him!

2   His wealth has not helped him nor anything he has earned.

3   He will burn in a Flaming Fire.

4   And so will his wife, the firewood-carrier,
5   with a rope of twisted fibre round her neck.

Sura 112

Al-Ikhlas
Sincerity

In the name of Allah, All-Merciful, Most Merciful

1   Say: 'He is Allah, Absolute Oneness,

2   Allah, the Everlasting Sustainer of all.

3   He has not given birth and was not born.

4   And no one is comparable to Him.'

Sura 113

Al-Falaq
Daybreak

In the name of Allah, All-Merciful, Most Merciful

1   Say: 'I seek refuge with the Lord of Daybreak,
2   from the evil of what He has created
3   and from the evil of the darkness when it gathers
4   and from the evil of women who blow on knots
5   and from the evil of an envier when he envies.'

Sura 114

An-Nas
Mankind

In the name of Allah, All-Merciful, Most Merciful

1   Say: 'I seek refuge with the Lord of mankind,
2   the King of mankind,
3   the God of mankind,
4   from the evil of the insidious whisperer
5   who whispers in people's breasts
6   and comes from the jinn and from mankind.'

Glossary of Terms

akhira	the Next World, what is on the other side of death.
Ansar	lit. the 'Helpers', the people of Madina who welcomed and aided the Prophet and the Muhajirun when they made hijra from Makka.
ayat	lit. sign, a verse of the Qur'an.
deen	life-transaction, religion in the broadest sense. The deen of Allah and the Muslim community is Islam but every society and cultural grouping have a deen which they follow.
dunya	this world, not as a cosmic phenomenon, but as experienced.
fidya	a ransom, compensation paid for rites or acts of worship missed or wrongly performed because of ignorance or ill health.
fatwa	a legal ruling.
fitna	civil strife, sedition, trial, temptation.
Furqan	something which discriminates between truth and falsehood; another name for the Qur'an.
hajj	the annual pilgrimage to Makka which is one of the five pillars of Islam.
halal	lawful in the Shari'a.
haram	unlawful in the Shari'a.
hijra	leaving one place and travelling to another for the sake of Allah and the establishment of His deen.
'idda	a period after divorce or the death of her husband for which a woman must wait before she may remarry.

ifreet	a powerful sort of jinn.
ihram	a state in which it is prohibited to practise certain deeds that are lawful at other times, in particular the state and dress assumed to perform the rites of 'umra and hajj.
iman	belief, faith, acceptance in the heart of Allah and His Messenger. Iman consists of believing in Allah, His angels, His Books, His Messengers, the Last Day, the Garden and the Fire, and that everything, both good and bad, is by the decree of Allah.
Injil	the Gospel, the revelation given to the Prophet 'Isa.
jihad	struggle, particularly fighting in the way of Allah to establish Islam.
jinn	inhabitants of the heavens and the earth made of smokeless fire who are usually invisible.
jizya	a protection tax payable by non-Muslims as a tribute to a Muslim ruler.
Jumu'a	the day of gathering, Friday, and particularly the Jumu'a prayer which is performed at midday on Friday instead of Salat adh-Dhuhr and which all the men in a Muslim community are expected to attend.
kafir	someone who rejects Allah and His Messenger and the deen of Islam.
kafirun	the plural of kafir.
khalif	someone who stands in for someone else or succeeds them, in Qur'anic usage it refers to man's position as vice-gerent of Allah on earth and in general usage to the ruler of all the Muslims.
kuffar	the plural of kafir.
kufr	disbelief, to cover up the truth, to reject Allah and refuse to believe that Muhammad is His Messenger.
Muhajirun	the Companions of the Messenger of Allah who accepted Islam in Makka and made hijra to Madina.
mumin	someone who possesses iman.
muminun	the plural of mumin.
munafiq	a hypocrite, someone who outwardly professes Islam

	on the tongue, but inwardly rejects Allah and His Messenger.
munafiqun	plural of munafiq.
mushrik	someone who commits the unforgiveable wrong action of worshipping something or someone other than Allah or of ascribing to something or someone attributes which in fact belong to Allah alone.
mushrikun	plural of mushrik.
nifaq	hypocrisy.
qibla	the direction faced in the prayer which is towards the Ka'ba in Makka but was, for a short time, towards Jerusalem.
riba	usury, which is forbidden, whatever forms it takes, since it it involves obtaining something for nothing through exploitation.
Ruh	the soul, vital spirit, the breath of life which emanates from Allah to His creatures. The Purest Ruh is a name given to the angel Jibril.
sadaqa:	voluntary charitable giving for the sake of Allah.
sadiqun:	truthful, true, sincere people, a term given to a high category of the muminun.
salat	the prayer, particularly the five daily obligatory prayers which constitute one of the pillars of Islam.
salih	someone who acts rightly.
salihun	plural of salih.
shaytan	a devil, particularly Iblis, one of the jinn.
siddiq	someone who is true to their word and absolutely sincere and unshakeable in their iman.
siddiqun	plural of siddiq.
sidq	truthfulness, sincerity, the quality possessed by the siddiq.
sura	a chapter of the Qur'an.
taqwa	awe or fear of Allah, which inspires a person to be on guard against wrong action and eager for actions which please Him.

tawba	returning to correct action after error, turning away from wrong action to Allah and asking His forgiveness, thus 'to make tawba'.
tayammum	purification for prayer with clean dust, earth, or stone, when water for purification is either unavailable or would be detrimental to health.
'umra	the lesser pilgrimage to the Ka'ba in Makka performed at any time of the year.
Zabur	the Psalms of Dawud.
zakat	one of the five pillars of Islam. It is an obligatory wealth tax paid on certain forms of wealth: gold and silver, stable crops, livestock, and trading goods when they are over a certain amount.

Glossary of Proper Names

Abu Lahab   'Father of Flame', the nickname of the uncle of the Prophet who was a fierce opponent of Islam. His wife was also renowned for persecution of the Muslims in Makka.

'Ad   an ancient people in southern Arabia to whom the Prophet Hud was sent. Their city was possibly Iram of the Pillars. (See Qur'an 89:6-8).

Ahmad   another name of the Prophet Muhammad.

Al-Ahqaf   'the Sand Dunes', the tracts of sand dunes where the people of 'Ad lived, next to Hadramawt and Yemen.

Ayyub   the Prophet Job.

Azar   the father of the Prophet Ibrahim.

Badr   a place near the coast, about 95 miles to the south of Madina where, in 2 AH in the first battle fought by the newly established Muslim community, the 313 outnumbered Muslims led by the Messenger of Allah overwhelmingly defeated 1000 Makkan idolaters.

Bakka   an ancient name for Makka.

Dawud   the Prophet David.

Dhu'l-Kifl   a Prophet mentioned in the Qur'an, possibly Ezekiel.

Dhu'n-Nun   'He of the Whale', another name for the Prophet Yunus.

Dhu'l-Qarnayn   lit. 'the two-horned', a name given to a great ruler in the past who ruled all over the world, and was a true believer. It is often thought to refer to Alexander the Great.

Firdaws   Paradise.

Haman	the minister of Pharaoh.
Harun	the Prophet Aaron.
Harut	Harut and Marut are two angels mentioned in the Qur'an (2:101) who were sent to Babylon and from whom mankind learned magic.
Hawiya	the abyss, a bottomless pit in Hell.
Al-Hijr	lit. 'the rocky tract', a town in Arabia about 150 miles north of Madina, where the people of Thamud lived.
Hud	the Prophet sent to the people of 'Ad.
Iblis	the personal name of the Devil, lit. 'seized by despair'. He is also called Shaytan or the 'enemy of Allah'.
Ibrahim	the Prophet Abraham.
Idris	an ancient Prophet, possibly Enoch.
'Illiyun	lit. 'the High Places', a name for the upper part of Paradise, where the register of people's good actions are kept, or a name for the register itself.
Ilyas	also Ilyasin, the Prophet Elijah or Elias.
'Imran	the Biblical Amran, the father of Musa and Harun. Also the name of Maryam's father.
Iram	possibly Aram, of the Aramaeans; or else the dam of Aram which engulfed the ancient city of Ma'rib in Yemen in about 120 CE, the city from which it is said Bilqis, the Queen of Sheba, originally came.
'Isa	the Prophet Jesus.
Ishaq	the Prophet Isaac.
Isma'il	the Prophet Ishmael.
Isra'il	Israel, the Prophet Ya'qub or Jacob.
Jibril	or Jibra'il, the angel Gabriel who brought the revelation of the Qur'an to the Prophet Muhammad, may Allah bless him and grant him peace.
Al-Judi	Mount Ararat, where the Ark landed.
Ka'ba	the cube-shaped building at the centre of the Masjid al-Haram in Makka, originally built by the Prophet

	Ibrahim. Also known as the House of Allah. It is towards the Ka'ba that Muslims face when praying.
Kawthar	lit. 'Abundance', a river in the Garden.
Luqman	a figure in the Qur'an, a sage
Lut	the Prophet Lot.
Madyan	Midian, the people to whom the Prophet Shu'ayb was sent.
Majuj	*see Yajuj.*
Maqam Ibrahim	the place of the stone on which the Prophet Ibrahim stood while he and Ismaiil were building the Ka'ba, which marks the place of the two rak'at prayer following tawaf of the Ka'ba.
Marut	*see Harut.*
Marwa	a small hill near the Ka'ba. (*see Safa and Marwa*).
Maryam	Mary, the mother of 'Isa.
Masjid al-Aqsa	the mosque in Jerusalem to which the Prophet Muhammad travelled during his 'Night Journey'.
Masjid al-Haram	the great mosque in Makka in which the Ka'ba is situated.
Mika'il	the archangel Michael.
Musa	the Prophet Moses.
Nuh	the Prophet Noah.
Qarun	the Biblical Korah, mentioned in Qur'an 28:76-84. He was famed for his incredible wealth and became arrogant on account of it. Allah caused the earth to swallow him up.
Quraysh	one of the most noble tribes of Arabia centred on Makka. The Prophet Muhammad belonged to this tribe.
Ar-Raqim	the tablet which contained the story of the Seven Sleepers, or possibly the name of their dog.
Rass	'the men of ar-Rass', a people mentioned in the Qur'an who were destroyed. Ar-Rass is possibly the name of a well.

Saba'	Sheba an ancient kingdom situated in modern Yemen.
Safa and Marwa	two hills close to the Ka'ba. One of the rites of 'umra and hajj is to go seven times between the two hills.
Salih	the Prophet sent to the people of Thamud.
Salsabil	the name of a fountain in Paradise.
Saqar	a place in Hell.
Shu'ayb	the Prophet Jethro.
Sijjin	the register where the actions of the evil are recorded, or the infernal place where the register is kept.
Sulayman	the Prophet Solomon.
Talut	the Israelite king Saul.
Tasnim	the name of a fountain in Paradise.
Thamud	a people to whom the Prophet Salih was sent, possibly Nabateans.
Tubba'	a South Arabian people, probably the Himyarites, of whom this was the title of their kings.
Tuwa	the valley in which Allah spoke to Musa.
'Uzayr	the Prophet Ezra.
Yahya	the Prophet John the Baptist, the son of Zakariyya.
Yajuj and Majuj	the people of Gog and Magog who are to burst forth near the end of time to wreak destruction.
Ya'qub	the Prophet Jacob, also called Isra'il.
al-Yasa'	the Prophet Elisha.
Yathrib	the ancient name for Madina.
Yunus	the Prophet Jonah
Yusuf	the Prophet Joseph.
Zayd	Zayd ibn Haritha, a freed slave whom the Prophet treated as his own son.
Zakariyya	the Prophet Zacharia, the father of Yahya and the guardian of Maryam.
Zaqqum	a tree with bitter fruit which grows at the bottom of the Fire. Its fruit resembles the heads of devils.